GENRE AND WRITING

Issues, Arguments, Alternatives

Edited by
Wendy Bishop and Hans Ostrom

Boynton/Cook Publishers
HEINEMANN
Portsmouth, NH

Boynton/Cook Publishers, Inc.
A subsidiary of Reed Elsevier Inc.
361 Hanover Street
Portsmouth, NH 03801–3912

Offices and agents throughout the world

The authors and publisher wish to thank those who have generously given permission to reprint borrowed material:

"Postings on a Genre of Email" by Michael Spooner and Kathleen Yancey originally appeared in *College Composition and Communication,* May 1996. Copyright 1996 by the National Council of Teachers of English. Reprinted with permission.

Excerpt from *The Alchemy of Race and Rights* by Patricia Williams. Copyright © 1991 by the President and Fellows of Harvard College. Reprinted by permission of Harvard University Press.

Library of Congress Cataloging-in-Publication Data
Genre and writing: issues, arguments, alternatives / edited by Wendy
  Bishop and Hans Ostrom.
       p.   cm.
    Includes bibliographical references. (p.   ).
    ISBN 0-86709-421-4 (alk. paper)
    1. English language—Rhetoric—Study and teaching.
2. Interdisciplinary approach in education.   3. Academic writing—
Study and teaching.   4. Literary form.   I. Bishop, Wendy.
II. Ostrom, Hans A.
PE1404.G39   1997
428'.007—DC21   97-18461
                                                                         CIP

Acquisitions editor: Peter Stillman
Production editor: Renée M. Nicholls
Cover designer: Renée M. Nicholls
Manufacturing coordinator: Louise Richardson

Printed in the United States of America on acid-free paper

02 01 00 99 98 97   DA   1 2 3 4 5 6

Contents

Acknowledgments

This book would not exist without the encouragement and support of Professor Anne Ruggles Gere. Thank you, Anne.

We deeply appreciate Peter Stillman's vision, good humor, and editorial confidence; he listened, understood, and acted—encouraging us to complete *Genre and Writing*.

The staffs of the Amistad Research Center, Tulane University, the Schomburg Center for Black Culture (Harlem), and Carolina Rediviva Library, Uppsala University, Sweden, provided generous assistance.

The many contributors to this volume shared drafts and disks, letters and emails—waiting when we were slow, speeding up when we were ready, and helping us whenever they could. Really, it is their book.

Our sincere thanks to Renée Nicholls and her associates at Boynton/ Cook for their expertise and good will. Jackie Bacon Ostrom, Spencer Ostrom, Morgan Pollard Bishop, and Tait Bishop Pollard shared us with our computer screens and welcomed us when we returned. Thanks to them all.

Introduction

I.

This book is about a variety of new concepts and applications of "genre," as viewed from several theoretical, critical, and pedagogical perspectives. The genealogical roots of genre are deep and far-flung. It has both pedigree and connections. With minor costume changes, it can move from an art historian's treatise to a college composition program to a drugstore shelf. It makes friends almost too easily; those who met it most recently think they know best what it means. Jealousies arise. We have been delighted, and also bewildered, to be under its spell, where we remain, further dazzled by the ways our contributors have put the word to work in yet more venues, exploiting its adaptability, indulging its appeal, using it as a golden machete to cut trails through the wilderness of discourse.

To start with the obvious, literary theory has happened to genre in a big way, inviting and cajoling writers and scholars to transgress. Closely and variously associated with "text (texte)," genre got itself deconstructed, psychoanalyzed, historicized, privileged, unprivileged (and yes, we know how violently some object to using privilege as a verb), punctured, poked, prodded, and reconsidered, reconsideration being what we do best, or most often. The (French, British, American, women's, Victorian. . . .) novel; the short story; the epic poem; the lyric poem; autobiography; comedy; tragedy; satire: these and other building blocks of the Old Taxonomy were suddenly up for (theoretical) grabs. The taxonomy imploded like an old demolished brick building in Chicago (Hotel Genre Decorum), depicted in slow motion on the eleven o'clock news; genres collapsed. The status and nature of these textual entities were destabilized; never mind that our course catalogues might still include "The Victorian Novel."

Simultaneously, on another part of the map, composition theory happened to genre. When Janet Emig, to mention just one name, began to ask, "How do students really write?", questions concerning kinds and forms and products had to follow—namely, How do students know how to write what they write? What do we tell them to write, and how do we tell them? How do we characterize the whatness of what they write? So a term that once applied mainly to certain French paintings now applied to the five-paragraph essay. An absurd stretching of a term, one might argue.

Still, it was no more absurd than not investigating how students (really) composed. No more absurd than not scrutinizing the forms of writing we asked our students to produce and ourselves to evaluate. To the degree students always had writing processes of one sort or another (no matter how little we or they knew about them), genre, at some level, always was a part of our teaching, and not just in the form of a novel we had assigned, or of an essay we kidded ourselves into thinking served as a model for student writing. To this day, after all, we assign things known as "papers": now *there's* a genre worth considering.

Then, more happened: The forms, kinds, types, codes, contexts, and contours of workplace writing, scientific writing, technical writing, and academic writing became sites of reconsideration, research, speculation. Paradigms of composing joined with ethnographic and teacher research. Once securely in the domain of humanistic taxonomy, "genre" was appropriated not just by new rhetorics but by methods and lexicons that looked very social-scientific. Who wasn't "doing" genre-criticism?

Let us not forget writers, who in all the critical confusion are so easy to forget. Writers have always happened to genre. Some have happened with such force and verve that the writing they serve up to subsequent generations upends the game-board—so that genre, with a vengeance, then happens to writers, a curious spin on the old melodramatic anxiety of influence. Basho, that is, happened to haiku, so much so that haiku now happens to everyone else. Fielding and Joyce happened to the novel, but not before Cervantes did. Austen, Balzac, Tolstoy, Raymond Chandler, James Michener, Janet Dailey, Harold Robbins, John Barthes, Ralph Ellison, Jane Bowles, Don DeLillo, Leslie Silko, and others—each in their own manner—all happened to the novel, too. Writing students in creative-writing classes happen to the novel, though the classroom situation tends to assure that the novel happens to the student first—not necessarily the better progression. In these ways, literary history concerns events arising from when writers happen to genres. Even the writing student breaks out of the workshop, tries to affect the form, tries to form an effect, inscribes herself/himself on literary history.

Beyond the canonized literary few, writers of dissertations, students at middle schools, tech writers at Boeing, and all the president's memoing men and women are writers, too; whether they set out to or not, they exert influence on genres and genre each time they write. Everyone who writes is a writer, a writer working in, on, and around at least one genre; a writer being worked on (worked over?) by genre.

From Johannes Gutenberg to Bill Gates, from hot type to hypertext, technology has also happened to genre. The billion blinking monitors around the globe sing the word (and the genre) eclectic. To the same extent a Dickens novel was shaped by—indeed "was"—inexpensive paper, quick typesetting, and an urban marketplace for books, genre today is shaped by—"is"—plastic, silicon, copper, programming, Anti-Trust Act violations, massive advertising budgets, telephone lines, satellites sent into space by NASA, and so forth. To what extent are we like so many wiggling silver fish scooped out of the sea of words by the Internet? To what extent are we impulses careening along the gossamer optical fibers of the World Wide Web?

Genre happened to itself, too—multiplying its meanings, attaching itself to innumerable critical discourses and academic conversations. Like language itself, this word seems to have its own protean energy. That, at any rate, is one story that might be told about an overworked word and some of the everything that's happened to it.

II.

This collection includes many essays that explicitly concern or at least take into account student writing; it includes essays exploring links between "process" pedagogy and genre, and between "social-epistemic" pedagogy and genre. Some essays explore the acquisition of genre-familiarity; others, the several possible social functions of genre. Also by design, such essays often echo one another, or implicitly quarrel with one another, or in effect collaborate with one another as they pursue arguments and lines of inquiry about textual forms, types, categories, disguises, erasures, enactments, and functions.

As often as possible, though, we and the contributors seek opportunities to link composition studies with literary theory, technological issues, more traditional genre theory and literary history, curricular politics, and research methodologies. We do so in part because genre itself is a natural bridge, but also because composition theory—like critical theory—has been known to circumscribe itself too much. We do so in part because of the likely audience for this book, an audience that probably feels as if it belongs to all (sometimes none) of the countries in the profession—literature, theory, composition, rhetoric, creative writing, linguistics.

What do genres of Japanese literature, the history and theory of elegy, and African-American literature have to do with compositionists' refigurations of genre, or with first-year college writing? Implicitly, our editorial response to this question and others like it has been twofold. "Good question." And, "Well, let's see (let's let our contributors see) what the connections might be."

In this spirit, some essays are conventional in shape, style, and argument, and are effectively so. Others operate more conversationally; others, meditatively. Still others are deliberately jagged, mixed like a gumbo or cioppino. Additionally, we have asked another team of contributors to write brief responses to some of the essays, as a way of building conversation and dialogue into the structure of the collection, as a way of inviting readers to imagine their own responses to these responses or to those essays that beg for a first response. Our purpose in stretching and teasing academic writing is not to be clever just for the sake of cleverness; instead we believe that a collection on genre should sweep around its own back door, so to speak;

also, we know the stretching and teasing and conversing will multiply useful connections, the ones most of us are trying to make these days between our lived lives, our teaching, our scholarship, and our research.

To showcase these different perspectives, we have divided this volume into four Sections, comprised of one to six essays each (some with responses), and three Intersections where two essayists were paired because their texts—it seemed to us—and topics, talked to, complicated, or illustrated each other. Intersections, of course, are political places—crossroads, trading posts—where ideas and individuals pass close, expressing opinions concerning race, class, and gender and how these phenomena affect writing students, teachers, and educators in academic and civic communities.

Caveat lector: The compositionist point of view guiding the collection brings with it some inevitable consequences. One of these is that *genre* often gets defined more loosely, more speculatively, more variously, and perhaps even more casually in this book than some literary historians and genre-critics will like. This treatment of the term is in the nature of compositionists' engagement with the subject, but it is also in keeping with the fluid, adaptable nature of the term itself. Second, kinds of student writing, classrooms and writing processes as research sites, and pedagogy are accorded roughly the same status as what some may regard as more literary, more traditional, more "serious" ways of framing questions about genre. Genre-critics and genre-theorists not accustomed to peering at the subject through the lens of composition and rhetoric may find this situation disruptive, unsettling, irreverent, perhaps just plain wrong. We know this. We believe, however, that the essays involved in such an unsettling equation of status will be convincing in their own right; but also, the very nature of our enterprise, and of contemporary genre theory, is to blur, dissolve, or at least cross boundaries; it is to violate decorum and trouble hierarchies. We place you in these sections and intersections intentionally.

III.

Now—after planning the book, envisaging its purposes and audiences, inviting proposals, whirling with contributors and anonymous reviewers through several cycles of revision and editing—we see before us at least two basic questions we want to address in plain terms.

First question: In relation to other recent books concerning genre, theory, and pedagogy, what new material does this collection bring to its readers? (The recent titles we have in mind include Berkenkotter and Huckin, *Genre Knowledge in Disciplinary Communication*; Cope and Kalantzis, *The Powers of Literacy*; Freedman and Medway, *Genre and the New Rhetoric* and *Learning and Teaching Genre*.)

From the start we sought this breadth of perspectives, as opposed to a deep but narrow exploration of a single genre-issue. For instance, many recent studies—including three of those just noted—take a highly focused linguistic approach to genre. Other work springs from sociolinguistic and sociocognitive modes of inquiry. Still other work maintains a tight literary focus on genre, even while acknowledging broader theoretical or ideological concerns.

In contrast, this collection draws on multiple traditions and modes of genre inquiry; it is panoramic in nature. The panorama stretches to include rhetorical criticism, critical pedagogy, feminist and psychoanalytical criticism, linguistic analysis, curricular debate, case studies, cultural criticism, autobiography, and personal reflection.

This multiplicity adds something new to current genre-inquiry because it reveals commonalities that have been incompletely explored or only barely acknowledged. Among these commonalities: the degree to which *rhetoric* makes its way into widely different sorts of genre inquiry; the extent to which *the history and politics of ethnicity and gender* shape questions of genre-inquiry; and the ways in which notions of *genre as a socially constructed phenomenon* inform a wide variety of genre theory, from composition to the history of elegy, and from autobiography studies to graduate curricula. These are commonalities in terms of topical focus, but not in terms of consensus; that is, different contributors may well disagree vehemently about what "rhetoric" is, about connections among genre, ethnicity, and gender, and about what "socially constructed" implies.

Additionally, the panoramic view begins to identify crossroads—sites of terminology where far-flung constituents can meet and speak a second language. In this sense the book is a trading post. "Social construction" is one such term, one such second language. So is the "dynamic" nature of genre— whether one speaks of genre as social action, as more of a site than a form, as a function of social capital rather than an insulated aesthetic entity. In these and other terms, at these and other meeting places, compositionists, literary theorists, graduate advisers, rhetoricians, literary historians, and creative writers have a lot to say to one another. As in any conversation, it can't all be said at once. This volume begins the conversation and invites readers to continue it.

Finally, the multiple perspectives here collectively mirror what we do every day—"we" as in we two, but more important, "we" as in thousands who by choice or circumstance or both become one-person collages of English studies; who (here's but one variation) might teach composition, teach literature, sit on a women's studies program committee, take a mainstream historical approach in a sophomore survey course, but pursue a feminist/cultural studies/genre studies line of inquiry while researching a book-in-progress. If it were just we two, we would not dream of insisting on multiplicity and panorama, but more than ever, English studies the macrocosm and genre studies the microcosm produce this collage effect in almost all who dare enter. Put another way, *genre* is often a point around which the one-person collage intellectually organizes herself/himself.

Which brings us to the second basic question: Where is the bedrock, or what connective strands run through the multiplicity? We see at least four strands binding these essays together:

1. Genre and *student writers*. Between essays that otherwise seem far afield from one another in the collection, often a concern for students provides a strong link. Sometimes the concern is explicit—how do students construct or acquire genres?—and at other times it manifests itself in terms of implications. For example, Allison Giffen's essay focuses chiefly on how some American women poets reconfigured elegy for themselves, but it also turns from literary history to speculate about important implications for young writers of composition, fiction, and poetry. Indeed, all of Section III attends to the writing classroom and student writers.

2. Genre *dynamics*. Fluid, protean, mercurial, historically conditioned, flexible, evolutionary. Different essayists use different descriptors as they inquire into the nature of genre, but throughout the book, from multiple perspectives, the contributors ponder the dynamic nature of specific genres, of genre in general, and of how genres function in our writing, our teaching, our theories of discourse, our literary histories. This occurs particularly in Section II.

3. *Genre and society*. As we noted, this collection is not nearly as tightly focused on a sociolinguistic approach to genre as are other recent related books. Nonetheless, genre and genres as "social" is a concept contributors work with, offering important linkages where otherwise a "fissure" might otherwise seem to be taking shape. The paired essays by William Lyne and Love and Hopkins are but one example. In style, ethos, and purpose, they are extremely different pieces, but they overlap not just at points where they concern race but also where they probe different ways in which genre can be a social tool—sometimes coercive, sometimes repressive, sometimes liberating. In other instances, classrooms, genders, historical moments, and curricula represent "society" or function as their own societies that shape and encode genres. Equally, what does the organization of our own graduate programs say about us as theorists, scholars, teachers; where will we and our genres and writing be situated as the next century opens?

4. The *means and material conditions* of genre-production. Dovetailing with the subject of "genre and society" is deep concern with how genres come to be genres, how writers of all sorts arrive at a point when they believe they perceive a discrete genre, how critics, theorists, teachers, and students do the same thing. Out of what

material and social conditions do elegies, autobiographies, ethnographic narratives, lyric poems, electronic mail, technical reports, and letters emerge? What are the circumstances under which genres invite or thwart participation by readers and writers? What are the connections among genre, teaching, and politics?

By means of this introduction and the general organization of the volume, we seek to highlight connections between and among the contributions. And that is why, as each Section and Intersection opens, you will find us still there, situating the discussion and inviting you to join us. And so, Dear Reader, it is time to begin.

Wendy Bishop
Tallahassee, Florida

Hans Ostrom
Tacoma, Washington

Part I

Setting the Scene
Genre and Composition

Several years ago, as we began to discuss this collection of essays, we felt those in composition were just beginning to break with scholarly conventions adopted from other disciplines, primarily those of the social sciences and literature. We felt the profession needed to do this more often and more vigorously because we saw that invested, personal writing was helping student writers as it could help us. A closer look showed us, however, that the field of composition was busily recasting scholarly genres—as liberating as well as constraining—and in doing so it was developing styles of writing more appropriate to our developing field. For instance, those attending composition conferences have steadily modified the MLA paper presentation model. Today, our conferences are filled with workshops and discussions, round-tables and forums, and classroom-practice presentations. In a parallel and connected move, composition journals have evolved from unjuried to juried to contested, as those wanting to redefine the system politick for symposia, forums, longer response sections, editors naming blind reviewers somewhere in the process, writers publishing memoir, and meta-professional, educational explorations. Therefore, our argument has shifted: We need to be aware of the power of discourses and genres that we have claimed for ourselves, and we need to return this power to our students, encouraging alternate understandings of genre as form *and* as social practice.

In this section, Wendy Bishop's essay examines the changing genres of composition studies and considers what those changes tell us about the field. Further, the essay argues that similar changes need to occur within the writing classroom—and for equally important reasons.

1

Preaching What We Practice as Professionals in Writing

Wendy Bishop

My daughter and son learn by pushing on limits; each evening, they try to stay up later; each trip to the store, they yearn for a new sugary cereal; each time they feel bad, they see if I'll put up with their concerns. They learn limits, then run back safely to the center. I'm the fulcrum, the representation of "parent," and their job is to learn "child" at continuously altering ages. Our relationships stay in constant flux, shifting with each inch of growth, each day of school and home learning, each new temporary negotiation we all complete and then immediately—it sometimes seems—begin again. In a similar way, as a transplanted southern Californian learning to garden in North Florida, I push the margins of memory and geography. I've come to appreciate day lilies, azaleas, and crepe myrtle, but I also plant oleander and cactus. Though I admire the astonishing toughness of monkey and centipede grasses, I miss eucalyptus and bougainvillea. I'm at the mercy of new climate and old expectations. Negotiating these changes, weaving together a microcosm of native and nonnative, I compound my learning about both ecosystems and locales, California past, Florida present.

We do this, too, as writers. I am a sneak-thief at the boundaries between prose and poetry, fiction and nonfiction. I steal from the seemingly richer genre (at any given time) and give to the poorer, plying boundary territories for resources. I find that sometimes telling teaching stories isn't enough, and I need to return to the class context, collecting more data. At other times, describing curricula sends me back to nonfiction for a different kind of grounding, as I explore my writing past and include poetry—and students' voices and writing—on the academic page. The issue isn't either/or (master *one* genre/discourse/community *or* the other: affiliate, dedicate), the issue is both/and (learn about both simultaneously because that's how we gauge and understand limits, boundaries, centers, edges, entry, and exit). I want the sure researcher's timbre and the exhilarated coauthors' word-play. Institutional boundaries between strands of English studies, theories of learning and teaching, territories of research, genres of academic writing, people who write, are still hard to breach for they trade in power, authority, and gender roles. Still, today, I want control *and* carnival—my voice on top, my voice lost and woven in. As a parent, gardener, writer, I've learned the exponential power of mixing and matching. I've learned to learn. Not either/or. But both/ and. To practice what I preach and preach what I practice. In parenting as in gardening as in writing as in teaching.

Looking at the last five years of journals on my office shelves, I find rich veins of both/and, convention-making *and* convention-breaking in alternately organized work. NCTE journals (*College English, College Composition and Communication, English Education, English Journal, Teaching-English in the Two Year College,* and *Research in the Teaching of English*) have re-evaluated their editorial policies to be more inclusive, and new, independent journals have altered our understandings of "what counts" in the academy (*Dialogue, Journal of Advanced Composition, Rhetoric Review, Pre/Text, Writing on the Edge,* among others). Thesis- and data-driven work now thrives side by side with narrative and metaphor-rich investigations. It is evident that scholars in composition *have* usefully broadened their writing/ thinking, in ways that I'll discuss farther below. But. I argue. We're still too often failing to share these options and alternate styles with our own students: graduates and undergraduates.

New ways of seeing and saying are invigorating our practices in composition and rhetoric because our practices grow out of our own resistance to needed but problematic professionalization. As we have resisted in order to *become* a legitimate strand of English studies, our own professionalization leads to a resistance to seeing first-year students as writers *like us.* I believe this has kept us from rethinking the ways we teach convention-making and convention-breaking in first-year writing classrooms. We have moved from a 1960s position of not practicing what we preached to not preaching in the 1990s what we practice. In the late 1960s and early 1970s, we learned more about writing and rebelled against teaching in a formulaic manner, but our own products were, at the same time, moving toward the scholarly mainstream so that writing teachers could hold on to or upgrade their jobs. Journals added blind reviews, and writing research incorporated more "rigorous" research methods. By the late 1980s and into the 1990s, composition writing has become increasingly more dynamic, yet composition textbooks and programs are as slow as ever to change. Certainly product talk often replaces process talk, but we still have fairly uniform accounts of what counts in writing classrooms (look at the table of contents of the five best selling handbooks and rhetorics and readers in any year). Students still produce "student papers." Lots of them. Sometimes more than the heart can bear.

* * *

I remember my army major father saying, "Do as I say, don't do as I do." As writers in composition, we're gaining through dialogic, multivoiced, personal, scholarly, experimental writing that aims to match, emphasize, underline, enhance our work; we're doing, but what are we saying? Our students are often still being asked to believe in the oldest of models. Master the (choose one)—academic essay, formal voice, discourse community—before you write (choose one)—exploratory, thought-provoking, genre-breaking, boundary-testing—prose. Despite process, despite whole-language, despite social constructionist and critical theories, a developmental view of writers is encoded, it sometimes feels, in the DNA of our writing programs. We continue to do *to,* not *with,* writing students.

In breaking free from one conservative model—product—we've entertained another: stylistic Grammar A precedes or dominates grammar(s) B, C, D, E, etc. (see Weathers 1980 for an introduction to the concept of dominant and alternate grammars of style). As we gain control of our field, we move from *other* to *center.* As we've done what I would have hoped—become writers ourselves—asserted our scholarly/research/pedagogical learning-through-writing as writing, we've not thoroughly enough transferred into our classrooms and programs the lessons we learn in learning through alternate styles, mixed genres, coauthored texts. By not allowing for more than a trickle-down of such power shifts into our classrooms, we're in danger of becoming discourse autocrats and monarchs (or army majors) instead of parents, gardeners, or writers who hope to enable, experiment, and explore with classroom writers.

It is possible, however, to look at innovations in our own scholarship in order to find practices we can rapidly and usefully adapt to our own writing classrooms and writing programs. Our professionalism should be in aid of students as well as in aid of our teacher/scholar communities. When it is, students benefit from the same writing-to-learn experiences from which we have benefited. I illustrate this argument in two parts. First, I want to review just a few of the many promising and innovative ways the text(s) of composition have been changing. Second, I suggest that similar changes can and should take place in writing classrooms and programs. This chapter asks that we look at the field of composition as one that is challenging scholarly genres and conventions and in doing so has the potential for giving our students similar needed tools for their own writing/discourse lives.

In our journals we still find exemplary single-authored academic essays that garner the Braddock (CCC) or Kinneavy (JAC) or the Berlin Award (RR). A rhetoric reading group in my program meets monthly during the academic year and often chooses essays like this to discuss. We can collect these "best of" essays; in fact, several editors/publishers are currently in the process of doing this, either as scholarly reprint editions like Hermagoras Press's Landmark Essays series (see Elbow's *Landmark Essays on Voice and Writing),* or as teaching ancillaries put out by textbook publishers for new teachers of composition. In this manner, we canonize and teach our central "literature," making our field-genres more explicit. With "best of" essays, we are usually looking at an identifiably scholarly genre of single or sometimes coauthored, specifically thesed and strongly organized scholarship/research: academic discourse. At the same time, there is ferment concerning this type of formal scholarship. Some of us would say that the composition conferences are getting too professionalized, too much like MLA, and the academic discourse essays too jargon-laden and distant from the concerns of classrooms and students, producing one dominant group of theorists talking only to one another (see Hairston; Sommers 1992).

Because they consolidate and further the knowledge in our field, I like, use, and need some of these essays. I regularly teach them to new teachers of writing. But sometimes I want to put down my journals and say, "No, that's not it. That's not it at all." To this end, I've collected alternate-style professional writing that I value. Coauthored research. Responses and interchanges. Imitations and parodies. Personal narratives and stylistic wordplays. When reading these essays, I find my thinking spurred; my desire to write back (or write at all) and to join the discussion begins. I've categorized some of these works and want to discuss what I see as useful in each category, but I note my own difficulty in category-making. When writers innovate, they often do so in more ways than one. I've listed examples here to *illustrate*, not to fix permanently these alternate styles. Then, of course, I'll be looking at how writing within and across these categories would broaden our students' writing and thinking horizons. The works I'll discuss might be grouped this way:

> Literacy Autobiographies
>
> Imitations
>
> Symposia/Forums/Dialogic Writings
>
> Collaborative and Alternate Research
>
> Metanalysis and Institutional Critiques
>
> Writings on How to Innovate/Alternate
>
> Innovative Textbooks

The last two categories of this list provide a segue from what we are doing in our professional writing into a discussion of what some are suggesting we can do in our writing classrooms to encourage writing in alternate academic genres *as a way of learning*.

Literacy Autobiographies

We seem to be in an age of narrative testimony. (I will highlight my preferences by saying, "*Luckily*, we seem to be in an age of narrative testimony.") Since composition has, for years now, been an undervalued, marginal field, seen as purveyor of service courses, asked to do the caretaking and remediation, configured as the drayhorse (see Schuster's analogy to Orwell's Boxer the horse) or wife of the English department (see Bloom's "I Want"), there has been a counterneed to testify to who and what we are. Literacy autobiographies serve an important function, announcing solidarity with our field while lodging complaints about how we are perceived and configured within the larger world of English studies. Literacy autobiographies also help us reduce our paranoia and insecurity, and assert our values (yes we care what we do, yes we chose this field). Not surprisingly, they often take the form of heroic narratives, becoming a rallying point for strong reader identification. Literacy autobiographies provide the mortar for the sometimes crumbling walls of our back room in the house of English. By sharing them, we create narrative selves able to survive (and even transcend) within our complex society with its complex architecture. We write to assert agency, arguing that since we come to where we are by choice, we should have the right to *affect* those choices and to have a voice in the field.

In a sense, our narratives are metaliteracy narratives since we often testify to our individual valuation of writing and reading and how that valuation led us to professional careers as literacy workers. Readers of this chapter will have their own lists of autobiographically based narratives they qualify as literacy autobiographies. Most of us might agree that books by Henry Louis Gates, Jr., Nancy Mairs, Richard Rodrigues, Mike Rose, and Victor Villanueva suit the definition, and some might stretch the genre to include portions of Peter Elbow's *What Is English* or Trinh Minh-ha's *Woman, Native, Other* (to choose two very different types of writings). Equally, it is a rare 4Cs Chair's Address of the last few years that hasn't relied on personal testimony (see Bridwell-Bowles 1995, Gere, and McQuade, "Living"). A great deal of the teacher-researcher literature highlights the same literacy narrative movement (for book-length treatments see Bissex, Calkins, Graves, and more recently Rankin, *Seeing*, O'Reilley, and Tobin; for essays see much of Tompkins and Sommers and Bloom, particularly her "Teaching College Writing as a Woman").

Imitations

When literacy narratives eschew the heroic quality I describe above, they may rely instead on imitation and parody. Wordplay asserts our double consciousness as members of the writing *and* the literary community, a membership that has sometimes seemed to be denied to us as soon as we affirm value in writing and pedagogy. Look at the number of literary puns made in conference titles (along with others, I've forever debased the worth of Ray Carver's story and collection *What We Talk About When We Talk About Love,* by turning it into a panel or paper take-off title). Jane Tompkins's often cited "Postcards from the Edge" borrows title and form from Carrie Fisher's novel of the same name. Lynn Bloom's "I Want a Writing Director" intentionally parodies Judy Syfer's

"I Want a Wife," which was a mainstay for some years of freshman readings and anthologies, while Nancy Sommers's "I Stand Here Writing" plays off of another equally anthologized work, Tillie Olsen's short story "I Stand Here Ironing." And, in our own composition journals, titles are grist for imitation, or we might think of them instead as jazz riffs, call and response, the carnival of masquerade and the homage of borrowing. For instance, Elizabeth Flynn answers her own "Composing as a Woman" with a meta-analytic "Composing 'Composing as a Woman'" followed some time later by Terry Myers Zawacki's "Recomposing as a Woman: An Essay in Different Voices."

Symposia/Forums/Dialogic Writings

As a field, we've shown a growing preference for interactive, dialogic discussions instead of traditional single-authored papers. This holds true in the many configurations of conference presentations I mentioned earlier, but it also becomes an identifiable theme in journals over the last ten years. *College Composition and Communication* has regularly hosted symposia, grouping essayists together, with room for reply and rebuttal. Examples include the "Symposium on The Professional Standards Committee 'Progress Report'" (see Merrill, et al.) and newly labeled "In Focus" sections like the one on "Feminist Experiences" (see Eichhorn et al.). The Ericka Lindemann and Gary Tate debate about the purposes of first-year writing has taken place across several years and engendered a number of readers' responses, as have the David Bartholomae (1995) and Peter Elbow (1995) essays and response essays (Bartholomae, et al.). This interactive impulse has played out in larger ways. New sites have been found and dialogic styles created; these include *Rhetoric Review*'s "Burkean Parlor" section, which allows for initialed-only or anonymous comment and response, and the many email lists that are being generated, including special lists for writing program administrators, writing centers and so on. Some journals continue to highlight the interview format (*Journal of Advanced Composition, Writing on the Edge,* and more recently *Composition Studies*). And one new journal developed around its editors' desire to change the review process itself (see Hunter and Wallace's introduction to the journal *Dialogue*). The review essay is popular in both *CCC* and *CE* (see North [1991] for a critique of book reviewing that probably influenced that renaissance), allowing reviewers to discuss several texts, placing the work of one author into dialogue with the works of others. Finally, definitions of coauthoring are being expanded in written research reports. But that takes me to another category.

Collaborative and Alternate Research

Research practices are changing, and that changes the way we must report data. The teacher-research movement has led to narrative and introspective practitioner reports and collaborative research projects in which students and teachers research and write together (see Anderson, et al.; Bishop and Teichman). Coauthored research like that of Lisa Ede and Andrea Lunsford in *Singular Texts/Plural Authors* can produce writing voices that are so clearly intertwined that the scholarly traditions of listing first and second authors has to be problematized. Lunsford and Ede introduced "Interchapters" to allow them to include the voices of others who influenced their work. This technique was adapted by Elizabeth Rankin several years later; she created interchapters where the "other" voice is her own, offering metacommentaries on the research process (*Seeing*).

Alternate research can require alternate styles of formats. Robert Connors and Andrea Lunsford "become" Ma and Pa Kettle. Sonja Wiedenhaupt's and Beverly Clark's "On Blocking and Unblocking Sonja: A Case Study in Two Voices" required two different typographies (see Love and Hopkins and Spooner and Yancey in this volume for further examples). Most recently, Janis Haswell and Richard H. Haswell's research report "Gendership and the Miswriting of Students" includes student texts as well as photographs of students. This report mixes first person singular and first person plural voices, asking readers to consider for themselves the reasons for switching from "I" to "We" at various points in the text. This stylistic move is not a trick; rather, the authors use it as a method for highlighting one of the concerns of the study itself: "Can you tell which section was written by the woman, which by the man? Did we try to write in the gendered style of the other, or to exaggerate our own gendered style?" (250).

Metanalysis and Institutional Critiques

Much of the innovative writing done in composition arises from the conditions of the discipline within English studies as a whole. While historians of English and composition from James Berlin to Robert Connors to Peter Elbow to Gerald Graff have been exploring the social/political/historical strands that comprise the field, compositionists in general have been using alternate styles of writing to launch their critiques and analysis as if the confines of traditional scholarly writing won't hold these necessary meditations. And perhaps those generic confines intentionally don't. As Pierre Bourdieu suggests, one function of genre-distinctions is to reflect status, and probably ossified scholarly rhetoric, diction, and form are there in part to preserve the status quo. It is possible, too, that MLA's ambivalence toward, even resistance to, composition studies springs partly from a reluctance to see scholarly genres questioned too closely. We have Elizabeth Flynn's "Composing as a Woman," which fits all of the categories above but served as a rallying point for feminist critique in composition. The writings of Jane Tompkins and Lynn Bloom work this way. In the last few years, Lillian

Bridwell-Bowles (1992) has been arguing that as our ways of thinking and research change, our ways of writing must also. She says:

> I have experimented with new forms to match my own changing scholarship, work that has become more and more cross-disciplinary. Just as I have moved from lines of inquiry exclusively based in social science and empiricism to those that are more oriented in humanistic, feminist, and liberation theories, so must my language change. (350)

Maxine Hairston launched an attack on the politicization of composition studies, critiquing the writing style and curriculums of certain authors in the discipline. Others are interested in investigating the scholarly structures of the field. Richard Gebhardt's "Editors Column" analyzes contributor diversity in submissions to the *CCC* journal, and his short essay "Thoughts" discusses issues of confidentiality in submitting and reviewing journal manuscripts; both were published during his years as *CCC* editor and are followed up in the more recent symposium on peer reviewing in scholarly journals (see Gebhardt, et al.) published in *Rhetoric Review*. Another can be found in *Writing on the Edge;* in this one, a Donald Murray essay was rejected from a journal for being too much like an essay by Donald Murray (see Hult, Murray, "A Preface" and "Pushing," Rankin, "The Second")

Scholarly and professional self-critique often takes alternate forms and has a rawness and newness that is impressive and disturbing. For instance, Bob Mayberry's account of life in one English department in the Spring 1995 issue of *Composition Studies* is tense with worry over his ability and right to testify to disturbing working conditions on personal grounds: "I don't write this article because my story is unique," he claims, "but rather because it is so common. I write for those whose departments resemble my former one, for those who continue the struggle in spite of unbearable conditions. I admire your perseverance; I admit it was more than I could bear" (79).

Others have mounted critical rhetorical analyses, counting or analyzing the texts of our profession (much as this chapter does); Ellen Strenski looks at writing program metaphors and Cheryl Fontaine and Susan Hunter examine the "voices" of composition, using a collage technique. Our institutional critiques, then, run the gamut of scholarly collections like that by Richard Bullock and John Trimber's *The Politics of Writing Instruction*, to literacy autobiographies like Rose's, to essayist calls for change like Mayberry's, to rhetorical analyses like those of Fontaine and Hunter. The thread that links these, though, is a willingness to engage in alternate and collaborative and mixed styles in order to say what must be said.

Alternative Style Explorations

Currently, there are more instances of explorations in style for the pleasures of style. Even though our business is writing, writing instruction, writing research, and reading in all those areas, we often forget the pleasures of style. We function for the institutions we serve. We strive toward acceptance and in turn ask those who come next to so strive (see Campbell, this volume, for problems inherent in this model). There has been some movement in changing our writing styles for the sheer pleasures of experiencing alternate ways of composing. Because exploring writing is our business. Because we care to celebrate the diversity of thought and expression available to us. The imitations and critiques I discussed above often register a sense of author's pleasure, of writer's breakthrough and play and pleasure. And such innovation is not restricted only to the well known compositionist like Bridwell-Bowles or Bloom (though it is more likely that these individuals will publish stylistically innovative work in mainstream journals). Some journals like *Writing on the Edge* and *Dialogue* intentionally solicit experimental writing, and others have accepted compelling examples of it. Examples, for me, include Carl Leggo's essay on voice in writing in *Rhetoric Review,* which offers teachers a list of one hundred questions to ask students before demanding that they compose in "their own" voices. Susan Wyche-Smith and Shirley Rose's essay on one hundred ways to implement the Wyoming Resolution, like Leggo's essay, reverberates with the serious play of listing and echoes Paul Simon's song about fifty ways to leave a lover. Toby Fulwiler's "Propositions of a Personal Nature" is a literacy autobiography composed in an alternately styled, numbered list. The same format guides my own "If Winston Weathers Would Just Talk to Me on E-Mail" (see Bartholomae, et al.), a response to the Elbow/Bartholomae debate concerning academic prose. Both use discontinuous narratives to make an implicit point, as does the essay by Monifa Love and Evans Hopkins in this collection. These are just a few examples, but clearly there is something to learn from alternate ideologies of style—particularly African-American styles—and other traditions to mine for ideas in this area (see Dubois, Gates, hooks, as primary texts, and Ostrom, "Grammar J" in Bishop, *Elements,* for a theoretical, pedagogical discussion). The informal essay is widespread and varied (see Auslander, Herren, among many others) and the academic poem (formerly published in *CCC* and occasionally still found in *WOE, EJ, RR*) could be considered an alternate form for commenting on the academic experience. One step further, WOE publishes short stories on teaching.

Writings on How to Innovate/Alternate

Although I don't think we're often enough preaching what we practice, there are appeals being made for the uses of alternate style for thinking in composition. Not surprisingly, I'm the perpetrator of some of this work (see "Risk-Taking" and "Teaching Grammar for Writers" and the forthcoming *Elements of Alternate Style*). My own work in this area was prompted by my grounding in creative writing, which allowed me to understand that writing a poem about a classroom or a student was a profitable type of research, a form of scholarly meditation, as valuable as was writing the teaching essay (North, in this volume, makes an argument for this at the curricular level). In this thinking, I am influenced by reading the work of Lillian Bridwell-Bowles, Peter Elbow, Toby Fulwiler, Donald Murray, Winston Weathers, and, of course, all the literary authors in my undergraduate literature courses and personal reading lists.

Clearly, too, anyone who has been reading critical theory in the last ten years has had to admit that alternate styles of writing are prominent, from Kristeva to Trinh Minh-ha, from Barthes to Bakhtin. Their writing calls for us to become different readers, and their theories, in practice, call for us to become different teachers of writers.

Innovative Textbooks

You may have noticed that my categories are less fully illustrated the farther I go. I began this chapter mentioning the lack of innovative textbooks. Our rhetorics still focus on the "paper" and the "research" essay. Our handbooks still promote dominant grammar. Our readers still offer literary texts by professionals but ask students to respond to those texts in limited ways. Innovation in textbooks often occurs by accretion, by the inclusion of a chapter on collaborative writing, inclusion of a chapter on varieties of reader response methods, and so on.

It seems to me that we need to rethink textbook formats entirely. I've had success teaching with texts that take an informal, personal approach, talking to (not down to) students; I've had better success after compiling a textbook for students that includes students' essays and essays by compositionists speaking about what they value in the field (*The Subject Is Writing*). Eve Shelnutt's *The Writing Room* includes writing and meta-analytic analysis of that writing, composed by her students. Donald Murray provides collections of writers' quotations (*Shoptalk*) and student writers' work (*The Literature of Tomorrow*). Innovative textbooks have at heart a sense of classroom collaboration, a doing *with* instead of doing *to* student writers, and, I would argue, they open the door for diversity in writing and thinking without sacrificing learning.

Simply, we should be preaching what we're practicing. I hope my categories and lists of examples show the many ways we're already practicing alternate styles of writing, profitably, professionally, in the field of composition. The strength of this argument is doubled when I reemphasize that my list is selective and eclectic; even as I describe this handful of authors and their texts, I know readers will add their own examples. By compiling lists together, we are pointing to a sea change that is occurring in our scholarly world that needs to be shared in our classrooms. As Lillian Bridwell-Bowles points out:

[S]tudents may need new options for writing if they, too, are struggling with expressing concepts, attitudes, and beliefs that do not fit into traditional academic forms. To give them permission to experiment, I simply tell them that they need not always write the "standard academic essay" and encourage them to write something else. Many continue to write in familiar forms, and I do not require that they do otherwise. They may need to adopt the standard conventions before they can challenge or criticize them (see Bizzell for an account of this position). But increasingly numbers of students take me up on my option and learn ways of critically analyzing rhetorical conventions at the same time that they are being introduced to traditional academic discourse communities.

When one attempts to write outside the dominant discourse, one often has to begin by naming the new thing. (1992, 350)

In first-year writing programs we have not been naming the "new thing(s)" that we and our diverse student populations represent. We inhabit a multilingual, multicultural world. And in composition, we have not offered a realistic breadth of genres to students who are already inhabiting the sophisticated text environment of email, the World-Wide Web, MTV, cinema, and new journalism. We bemoan disengagement when we could reduce it with more inviting and inclusive curricula. To teach alternate style, by the way, is not to risk everything tradition holds dear. For instance, in teaching alternate style, like Bridwell-Bowles, quoted above, I never abandon the essay, for it is only by putting the traditional and experimental in dialogue that we learn about convention making and breaking, who is doing what, in what manner, and why. And contributors to this volume, invited to write in alternate styles, often, rightly, found traditional genres more appropriate to their subjects.

However, for students stunned by up to twelve years of rule-bound writing instruction, it is a decided relief to find a name for what exists: discontinuous prose paragraphs (Winston Weathers provides the term "crot") or multivoiced writing (Bakhtin provides the term "dialogic") and so on. Students need to name the alternatives they've experienced. For instance, MTV video producers rely on the techniques of montage and collage, as can writers in their writing.

While we shouldn't abandon the academic essay, I feel that we have not made convincing cases for the relevancy of the forms of academic discourse we currently ask students to compose. Students, if invited into a dialogue on discourses, have a lot of school knowledge and are very canny about genres of writing:

Our texts are "safe" when we do what we know we've gotta do to get a good grade, rather than approaching a paper creatively. Regardless, you must make your point, but a safe paper is one you write, stylistically, for others, not yourself. I hate safe. Freshman English teachers try to "unteach" this style, yet freshmen must stick to it in history classes and humanities (sometimes).

My student explained these clear subtleties as our class completed a sequence of assignments experimenting with style during revision (see "Risk-Taking"). In fact, she is no more "fooled" by my encouragement to explore than she is by another teacher's warnings not to. By examining her writing actions, she is doing both, conforming *and* innovating, adapting to the genre demands of different academic contexts. This student may like creative options but also knows that she can't import such a style wholesale into most history classes. She can, though, name what she is doing and discover what choices she has available when offered stylistic revision options (see Bishop 1995, Bridwell-Bowles 1992, and Fulwiler 1992 for more of these).

What might our writing classes take from our own writing experiences in composition?

I return to my original categories.

Literacy Autobiographies—Many composition teachers are assigning these as initial exploratory writings for the term. These narratives initiate many of the writing about writing discussions that need to take place in our classrooms. *Imitations*—writers learn the moves of professional writers inside out when they imitate. Students may be asked to fill in gaps (missing chapters/stories/stanzas) in an author's work, to extend the work (to an hour, day, or year beyond the text's ending) or to write their own piece of literature, imitating authors' styles and/or subject matter. By writing rhetorical analyses of essayists or magazine styles, students can work on issues of rhetorical form and audience development (I've asked students to analyze the prose of essayists they like—from Dave Barry to Janet Malcomb—or to write a rhetorical analysis of the campus newspaper or popular magazines they read; we publish these as a class book of style options that they'll borrow from throughout the term).

Many programs publish their own readers, collections of exemplary student essays, and many writing classes publish collections of student work in the form of textbooks (students writing teaching essays), preparatory to response workshops (books of class drafts), or simply to celebrate the term's work (final individual or collaborative class projects). A class book published mid-semester can be the occasion for response essays published at the end of term. Computer classrooms offer a variety of new options for *Symposiums/Forums/Dialogic* writing of this sort.

In some writing programs, students are encouraged to undertake literacy research and collaborative research projects. Research is configured as a process, a movement first encouraged by Ken Macrorie's influential I-Search assignment and now augmented by current field interest in ethnographic methods. Students are encouraged to research family and community history, to interview members of different cultures and speech communities, to explore their own writing process and the writing processes of others. As they conduct *Collaborative and Alternate Research,* students often become involved in *Metanalysis and Institutional Critiques,* whether these consist of exploratory writing on themes like those posed in the curriculum of David Bartholomae and Anthony Petrosky (1986), or in attempting traditional critique-based forms like the letter to the editor and movie review or the more recently introduced metanalysis techniques like process narratives and self-analysis essays often found in end of term writing portfolios.

Students often respond well to developing authority-based writings, when this writing taps their actual expertise. *Writings on How to Innovate/ Alternate* can be written from one class to another or written as "How to Survive at College" essays for peers, entering high school classes, or younger family members. Students can review handbooks and make necessary editing presentations and compile those presentations into class books. In fact, writing classes thrive on textbook production. For instance, Toby Fulwiler conducted a writing course whose goal was to write a writing textbook; that book is now under contract to Blair Press. Other class publishing ventures can produce valued holiday presents for family members, collections of exemplary essays from all sections of a writing program, class books that a teacher highlights in her next class, showing students the professional journey they're about to embark upon, and so on. Writing teachers reading this chapter may find some of these categories and practices "old news." I'd argue, however, that they could become important news if we allow them to influence more than individual classes. My thinking goes like this: Alternate styles produce alternate classrooms produce alternate writing programs, alternate writing programs produce . . .

Now, imagine this.

To institute innovative practices, our program (yours and mine) has to develop a functional theory of genre along the lines being worked on by the many authors in this book. We have to discuss what we're teaching and why. We have to share results, good and bad ones. We're no longer a cell of individual class communities, worker bees feeding royal jelly to our charges in the comb, keeping the hive well nourished and in order. Instead, we create program practices that put classes and colleagues in communication with each other. We need to develop new models for our writing programs, ones that don't feed knowledge to new teachers in one room and then send them out to their separate universes to teach their version of what they *think* they just heard.

We know that teachers talk to and grow from interactions with other teachers. We know that students talk to friends in other classroom sections (compare and complain about, but talk and communicate nonetheless). Both sets of interactions need to be more productive. We need to be publishing more classroom writing, teaching more classes together or in pods, allowing students the chance to develop a sense of larger communities and a more extensive understanding of a "general college reader." Our classes could be producing textbooks for each other, giving presentations, performing, holding conferences, evaluating and responding to work from other classes, and so on (see Graff's *Beyond* for initial ideas, though I doubt his conflictual model is our only or best option).

Finally, I'm fully aware, as is any reader of this chapter, that there are true and real and limiting institutional constraints placed on our programs, teachers, and students. But this has always been the case for those in composition. Regularly, we've overcome a lack of money, prestige, and possibilities; we've *worked around* many of these same constraints for ourselves. How might we learn from those experiences? How might we preach what we practice and practice what we preach? Finally, both/and. In the classroom and across the programs? I suggest we can do this by exploring alternate genres of writing and their concomitant alternate models of interacting, but also that we do this as an integrated part of the curriculum, not as "special" events, things done after the basics. Our students can benefit from what we've learned professionally in the last twenty or more years. They can learn from our own learning, as parents, gardeners, and writers. They do this when we create opportunities for them to act as involved writers, as we have had to do for ourselves in order to stay involved in our own difficult but satisfying communities of college composition. As our "required enrollment" students must do if they are ever to become involved in writing lives.

Part II

Understanding and (Re)Defining Genre

The authors who define genre in this section do so through analysis but also through metaphor. Exploring genres as "frames for social action," Charles Bazerman presents textual genres as only the tip of the iceberg—"the visible realization of a complex of social and psychological dynamics." Genres, he continues, are about complexity, not conformity. And complexity challenges us to be creative teachers. When we show how the familiar and the strange intersect, how blurring genres is not tantamount to abandoning genres, we encourage students to inhabit one place well and also give them the tools to understand new territories when their lives take them to other locations. For Thomas Helscher, "The Subject of Genre" leads to an investigation of the way genres encourage us to occupy subject positions within discourse communities. Here the metaphor of generic restraints as a counterweight against (overly swift or disruptive) change presents genre as an instrument of tension, (sometimes) stasis, and (sometimes necessary) balance. While genres facilitate, mark members, socialize, and so on, they also constitute and create subjectivities. Helscher considers the challenges raised to genre, identity, and subjectivity by the autobiographical impulses of postmodern scholarship, challenges examined again in this volume in an Intersection on autobiography.

Consider the metaphor of genre as a magical act, creating an illusion that genres—particularly textual genres—are out there in the world rather than in here in the head of the subject who exists in a discourse community. Such an illusion helps us develop schemas for negotiating the world, and Irvin

Peckham explores some of those schemas, the relentless way that genre leads to dichotomization (often based on the power of class and gender—for example, literary provides the "better" generic envelope and patriarchal discourse provides the more authoritative discourse). Once we see the privileging at work in genres, Peckham believes, we begin to see, and help our students see, what is at stake in writing in and out of forms, of working inside and outside the academy. Like Bazerman and Helscher, Peckham argues for exploring genre and genre issues as the best method of defusing genre inequities and (overly) restrictive community constraints, while, in a second take on constraints, Amy Devitt asks us to consider the metaphor of genre as a language standard. Genre in this manifestation presents us with etiquette, appropriate behaviors, manners. These social conventions—like language conventions—are evolutionary, for language evolves as language users make and agree upon new choices for language use. For Devitt, genres are socially structured and socially complex just as language is, and both are less about dictates than about choices, choices we and our students need to investigate. She predicts that our attitudes toward our genre manners may be more important than the genre rules themselves, and, like Peckham, she argues for a balance—a yin *and* yang, an attention to rules *and* the innovation that leads to new choices. Not either/or, but both/and.

We have been looking inward at the discourse communities of our classrooms. Debra Journet shifts our gaze outward, to the edges of our community. The very territorial imagery that we, editors and contributors of this volume, use so readily poses its own problems: like our students, we ply boundaries, cross disciplinary territory, advocate moves that require constant mediation and negotiation. Whose territory, authority, conventions, rules, and why? She proposes a boundary rhetoric where "writers may sublimate differences not just by articulating connections but also by recasting the knowledge claims of one discipline into the generic forms of the other." As in other essays, perceived dichotomies become the site of productive thought by offering us a new move—instead of sublimating one discourse or set of conventions to the other, Journet argues for intentional interpenetration, the creation of what she calls boundary rhetorics.

While undefining, defining, and redefining genre, these authors have created a definitional new frontier. In that vital area, we trust readers will consider what these issues might mean to their classes and to their students, just as Carrie Leverenz does in the response that closes this section.

2

The Life of Genre, the Life in the Classroom

Charles Bazerman

Genres are not just forms. Genres are forms of life, ways of being. They are frames for social action. They are environments for learning. They are locations within which meaning is constructed. Genres shape the thoughts we form and the communications by which we interact. Genres are the familiar places we go to create intelligible communicative action with each other and the guideposts we use to explore the unfamiliar.

But the symbolic landscape we have constructed to live in is precisely that which most fits us and the others with whom we share it. Even when we find that the genres we become habituated to are filled with dissension, dysfunction, or even deception, and we want to seek alternatives, they still have formed the discursive and cognitive habits we bring with us.

Other people have other places they have constructed where they regularly go to interact. When we travel to new communicative domains, we construct our perception of them beginning with the forms we know. Even our motives and desire to participate in what the new landscape appears to offer start from motives and desires framed in earlier landscapes.

In our role as teachers we constantly welcome strangers into the discursive landscapes we value. But places that are familiar and important to us may not appear intelligible or hospitable to students we try to bring into our worlds. Students, bringing their own road maps of familiar communicative places and desires, would benefit from signs posted by those familiar with the new academic landscape. However, guideposts are only there when we construct them, are only useful if others know how to read them, and will only be used if they point toward destinations students are attracted to.

So we should not take lightly the choice of which genres we ask our students to write in. Nor should we keep those choices invisible to students, as though all writing required the same stances, commitments, and goals; as though all texts shared pretty much the same forms and features; as though all literacy were the same. Nor should we ignore students' perceptions of where they are headed and what they feel about the places we point them toward.

The picture I have drawn of the role of genre as it shapes educational activity is informed by developments in linguistics, rhetoric, psychology, and sociology. These areas of inquiry consider genre and related concepts in ways alternative to those offered by the literary tradition. These alternative traditions differ not only in the intellectual and investigative tools brought to bear on genre, but in the range of genres considered.

For almost two centuries, *genre* has been an important term in the arts and art criticism, first brought to the English language in relation to a kind of painting of rustic scenes favored by the French Academy, but the term spread to the literary and other arts. Although the term *genre* is now used widely to identify the distinctiveness of various kinds of creations in all creative realms, it still bears the stigma of a shallow formulaicness and a limited vocabulary of stylistic and organizational gestures. Artistic productions considered as being primarily within a genre are frequently set in contrast to richer, more creative works of art that are thought to transcend the limitations of genre.

In literary studies the modern consideration of genre invokes an ancient tradition of evaluating works according to their species, a tradition stretching back to Aristotle, but which in the seventeenth and eighteenth centuries had become moribund within a rule-determined version of artistic decorum. The romantic rejection of this tradition in the name of individual expression, originality, organic unity, and the chaos within added to the stigma of those works labeled as generic. Even among those literary critics who have seen past such stigmas, literary studies still have traditionally concerned themselves with a limited range of literary genres already embedded within practices and assumptions of the literary system, so that literary thinking about genre is more adapted to thinking about the lyric than the comic book, and to both of those more than to the environmental impact statement. Moreover, because literature is often written and read in contemplative circumstances, apparently (but not thoroughgoingly) removed from immediate exigencies of life, the social embeddedness of genre has been less visible. Moreover, insofar as literary texts advance recognizable social designs, reminding us of their social positioning, they are typically considered as propagandistic and coercive, and thus of less literary value. Genre in literary studies has therefore come to signify more matters of textual form or of effect upon ideal readers than of social relations (see, for example, Dubrow, Fowler, Hernadi, Strelka). Curiously, because schooling also apparently (but again far from thoroughgoingly) has elements of removal from immediate exigencies of life and from overt designs, other than the development of mind and reflection, the apparent contextlessness of the literary can translate readily to the apparent contextlessness of classroom language. Consequently, the literary genres can readily appear as models for the genres of classroom writing, and both can appear as the universal forms of knowledge and thought. Literary literacy can, on the face of it, appear equivalent to all literacy.

Recent literary theory, noting the indeterminacy of literary forms, the novelty of individual texts, and the idiosyncrasy of reader response, calls formal or textual definitions of genre (Derrida; Foucault 1972, 22; Hernadi) into question and sees the identification of any text as being essentially of one or another genre as chimerical. Both Bakhtin's and Cohen's rehabilitations of genre are dependent on placing symbolic types into psychosocial history. Bakhtin, viewing utterances as communicative, sees in speech genres a situational stabilization influencing referentiality, expressiveness, and addressivity; generic shaping of communicative action thereby regularizes our subjects of discourse, our emotional stance toward those subjects, and our relations to those we communicate with (*Speech Genres*). Cohen argues that genres are historically constructed and evolving, as parts of changing social expectations as perceived by each individual. Thus not only do genres change, but what counts as an example of a genre is historically determined, how readers apply generic expectations changes, and each text transforms the landscape of generic expectations (1986).

These most recent turns in literary understanding of genre match well with work already preceding in linguistics and rhetoric. Moreover, since much of the work in applied linguistics and rhetoric was done precisely to make visible the particularity of academic and pedagogic communicative practices, the implications for the teaching of writing are already drawn, in ways that do not conflate literacy and literary—although recognizing that the literary encompasses many varied and rich forms of literacy.

The work from linguistics can be seen as arising from concern for register: the varieties of language deployed in different circumstances, consisting of features of language that covary (Biber; Devitt 1993, 1989). Further, some forms of linguistic analysis have attached these features to intellectual and social relations created by the deployment of various features (Halliday 1989; Hasan; Halliday and Martin; Kress 1987; Kress and Threadgold; Martin; Cope and Kalantzis, *Powers*). Further, some have used genre to understand textual organization in terms of the typical meaning-making moves the writer takes appropriate to regularized discursive contexts, as in Swales's analysis of article introductions in science and Dudley-Evans's analyses of dissertations (see also Bhatia). Cognitive linguistics work on prototypes, although not yet extended to considering larger discoursal units, also provides a potential resource for considering genre (Rosch; J. Taylor).

Rhetoric, since its founding 2,500 years ago, has had an interest in genre or types of utterance, for rhetorical practice is concerned precisely with determining the effective utterance appropriate to any particular circumstance. The rhetorical concept of genre has from classical times associated the form and style of the utterance with both the occasion or situation and the social action realized in the utterance. Carolyn Miller, in reviewing the rhetorical discussion of genre and associating it with sociological concepts of typification, has defined genres "as typified rhetorical actions based in recurrent situations" (1984, 159). That is, rhetors become aware that a particular kind of utterance has proved effective in certain kinds of circumstances, so that when they note similar circumstances they are likely to try a similar kind of utterance. Over time and repetition, socially shared patterns and expectations emerge to guide all in the interpretation of circumstances and utterances. In Miller's account, perception is a key to recognition of recurrent circumstances and of typified actions, so that the emergence of recognizable genres increases the recognition of situations as alike or recurrent. For example, once one is familiar with business letters of complaint as a kind of response to particular circumstances, one may begin to identify a situation as one calling for a letter of complaint. Moreover, the recognition of genre typifies possible social intentions and actions, as one realizes a letter of complaint is a possible response to some commercial injustice.

The implications of this socially embedded account of genre have been explored by placing it within social structural and social psychological theories, seeing the rise of genres in relation to regularized social relations and institutions of communication and in relation to socially shaped psychological practice (Bazerman, 1988). That is, genres, as perceived and used by individuals, become part of their regularized social relations, communicative landscape, and cognitive organization.

The social and psychological implications of genre have been further elaborated in relation to speech act theory and the structurationist accounts of Bourdieu (1991), Giddens, and Luhmann. Structurationist theory points to how larger patterns of social regularities are created and maintained through the many individual acts that establish, reassert, and modify patterns and expectations. These patterns provide social locales for speech acts as well as shape the requirements for successful action (Berkenkotter and Huckin 1994; Yates and Orlikowski). Structurationist accounts of genre thus provide a means of analysis of the social and institutional conditions of speech acts called for by Austin while avoiding the abstracting and decontextualizing tendencies of Searle's analysis. Moreover, in providing socially and historically shaped locales within which we must speak in recognizable and appropriate ways, genres present environments or habitats within which we perceive and act (Bazerman, "Whose Moment" and "Systems of Genre").

Historical and ethnographic studies in various domains have been pursued using these linguistic, rhetorical, and sociopsychological approaches to genre, including scientific and technical communication; medicine and veterinary record keeping and diagnosis; business and policy communication; primary, secondary, university, and graduate education. (See for examples, D. Atkinson; P. Atkinson; Bazerman and Paradis; Blakeslee; Campbell and Jamieson 1990; Casanave; Connor; Fahnestock; Freedman and Medway, *Learning, Rethinking*; Freedman 1993; Hunston; Myers; Prior; Schryer; Smart; Yates; Yates and Orlikowski.) These studies have examined how the various sites of work and social interaction are organized around structured sets of genres, how the production of those genres is an essential part of the work and interaction at those sites, and how thought and meaning are framed within generic tasks. These studies draw the work in rhetoric, communication, and linguistics ever more closely to work in psychology (see Vygotsky), sociology (see Luckmann; Luhmann), and anthropology (see Bauman; Gumperz; W. Hanks), finding shaping mechanisms for our internal and external lives in the mechanisms by which we organize our communication. This work holds much promise for drawing humanities' understandings of the workings of language into relation with the social sciences' understandings of human relations, behavior, and consciousness. By forging closer links with the related enterprises of conversational analysis, ethnomethodology, and other forms of discourse analysis, genre analysis can play a major role in the current investigation into the communicative grounds of social order (see, for example, Boden and Zimmerman; Ochs).

These investigations reveal that what emerges from these various studies is that genre is a rich multidimensional resource that helps us locate our discursive action in relation to highly structured situations. Genre is only the visible realization of a complex of social and psychological dynamics. In understanding what is afoot in the genre, why the genre is what it is, we become aware of the multiple social and psychological factors our utterance needs to speak to in order to be most effective. Once we understand the dynamics and factors, we may have a range of choices available to us, including choices that are far from traditional in appearance, but which nonetheless speak to the circumstances. What we might feel as the weight of living up to the expectations of a particular genre is in fact rather the reminder of all the complexities at stake in the form. The pressure of genre is not of conformity so much as of response to complexity, and insofar as we feel drawn to or seek traditional formal solutions, those standardized forms provide a means to begin to address the situation in a focused way.

When we invoke a genre such as a newspaper editorial, we are invoking not just a pattern of timely topic, evaluative and emotional words, and policy recommendations—we are invoking the role of journalism and commentary in contemporary politics, the civic and economic power of a particular newspaper, the public reputation of its writers, and the influence of its readership. We are invoking unfolding events in which there are many players, a changing topology through time, and a deft sense of timing necessary for any editorial to be successful. We are invoking the standards of taste and criticism within a community, current attitudes toward political figures, and the emotional hot buttons of the moment. It is in this complex environment that the editorial must act.

Similarly, genres enacted in the classroom are more than a ritual repetition of standardized statements. If they fail to be more than that, it is only because we so strip the meaning from the classroom activity that generic productions become only formal exercises. It is up to us as teachers to activate the dynamics of the classroom so as to make the genres we assign alive in the meaningful communications of the classroom. This may be by drawing on the students' prior experience with genres in social situations that they have found meaningful or by tapping into students' desires to enter particular new discursive situations, or by making vital to students' concerns the discursive realms we wish to invite them into. And we must do this within the institutional definitions of our courses, so that students accept the appropriateness of what they are doing in the classroom.

As teachers, we all know in class discussion we are expected to ask certain genres of questions. We all know it is easy enough to make up a question on the assigned topic of the day, but we all also know how difficult it is to come up with a question that effectively engages the students and evokes reflective responses. In finding the right question, we need to search for what is already alive or what we can make come alive in the classroom, within all that constrains and defines that particular class setting. The study of classroom genres is not about defining the minimal requirements of any old statement, but about releasing the full power of the well-chosen statement that speaks to the full psychological, social, and educational dynamics of the setting. In any classroom's discourse, how fully alive any student's generic productions are depends on the life we invest in our comments and assignments that model and prompt students' utterances as well as on what the students bring to the task. Our assignment questions not only identify the genre we are asking students to produce, but also provide an environment for students to speak within, a place for them to invest their energy and concern.

Moreover, genre is a tool for getting at the resources the students bring with them, the genres they carry from their educations and their experiences in society, and it is a tool for framing challenges that bring students into new domains that are as yet for them unexplored, but not so different from what they know as to be unintelligible. As creative teachers, desiring to increase our students' rhetorical skill, flexibility, and creativity, we can try to locate those kinds of utterances our students are ready to make if they are given the challenge and some guidance in what such statements do and how they do it. That is, our strategic choice of genres to bring into the classroom can help introduce students into new realms of discourse just beyond the edge of their current linguistic habitat.

What genres we choose to bring into the class through our comments and assigned readings, and which genres we ask students to communicate in as we signal by our questions, assignments, models, and instructions are matters that need to be worked out in each individual circumstance. But if we find the right generic locations within which to place the communicative activity of each class, students may become capable of remarkable performances as they speak to environments they grasp and they want to speak to. Many years ago, teaching third grade in an inner city school, I found that children whom the system had given up on were able to create complex play scripts based on television cartoons popular at that time—they knew the genre of "Crusader Rabbit" and they very much liked playing in that generic space. More recently I found that urban college students in a business program, who were not much motivated toward autobiographical revelation nor toward social science analysis, came alive with wonderful discussion and papers when we put together social structural analysis of social and economic mobility with their individual and family sagas. Immigrants from Asian peasant families or fallen Iranian aristocracy had remarkable things to say about how political and economic structure affected their life chances. African-American students had precise understandings of the barriers placed to social mobility in both rural and urban settings, North and South.

But among a group of equally ambitious and academically more advanced engineering students the social mobility assignment fell flat, because their privileged cultural homogeneity had given them few opportunities to think about how they and their families' fates were dependent on social factors. Rather, their individual and family sagas were built around tales of individual initiative and character. In this class the genres of social analysis and personal narrative intersected in a different and less intellectually exciting place. However, the right generic mix for this class was found in an assignment that coupled the ambitious stories of their own lives with descriptions of technological progress. Their research papers, describing leading-edge developments and ten-year projections for fields they hoped to contribute to, led to remarkably sophisticated and interesting papers, which, for example, argued for the increasing role of architects in space station design or set out new directions for microchips.

So which genres work in any classroom circumstance depends on a negotiation among institutions, teacher, and students. That negotiation determines where the journey of the class can most successfully go while meeting the goals and needs of each. Sometimes institutions have clear imperatives, as defined through professional accreditation requirements or faculty senate mandates. Although we at times may see these demands as rather blunt, if not stupefying, instruments, they do assert the stakes the several professions and disciplines have in the specialized literacy of students entering their domains. We as teachers often have strong opinions about the kinds of writing we feel will lead to most growth. And students may have strong attractions and aversions to discursive domains offered in the university and the professional worlds beyond.

Since without student motivation little happens in a writing class, motivation must always be attended to. Learning to write is hard work, requiring addressing ever more difficult writing problems, so that if we want students to learn to write we must locate the kinds of writing they will want to work hard at, the kinds of writing problems they will want to solve. Once students learn what it is to engage deeply and write well in any particular circumstance, they have a sense of the possibilities of literate participation in any discursive arena. Moreover, in any new discursive circumstances they may enter into, they will have at least one set of well-developed practices to draw analogies from and contrasts to. Further, if we provide students some analytical vocabulary to reflect on how genres relate to the dynamics of situations, they will be able to observe and think about their new situations with some sophistication and strategic appropriateness.

Thus while studies of genre point to how different discursive practices are in different circumstances, we need not worry too greatly that in helping students down any particular path—one they are interested in pursuing or one appropriate to the particular career goals they have chosen—we are shutting them off from other practices that we as teachers of the humanities value highly. Rather, students are likely to learn how powerful a tool writing is to carry out specialized work and how empowered they are in entering focused, specialized discussions in appropriately forceful ways. With that knowledge they are more likely to respect alternative discourses and their own ability to enter those discourses when they are interested in doing so.

After all, having learned to inhabit one place well and live fully with the activities and resources available in that habitation, no one is likely to mistake it for a different place. Nor having moved to a different place do people stint on learning how to make the most of their new home. It is only those who have never participated more than marginally who do not notice where they are, because they do not perceive why all that detailed attention is worth their effort. Once students feel part of the life in a genre, any genre that grabs their attention, the detailed and hard work of writing becomes compellingly real, for the work has a real payoff in engagement within activities the students find important.

3

The Subject of Genre

Thomas P. Helscher

A black woman sits propped up in bed typing into a laptop computer her experiences as a professor of law. She believes these experiences are inextricable from her position as a black woman, yet her inclusion of them in her writing produces a kind of discourse alien to traditional legal writing (always public, rational, universalizing). Along with her personal experiences, the book contains a series of more traditional legal analyses of cases in commercial law, the constitution, and affirmative action. She describes her efforts as a self-conscious attempt to change the conventions of legal writing, conventions she believes restrict the range and effectiveness of legal discourse: "I am trying to create a genre of legal writing to fill the gaps of traditional legal scholarship" (7). Her new kind of legal writing is based on the proposition that "subject position is everything in my analysis of the law" (3).

I would like to use this example of Patricia Williams revising the genre of legal writing in *The Alchemy of Race and Rights* as a way into the tangle of issues surrounding not only what constitutes a genre, but how genres serve to constitute, support, and regulate discourse communities. As I'll explain in a moment, this regulatory function of genres has been well documented; what is much more interesting and less familiar are the ways in which genres serve as the site for change and conflict within discourse communities. I believe that this neglect is not accidental, since it is part of the irresistible attraction of genres, and perhaps their primary effect, to normalize, regularize, unify, impose order and identity. In fact, I would argue that the theoretical discourse about genres tends to fall under the spell of genre's normalizing force, what Derrida calls "the law of genre." It is for this reason as well then that the example with which I began focuses on the genre of legal writing.

Recent work in composition theory has found it useful to link the notions of discourse community and genre (Swales; Freed and Broadhead). According to this line of reasoning, discourse serves to mark off the boundaries of communities, initiate new members, and can even be seen to constitute the field of knowledge for a given community. John Swales, for example, argues that

> Discourse communities are sociorhetorical networks that form in order to work towards common sets of goals. One of the characteristics that established members of these discourse communities possess is familiarity with the particular genres that are used in the communicative furtherance of those sets of goals. (9)

Thus genres serve important functions within discourse communities: they facilitate communication by offering a common code of assumptions, procedures, concerns, and goals. They also help mark a user as a member of the discourse community—an important part of the socialization process of an initiate in one of these communities is learning to work with the genres. Sometimes this process is explicit and shaped by instructors, as in law schools, which hold legal brief-writing workshops, and often it is implicit, as in many on-the-job training situations in which a new member is initiated by working up the same genre repeatedly. Academic subjects typically fall between these two poles, sometimes offering workshops on how to write a history paper or lab report, and sometimes shaping the students' understanding of the generic conventions through trial and error. These communities can be ranged across a continuum of self-consciousness about such acculturation, from those that train their new members carefully in the generic techniques to those that for whatever reason require the initiates to master the genres on their own. Interestingly enough, English graduate programs, particularly those in literature, tend to avoid much explicit discussion of the genres in which they work. One reason for this reticence is as Alastair Fowler notes the (misguided) notion that teaching genres stifles creativity (20–36). A slightly more sinister explanation might be that by not revealing the "secrets" of the profession, professors can continue to function as priests in touch with the profound mysteries of literature that students can only glimpse dimly.

As part of a general trend toward what is often called social constructionism in the humanities, social sciences, and professional education programs such as law and business schools, this recent work on genre assumes that writing is fundamentally a social act. Therefore the notion of individual expression must be subordinated to the particular discourse communities within and across which an individual expresses him or herself.

Writers disagree, however, on whether participation in a discourse community bears any fundamental connection to the identity of the members of that community. Patricia Bizzell argues that "if we acknowledge that participating in a discourse community entails some assimilation of its world view, then it becomes difficult to maintain the position that discourse conventions can be employed in a detached, instrumental way" (quoted in Swales, 30).

John Swales, on the other hand, argues that genre use is often purely instrumental, citing as an example his experience with the stamp collecting group the "Hong Kong Study Circle," which uses its own genre for discussing the history, classification, and use of the postage stamps of Hong Kong. Swales describes his own difficulties mastering the proper tone, codes, and kind of message appropriate for the HKSC's *Bimonthly Journal and Newsletter*. While acknowledging that to work as an effective member of this community depends upon one's ability to master the nuances of the genre, Swales denies that "participation entails assimilation" (30).

By focusing on the individual and stressing the instrumental value of genre, Swales implicitly repositions genre theory in the liberal rhetorical tradition against which social constructionism arose. The question that I think needs to be addressed, in other words, is not whether discourse communities and their genres are constitutive of individuals, which is by definition fairly ludicrous, but whether they are constitutive of subjects, and if so, how precisely. I would argue that through the specific genres that they use, discourse communities do in fact constitute specific subjects. At its simplest, this means that to do business within a specific community, we occupy the subject position offered by the genre or genres at hand. For example, I may be a professional poet, but if I choose to defend myself in a court of law, I need to write briefs and not sonnets to transact my business with the court. I suspend for this act of writing my personal identity as a poet to function as a legal subject. I signal my acceptance of the conventions governing legal subjects by writing a brief rather than a poem. The conventions of legal subjectivity demand that I bracket my profession as poet in order for the court to treat my business with the court according to its legal merits.

By linking identity to subject position rather than some non- or extralinguistic concept like individuality, we necessarily shift from a unitary model of personal identity, founded on some essential core, to a sense of identity as a shifting and fluid composite of the multiple subject positions we occupy. Within this latter model, certain positions may be more and others less contingent. Thus, for the stamp collector like Swales, writing as a stamp collector, within the genre of the HKSC's *Bimonthly Journal and Newsletter,* may feel less perdurable or "essential" than his writing in books and articles on applied linguistics. Or the poet may write as a lawyer for a single instance, yet would never consider that her experience with that genre constituted her as a "lawyer."

Am I arguing that the constitution of subjects by genres is oppressive? Not at all. In fact, the stability of this process is essential to the stability and coherence, the efficacy, of discourse communities. If lawyers were to perform stand-up comedy, or otherwise adopt an ironic stance toward the proceedings of the court, our already overburdened legal system would face meltdown. (Conversely, such an event must serve as a symptom of a certain revolutionary moment in the history of the larger community served by the court—I'm thinking of the parodic Chicago Seven trial here.)

I believe it is important to note, however, the way this effect of genre on the rhetorical constitution of discourse communities operates as a counter-weight to the process of community growth and change. These forces for change often manifest themselves in the evolution of the subject or subjects within a given community; when the limitations of the subject position at hand become too apparent, when the pressure to redefine the subject of a particular discourse community reaches a certain level of intensity, the genre or genres are revised to create new subject positions. For example, as part of a broader deconstruction of traditional generic hierarchies, one of the most important developments feminism brought to the discourse community of literary critics was an explicitly autobiographical element.[1] This change resulted from the sense that the subject of traditional literary scholarship—detached, objective—was in fact exclusionary.

There are two ways of explaining this particular revision of the genre of literary criticism that stem from the divergent notions of identity I sketched out above. First, many feminists would argue that women's experience is somehow essentially more grounded in the personal, the contingent, the par-ticular than male experience, and that therefore the subject of traditional scholarship was essentially male. To transform the genre to include autobi-ography is, according to this line of reasoning, to create an essentially femi-nine subject within this discourse community—that is, to create a genre that expresses some essential feminine identity. At its most radical (a point where it exceeds the logic of social constructionism), this argument calls for a new genre, "feminine ecriture," for example, that is an expression of a new and separate discourse community. While eschewing the biological or essential-ist premise of French feminism, Catherine MacKinnon has argued that gen-der is the primary social division, upon which all other discourse communi-ties are founded (and to whose maintenance they are dedicated). For MacKinnon, under patriarchy, all discourse communities and all genres work to support the fundamental division of society into men and women.

The strong argument for this link between genre and identity is thus that forms of writing must express some core experience or essence of some socially or biologically defined group. The move to autobiography or more explicitly subject-centered kinds of writing for these critics represents, then, the flowering of multiculturalism, in which a diverse range of ethnic, racial, gender, and sexuality-based subjectivities are free to express themselves, to give themselves an authentic voice for representing their diverse experience. For them, the attempt to historicize or deconstruct subjectivity, to disperse it into some generalized field of textuality, represents a hegemonic effort to muzzle these groups at precisely the moment they acquire a voice. For exam-ple, in "The Master's Pieces: On Canon Formation and the African-American Tradition," Henry Louis Gates, Jr., argues:

. . . while we readily accept, acknowledge, and partake of the critique of this [the Western male] subject as transcendent, to deny us the process of exploring and reclaiming our subjectivity before we critique it is the critical version of the grandfather clause, the double privileging of categories that happen to be *preconstituted*. Such a position leaves us nowhere, invisible, voiceless in the republic of Western letters. (111)

Thus the question of the relation between genre and identity or subjectivity I raised earlier proves more complex and politically loaded than when it seemed simply a matter of deciding whether writing for the HKSC *Bimonthly* marked one essentially and finally as a stamp collector. By loosening the fit between subjectivity conceived as some more or less unitary nonlinguistic phenomenon and the subject-position implicit in any act of writing or reading ("writing as . . ."), we risk being accused by proponents of multiculturalism like Gates of trivializing the experience of traditionally marginalized groups, of instituting a "critical version of the grandfather clause." In a sophisticated attempt to straddle this essentialist-constructionist divide, Teresa de Lauretis in *Technologies of Gender* turns to a concept of "lived experience," which she defines as an interrelated web of social experiences and closely aligned subject-positions, to create a more or less stable subjectivity for women that transcends any particular instance of reading or writing, yet that is not dependent finally on some biological or nonsocial (ahistorical) essence of femininity. De Lauretis invokes this category to dismiss Jonathan Culler's claim to be able to read "as a woman," while not falling into the "anatomy is destiny" trap. I would argue that de Lauretis's use of "lived experience" offers us a middle ground in the continuum of identity-subject position between biological essentialism and pure deconstruction (each instance of writing or reading "as" constitutes us as subjects in particular ways). Eve Sedgwick in *Epistemology of the Closet* also refuses to be bound by a strict "either nature or nurture" (essentialism versus constructionism) choice in defining the source of homosexual identity, arguing that we need to think about these questions in terms of political effects rather than epistemology. (For what really hangs on *knowing* whether homosexuality is biological or socially constructed? Any interesting answer to that question will depend more on the particular construction of "knowledge" as well as the consequences of that construction than the fact itself.)

Taking my cue from Sedgwick, I would like to suggest a purely strategic way of reading this generic transformation and its accompanying revision of the subject in question. I would argue that it represents a specific intervention into institutions like literary criticism (the law, the social sciences) designed to call attention to its dominance by white male practitioners. Feminists called attention to the gap between the universalist pretensions manifested in the subject of literary criticism and the reality of its being the almost exclusive province of men. According to this line of reasoning, writing within discursive formations always implies a certain situatedness. The denial of one's place is one of the most insidious effects of ideology or power. Paradoxically, calling attention to one's particular subject position constitutes perhaps the only liberatory gesture left. As of this moment, the autobiographical impulse has included African-American studies, queer theory, postcolonial studies, and with Patricia Williams and Catherine MacKinnon, legal scholarship.[2]

The autobiographical impulse, however, is only one expression of a larger movement against objectivism in the social sciences and humanities, a movement that has resulted in fundamental changes in the research genres in these fields. Social scientists have turned to Clifford Geertz and James Clifford's anthropological and ethnographic writing for ways of reconfiguring the relation between the discursive subject and the field of research in these genres as well as systematically revised the research methodologies, procedures, and goals. Indeed, the combined effect of these changes has been to call into question what constitutes knowledge within these fields.

I would argue, then, that we need to see the reconfiguration of the subject as part of a larger historical phenomenon and not an isolated incident or the whole story. This particular transformation of the fundamental generic conventions by which communities constitute themselves is, I would argue, paradigmatic of the process of social transformation.

Implicit in my argument about the relations between discourse communities, genres, and the subjects they constitute is the assumption that genres are always mixed. Any important genre is composed of a mixture of kinds of writing. This mixture is more often than not in a constant state of revision. Thus the example of the incorporation of autobiography into the genre of literary criticism is typical of the kinds of transformations genres undergo.[3] The mixture of genres within the "new genre" Patricia Williams wishes to construct to "fill the gap in traditional legal scholarship" represents, then, a significant but not atypical example of this process of historical change that genres undergo. Obviously, we need to keep in mind that discourse communities range across a spectrum of resistance and openness to change in the repertory of genres they contain within their dominant genre or genres. We must also keep in mind that the shuffling of constituents within a given genre can be relatively minor or it can represent nothing less than a realignment of the fundamental paradigms underlying a discourse community and its subjects. Thomas Kuhn's distinction between normal and revolutionary science comes to mind as a useful analogy, although my own sense is this dichotomy is too rigid to account for the regular, ongoing process of change genres undergo.

While it is in the nature of genres to be mixed, to contain and be contained by other genres, I would argue along with Thomas Beebe that it is the ideology of genre to deny such mixture or contamination by other kinds of writing. In his discussion of the genre of legal discourse in *The Ideology of Genre*, Beebe notes that law in particular attempts to define itself as a "pure" genre, free of the contaminating influence of other kinds of speech and writing. He argues that the power of legal discourse, what he describes as its "power to act," is precisely its ability to "forget" its own historical roots in the negotiation among "successive kinds of heterogeneity" (150). The legal system attempts to present itself as a "closed society," "embodying fixed and eternal values" (153). In its practice, however, legal discourse is constantly appropriating and competing with other discursive systems—religion and psychology, for example. Looked at pragmatically, what Beebe calls the ideology of the genre of legal discourse, its capacity to deny its construction out of other competing genres, is a necessary fiction. What Patricia Williams attempts to do in *The Alchemy of Race and Rights* is to assess the cost of that fiction in the law's ability to respond to the richness and complexity of both its practitioners (judges, lawyers, law professors, and law students) and those who find themselves caught within its proceedings (defendants and plaintiffs).

Yet Williams's response—to attempt to incorporate autobiography in the genre of legal discourse—ultimately does not address what Beebe describes as the law's ideological forgetfulness. In fact, the autobiographical turn in legal studies, as well as in literary criticism and the social sciences, obscures the real issues at stake in the social construction of the discursive subject of professional communities. Most of the efforts to make colleges, universities, and by extension, the professions, more multicultural have focused on the content of courses rather than the genres in which they operate. Literature and social science departments have dramatically expanded their offerings on multicultural topics and made concerted efforts to hire faculty from traditionally underrepresented groups to teach them. While these are obviously important first steps, by not revising the genres within these fields, we risk reproducing the same kinds of subjects and discourse communities with the same core identity. Students who major in African-American literature, for example, may be well versed in the slave narratives and their fictional derivatives, but function in their courses—writing papers, theses, and dissertations—as traditional students of literature. Those who go on to graduate school have been shaped by genres that essentially reproduce the kinds of academic professionals, and the kinds of academic communities, that have existed for the last thirty or forty years. Whatever diversity may exist has been contained by the process of professionalization that begins with assimilation of the basic genres. A slightly paranoid interpretation of this phenomenon would be that this is precisely the point. In a fittingly postmodern version of the parable about old wine in new skins, this strategy of political containment might be described as packaging new wine in the same old academic bottles. The problem is that having African-American or African-Americanist academics producing the same kinds of papers and articles does not alter our academic or professional communities in any fundamental way. In fact, it constitutes a failure of the academic community to acknowledge that new fields of knowledge require new forms of representation, thus new genres. Without a revision of the genres that allow us to give a meaning and context to the material we study, we risk denying the differences in the experiences articulated by new material. What we get instead is a normalization of experience and a leveling of differences that preserves the identity of the academic or professional community at the expense of what de Lauretis calls the lived experiences of those who have recently been admitted to it.

The autobiographical turn, however, represents too concrete a response to the deeper theoretical problems of professional identity. It fails to acknowledge the inherently communal nature of professional identity as defined by the notion of discourse community. Including autobiography as a response to the rigidity of institutional genres risks recasting the problem in terms of the older paradigms of expressionism. It offers as a corrective to the problem of a specific configuration of generic procedures that has produced a more or less uniform subject and a homogenous community the illusion that we can somehow simply incorporate new experiences directly through autobiographical accounts of the new members. As an interim solution that points to the gap between the lived experiences of these members and the official genres in which the community's business is transacted, the inclusion of autobiography is useful. This is precisely the value (and the stated intent) of Patricia Williams's efforts in *The Alchemy of Race and Rights*. Yet to the extent that the ground for including these new experiences remains the authority of individuals' experience apart from their participation in the community, the inclusion of autobiography reproduces the original problem by setting the individual against the larger community. Even if the intent is to stake a place for smaller communities within the larger group, the problem remains, since the goal is to define a subset of the community against the identity of the larger group. The strategy behind the autobiographical turn is thus based on a denial of the institutional power of genre as constitutive of discourse communities. Relying on the authority of lived experience risks trivializing the contributions of those whose experiences are represented, since it offers the fiction of a more authentic "experience" as a corrective to a constructed professional identity. Professional identities are always necessarily constructed, however, and to deny that is to deny those who have traditionally been excluded a role in redefining the genre, and thus the subject-position, of the community. We need African American professors, but we also need African Americans who participate in the ongoing redefinition of what it means to be a professor, whether white or black.

As a particular example of the way revising a genre reshapes the subject of the discourse community, the autobiographical turn represents an important intervention. By focusing on a split between the professional and the personal, this change obscures the broader implications contained within it. To turn Gates's argument on its head, I believe we risk losing the sense of the constructedness of our professional selves at the very moment that we become conscious of it.

We face two related problems in our efforts to act on our understanding of the ways in which genres create the subjects of discursive communities. Using the writing classroom to foster a sense of community—to constitute a particular writing class as a fragile discourse community—represents a significant advance on the older individualist, expressionist tradition. Yet my analysis of the way genres can inhibit participation and often tend toward a universal subject suggests we need to be wary of assuming or imposing a communal identity. The first danger I see is that in our desire to create a harmonious and stable community, we will attempt to fix the limits of our genres in ways that inhibit healthy change and growth, and particularly discourage the social transformation of the community through revisions of the genres and the subjects they constitute. While we needn't fall back on an expressionist explanation—the individual must be free of the fetters of oppressive social institutions—we should be conscious of the normalizing or universalizing tendency of genres. Let's imagine the student who produces an essay on affirmative action like Patricia Williams's chapter "The Obliging Shell," which begins and ends with personal narratives, for an instructor not sympathetic to this autobiographical turn, whether for practical (you won't be able to get away with that kind of thing outside of this class) or ideological reasons. Examples like this suggest that in order to allow our communities to remain open and accommodating to diverse experiences, to diverse subjectivities, we need to keep our genres fluid.

On the other hand, we need to be aware that the kind of relativism introduced by the mere inclusion of autobiography limits our ability to intervene in the ongoing process of our self-creation as "professional" subjects. To return to the example of the student who wants to include autobiography in her essay on affirmative action, the professor's objection that "you won't be able to get away with that kind of thing outside this class" raises an important point about our ability to effect such changes on the kind of local, ad hoc basis implied by the proponents of autobiography. As social institutions that regulate the way we do business in the world, generic conventions carry the weight of tradition. We don't do our students any favors by letting them assume that they can violate the conventions of genre without suffering any consequences. As much as we in academia would like to believe in our capacity to make the genres of our professional communities more fluid and open to new experiences, the reality of institutions is that they resist change and growth. Thus, the process of (re)defining the discursive subject of a community is ongoing, but one characterized by a kind of formal resistance built into the nature and function of genre.

I find it useful to conceive of genre, then, as a site for the struggle over the (re)definition of our discourse communities. To teachers of writing, genres are in many ways the only direct access to the social real. For the sake of our students as well as our own effectiveness, we need to be aware of the power of genre. We need to be aware not only that genres are socially constructed but also that they are socially constitutive—in other words, that we both create and are created by the genres in which we work.

Notes

1. It is important to note that this phenomenon is not confined to literary criticism, nor can it be simply defined as an effect of seventies feminism. To understand the overdetermined nature of complex events like this major transformation of the genre of literary criticism, we would also have to recognize the rise and fall of structuralism and its scientific pretensions, the emergence of a left political criticism, and the broader "linguistic turn" in philosophy that has helped undermine positivist epistemology in this century and created a climate conducive to elevating the importance of the subjective.

2. For an example of queer theory and autobiographical criticism, see Sedgwick's *Tendencies*. Gates's most recent book, *Colored People*, is pure autobiography. For an argument for the need to create a complex feminist/Chicano political subject, see Angie Chabram.

3. For an excellent response to Derrida's deconstruction of genre as well as a lucid explication of this notion of genre as historical process undergoing constant revision, see Ralph Cohen.

4

The Yin and Yang of Genres

Irvin Peckham

I apologize for the obscurity of my title. I have had third thoughts about letting it stand because I am hesitant to break the academic title tradition of telling readers up front what the essay will be about. Anticipating your confusion and several of my colleagues' sneers, why, then, did I choose this new age or old hippie title for what is intended as serious discourse? Well, there is a residue of old hippie in me that cannot resist saying what I shouldn't—although I have learned to curb this tendency as the years have worn me down. There is also a serious side to my title, for the yin and yang of existence offered me a frame for my purpose, which is to bring to the surface the sociopolitical and gender-based subtexts underwriting the current debate over the place of genres in writing instruction.

But before exploring the yin and yang of genres, I want to lay a little groundwork by (un)defining genres and addressing a few misconceptions that frequently surround genre discussions. By genre, I mean something more than, for example, the logical, stylistic, and organizational features that can be found in the objective reality of texts (Kinneavy). In line with most current genre theorists, I interpret genres within the interplay of recurring rhetorical situations and texts. As Kenneth Burke has pointed out, rhetorical situations do not, however, exist in isolation; like texts within texts, they are always embedded in other rhetorical situations, which are in turn embedded in others until we get to what might be called the rhetorical situation of life. In addition, genres are generally a matrix of other genres as texts are a matrix of other texts (see Bakhtin, "Problem," 62; *Dialogic* 48–49). Were I to hazard a definition, I would paraphrase Kathleen Jamieson and Karlyn Campbell's claim by saying that genres are a constellation of features that make a group of completed utterances—located within recurring rhetorical situations —seem similar (1978, 18). These features act like internalized schemata that help us respond and interpret how others have responded to similar situations. Unfortunately, as one gets older, life seems to present itself as an unbroken series of recurring rhetorical situations.

This fuzzy definition leads me to some misconceptions one frequently meets upon carelessly declaring one's interest in genres. First is the belief in, as Richard Larson has called it, the "objective existence" of genres (207). James Kinneavy in fact predicated his theory of genres on their objective existence and on his ability to discover them (see 35–49). Even Walter Beale, who generally understands truth as a rhetorical construct, speaks about "discovering" genres (13, 20) as if they were "out there" to be discovered. But genres are not "out there." They are in writers' and readers' heads—and in the collective head of discourse communities that operate under the necessary illusion of genres. I would compare this illusion to the illusion that words have fully determined meanings. We need this illusion of referentiality in order to carry on discourse, but as Wittgenstein remarked, meaning is use (20^e). Likewise with genres. Having said that, I need to hedge a bit by acknowledging that some genres seem more "out there" than others.

Their degree of "out-thereness" depends largely on their level of abstraction. I am using James Moffett's meaning of abstraction (18–23). According to Moffett's notion, a category at one level is an abstraction of (in the sense of taking out) similar features from categories at lower levels. Thus, one arrives at a category that is more general and broader than categories that lie below it. The features one abstracts depend on one's purpose and on socially constructed patterns of signification. We have been socially constructed, for example, to value a distinction between what is real and what is imaginary. Consequently, at a very high level of abstraction, we have genres of fiction and nonfiction prose. At a lower level, we can subclassify nonfiction prose into expressive and transactional prose (Britton, et al.). One can further subdivide (always with the caveat that one is not offering the *real* categories) each category, working downward, perhaps, through transactional to informative discourse, until one gets to de facto genres like obituaries or instruction manuals. Although one might quarrel about genres at higher levels of abstraction, one will more likely admit the "existence" of de facto genres, which are, by Jackson Harrell and Will A. Linkugel's definition, the genres that "common-sense" perception readily recognizes (266–67; Beale, 23–25; see also Kress 1993, 36). One might even dispute the existence of obituaries as a genre by pointing out the differences between obituaries of famous and obscure people (and these differences are significant), but the point is that obituaries seem to be more "out there" than genres like informative or transactional discourse. When we talk about the "objective reality" of genres, then, we need to ground our discussion in some awareness of our level of abstraction, for higher levels of abstraction increasingly reflect the mind's (and society's) way of organizing categories and decreasingly refer to empirical reality (Moffett, 22–23).

Next is the misconception that genres are equally restrictive. One could compare, for instance, obituaries to the novel. Less restrictive genres—like the novel—give writers far more room in which to insert new turns and in those turns reveal themselves. Similarly, one can see that all genres are not equally stable. Bakhtin describes the novel, for example, as volatile by definition (*Dialogic,* 39). Obituaries, by contrast, are exceedingly stable. In genres—as in social structures—stability and restrictivity might in fact be directly proportional to each other. Interestingly enough, they might also have something to do with the social status of people who use them. So much, then, for the ontology of genres. I can now return to why I risked the sneers of certain colleagues by my spacey title: although I hesitate to bore other ex-hippies who yinyanged their ways through the sixties, let me rehearse a few of the notions involved in the Chinese dichotomizing of existence because they illuminate some of our Western concerns about how genres function—both in the classroom and in the sociopolitical arena. Yin and yang are associated in ancient Chinese thought with the cyclical nature of becoming and dissolution. These states of being and nonbeing are in turn associated with some wildly sexist notions of the male and female principles of existence. I apologize for mentioning these—indeed, I would submerge them if it were not for some sexist notions that play themselves out, as Bill Green has argued—in the genre debate over whether, how, and which genres should be taught. The yin, with its softer final consonant, represents the female principle; yang, with its hard terminal consonant, represents the male—I will resist the temptation of devolving into an X-rated analysis, but I have to mention that the yin is the valley, the yang is the mountain, the yin is passive and absorbing, the yang is active and penetrating, and, finally, the yin is the earth and the yang is the sky in a missionary model of metaphysical copulation. In Figure 1, you can see we might further derogate the female principal by comparing yin's dark to yang's light, yin's broken (curvaceous) to yang's straight line, the yin as the moon who can at best in a dissipated fashion reflect the yangish and quite logical sun. According to the ancient and obviously male philosophers, these two forces existing in harmony represent the creative principle of life.

But yin overlapping yang generates chaos; yang overlapping yin brings stasis. This overlapping concept has gender and sociopolitical implications. Mr. Yang—with his emphasis on straight lines, daylight, and patriarchal interpretation of rational discourse—represents authority, the social structure, laws; Ms. Yin—with her broken lines, moonlight, and patriarchal interpretation of emotional discourse—represents rebellion, the individual, anarchy. Pandora and Eve are the most obvious examples of the complementary Western tradition of situating the female as the site of rebellion, the individual resisting the confining presence of laws—or, one might say, genres of behavior.

In his analysis of language, Bakhtin circumscribes the play between these dichotomies with his centripetal and centrifugal tropes (*Dialogic,* 270–274). His centripetal trope represents an alignment of the forces that coalesce, that make things smaller, more governable, more recognizable, more imprisonable. These are the forces that nail meaning down so that when you

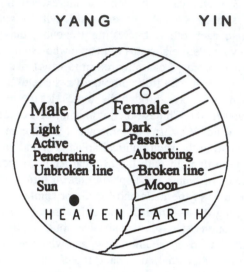

YANG   YIN

BECOMING   DISSOLUTION
Figure 4–1

say a Word, by God, it means something, something definite, something clear, something rational—like a law, like logic, like the male interpretation of male discourse. This pushing of meaning into a recognizable entity is the *becoming* of yang.[1]

Bakhtin's centrifugal trope represents the forces that cause things to fly apart; this is the *dissolution* of yin. When the yang or centripetal force dominates, we have dead words characterizing inauthentic language (*Dialogic*, 60). But when the yin or centrifugal force dominates, words lose their meanings; they dissipate into space. We use dictionaries to freeze words. And we speak to unfreeze them, to give them life overflowing with heteroglossia. In that borderland between yang and yin, or in the tension between the centripetal and centrifugal forces, new meaning (rather than iteration) occurs. And that's why the yin and yang represent the creative principle not only of existence but also of language—and they might be the same thing.

The centripetal and centrifugal tropes also apply to genres. As they work to freeze words, the centripetal or traditional forces of a society work to make genres into rigid units of discourse with predictable features such that texts, to be legitimate, have to fit those rules (the ones normative theories of genres, like Kinneavy's, set out to discover). The centrifugal or revolutionary forces work to break genres, to make them fly outward so that individual texts are only instances of themselves and have only their own criteria to account for. As it is for the word, meaning in completed utterances is created in the tension between the centripetal and centrifugal forces that work to stabilize and destabilize genres.

Several dichotomies echoing these Chinese and Bakhtinian tropes are frequently associated with the debate over the place of genres in writing instruction. I recognize that by dichotomizing the swirl of arguments into the following list of antinomes, I am reifying what I want to diffuse. My only excuse is the traditional one that we often have to look at the parts in order to understand the whole—with the understanding that when we decontextualize the parts, we are transforming them. I do not believe these dichotomies are any more "out there" than genres are. But by viewing them through the double lenses of the Chinese and Bakhtinian tropes, I am trying to highlight the gender and sociopolitical subtexts underwriting the genre debate.

[Centripetal/Yang/Male]	[Centrifugal/Yin/Female]
PRO GENRE	NO GENRE
Form	Content
Text	Context
Product	Process
Closed	Open
Objectivity	Subjectivity
Conformity	Individuality
Traditional	Progressive
Stability	Flexibility

At one level of abstraction, the yangish advocates of genres are associated with privileging form. The yins vote for content. The form is the Platonic abstraction—one might say the Father Heaven of discourse; the content is the instance—or the Mother Earth. On a different level, the form is the social structure; the content is the individual. Socialization is a process of learning to conform to the forms of society—or, in our particular area of concern, to the genres of discourse. Writers resist socialization by resisting genre constraints. When Maurice Blanchot insists that "the book alone is important, as it is, far from genres, outside rubrics . . . under which it refuses to be arranged and to which it denies the power to fix its place and to determine its form" (qtd. in Todorov 1976, 159), he is asserting the integrity of the text and of the artist who refuses to be pushed into meaning by the centripetal forces of society. The danger of this "arrangement," to genre resisters like Blanchot, is that it may lead to a mindless conformity, an erasure of self that becomes a habit of both thinking and being. Genre advocates, on the other hand, might claim (or at least believe) that acceptance of this socialization process marks maturity. As one grows up, one learns one has to live within the institution—that is to say, speak within genres, inserting one's individuality within whatever wiggle room the genre allows.

From this kind of sociopolitical perspective, the other antinomes in the series of dichotomies associated with the genre debate generally align themselves with the Centripetal/Yang/Male or the Centrifugal/Yin/Female forces. To add other lenses through which to see this issue, one might say the Yangs are neoclassicists; the Yins are romantics. Or the Yangs are hard-edged rigorists; the Yins are the soft nurturers, returning us to Bill Green's thesis, albeit in different tropes: the Yangs are men; the Yins are women. Yangs (objectivists) disregard themselves and write in forms. Yins (subjectivists) disregard forms and write themselves. It is not too difficult to see how these alignments play themselves out in the classroom—and why, consequently, the debate over genres frequently takes on a sharp edge. When we are talking about whether and how we should teach students to write "in genres," we are really talking about a host of other issues that have everything to do with who we are and how we see ourselves as subjectivities being pushed and pulled, shaped and reshaped by the different positions in which we sometimes surprisingly find ourselves. Some of us yearn for objectivity; we like tradition, the stability of forms. Some of us revel in our subjectivities; we like change, movement. We travel. We greet with enthusiasm the differences in content.

In *Distinction: A Social Critique of the Judgment of Taste*, Pierre Bourdieu reads these different orientations as markers of social class—or, more accurately, of class fractions.[2] The "upper" classes play, as it were, in the Heaven of forms. The "lower" classes work in the earth of content. A focus on the form of something highlights how it is constructed, the relationship of the parts; a focus on the content highlights what it is—which, in the lower classes, is defined by what it does. Bourdieu very interestingly extends these orientations toward diet, table manners, clothes, sports, entertainment, art, social customs, gestures, and language. Within the genres of writing, one finds the upper classes privileging literary genres, where the focus is on style and organization—that is, on the text as text. The lower classes privilege—in Britton's terms—transactional texts, the kind that "gets things done" (88). There are of course wheels within wheels: within the wheel of transactional genres, the upper classes read texts featuring concepts, that tell *about* things; the lower classes read texts that tell how to do things. Within the wheel of literary genres,[3] the lower classes read stories with strong narratives that allow readers to escape their everyday lives. The upper classes read literature that draws attention to the text as being other than what it represents. This foregrounding of text allows the reader to maintain a distance from the narrative. This distance, marked by the ironic gaze, reflects the upper class distance from the gross materiality of the world (Bourdieu 1984, 32–35). That is to say, the upper classes don't have to clean their bathrooms; the lower classes do.

Let me end this speculative essay with an interpretation of how gender and sociopolitical subtexts are written in the genre debate. The play of these subtexts on the field of genres is a manifestation of a society's self-authorization by dichotomizing experience and then socializing people by impressing these dichotomies into them as if they were real. The key to this self-authorization lies in the implicit privileging of one member of the dichotomy. Although I may be accused of having created them, I have tried to interpret in this essay a series of dichotomies embedded within the Chinese metaphor for the nature of existence, within the Bakhtinian metaphor for describing the nature of language, and within the arguments for and against the use of genres in writing instruction. Taken together, the series of dichotomies reveal an ideological privileging that has crossed cultures and time, reflecting patriarchal and class-based values. Although lip service is paid to the dark, feminine side of the master trope, there is never any question that the real power lies with those who associate themselves with the Centripetal/Yang/Male forces. Within the genre debate, society's urge to reproduce itself is perhaps reflected in the privileging of "rigorous" (read hard, penetrating, the desired phallic state) educators who make their students shape their texts/selves to fit genre conventions. These rigorous educators, in turn, favor the more restrictive, "objective" genres (see Martin and Rothery, Christie). They are, after all, the genres of power, the genres that "get things done" in the world. Less privileged are the nurturing (read soft, yielding, receptive) educators who encourage students either to ignore genres or to write themselves in the warm, fuzzy subjectivity of expressive genres, such as journals, autobiographical incidents, or—somewhat more respectably —personal essays. The rigorous educators are of course masculine; the nurturing, feminine. Or to shift the perspective, the men are upper, and the women lower class—an association that accounts for the current commonplace that narrative represents women's way of knowing.

But rather than end with a point, let me conclude with a story. I remember walking when I was young in the hills behind our Wisconsin farm and coming across the old deserted Snyder house in some forgotten valley. I was surprised to find the large living room window still intact. I did what any young boy is supposed to do. I found a rock and threw it through the window. The sound of the breaking glass, although frightening, brought pleasure. So it is with genres.

Notes

1. Although Heaven seems to work azgainst Bakhtin's centripetal trope, if we interpreted Heaven as the site of God (rational discourse, the head) and Earth as the site of humans/animals (of irrational discourse, of the body), we can appreciate the patriarchal logic governing this distribution of attributes. Heaven, although it would seem to be centrifugal, is actually centering, the locus of law and logic. Earth is the locus of irrational, dispersive behavior.

2. Bourdieu recognizes that a social class is a category and, therefore, conceptual only. He points out that one creates a category of social class by choosing the features that count (12, 479–84).

3. I am interpreting "literary" genres as fiction and poetry that makes no pretense to verisimilitude. I am collapsing the class-based distinction between such things as "literature" and pulp novels.

5

Genre as Language Standard

Amy J. Devitt

Although genre is currently being redefined (see Bakhtin, "Problem"; Carolyn Miller, "Genre"; Swales; Berkenkotter and Huckin, "Rethinking"; Devitt, "Generalizing") as an active social and rhetorical construct, we have not yet come to terms with the constraining power of genre, with genre as restrictor of individual creativity and originality.[1] Frances Christie has argued that genre and choice are not inimical and that genre enables choice, but, as convincing as many of Christie's arguments are, her perspective still implies that constraint is bad and choice is good. Instead of seeing a dichotomy between constraint and choice, my argument in this chapter is that we must see both constraint and choice as necessary components of genre—both/and instead of either/or. This complementary relationship between constraint and choice within genre can be clarified by comparing it to standardization and variation within language. Using the metaphor of genre as a language standard (and I will treat it now as a metaphor, though it becomes more literal by the end of this chapter), I will argue that genres, like language standards, interlink standards/constraints and variation/choice, an interlink essential to the construction of meaning.

We cannot deny that genres do in fact constrain and limit the possibilities of what people write. As long as I want to "reach" my audience and accomplish my goals, I will not write up the results of my college laboratory experiment as a first-person narrative of my experience, including all my hopes and fears and mistakes. Once I accept that my rhetorical and social goals will best be accomplished by writing a school lab report, my writing will follow an expected organizational pattern, including sections of introduction, methods, results, and discussion, will use passive voice freely to avoid first-person pronouns and to avoid calling attention to the researcher, will present results in numerical and tabular form, and much more. The established genre of the school lab report will dictate much of what I write.

But pause for a moment to consider alternatives: How does an inanimate genre "dictate" my writing? What if I have never written or read a lab report before and do not know what is expected? What if I do not want to "reach" my audience in the expected way? What if I do not want to accomplish the assumed goals but rather my own goals, perhaps to startle my rigid teacher and to subvert the conformity required in my science class? The existence of a genre in an established rhetorical and social context does not "dictate" any writing: it is a choice that can be made. Yes, it is a "choice" with powerful incentives and punishments attached, and the embeddedness of genres within ideologies and power structures will be considered toward the end of this chapter. For now, it is enough to notice that the existence of genre as a constraint on writing is not as simple as might be expected.

With a beginning nod to the complexity of constraint, let us return to acknowledging that genre does, of course, represent established expectations of what "good" writers write in particular contexts and that to subvert those expectations entails consequences of various kinds, good and bad. (To conform to those expectations also entails consequences, good and bad.) Genres do constrain writing in that sense, and in that sense, genres are also like language standards. Language standards are the rules of linguistic etiquette—rules of punctuation in writing, usage standards in speech and writing (subject-verb agreement, pronoun case, verb tenses, and so on, what some have called "grammar" but what is more precisely called "usage"; see Hartwell). Language standards, like genres, represent established expectations of what "good" language-users do in particular contexts; to subvert those expectations of language standards is to invite consequences, both good and bad.

The constraint of language standards has been reviled by some English teachers as a constrictor of individual freedom in the form of individual idiolects, as restrictor of the home dialect and all it stands for, and as senseless formula contrived by members of the upper class to oppress members of the lower classes. It has been revered by others as keeper of the gate against anarchy and unintelligibility and as the tool of empowerment for the disadvantaged, who can gain access to the circles of power if only they have access to the standard language. These two perspectives on language standards represent ends of a spectrum. A similar spectrum concerning genre has begun to appear. The debate about whether or not to teach genre explicitly, as has been done in the Australian curriculum, revolves around whether the teaching of genre liberates the socially excluded or enforces artificial formulae (see, for example, the chapters in Reid, in Cope and Kalantzis, *Powers*, and the discussion around Aviva Freedman's article "Show and Tell?" in *Research in the Teaching of English*). I do not intend to join the fray about explicit teaching in this chapter, although I will consider the implications for teaching at the end. Instead, I want to stress that the similarity of the debates about teaching genres and teaching language standards further suggests that we can better understand the constraints and choices of genre if we examine genre's similarities with the constraints and choices of language standards. Both genre and language standards are, at least in part, standardizing influences on discourse. Both bring greater uniformity to language use, greater homogeneity; both act as centrifugal forces, holding language use together (for perspectives on language standards, see, for example, Devitt 1989, Heath 1980, and other articles in Shopen and Williams, Haas, Crowley, and Joseph). That both also encompass centripetal forces is the crux of my later argument.

As we now understand from recent arguments about genre and long-standing views of linguistic standards, both genres and language standards are socially constructed. Without recapping all the arguments and their critiques in detail, I will simply refer to major theses about the construction of genre and standards. Genres develop within groups, discourse communities with common purposes (Swales), and are situated within groups (Berkenkotter and Huckin 1993). They respond to rhetorical situations that recur within particular groups (C. R. Miller, Devitt 1993) and fulfill the functions of those groups (Devitt 1991). Genres serve to construct the situation as well as to be constructed by the situation (Devitt 1993). Historically as well as theoretically, genres can be seen to develop within contexts (see Yates or Jamieson, for example), responding to individual and group influences in such ways as to serve the needs of both and reciprocally shaping and being shaped by social and rhetorical context. Our perception of genres also results from our social and cultural context.

Genres, then, are not arbitrary or random, being tied to rhetorical and social purposes and contexts, but neither are they necessary and inevitable, being shaped by various influences at various times. Similarly, language standards are neither wholly arbitrary nor predictable. The history of Standard Edited English (SEE), a standard for formal written texts, is complex and multiple (see Heath 1980, Fisher, and Crowley, for three examples). It may have first developed from scribal practices in Anglo Saxon times; it was shaped by explicit commentary in the seventeenth and especially eighteenth centuries. Whatever history is traced, however, it is clear that SEE developed partly out of social context for social purposes. The prestige and power of the London-Cambridge-Oxford area shaped the initial spoken dialect, as did the dialect of William Caxton and the first printers; the need for a common dialect for printed texts may have encouraged the promotion of a single dialect while at the same time the erosion of class distinctions may have encouraged the promotion of linguistic distinctions in the form of a more rigid prestige dialect. As historians trace these and other contextual factors in the development of SEE, it is clear that this language standard is neither wholly arbitrary nor inevitable. Both genre and language standards are socially constituted.

For both genres and language standards, formal features can be specified. The genre of lab report includes an organizational pattern, stylistic features, and textual appearance that I described earlier. The language standard of SEE includes such formal features as the use of "whom" in objective case, use of a comma between independent clauses joined by a coordinating conjunction, use of "doesn't" to agree with third person singular subjects, and so on. In fact, for SEE we have a complex vocabulary for describing such formal features, called "school grammar" in Hartwell's terms.

These formal features can and will change, however. In SEE, multiple negation was standard in Chaucer's time, and the once standard distinction between "less" and "fewer" is apparently becoming obsolete. The changes in the form of the experimental article have been traced in detail by Charles Bazerman (1988), including changes in the use of first person, of tables and graphs, and of organization. The history of the memorandum has similarly been described by JoAnne Yates. Even though the formal features of a genre can be specified, they do not constitute the genre. As these historical cases demonstrate, the genre exists even as its formal features change. The same might be said for a language standard: its specific features can change and the standard, as a social construct, can remain in place. We do not claim that SEE no longer exists just because multiple negation is no longer acceptable and "less" more generally is. Conceivably, a genre or a language standard could undergo so many changes in formal features that we would indeed perceive and define it as a new genre or different language standard. In terms of language standards, however, such redefinition tends to occur as a political rather than a formal statement: for example, a government declares for political reasons that a new standard will be imposed, a standard that is a version of an existing standard. I suspect that renaming of genres similarly tends to result from political rather than formal changes: "creative non-fiction" may differ formally from "essays," but the essay genre might have continued to encompass a wide range of forms were it not for the negative connotation of the freshman or school essay. Another factor in genre definition may be simple frequency: the popularity of the "nature essay" may move it from its perception as a subset of one genre to a genre of its own. Political and popularity forces combined may lead to the academic essay subdividing into traditional or scholarly essays and "new" or personal academic essays. Changes in formal features alone, I suspect, are not enough to cause renaming of a genre or language standard without political forces encouraging such redefinition. The genre and the standard are much more than listings of their formal features.

Although the specific formal features of genres and language standards may change, readers/listeners expect some common features and may notice if there are variations or violations. That is, genres and language standards have a "reality" for readers/listeners. The student who includes no "Methods" section in her lab report will probably receive a lower grade; the student who writes "The chemical don't work" will probably be noticed negatively. As Joseph Williams points out in his important article "The Phenomenology of Error," however, not all variations are noticed equally, and neither is conformity to all rules. Some features of SEE are noticed only when they are violated (using "doesn't," for example, or beginning a sentence with a capital letter) and others only when they are met (using "whom" and "fewer" may soon fit that category). Some features are noticed neither in their violation nor in their conformity (the split infinitive may fit that category for many people; using a comma after an introductory phrase may as well).

A case could be made for the same being true of genre features. Some are noticed only when they are violated: the aforementioned absence of a "Methods" section in a lab report, perhaps, or the inclusion of numerical results in prose form. Others are noticed when they are met: perhaps the poetic form of a sonnet written today. Still others are not noticed at all, in agreement or in violation: perhaps the use of passive or active voice in a lab report would not be noticed but only the use of "I." Both genres and language standards, therefore, are connected to specific formal features, which may change over time, and readers/listeners come to expect certain features and, at times, to notice how those expectations are met.

So far, I have been writing as though SEE is the only language standard while drawing examples from multiple genres. In fact, both genres and language standards are multiple and vary in different contexts. Contrary to popular opinion, SEE is not the one and true standard for all occasions. Linguists have long noted the multiplicity of standards (see Krapp, for example), from a national standard like Received Pronunciation (RP) in England to regional standards like upper-class Southern American English. If a language standard is acknowledged wherever a group expects a set of features from its members, then the multiplicity of language standards can be seen to extend across situations as well, with the same speaker using a different standard in intimate conversation from the standard used in formal written academic essays. (For more on this view of standards see Chapter 1 in Devitt 1989.) If one were to use SEE on the playground or in a letter to a friend, one would be considered "wrong," as using inappropriate language. Use of the subjective case of the pronoun in the subject complement position after a copulative verb may be "correct" in SEE, but "It is I" would be considered a joking response to the question "Who's there" after a knock on a dorm room door. The child who uses "whom" while playing marbles is likely to be laughed at. On the other hand, the child who does not use nicknames and slang is equally inappropriate. The African-American living in a lower class section of Detroit who speaks to friends without using African-American English Vernacular may be seen as speaking inappropriately. That is, a language standard exists on the playground and among less powerful groups in society as well, a standard in which the participants expect some features and not others. The standard of the less powerful or of the playground is no less a standard for not being institutionalized; its rules may be just as rigidly and even harshly enforced, and it may just as well mark insiders and outsiders. Language standards are also multiple across speakers, for different speakers apply different standards and in different contexts. The aforementioned African-American may use SEE in school or at work; a college professor may use Appalachian English when visiting at home. There are some who never use SEE, just as there are some in England who do not use RP. To some, even upper-class Southern American English seems "wrong" and non-standard; to others that dialect seems affected and inappropriate for casual conversation. These multiple language standards with their different sets of features shift for everyone across context, situation, and individual.

That there are multiple genres, like multiple standards, is obvious, but the multiplicity of genres goes beyond that obvious statement. Like language standards, genres shift across context, situation, and individual. The extensive variety of genres in different contexts has been established by many researchers, in literature and composition studies, as has the development of different genres in different rhetorical situations. Many scholars, grounding their theories of genre in the theory of M. A. K. Halliday (1978), have stressed the functional nature of genres as they respond to the situations and serve the needs of different communities (for example, Swales, Reid, Devitt 1993). Since genres function to fulfill the needs of their users, different situations for different users in different social and cultural contexts create different genres. The multiplicity of genres is inherent in a functional view of genre. The related view of genres as socially constructed further reinforces that our perceptions of genres will be multiple. Just as standards depend on whose standards, genres depend on whose genres. They can be perceived, described, and classified in different ways depending on who is doing the classifying. Like national versus regional language standards, a genre can be classified as narrative or fiction or novel or Bildungsroman; another as persuasion or argument or essay or article or editorial. Different genres exist for different people in different contexts as well as for different purposes in different situations. Both genres and language standards are multiple in multiple ways.

As we pursue the metaphor of genre as language standard, genre comes more and more to be tied not just to function but also to appropriateness. Standards of language use, commonly metaphorized as linguistic etiquette, involve expectations of appropriate behavior. The standard of SEE entails certain features that have come to represent formality and education. The standard of upper-class Southern American English entails certain features that have come to represent education, breeding, and regional loyalty. The standard of African-American English Vernacular entails certain features that have come to represent ethnic identity and loyalty. The standard of the playground entails certain features that have come to represent intimacy, playfulness, and "coolness." Whereas language standards have come to be viewed in terms of appropriateness, genre has come to be viewed by recent theorists primarily in terms of function. The metaphor of language standard allows us to emphasize that genres, like language standards, are both functional and appropriate.

Although well established as conventions marking appropriateness, language standards, like genres, are also functional: they serve the needs of the community both for markers of membership and for increased intelligibility.

In reducing variation, they increase intelligibility across time and space; and, in restricting variation, they encourage conformity of group members and give them linguistic signals of who belongs and who does not. Although well established as functional, genres, like language standards, are also appropriate. Genres, too, are linguistic etiquette, exhibiting the "proper" (that is, appropriate) behavior at the proper occasion. Once genres have become well established, they are not just, as Bitzer described them, "fitting" responses to rhetorical situations and therefore functionally and rhetorically effective, but also appropriate behavior in conventional social contexts and therefore socially effective. They meet our expectations for proper behavior, for generic etiquette.

Extending the etiquette metaphor from standards to genres can clarify one aspect of generic constraint. The functional nature of genres and language standards constrains the writer/speaker because they represent effective means of fulfilling some purpose. Following the generic "rules" enables one to achieve a goal; not following them potentially leaves some important function unfulfilled. The appropriate nature of genres and language standards constrains the writer/speaker because they are conventionalized proper behavior. Following generic etiquette "rules" enables one to "fit in," to be marked as belonging to the group; not following generic etiquette marks one as not belonging in some way. One must learn or acquire the rules of generic etiquette. Some acquire even the most advanced rules early, as parents and friends and schools provide an environment in which the etiquette of many sophisticated genres is followed regularly; others must make an effort to learn the etiquette rules of some genres later and may never learn the rules sufficiently to fit in completely. Different societies may make that generic etiquette more or less accessible, depending on the strength of their desire to include and exclude people.

In addition to genre constraining people because it is functional, then, generic etiquette constrains people if they want to belong to a group. That constraint is powerful, more powerful perhaps than the trivialized notion of etiquette can capture. Depending on the society, the need to belong to a group—or the power of membership in a particular group—may be so strong that individuals choose to violate such etiquette only at great risk to their well-being. Or the social training to that etiquette may be so ingrained that individuals can "choose" to violate it only with great difficulty, so ingrained that many, in fact, may be unable to "choose" to do otherwise. Again, the comparison with language standards illuminates the difficulty, for sociolinguists have long recognized and amply demonstrated that individuals have strong and unconscious attachments to the dialects and standards they have been raised with, attachments that appear in the language they "choose" to use. Most noticeable to the nonlinguist perhaps is the virulence with which variations on an established language standard are attacked in letters to the editor and editorials by linguistic prescriptivists and purists such as William

Safire. How dare we use "flaunt" when "flout" is intended! The constraint of linguistic, and so perhaps generic, etiquette is personally, socially, politically, and ideologically loaded. It is a powerful constraint, indeed.

But even the most rigid and institutionalized language standard does not constrain all linguistic behavior, does not proscribe and prescribe every element of every word that is said or written. Broadening language standard to encompass all "rules" for language use in different settings still does not provide rules for every utterance. Even the sociolinguists who attempted to state rules for every usage and pronunciation called them "variable rules," ones that did not apply 100 percent of the time, and they allowed for what was once called "free" variation, unexplained differences in what individuals said. Within each language standard, in fact, remains great variation, both free variation and variable rules. SEE specifies that "whom" be used in objective functions, but it does not specify when "use" rather than "utilize" must appear. It specifies what will constitute subject-verb agreement, but it does not specify which verbs should be used. Added to such free variation are the many variable rules: use a comma after an introductory phrase, unless the phrase is short (how short? it varies); collective nouns are singular or plural, depending on context. A great deal of the language remains as individual choice, necessary flexibility without which individuals could not mean different things. The same is true, I argue, for genres.

Genres, too, permit a great deal of individual choice, for not every aspect of every text is specified by any genre. The lab report, for a continued example, may seem a relatively rigid genre, yet it does not dictate how the research question will be worded or which apparatus will be described first. Within any genre, there is a great deal of "free" variation. Even the generic rules that we might consider specified are often really variable rules: the passive voice is common, but the researcher's activities can be and are described actively sometimes; the Results section precedes the Discussion section, except sometimes when a writer combines the Results and Discussion into a single section. Variation is permitted to the degree that it does not negate either function or appropriateness. (An interesting question for future research is how much and what types of variation retain function and appropriateness.)

Such variation is not only available within genres and language standards; it is necessary for genres and language standards to exist. Without variation, it would not be possible to perceive standardization; without generic choice, it would not be possible to enact generic constraint. Language standards imply the existence of linguistic variation; generic constraints imply the existence of generic choices. If there were no variation in how people used the language, all people would speak exactly alike (a linguistic impossibility, in fact, but a hypothetical case that will serve for illumination). If all people spoke exactly alike, their similarities would probably go unnoticed, for there would be no contrast to call attention to any feature. As long as all humans have eyes, noses, and mouths, poets will not sing praises to the fact that their lovers have mouths; it is the way the lover's mouth differs from others that is noticed, is, in fact, the contrast with others that gives the lover's facial features meaning. It is, similarly, the contrast of one language feature with another that constructs meaning. It is in the "not-statements" (Freadman), in the semantic and semiotic relationships (Halliday 1978), in the variation within standardization, in the choice within constraint that meaning resides. Without the possibility of an alternative, no standards need develop for no meaning is made.

That is in fact the case for linguistic and textual features that have no alternatives. In English, no language standard specifies that the definite article precedes rather than follows the noun; grammarians specify it, but it is a descriptive, not prescriptive rule. (No native speaker will utter "dog the.") The meaning resides in what the standard does specify, the contrast between a noun phrase with a definite article (the dog) and one without (a dog). Similarly, the lab report genre does not prescribe that the text will break into paragraphs, that it will be written in sentences, or that it will be written and not sung. The meaning of the lab report genre resides where it does contrast with other texts, in the expectation of a Methods section, in the avoidance of active agency, in the dependence on visual aids. Where there are no alternatives, there is no standard. Where there are both standards and variations, there is meaning.

Too much choice is as debilitating of meaning as is too little choice. In language, too much variation results eventually in lack of meaning: mutual unintelligibility. As the Latin-derived languages came to vary in more and more ways, they came to be so distinct as to be unintelligible, unmeaningful, to speakers of the other language—hence French and Italian. In genre, perhaps some genres permit more variation than others (the novel comes to mind), but variation cannot be infinite or the discourse might be unintelligible. Even the varied *Finnegans Wake* plays with narrative structure and stream of consciousness, traits of the novel genre. Even choice that is less than infinite can be paralyzing. Can each language user respond to each rhetorical situation anew? Can each utterance require a new organization? It is with some reason that many students panic when the assignment "allows" them to "write on any topic." As Christie argues, choice is enhanced by constraint, made possible by constraint. Further, I argue that meaning is enhanced by both choice and constraint. Meaning exists in the interaction of choice and constraint, in genre no less than in words.

Every utterance is constraint and choice, within the language itself, within the situation, within individual ability and characteristics, within the ideological and social context. Genre and language standards point out the places of variation and choice by delimiting that variation and choice. Rather than genres and language standards inscribing only constraints, then, they encompass both constraint and choice. No longer a metaphor now, genre and language standards share the same fundamental trait of language, considered from two perspectives. Both constraint and choice, standardization and variation, are necessary for utterance, for meaning. Too much or too little of either is linguistically and rhetorically paralyzing. Language and utterances require both a centrifugal and a centripetal force to maintain the balance of meaning. Genre and language standards both exhibit that fundamental trait of language, a balance of standardization and variation.

If the metaphoric and more literal connection of genre as language standard has illuminated the role of constraint/standardization and choice/variation, then perhaps it can illuminate the place of genre in the writing classroom. With language standards, many of us have come to an uneasy compromise: we teach the diversity and social constructedness of language standards, and we teach the possibility of resisting those standards, while we also teach the one language standard, SEE, that "educated" contexts require. What matters most is more an attitude toward standards that we teach than a particular pedagogy or set of skills. A similar approach to genre would seem to me to be appropriate. Our attitude toward genres in the classroom could include: that genres are diverse, including the formal research paper and the friends' conversation; that their expectations are constructed in response to social and rhetorical contexts; that it is possible to violate any generic expectations; while at the same time we might teach and expect the genres most important to "educated" contexts. Whether those genres ought to be taught explicitly I leave to debates about the issues Freedman (1993) has raised so clearly and about other issues to be raised in the future.

What I am sure of is that the existence of genres and their power to constrain and enable choice is something we should confront directly. We can confront it when we teach first-year writing and decide whether to teach "the essay" or how much to insist on the conventions of "academic writing." We can confront it when we begin our dissertations and consider the attitudes toward knowledge and personal experience that we must adopt if our dissertations are to be passed—or when we direct our student's dissertation and decide how much "dissertationese" we must require for our colleagues to accept it. We can confront it whenever we "do" scholarship on composition and select the genres within which our participants will work, a choice that may determine a community, an ideology, a voice, and much more. When in our past we failed to examine language standards, we taught them to our students unthinkingly and uncritically. When we saw language standards as evil constraints only, we failed to enable our students to use the prestige dialect to achieve their own goals. Only when we see language standards as both inhibiting and enabling, can we give students the power to use them critically. Only when we understand genres as both constraint and choice, both regularity and chaos, both inhibiting and enabling will we be able to help students to use the power of genres critically and effectively. In such power is individual freedom.

Notes

1. My ideas in this paper have advanced considerably through discussions with many people, especially James Hartman and the members of my seminar on genre theory in the spring of 1994: Anis Bawarshi, Lara Corkrey, Angela Crow, Wendy Doman, Scott Hendrix, Lee Hornbrook, Daniel Kulmala, Susan Malmo, Andrew Moody, Mary Jo Reiff, Jean Reitz, Aaron Rosenberg, Elizabeth Rowse, and Amy Southerland. I owe them all my thanks, but they would not all agree with all of what I argue here, so the responsibility for the ideas remains mine.

6

Boundary Rhetoric and Disciplinary Genres:
Redrawing the Maps in Interdisciplinary Writing

Debra Journet

It is now commonly accepted that the genres through which a discipline embodies its knowledge are not essentialist types but socially constructed codes of behavior: they are the necessary language and customs one must learn when entering the territory of any disciplinary community (Bakhtin, "Speech"; Berkenkotter and Huckin, *Genre*; C. Miller, "Genre"). It is also true, of course, that the territorial boundaries dividing disciplines are commonly understood as socially constructed rather than as preexisting distinctions between different types of knowledge (Foucault 1972, Messer-Davidow et al., Rorty). Nevertheless, despite their constructed nature, genres—and the disciplines they constitute—are powerful operative categories with real historical, rhetorical, and even political force. Genres allow disciplinary communities to do their work. They embed and encode communal assumptions and values, thus enabling groups of people with shared interests to advance claims and move toward consensus. Genres bring together not only discursive forms and vocabulary, but the common problems or representations of reality, the preferred methods and techniques, and the whole range of theoretical, methodological, and epistemological commitments that constitute a discipline.

The political as well as intellectual power of disciplines is reflected in the very language we use to talk about them, especially the territorial image of disciplines as self-enclosed entities. Klein has described the dominant metaphor of disciplinarity as one of "geopolitics," particularly the language of imperialism, and has discussed the way images such as "turf," "property," "boundaries," "borders," as well as "territory" pervade and structure our thinking. Such imagery, she argues, reflects most importantly the sociopolitical reality of disciplines, particularly the degree to which they are embedded in academic institutions (77–78). It also reflects, I would argue, the idea of shared language and customs I am associating with genres.

Research in composition has devoted some attention to the difficulties writers can face as they learn the customs and language of new territories, especially the complex genres of academic disciplinary writing (e.g., Berkenkotter et al., Myers). But alongside the problems of becoming acculturated to the "strange land" (McCarthy) of new disciplinary genres is another issue: the growing phenomenon of interdisciplinarity and the rhetorical challenges it poses. The presence of territorial images of disciplines suggests some of the problems inherent in interdisciplinary discourse, particularly the often political and social as well as theoretical and methodological differences writers must mediate. If genres reflect shared disciplinary commitments— commitments often built up through lengthy negotiation (Bazerman 1988)— then dismantling disciplinary boundaries may mean reformulating generic modes of expression. This tension between genres may pose particular difficulties when writers try to communicate with diverse groups of readers about phenomena each claims as its own.

Others have written of some of the rhetorical challenges of straddling disciplinary boundaries (e.g. Klein, Lyon, Roberts and Good). It is these challenges I wish to consider by suggesting an interdisciplinary rhetorical strategy I have labeled boundary rhetoric (Journet 1993). One of the most complete considerations of interdisciplinary rhetoric is that of Fuller, who has offered the metaphor of "interpenetration" to describe dialectical models of interdisciplinarity that "call into question the differences between disciplines involved and thereby serve as forums for the renegotiation of disciplinary boundaries" (33). Fuller describes several rhetorical modes for interdisciplinary work. The boundary rhetoric I am proposing is closest to the one he calls "sublimation": an interdisciplinary rhetoric in which "each side- ... export[s] ideas that are essential to the other's project. Thus differences are 'sublimated' by showing them to be natural extensions of one another's position" (63). My conception of boundary rhetoric suggests that in certain situations writers may sublimate differences not just by articulating connections but also by recasting the knowledge claims of one discipline into the generic forms of the other. That is, the boundary rhetorician's interdisciplinary theory is paralleled by her intergeneric discourse, a new hybrid genre that reshapes the values and assumptions of each discipline into the discursive forms of the other. These new genres do not simply juxtapose disciplinary perspectives; instead, they demonstrate the subtle and familiar ways in which one kind of knowledge can be made to seem related to another.[1]

The problems and challenges of crossing disciplinary borders seem to me a very important issue in many areas of scholarship today. Certainly, they are crucial in composition studies, which has always been interdisciplinary in its objects of investigation as well as methods of research and generic modes of discourse. Most immediately, these issues seem relevant to the central debate between cognitive and contextual approaches to writing research and instruction, a debate that has been the focus of our attention since the early 1980s. Much of this debate has been polarized, I think, because writers depend on colonizing strategies, even when they are making concessions toward the other position and ostensibly arguing for reconciliation. Instead, I think we need to look for possibilities of boundary rhetoric. To illustrate these possibilities, and to clarify the relation between epistemology and genre, I want to look at how similar issues are treated by a group of writers in another field: an interdisciplinary attempt to connect neurology and psychology as competing ways to explain particular phenomena. The generic innovations produced by the medical writers I describe may offer possibilities for an interdisciplinary boundary rhetoric useful to composition studies. We find the beginning of such boundary rhetorics, I will argue, in manifestos and in research projects that explicitly try to incorporate multiple perspectives. But the interdisciplinary possibilities of such multimodal research may be inevitably limited without generic innovations to reflect our ambitious multidisciplinary goals.

Interdisciplinary Knowledge, Boundary Rhetoric, and the Human Sciences

The debate about cognitive and contextual perspectives in composition is more than a debate about writing theory; it is also a product of significant methodological and epistemological differences—differences which result in very different generic forms of research. While the specifics of this debate are technical and detailed, its general parameters can be seen in the various ways it has been characterized: researchers, for example, speak of differences between general and local (Carter) or nomothetic and ideographic (North 1985) knowledge; between empirical, experimental or positivist and interpretive, hermeneutic or constructivist epistemologies (Berkenkotter 1991, Brandt 1992, Heap); between quantitative and qualitative methods (Hillocks). Such a debate is not unique to composition studies, but is, in fact, central throughout the human sciences (Berkenkotter 1991). I want to gather these differences under umbrella terms proposed by Bruner (1986), who differentiates these positions—in terms of both knowledge and discourse—as logico-scientific (or paradigmatic) and narrative modes.

The general questions faced in these debates concern the degree to which human behavior can be objectively described or must be subjectively interpreted, as well as the extent to which the researcher's observations are generalizable over more than one group of individuals or are seen to be true only of individual cases. Arguments aimed at verifiable reference and empirical truth usually emphasize covering laws that govern the phenomena under study and reduce individuals to examples of universal principles. Arguments aimed at interpretation usually emphasize the particularities of phenomena and the uniqueness of individual cases. These differences in epistemology and methodology are intimately related to differences in genre and modes of argumentation. Researchers who adopt the first mode construct empirically verified, general explanations and tend to produce genres that rely on logico-scientific analysis and exposition, that try to efface the character of the researcher, and that limit or suppress unique personal or social complexities of the situation. In composition, such genres include experimental reports (usually presented in the introduction, methods, results, discussion format) or other forms of quantitative, statistically interpreted research. Researchers who adopt the second mode construct interpretations of particular cases and tend to produce genres that rely on narrative, that recognize the situated position of the researcher as interpreter, and that stress the cultural and social complexities of the individuals and situations being observed. Prominent genres for this kind of research in composition include qualitative case studies or ethnographies. That is, logico-scientific genres and narrative genres construct different *kinds* of knowledge.[2]

The particular debates between cognitive and contextual approaches that have concerned us are not, of course, that direct or simple. Nevertheless, the presence of different traditions of research and the genres that construct them suggests that if we are to combine cognitive and contextual approaches, as so many have advocated, into more inclusive approaches to writing research, we may also need to combine the generic characteristics of each research tradition. That is, as we renegotiate disciplinary boundaries, we may need to create new genres to embody our interdisciplinary research.

If we look at a different field that faces a similar debate and hence a similar rhetorical problem we may find possibilities for this boundary rhetoric. For the past several years, I have conducted research on several neurologists—including Oliver Sacks, A. R. Luria, and Smith Ely Jelliffe—who were all dissatisfied with the limitations that the neurological paradigm imposed on their understanding and treatment of patients with specific brain disorders (Journet 1990, 1993). Neurology, they argue, typically explains the consequences of brain injury or illness in positivistic, reductive, physiological terms—logico-scientific explanations that are valid but by themselves partial and inadequate. In response to these perceived limitations in their own discipline, the writers I've investigated turn to other, sometimes competing, disciplines—such as psychology, psychiatry, or psychoanalysis—to explain their patients' conditions. The holistic, interpretive, narrative explanations offered by psychological disciplines become, for them, a way of enlarging the deterministic knowledge produced by neurology.

What makes these writers so interesting to me, though, is that they try to do more than merely encompass other disciplines, such as psychology or psychoanalysis, into the territory of their home discipline, neurology—a not uncommon strategy in medicine. Instead, as they try to reconceptualize their discipline, they also redefine or expand the genres in which their disciplinary knowledge is constructed. Specifically, their solution to the interdisciplinary challenge they face is to write extended case histories that combine the logico-scientific analysis and exposition that is paradigmatic for neurology with the individual and subjective narrative that is so important in psychological traditions. In effect, they invent a new genre which Sacks calls "neurography" (1984, 15), a combination of science and art, or general neurological principles and individual psychological biography. This new blurred genre implies new relations among relevant disciplines and hence a new revisioning of what counts as disciplinary knowledge.

The formulations of this interdisciplinary genre vary. Luria, for example, in his famous case study of a patient with a severe brain injury, *Man with a Shattered World* (see also *Mind of a Mnemonist*), produces a kind of dialogic text that intersperses the patient's personal and ongoing account of his illness, excerpted from his journal, with Luria's summary discussions of his neurological condition. Sacks, in his collection of case studies of patients suffering from postencephalitic Parkinsonism, *Awakenings*, yokes two perspectives on illness or two ways of writing about this phenomenon: detailed scientific analysis of the general characteristics of this disease, typical of neurological genres; and individual and interpretive narratives of each patient's illness in the context of familial, biographical, and even cultural background, a discourse form more typical of psychological and even psychoanalytic genres. Jelliffe offers a complex psychosomatic theory of organic illness that unites neurology and Freudian psychoanalysis, and writes case studies that not only offer explicit arguments about the need to combine these disciplines, but that also show how knowledge claims from both fields can be recast into the generic expressions of the other; specifically, he places neurologic data into the narrative logic characteristic of psychoanalytic discourse, and analyzes psychoanalytic data through what he calls the "syllogistic logic" (158) of neurological discourse.

Neurology and psychology are, of course, quite different disciplines from composition studies. Despite their obvious differences, though, these are all fields concerned with somewhat similar phenomena—understanding the nature of the human mind and its productions, including the way those productions are implicated in a social context—and are all fields involved in a somewhat similar epistemological debate about the relative importance of cognitive and contextual forces. Thus, possibilities for boundary rhetoric in these related disciplines may have implications for composition studies.

Boundary Rhetoric and Composition Studies

The debate about cognitive versus contextual approaches to composition has often polarized into a dichotomous choice: cognition *or* context. I want to look, though, not at these polarizing moves, but at two kinds of research genres that try to recast the debate in more positive terms: theoretical manifestos and research reports that combine disciplinary perspectives. Both, I will argue, point the way to the kind of generic innovations that may be necessary for breaking down boundaries between cognitive and contextual perspectives, but both stop short of the generic innovation of true boundary rhetorics of the sort I have just described.

Arguments for the need to unite the cognitive and the contextual often appear as manifestos or calls to action. Such articles, frequently written by someone firmly identified with one perspective, explicitly argue for the compatibility of both perspectives, but often do so by showing—either implicitly or explicitly—how one discipline, or in this case subdiscipline, can be subsumed into the other. Furthermore, they sometimes have as an unstated purpose a kind of hierarchizing strategy that places one perspective in the center and brings the other into its purview.[3] Two examples of such manifestos include recent articles by Linda Flower (1989) and Deborah Brandt (1992). My argument is that these manifestos begin to offer a basis upon which a boundary rhetoric can be built because each, in Fuller's terms, tries to "sublimate" the competing perspective into the writer's home discipline; in both cases, the primary sublimating strategy is "translation"—transforming concepts from one perspective into the vocabulary of the other. But I also want to argue that the "exporting" strategy Fuller describes may be only a partial basis for a fully integrated boundary rhetoric.

In "Context, Cognition, and Theory Building," Flower directly states her desire to go beyond what she sees as the dichotomies of current composition research—polarities that lead to "reductive, simplified theories" and a "reductive vision of what we might teach." Her goal instead is to move toward a "more integrated theoretical vision which can explain how context cues cognition, which in turn mediates and interprets the particular world that context provides" (282). Specifically, Flower wants to bring together theories and methods that draw on cognitive psychology—her "home" discipline—with theories and methods—such as ethnography, textual analysis, or historical reconstructions—that draw more heavily on humanistic disciplines. Despite the language of equality, however, I think the underlying rhetorical strategy of this article is to demonstrate how contextually oriented research can be seen as a version of cognitive research. That is, Flower works to recast the generic goals, assumptions, and methods of contextual research into those of the cognitivist's research agenda. In Fuller's terms, she exports cognitive ideas into the contextualist camp, offering to sublimate the differences between them by showing how social approaches are a natural extension of cognitive research. She does not, though, show how cognitive approaches are a natural extension of contextual research.

One of Flower's most powerful strategies for renegotiating boundaries is her demonstration of how social or contextual research can support insights produced by cognitive research.[4] She does this, in essence, by translating contextual research into cognitive terms. For instance, when she talks about rhetoric's traditional concern with the "rhetor/writer as a social actor within a public forum," she does so in order to argue that such an account is compatible with the *"language* of 'problem-solving' [that] itself places the writer in a responsive stance" (287; emphasis mine). But when Flower presents cognitive research, she does not recast it into the contextual. Instead, contextual factors are usually described as some sort of nuisance, as when "the very lively social classroom process" interferes with the students' ability to remain on task in peer response groups (285) or when the "legacy of school" assignments gets in the way of how a student "represents a writing task" to herself in college (289).

Flower's rhetorical goal may, in fact, be less to sublimate differences than to hierarchize the two approaches. While she is careful to indict both "the armchair of social theory" and "the mind in the belljar" of cognitive research" (286), there is a subtle dichotomy running through her article that constructs contextual research as abstract, theoretical, or speculative, whereas cognitive research is presented as empirical, scientific, or observational. Further, though Flower points out the limitations of focusing solely on either social context or individual cognition, she is much more interested in explaining how the early "strong claims" of cognitive research (283) have been expanded. The most important question still seems to be: "But what actually happens in the minds of students?" (285). The effect is to suggest that while contextual research may provide one source of theory, it is cognitive research that confirms or disconfirms that theory.

A related attempt to show how the cognitive can be "sublimated" into the contextual is Brandt's article, which announces its intent in its very title: "The Cognitive as the Social." Like Flower, Brandt begins by talking about polarized positions, though she more firmly locates them in different epistemological stances of empirical and hermeneutic research traditions. Also like Flower, she asks for integration, what she calls a "third way" (317), in this case one supported by the research agenda she advocates: ethnomethodology, which she also describes as "empirical hermeneutics" (318). Ethnomethodology thus has the potential, in Brandt's terms, to "find better ways to articulate how the cultural activity of literacy is manifested in the cognitive processes of writers and readers" (317).

In direct reversal of Flower, Brandt fulfills her task of sublimating differences by exporting contextualist ideas into the cognitivist camp. The goal of her article, as announced in the abstract, is to use "ethnomethodological perspectives to *translate the language* of Flower and Hayes' cognitive theory of writing into a more thoroughly social vocabulary" (315, emphasis mine). Specifically, Brandt asks "how might the main elements of a cognitive model of composing be translated to reflect their public 'anchorings'?"

(327). Her response is to take certain central cognitivist terms—such as "purpose," "plans," and "recursion"—and show what they mean from an ethnomethodological perspective. "Purpose," for example, "instead of [being] conceiv[ed] . . . as an 'internal, cognitive construct' (Flower, 1988, p. 531)," becomes "the way writers display . . . . their orientations toward public situations" (317). Similarly, she argues that "what Flower and Hayes call recursion . . . ethnomethodologists, from their public perspective, would call the reflexivity of practical reasoning" (328). Brandt does not, however (because like Flower it is not part of her conceptual or rhetorical purpose), translate contextual terms into a cognitive vocabulary.

Brandt is careful to point out the ways "process studies, especially the think-aloud studies undertaken by Flower and her colleagues over the last 15 years, share some key perspectives with ethnomethodology" (324). Nevertheless, part of her goal is to identify some of the deficiencies in cognitivist research that contextual research, in this case ethnomethodology, can remedy: "The fact that writing process studies draw their theoretical sustenance from cognitive science has tended to mute the social interpretations of the language that is captured in oral protocols" (324). The article concludes with an illustration of ethnomethodological research: an analysis of a think-aloud protocol of a writer at work on a real-life task, in terms of his "sense-making practices" and the way those practices "are indexes to the social structures that bear on literate interpretation" (343).

Boundary manifestos of the sort produced by Flower and Brandt are important because in working out theoretical ways in which one disciplinary perspective can be sublimated into that of another, they show how assumptions can be translated into a different generic vocabulary and thus point to possibilities of boundary rhetoric. But because translating primarily involves staying at home while exporting one discipline's generic assumptions and terminology to another, these boundary manifestos do not yet create the new genres that may be necessary for full integration of cognitive and contextual perspectives—as well as the empirical and hermeneutic research traditions they spring from.

The beginning of this kind of generic innovation may be present in a number of innovative studies—including research by Flower (*Construction*) and Brandt (*Literacy* and the second part of "Cognitive")—that in the process of combining cognitive and social perspectives also begin to combine logico-scientific and narrative genres. The more innovative aspect of this combination is, of course, the addition of narrative. As Luria, Sacks, and Jelliffe also realized, narrative is a potent way to expand the quantitative and analytic explanations offered by logico-scientific perspectives. And since composition studies has borrowed heavily from the prestige of logico-scientific genres, our growing acceptance of the epistemological function of narrative (Brodkey, "Ethnographic"; Bishop, "I-Witnessing"; DiPardo), as well as our increased awareness of the assumptions operating behind the particular narrative representations we choose (Newkirk, Detweiler), indicates our willingness to enrich these research traditions.

Narrative has become a particularly important mode of knowledge in composition studies, not just in primarily narrative-based genres, such as the contextually rich stories we tell about writers, but also in research that tries to connect detailed textual or cognitive analysis with narratives of social and political contexts. Several innovative studies point to these connections offering possibilities for multiple perspectives to be heard. Hull and her colleagues, for example, combine close analysis of the talk between teacher and students in a fifty-minute classroom lesson on writing with consideration of the larger cultural assumptions that affect classroom practices, telling, in the process, a detailed story of Maria and June; "moving between micro-level, close examination of oral or written discourse and macro-level investigations of society and culture" helps them, they explain, make "connections between language, cognition, and context" (321). Similarly, Berkenkotter et al. combine close linguistic textual analysis with a detailed narrative account of Nate's experiences in a Ph.D. program. And Nelson employs writing process logs and other descriptive data to examine how specific classroom situations affect task representation of students, constructing case studies that present stories told from perspectives of professor, teaching assistants, and student. Other dialogic texts, such as that of Flower et al. or Anderson et al., present the multiple voices of researchers, teachers, and students. Such studies do more than argue for the compatibility of cognitive and contextual approaches. They begin to show these connections by combining the generic features of different research traditions.

Akin to these dialogic texts are research reports that use narrative to reflect upon our methodologies and larger disciplinary practices, as a recent issue of *College Composition and Communication* (Vol. 43, February 1992) devoted to articles displaying "strong personal voices" demonstrates. In this issue, Geisler, for example, offers an account of her research which juxtaposes four "layers": a "Scientific Report" describing her research on expertise from a cognitive, social, and cultural perspective; a "Reflexive Analysis" evaluating the costs and benefits of her multimodal methods; a "Personal History" relating her intellectual position to personal narrative; and a "Deliberative Appeal" asking for "a new discourse of knowledge-making" (50). Other examples of narrative reflection include Hayes's exploration of the "complex roots" of his literacy research not just in the cognitive psychology paradigm but also in personal and disciplinary history; McCarthy and Fishman's "boundary conversation" or "narrative of research collaboration" (460), which concludes their interdisciplinary ethnographic study; or M. Rose's famous autobiographical and historical account of "the cognitive and social reality" (xi) of literacy in this country.

"Experiments in composing" (Geisler) such as these are important not just in negatively deconstructing logico-scientific accounts, but, more positively, in helping us see the constructed nature of our knowledge and the way interpretation and narrative can be joined with empirical verification or quantitative analysis. Nevertheless, manifestos and these multimodal research studies do not present the full range of generic innovation possible in boundary rhetorics. Boundary rhetorics, as I anticipate them—and as Sacks, Luria, and Jelliffe illustrated—will go beyond combining or juxtaposing disciplinary genres. More radically, they will blur the generic conventions and expectations of the constituent fields and recast the values and principles of one discipline into the language and discourse forms of the other. This disciplinary "interpenetration" thus means a revisioning not only of conventional forms of discourse, but also the methodological and epistemological assumptions that animate those forms. That is, boundary rhetorics do more than renegotiate the borders between disciplinary genres; they open up new territories to explore.

If genres represent historically constructed ways of achieving consensus within disciplinary communities, reformulating those genres will present a complex challenge. First, there is a difficult line between what J. Harris has called the "confessional" and the "situated," and in arguing for the expansion of genres, it is important to emphasize that boundary rhetorics will also require care and attention. Moreover, established academic genres carry with them a set of conventions that are frequently perceived as being *inherently* more "objective," "impartial," or "accurate," and these perceptions can be difficult to resist. It is therefore not uncommon for innovative rhetorics to be characterized as less than "rigorous"—though, in fact, boundary rhetorics may help us redefine "rigor" by interrogating conventions that have gone unchallenged for decades. Finally, critiquing genre traditions is, as Berkenkotter (1993) has recently argued, a politically difficult business, at least for those who are not influential senior scholars. Nevertheless, I believe composition is a field more open than most to boundary rhetorics—in part, because we are and always have been interdisciplinary, and in part, because we are perhaps more self-conscious than most fields about our discursive practices.

Notes

1. The other frequently discussed strategy for interdisciplinary rhetoric, which I will not be able to consider here, is intertextual refashioning of a field through selective citation. For discussions of the rhetoric of citation see, for example, Bazerman (1988); Bazerman and Paradis; Berkenkotter and Huckin; Myers; Journet (1993); Selzer.

2. Narrative is now recognized not simply as storytelling, but as a complex mode of knowing that is important in both human and physical sciences (e.g. Shafer, White, Bruner 1990, Geertz 1988, Gould, Mayr).

3. Kirsch (in Kirsch and Sullivan 1992) makes the related point that "research-ers steeped in different research traditions often speak different languages," and even when they argue for methodological pluralism often highlight their own paradigms while describing other methodologies as supplementary (256).

4. She, like Brandt, below, also uses intertextual citation to establish connec-tions with researchers of other perspectives.

Response to Bazerman, Helscher, Peckham, Devitt, and Journet, by Carrie Shively Leverenz

Recently, I asked students in a first-year writing class to respond to my evaluation of their midterm portfolios. Although most students told me they approved of their grade, and understood the criteria I used to evaluate their work, one student, who had received an "A–" at midterm and who was motivated to do even better on her final portfolio, took the opportunity to interrogate my response to her writing. One of the questions she asked opens up the issue of what genres are and how we ought to go about teaching them: "On a lot of my writing, you told me that all of my points need to relate. Was that something I have to do, or was it just a suggestion?" In an earlier phase of my teaching, I would have responded, authoritatively, that essays should be organized around a central idea and that everything in the essay—evidence, arguments, descriptive details—should advance or support that idea. Although in that earlier phase of teaching, I was progressive enough not to insist on a thesis statement in the first paragraph, the "central idea plus support" model of writing seemed beyond question. All first-year writing textbooks espoused that model, every writing teacher I knew required some version of it, and my own writing was based, unquestioningly, on the same model.

As the essays by Charles Bazerman, Thomas Helscher, Irvin Peckham, Amy Devitt, and Debra Journet contend, such assumptions about the "essen-tials" of effective writing are more a product of membership in a particular discourse community than the distillation of universal principles of commu-nication. The question of whether all the parts of an essay have to "relate," as my student put it, a question that some researchers in composition have tried to answer by investigating the cognitive processes involved in generat-ing or making sense of written texts, is now more profitably addressed by examining the context in which an essay is written. If a piece of writing must advance a single claim, be organized in a logical way, present authoritative evidence, use concrete language, these requirements reflect standards agreed to by a particular group of readers and writers. Understanding and making use of these generic standards marks one as a member of a particular knowledge-making community and gives one the ability to do business within that community. As Bazerman and Devitt argue, without some generic constraints on discourse, there would be no communication.

But the essays that open this volume do more than argue for the efficacy, indeed, the inevitability of discourse communities and their attendant genres. They also begin to problematize the ways genres function as borders that outsiders must negotiate if they want to become insiders. Implicit in these essays is an awareness of the power that is at stake in accommodating one's writing to a discourse community's genre expectations. Charles Bazerman acknowledges that students have their own ways of making knowledge that probably do not match those we wish to educate them into, raising the question of how to be sensitive to students' interests while teaching them the genres that we deem most important for them to know. Thomas Helscher notes the "regulatory functions of genres," accomplished in part through the construction of a limited number of subjectivities for community members to inhabit, but argues that when the available subjectivities become inadequate or too constraining, genres adjust to create new subject positions. Irvin Peckham uses the metaphor of yin and yang to illustrate how genres get constructed as good and bad, high and low. Amy Devitt sees similarities between genres and language standards, noting that although both involve constraint and variation, it has been the constraints that have received greater attention. And Debra Journet connects disciplinary genres with the control of realms of knowledge, noting that most writing that claims to be interdisciplinary is really an attempt by one discipline to claim the turf of another. All of these essays suggest that knowledge-making groups gain and maintain power by marking out a region of knowledge that is contained in and by the use of specialized discourse forms that we might call genres.

Back to my student's question: Is abiding by genre conventions something I have to do or is it just a suggestion? Bazerman might respond that teachers and students should work together to find some way for students to inhabit meaningfully what Helscher calls the subjectivities made possible by existing genres. Doing so, presumably, would enable students to succeed in particular classrooms and their chosen professions while allowing them to do writing they care about. In fact, Bazerman implies caring about what they write would motivate them to learn genre conventions. Devitt also seems to argue that because there is room for variation within genres, asking students to accommodate their writing (and their subjectivities, according to Helscher) to genre constraints is not such a bad thing and may, in fact, give them access to discourses of power. But what kind of power? The power of an insider who knows how to play according to the rules? Peckham attempts to deconstruct the yin and yang of genre to show how those in power maintain their position by creating binary oppositions that elevate their own forms of knowledge-making at the expense of "Other" forms, but he acknowledges that resisting or challenging discourses of power can have serious consequences if attempted by novices. Although Peckham may have found it irresistible and intensely pleasurable to break the rules by shattering the window of an abandoned house, should that house have been inhabited by, say, a teacher or his boss or a police officer, there might have been hell to pay.

Although these authors recognize the power that comes from being an insider, one who knows and can use the language of the land, so to speak, they also acknowledge the power of genres to exclude those who do not or cannot conform. In spite of this exclusionary function, Bazerman, Helscher, and Devitt insist that genres allow for personal meaning-making, for the creation of new subject positions, for individual variation. They suggest, in other words, that working within the constraints of genre need not be inhibiting, oppressive, silencing. But I'm not so sure. I still remember trying to write the first draft of my dissertation, an ethnographic study of collaboration in multicultural writing classes, without using "I" and without being conscious that I was not using "I," so hidden were my assumptions about the conventions of a dissertation. And when an editor commented that my writing was earnest but clinical, I explained my distanced, objective tone as a sign of my status as a novice whose anxiety regarding her professional authority was exacerbated by a working-class background that seemed to conflict with her membership as a professional academic.

To the student who wanted to know if she *had* to make all of her points relate, I wish I could have said "No. Write what you want. It's more important for you to care about what you write than it is for you to do what I *suggest*." But like Irv Peckham, I used the scapegoat of "other teachers" who, in his words, "get very excited" about the issue of a clearly articulated main idea and logically related points. And in Florida, where all students in the state university system have to pass a competency test that includes writing an essay with just those characteristics, I would be doing my students a disservice not to warn them of the genre expectations of the "other teachers" who will be reading their essays. As a teacher and a writer, however, I still have mixed feelings about the way that discourse communities routinely—and perhaps inevitably—create boundaries that keep out those who make knowledge differently. In writing this response, for example, I have been acutely aware of the constraints imposed by the genre of a "response essay" that would appear in a book addressed to composition scholars, worried that my response would not be academic enough, that I wasn't citing sources, that I was using "I" excessively and including too many personal anecdotes. If Bazerman is right, I simply found a way to imbue a genre form with meaning that matters to me; if Devitt is right, I have just taken advantage of the variation that is possible within the constraints of a genre. And if Helscher is right, I have just constructed a new subject position when the existing ones seemed inadequate. But if all of these essayists are right, it is you, the readers of this collection, who ultimately decide if my response is *acceptable*. Because I want to be accepted, I care about abiding by conventions, but I also feel limited and sometimes silenced by them. Students in my first-year writing class are likely to feel similarly limited and silenced. It doesn't seem enough to say simply, "That's the way discourse communities function; communities make the rules and members follow them." As teachers and scholars, we are the communities, the rule-makers. We can accept our complicity with the exclusionary function of our communities' genres or we can interrogate our complicity—though interrogating it is not the same as escaping it. Rather than answering my student's question, we need to continue asking it: Must I accommodate my writing—or is it just a suggestion?

Part III

The Intersection of Politics and Genre
Race and Class Inside and Outside of Classrooms

Consider this disturbing equation: composition studies thrives *because* Johnny Can't Write. William Lyne argues that Johnny *never could* write and that we find our community today built on the institutionalization of a literacy crisis which is itself institutionalizing an underclass of students (required to take first-year writing) and teachers (adjuncts, graduate teaching assistants, part-timers, freeway flyers). One of our responses has been to teach antifoundational theory, but Lyne's essay "White Purposes" finds this a self-serving move. Teaching genre-theory, discourse communities, cracking the code, and how to get a piece of the pie doesn't teach disenfranchised students (if they are even allowed into our increasingly more competitive state university systems) how to confront institutionalized inequities. Lest our teaching of difference boomerangs, sustaining inequities, as Lyne argues it probably does, lest we teach "difference" but make no difference, our courses may do their best work when issues, activities, and discussions make privileged students uncomfortable with the status quo.

Through their use of alternate style—a fluent version and subversion of dominant discourse—Monifa Love and Evans Hopkins enact the very issues Lyne raises, and their words become a found poem:

We work against and in the name of invisibility.
I was going to write yesterday, but I was too pissed off.
What joy your letter brought me!
I can't see ahead of me and I don't know when to get off.
I hadn't expected to say that.
Be well.

Mary Rose O'Reilly, in her powerful narrative study of teaching, claims that we must "examine our subject matter, whatever it may be, through a glass of tenderness as well as through a glass of reason" (82). Lyne and Love and Hopkins examine their subjects, their selves, through a glass of tenderness as well as through a glass of reason—and through glasses of rage and grief and loss and love—lenses we do not expect (and perhaps sometimes still wish to keep banished?) from scholarship and criticism. We see Love and Hopkins writing out of the powerful arena of intentional resistance, where "composing" oneself does not mean harnessing thought and emotion in expected ways. In fact, as Allison Giffen suggests in our next section, we might do a better job of composing ourselves by not composing ourselves, by looking for the constructive dimensions of alternate emotions as these authors do here.

7

White Purposes

William Lyne

> The brutal truth is that the bulk of the white people in America
> never had any interest in educating black people, except as this
> could serve white purposes.
>
> —James Baldwin

I.

Freshman writing is moving from genres to genre theory. Instead of teaching our students to inhabit and reproduce various officially sanctioned rhetorical genres, we have begun to teach them to recognize the cultural and ideological assumptions that go into the construction of those genres. We have begun to "try to make a pluralistic study of difference into a curriculum" (Bizzell, 269), creating writing courses that "enable students to learn something . . . about the often-unstated assumptions on which their lives are built" (Berlin 1987, 189). This sort of course attempts to use postmodernist insights for empowering or liberatory purposes. But even as we try to convince ourselves and our students that escape from Oz lies in the close scrutiny of the man behind the curtain, we may be overlooking some of the often-unstated assumptions on which this genre of composition course is built. Along with the liberating possibilities that many composition theorists envision, the recent history and current institutional practice that define and shape the genre theory or "antifoundationalist" composition courses have also created some dangerous cul-de-sacs.

Composition historians generally peg the open enrollment programs of the 1960s and *Newsweek's* "Why Johnny Can't Write" article as points of origin for contemporary composition studies. The rhetoric and composition industry was created largely in response to a perceived "crisis" in literacy. But, as Mike Rose points out, Johnny has never been able to write:

The more things change, the more they remain the same. In 1841 the president of Brown complained that "students frequently enter college almost wholly unacquainted with English grammar." In the mid-1870s, Harvard professor Adams Sherman Hill assessed the writing of students after four years at America's oldest college: "Every year Harvard graduates a certain number of men—some of them high scholars—whose manuscripts would disgrace a boy of twelve." In 1896, *The Nation* ran an article entitled "The Growing Illiteracy of American Boys," which reported on another Harvard study. The authors of this one lamented the spending of "much time, energy, and money" teaching students "what they ought to have learnt already." There was "no conceivable justification," noted a rankled professor named Goodwin, to use precious revenues "in an attempt to enlighten the Egyptian darkness in which no small portion of Harvard's undergraduates were sitting." In 1898 the University of California instituted the Subject A Examination . . . and was soon designating about 30 to 40 percent of those who took it as not proficient in English, a percentage that has remained fairly stable to this day. (5–6)

Composition theory, then, owes its growth not to increasing numbers of students who can't write, but to the kind of students who can't write. As long as it was just Harvard men who couldn't write, composition theory was limited mostly to the harumphing of professors and college presidents and calls for more rigorous instruction in grammar. Only once the race, class, and gender makeup of the American university began to change did composition theory become firmly institutionalized. This would suggest that the growth of composition studies was a response to a political, not a literacy, "crisis." As high-profile underclass students begin to trickle into the university, composition becomes one of the primary sites for the battles over what to do with these students—a place to focus the contest between support and demonization, assimilation and ghettoization, liberation and oppression.

The ways in which the university and the larger society have decided this contest have had a tremendous influence on the current shape of rhetoric and composition programs. We need not look very closely to see that, especially for African Americans, demonization, ghettoization, and oppression have won the day. The material lives of a disproportionate percentage of African Americans are circumscribed by subtle and not so subtle forms of racism and continue to get worse. The few real gains of the sixties have been rolled back, leaving a slightly expanded middle class, a holiday, and a lot of academic interest in things ethnic. The classroom space that *Brown v. Board of Education* was supposed to have created for black bodies has been filled by black texts.

The impulse toward social change behind composition studies has been stifled in much the same way. The marginalized students who precipitated the "crisis" that gave composition theory an institutional toehold have been excluded, in the last two decades, from the university just as systematically as they have been excluded from other avenues to power. Those who do penetrate the playground of the leisure class are safely segregated into courses taught by the academic underclass—the exploited adjuncts, part-timers, and graduate students who actually teach freshman composition and remain the lowest paid and least respected members of English departments. The politics of the dispossessed may have helped create composition studies, but expansion has come as faculty have been able to scramble away from the teaching of basic writing and up to the more prestigious world of directing programs, doing research, teaching graduate students, and writing theory.

It comes as no surprise, then, that the genre-theory composition classes that are touted for their liberatory possibilities also happen to have the kind of contours that give composition studies institutional status. Rhetoric and composition has traditionally struggled to establish itself as a discipline, often receiving some rather dubious looks from the more established domain of literary studies. But more and more, composition theory finds itself very much in fashion, having dovetailed with literary theory's renewed focus on rhetoric. Composition scholars have found fertile ground in the work of anti-foundationalist theorists like Mikhail Bakhtin, Richard Rorty, and Stanley Fish, and literary theorists like Fish, E. D. Hirsch, Jr., and J. Hillis Miller have turned some of their attention to composition questions. The condescension and neglect that spawned CCCC and *College English* have been overcome to the point where composition panels are a regular part of the MLA convention and tenure track positions in rhetoric and composition outnumber those in most other categories in recent MLA Job Lists. The institutional space cleared for the Johnnys who can't write has been filled with autonomous departments, doctoral research programs, and chaired professorships devoted to the philosophical and social-scientific investigation of composing.

The genre-theory type of composition class is a natural outgrowth of this shift. Teaching composition students difference or the deconstruction of hegemonic assumptions retains the political look of composition studies' origins while at the same time consolidating and expanding composition turf. We show our students how to recognize the forces that oppress them while at the same time showing our colleagues and deans that composition is a *discipline*, not just a skill.

II.

Teaching antifoundationalist theory may help expand and solidify the political position of composition within the academy, but there is still some question as to whether it is a useful device for empowering marginalized students. Stanley Fish, in "Anti-Foundationalism, Theory Hope, and the Teaching of Composition," offers a typically clever antitheory argument:

Ah, you say, but now we really *know* it because we know it self-
consciously. But to say that is to make self-conscious knowledge a knowledge more firm and more "true" than the knowledge we have without
reflection. That is, of course, a general assumption of liberal thought—that
the only knowledge worth having is knowledge achieved disinterestedly, at
a remove from one's implication in a particular situation—but it is an
assumption wholly at odds with anti-foundationalism, and it is certainly
curious to find it at the heart of an anti-foundationalist argument. That is, it
is curious to have an argument that begins by denying the possibility of a
knowledge that is independent of our beliefs and practices and ends by
claiming as one of its consequences the achieving of just such an indepen-
dence. (348)

This demonstration of antifoundationalist paralysis is philosophically
interesting, but when we are talking about composition courses, perhaps we
should take the pragmatic approach of antifoundationalist philosopher Richard Rorty and ask whether antifoundationalist theory (even with its self-
defeating conclusions) is a useful *tool* for our marginalized students. That is,
does showing our students that all knowledge is situated and contingent, that
even the Olympian view is a point of view, help them negotiate their situation? A composition theorist like James Berlin would certainly answer yes,
that exposing the "unstated assumptions" would help our students attack,
sidestep, or otherwise rearrange those assumptions.

The problem with this position becomes clear when we move from the
work of Stanley Fish to that of another antifoundationalist giant, Mikhail
Bakhtin. Bakhtin's notion of dialogue and his contention that all language is
socially constructed (or "heteroglossic") have been tremendously influential
in both literary and rhetorical studies. But too often academic writers who
apply Bakhtinian theory forget that Bakhtin's is always, in the words of
Michael D. Bristol, a "sociological poetics" (19). This is especially true of
those Bakhtinian concepts that we might label antifoundationalist. The rhetorical forms that most acknowledge and exploit dialogue and heteroglossia
(such as stylization, parody, and pastiche) always originate in the economic
underclasses and tend to become more "monologic" and "centripetal" as they
move up the social ladder. Consider, for example, this discussion of the differences between poetic genres and the novel:

At the time when major divisions of the poetic genres were developing
under the influence of the unifying, centralizing, centripetal forces of
verbal-ideological life, the novel—and those artistic-prose genres that gravitate toward it—was being historically shaped by the current of decentral-
izing, centrifugal forces. At the time when poetry was accomplishing the
task of cultural, national, and political centralization of the verbal-
ideological world . . . on the lower levels, on the stages of local fairs and at
buffoon spectacles, the heteroglossia of the clown sounded forth . . . where

all "languages" were masks and where no language could claim to be an authentic, incontestable force. (272–73)

The places where foundations are most likely to crumble and show their cracks are "the lower levels," the socioeconomic zones where there is little to lose by acknowledging that "truth" is really ideology. Dialogic insight is most likely to take place in what Michael G. Cooke calls "the paradoxically favorable environment of suffering" (ix).

Thus, it is perhaps rather presumptuous to suggest that a university professor has anything to tell a student from the margins about antifoundationalism. The lower middle class woman with an ethnic accent who faces this society's sexist distribution of resources every day, the young black man from Compton who knows firsthand the distance between law and law enforcement, the gay student who must choose between the closet or legal discrimination and violence, all know about double voicedness and constructed realities without ever having read Bakhtin, Rorty, or Fish. The militant, parodic, or assimilationist strategies for dealing with oppressive institutions are more often brought to the classroom than they are devised there. Teaching the marginalized student genre theory often becomes nothing more than teaching him or her another privileged genre, another way to "write like the Man."

There is a school of thought that suggests that this is exactly what we should be doing. E. D. Hirsch, Jr.'s "Cultural Literacy" program, for example, attempts to make the dominant culture more available to students from whom it has traditionally been withheld. In his own eccentric way, Hirsch extends the work of theorists like Richard Rorty and Jean-Francois Lyotard, taking antifoundationalist and neopragmatist insights seriously. Where Rorty advocates a vision of language as a tool and Lyotard describes the impossibility of overarching metanarratives, Hirsch pushes these theoretical insights toward a practice that looks all too familiar to some commentators. Along with his collaborators at the University of Virginia, Hirsch turns theory's abstraction into practice's list: a group of tools ("What Every American Needs to Know") for negotiating the local narrative of America. Cultural Literacy, as Hirsch sees it, becomes a way to demystify the dominant ideology, a set of practical keys that every American can use to crack the codes of newspapers, privileged discourse communities, and standardized tests.

Contemporary composition theory has, for the most part, defined itself against this kind of thinking. To many critics, Hirsch's list, despite its occasional nods toward minority cultural referents, looks too much like the master race narratives of Allan Bloom, William Bennett, and old-fashioned prescriptive reading lists. The expressionist and social-constructionist perspectives that have dominated composition theory since the seventies see programs like Hirsch's as driven by an ideology that "may indeed threaten students with cultural assimilation and the loss of their native discourses"

(Bizzell, 212). Along with this perceived danger to students, back-to-basics programs like Hirsch's also pose a threat to composition's institutional turf. Teaching students genre conventions, teaching them to write academic prose in a way that will help them through their college careers and perhaps beyond, nudges composition back toward the realm of the "service" course and undermines the epistemology on which composition studies is built.

Unfortunately, a faithful application of Bakhtin's vision of the underclass suggests that, if we are trying to empower the disenfranchised, we should be teaching genres. For the marginalized student entering the racialized, classed, and gendered discourse communities of political power and economic survival, empowerment comes from getting a piece of the pie, not from understanding all the reasons why you are never served. Strategies of resistance such as satire and signifying, parody and passing take antifoundationalism as their starting point, but gain their power from a deep understanding of and ability to mimic the dominant discourse. Caliban's curse meant nothing until he articulated it in Prospero's language, and Frederick Douglass wrote himself out of slavery by first relentlessly copying his master's children's workbooks. Richard Wright and James Baldwin both developed their own voices by reading the classics in white people's public libraries. Bakhtinian antifoundationalism seems to lead where Henry Louis Gates, Jr., points when he writes, "only the master's tools will ever dismantle the master's house."

But when Audre Lorde tells us that "[t]he master's tools will *never* dismantle the master's house" she describes the problem with a pedagogy grounded in teaching genres. Bakhtin's genre of subversion is "carnival," Gates's the similarly double-voiced "signifying." Both are quite capable of empowering individuals (Caliban, Douglass, Baldwin, etc.), and both may disrupt the master's house from time to time, but they will never dismantle it. The problem with a program like Hirsch's is not that it may threaten to rob a marginalized student of his or her "native" discourse. Along with the problem of categorizing native and alien discourses, the dynamic of cultural assimilation is very complex, and teaching the master's tools is as likely to produce a Clarence Thomas as it is a James Baldwin. Cultural Literacy may be an empowering device for individuals, but it does nothing to dismantle the institutions that exclude all but those few individuals.

III.

If we are going to utilize the institutional space that composition theory has created and make good on the empowerment promise, we must face this paradox: teaching genre theory is not the best way to empower marginalized students and teaching genres does nothing to dismantle the systems and institutions that exclude the dispossessed. The way out of this paradox is to face a bitter and more important reality: that no matter what kind of composition course we teach, we are in all likelihood teaching it to students from relatively privileged backgrounds. Despite all the rainbow rhetoric, our larger social structures continue to exclude the students who sparked the composition "crisis." It would seem, then, that our pedagogical efforts should move from empowering the "marginalized" to educating "centered" students as to how those larger social structures are robbing them of their humanity.

The genre-theory composition course can be a very useful tool in this effort. For it is the "centered" student, the student whose experience validates foundational "truths," who is most likely to benefit from a strong dose of antifoundationalism. As we can see in the work of Pierre Bourdieu, our arrangements of symbolic power and our educational systems conceal "the link between the qualifications obtained by individuals and the cultural capital inherited by virtue of their social background," and enable "those who benefit most from the system to convince themselves of their own intrinsic worthiness" (Thompson, 24–25). We see this dynamic at work everywhere, especially in the mainstream popularity of books like Allan Bloom's *The Closing of the American Mind* and Shelby Steele's *The Content of Our Character*, books that attempt to reassert the authority of the privileged and blame society's victims for their status. Patricia Bizzell describes Bourdieu's theory writ small in the composition classroom:

> James Berlin has designed an experimental course to replace traditional freshman composition at Purdue University. His course asks students to deconstruct dominant ideologies on relations between the sexes and between employers and workers. Berlin has found that students hold firmly to the ideologies they are supposed to question. Women and men defend prostitution as a woman's right to make money any way she sees fit; and they explain unjustified pay cuts, unsafe working conditions, and other oppressive job situations which they have experienced as "good lessons" that toughen them and so will help them get ahead in the future. (269)

Since it should come as no surprise that many students in American universities (the postmodern bourgeoisie) defend dominant ideologies, this situation should provoke neither our alarm nor our dismay. On the contrary, we should see these points of friction as opportunities to do some of our most important antifoundational teaching. Too often our teaching of "difference" (in both literature and composition programs) becomes just another "mechanism for creating and sustaining inequalities" (in the same way that composition studies has too often become a mechanism for sustaining academic hierarchies) (Thompson, 24). In "The Multicultural Wars," Hazel V. Carby delineates this danger:

> The cultural, political, and social complexity of black people is consistently denied in those strands of feminist and multicultural theory that emphasize "difference" and use it to mark social, cultural, and political differences as

if they were unbridgeable human divisions. This theoretical emphasis on the recognition of difference, of otherness, requires us to ask, different from and for whom? In practice, in the classroom, black texts have been used to focus on the complexity of response in the (white) reader/student's construction of self in relation to a (black) perceived "other." In the motivation of that response, the text has been reduced to a tool. The theoretical paradigm of difference is obsessed with the construction of identities rather than relations of power and domination and, in practice, concentrates on the effect of this difference on a (white) norm. Proponents of multiculturalism and feminist theorists have to interrogate some of their basic and unspoken assumptions: to what extent are fantasized black female and male subjects invented, primarily, to make the white middle class feel better about itself? And at what point do theories of "difference," as they inform academic practices, become totally compatible with, rather than a threat to, the rigid frameworks of segregation and ghettoization at work throughout our society? (192–93)

Carby's analysis is a clear challenge to those academic programs whose origins are in the political plight of various marginalized groups—women's studies, black studies, composition studies. Well-financed, muddle-headed programs aimed against the "politicization" or "balkanization" of the classroom have generally kept our composition courses from clearly focusing on "relations of power and domination." If we are to keep our antifoundationalist courses from functioning like the King holiday or Black History Month, if they are indeed to be threats to social inequality, then we must push them beyond Fish's deconstructive paralysis and comfortable paradigms of difference. Bakhtin's carnival always comes from below and it always has very specific authority targets. Our antifoundationalism must do more than show the contingency of all foundations, it must engage our social reality and point toward historically dominant foundations and their oppressive features. The most effective genre-theory courses will be those that make privileged students uncomfortable, those that lead them to question genres that have always worked well for them.

8

Deep-Rooted Cane
Consanguinity, Writing, and Genre

Monifa A. Love and Evans D. Hopkins

They led him t th coast, they led him t th sea, they led him across
th ocean an they didnt set him free. The old coast didn't miss him,
an th new coast wasn't free, he left the old-coast brothers t give
birth t you an me.

—Jean Toomer

First recollections of writing are marks on the sidewalk, ciphers on a wall,
ardent loops swirling not-quite-between sky blue lines. At six, writing was
swinging high and my toes touching clouds. It is still that reaching and
pressing back, that lean into and against the air, the exhilaration and queasi-
ness of pumping, being still, letting go, and sailing. Like swinging, writing is
closest to what I imagine freedom to be.

In the space above are prefatory words from Evans. Bordering the paragraphs that follow are Evans's insistent notes, his hard-to-read writing rein-
serting and reasserting what I have left out, what I have set aside as too pun-
gent for the page, what I have surrendered because he and I have not had
enough time to piece *together* our thoughts.

In the space above and below are efforts to blur and distinguish lines: blood lines, line ups, lines of communication. To discuss the territory and politics of literary genres, crossing and stepping on lines is necessary. Natural. In this space

are Evans's warnings about essentialism, his lockdown commentary on what is and isn't natural, and his quotes from Ellison. His commentary makes me try again. To write across the territory and politics of literary genres is to live with your head in the lion's mouth. You're mindful of false moves.

Picture the 1969 Perennial Classic Edition of *Cane*. See the cover. Study the outline of the face. The quiet images of planting that fill it. Turn to pages 68, 69. Yes, they are blank except for an arc that hovers in the upper right hand corner. Evans and I and our words on writing, relationship, and genre are like the cover and those always surprising, seemingly empty pages. We work from the small arc of our mutual understanding. We work from our imaginings of home, history, and the harvest to come. We work from an understanding of corners and a longing for unfettered space. We work against and in the name of invisibility.

It is 1981. In the small southside Virginia city of Danville, a mill town whose claim to fame is being "The Last Capital of the Confederacy," I stand before 12 of its white citizens, my jury of peers.

"We find the defendant guilty of robbery and the use of a firearm in the commission of a felony, and recommend the punishment of life and one year in the state penitentiary."

I am stunned. Now. I had expected a long sentence, having provoked the jury's ire and invited their contempt by presenting a pathetic alibi defense (which consisted of a half-hour of testimony concocted by the fiction-writer-to-be the night before, and delivered by the terrible actor doped up on pills from the jail psych) . . . But life for a robbery in which no one was injured?

My attorney, perhaps slightly embarrassed at his part in helping to get me the max, leans over and whispers to me, "Don't worry. Life is only 12 and a half years in Virginia." It has now been about 12 and a half years. And here I am at central Virginia's Nottoway Correctional Center, a complex of gray concrete buildings surrounded by gun towers, double-fencing and miles of concertina wire.

* * *

Dear Cousin,

I've been writing this letter for years. Since you went back in. Yes, I've written other letters but many of them (most of them) are selfish and puny. Rereading them causes me pain. I wish I could take them back, erase the glibness, begin again. When we were children, we played with an intensity and compulsion that I have not found with anyone else. Luckily. Unluckily. I have looked for it. I think you are right, we must be twins. Separated at birth, stolen by gypsies. That's how the mythology goes, right? [Have you ever wondered why gypsies are so deeply associated with issues of blood and the future, what crossings of culture make us (and I use the term liberally—smile) cling to and repudiate them? You know I get lost and found in these tangents.] Anyway, sometimes you are so close it is destabilizing. This sense of disequilibrium is eased (and not helped in the least) by the fact that you agonize over words on the page, too.

I received your letter—this work, after a day of napping fitfully, hoping for something to reignite the fire to write again, to finish the political/personal piece for the Post *on incarceration, to give the momentum for the resumption of my book, my film, my play. Knowing that someone cares enough for my words, my thoughts, to read and share and give them back to me makes me anxious to get back.*

There is little reason for you to be where you are and for me to be where I am. I fool myself into thinking there are remedies to the problems that face us. I deceive myself so that I don't feel like such a collaborator. But of course, I am. It's funny looking back at "collaborator." The word makes me think of COINTELPRO and the Vichy provisional government. Ironically, I write this letter to propose our collaboration. [This is a side trip but I cannot resist it. As I struggle to master English (with all the connotations of control lurking inside "mastery"), I am constantly amazed by the ideas embedded in words and how hard it is to unrun the shades of meaning.]

Up late, but not feeling up to serious composition, heavy thinking, or reading. Just finished reading part of the Greenberg piece from the AWP paper and thought I might pen a note, though I've so much to write to you I feel hesitant.

We must strive for mastery. A lesson from John Gardner, and from Ellison—"One works to become a master not a student," he said in referring, I think, to Richard Wright. "Sons must slay their fathers."

I recall talking to Colin Turnbull ten years (or so) ago, when he came into the penitentiary to talk to a group of us, about this confluence of my artistic and scientific interests. He said that the best anthropological study was a form of poetry.

Excuse the mixed metaphor. It's actually not a side trip at all. It gets to the question of whether we can write across the wall that separates us. No, it gets to whether I can edit your words responsibly, not transform them into my own. I am reminded of our last discussion on reader response. I wonder if all I can do is make your words my own.

As an aside, the writer friend who brought Turnbull in recently told me he's gone into seclusion at some Buddhist retreat somewhere.

It's so much easier pretending there are remedies and choices. Easier acting as if my doctorate will make some kind of difference. One thing I have learned in graduate school: "easy" is a runaway constantly on the move. By the way, Turnbull has passed.

I look forward to the night's work, with some confidence, for a change, with the thought, "I must feed my people . . ."

Not much of a holiday message is it?

The people outside or the people inside?

Enclosed is a copy of my novel. It is more master's thesis than book but I am working on helping it to grow up. I have been afraid to show it to you. I am afraid it would be so far off the mark that you would think of it with disdain. It is, in many ways, a message of love to you and I hope that's what you find in the pages.

The question for me at the moment is can I afford to dwell in anthro-poetic meandering, lost in artistic thought, rather than putting it in gear (I hate mechanical metaphors), pulling my work together, and testing the marketplace. The communist in me rebels at that last thought. Am I afraid of fame, or afraid my work is not worthy of note; or not powerful enough to achieve the cultural/political impact I desire/need it to?

Rereading this letter, I find in it my search for the volume control, for some grammatical/literary mechanism that will allow me to reflect the intensity of my feelings. I find myself reaching to connect or disconnect the cable that links us. (I know, you dislike mechanical metaphors.) "So" has performed many duties, tasks that are perhaps too large for it. I think the rereading has helped me see metaphor in another way, as a search for amplitude instead of poetry.

Fear of self-disclosure cannot be allowed to slow me.

When I first thought "amplitude instead of poetry" I thought I had found something. But now I'm not sure what the big deal was. My letters to you seem to contain glimmers that mean everything and nothing. I feel like an astronomer watching the sky for an event I can sign my name to. By the way, I have always wanted to ask you about writing for the paper, life in Oakland, and the Party. I don't know where to start.

I made a note in my journal early this morning, after seeing a news clip of Huey Newton (his death was five years ago today), recognizing people in the clip, remembering their youth, resoluteness, and determination. I recall a recent dream, one that told me how I still hold so much of that time that forged my adulthood. The authoritarian Leninist seed that led to gang-sterism and the demise of something so beautiful.

I try to be cutting-edge, even if it now means the courage to reassess how we strayed from basic moral value and the enduring human themes in the attempt to be "vanguard"—maybe having the vanguard concept I've felt that whatever I write is not just for me, but for the all-encompassing struggle, for "the world," posterity, etc. IT is a conceit that has had me being selfish while thinking I was selfless, but now that I am again getting a sense of my place, it may help me to feel my worth—which at times, in here I have little idea of.

I'd wanted to do several more pages, there is so much to share. I especially wanted to pique your interest in my play. I just leafed through a synopsis I wrote five years ago. I thought about sending it to you, but the story has changed and developed so much from what was once mainly a historical play. More on this later, perhaps writing to you will help resuscitate this project. Yes, I've become quite the playwright. (Recall May's quote of Ellington in "Courage to Create." "It is good to have to submit to a form.")

I have enclosed a copy of my D.C. Incarceration article. I'm in the process of finishing a poetry manuscript for a 2/28 deadline. This note will be very brief. As far as my writing is concerned, I understand that my purpose is poetic, by which I mean what is important to me are glimpses and fragments.

I slept til 3 P.M. and wrote til 5. Watched "Viewpoint" on ABC earlier. Read some Yeats (seeing much of me in him, how modest) and thought about the poetry manuscript you sent me and found it amid my debris. Got out your letters a few minutes ago. Still debating punctuation and form of my verse. Agreed with the revelation from earlier today that the poem I have been working on, "Herein," is a great one. Cane *floored me tonight, too. I want to write a screenplay from Karintha.*

I read somewhere that August Wilson calls himself a collagist.

I am told there is already a movie of *Cane*. I have never seen it. I think there has also been something done on "Karintha." *Cane* may be the reason I married my first husband. He was the first person I'd ever met who felt as passionately about the book and as confused about Toomer as I did. There are probably stranger reasons for marrying.

Reading Claude McKay's autobiographical A Long Way from Home *and working on another article for the* Post *I am getting very personal in my nonfiction, and more so with my fiction. This may have something to do with the characters in your novel.*

The structure of short fiction doesn't make sense. Short fiction writers must have clarity about fear, weakness, good, and evil. I don't. It seems to me the sum of a moment is mystifying. Short fiction seems particularly god-like at least tonight while I'm writing this letter. But who knows. More later.

I have not meant to neglect writing you. I have two or three typed pages I wrote just after receiving your letter of early April somewhere within this welter of paper in my cell. I have been in something of a mild funk from having no ribbons for the printer and trying to pull together a manuscript of poetry for the Virginia Prize. We were locked down (again) and I couldn't get copies done and had to do some serious rewrites. I had hoped to see you by now. There is much I need to discuss with you. There has been no change as regards my visits. I hope that you'll be able to visit soon; we can talk and get a feeling about our working together.

Getting back to collaboration. I'm trying to work it through, see what it means to me to allow a place for our closeness. I thought we might aim towards a collaborative writing project. You mentioned this long ago. I think it was after reading *Brothers and Keepers*. Uncle C. has also been asking me why you and I couldn't do something together. A family story. Something that would sell. Yes, the marketplace rears its ugly head once again. I'm fooling around on the page now because I am afraid. I'm not sure of what exactly. You'll have to decide if you're willing to take it week by week, if you're able to trust that I'm struggling to do the best I can by you and with you. I guess I will, too. And that somehow I will bend the words and say what I am thinking.

When you told me that you thought I had the narrative gift (more so than a poetic vision) you hurt my feelings, but I decided you were right and have begun to concentrate on prose.

Did I say that?

I agree and disagree about the goodness of con-forming. Writing form poems are extremely gratifying. When they come out right. But writing against form, writing through form seems to get me closer to seeing what I really think and feel on the page. I don't know if it's a question of lack of discipline or conscientious rebellion.

We were on lockdown for the past couple of weeks, so maybe that accounts for the delay in the mail. In any case, the delay in my getting your letter does not leave us with the time to exchange ideas although it might be possible to respond to something. I would have enjoyed an excursion into literary theory. I may still be able to riff off a few pages of comments from which you could perhaps glean something. I would have liked to explore ideas on the epistolary novel—or something. I am not thinking clearly tonight. I have engaged to do a piece for the Post *next month and am struggling between* New Yorker–*long narration and "Outlook" op-ed ese. May submit to both—if I can just finish something. I must get this in as the crime bill hits the floor, and prepare something to weigh in against the Governor's attempt to abolish parole in September. I've got an important piece to finish by July 4th on race and imprisonment, the crime bill, and my personal history.*

Please keep me up to date on the project.

You're right, we should just start. I may help motivate you to do some thinking and working that you haven't gotten to yet and you may do the same for me. But a part of me keeps asking, "what are we doing?" "where are we going?" "what form are we working in?" I wish I didn't need an anchor. Without one I don't get anything done and drift in rather annoying circles.

I just finished reading your excellent article in *The Post*. It was wonderful seeing you in print.

I received your book this afternoon and read it straight through, just finishing it. I don't want to respond at length to it now, must wait for it to sink in, and see how it affects me. The editor in me did take a page of notes you might find helpful, should you plan to do another rewrite, though I shouldn't be afraid to submit it as is, if I were you.

I found your letter regarding the denial of your parole to be quite admirable. I don't know that I would have the grace, the restraint, the care you demonstrated. I think I would have exploded across the page.

Been thinking about Freedom *a bit since my last message, think I may give it a little more thought and possibly a re-reading before elaborating some on the literary tip. Thought I'd pen a note to go with this card while waiting for Nathan McCall to come on Arsenio. Have you read McCall? Turns out he worked with me in the library at Southampton on my first bit. I happened to be talking to the editor of the "Outlook" section, a couple of years ago and found out he was at the paper. Kicked it with him a few times over the phone afterwards. I'm glad to see his success but have had to get over the fact that he got out and made it and I came back when I was the first young Black writer he'd ever met.*

Despite the fact that other women came through the waiting room with less clothing than I and were admitted, the guards were adamant. They also did not seem to believe that a cousin would drive so far to see you. I asked for them to allow me to contact you in some way to let you know I had come as promised.

I was going to write yesterday, but I was too pissed off.

I'd hesitate before expanding a work which obtains such beauty from the untold story—the silences and distances and the central irony of these two people never meeting again—which is another reason I am reluctant to say any more just now.

What joy your letter brought me! I am so glad that you were able to get the manuscript.

The version that you got is a long way from being finished. I have many, many thoughts—probably another 100 pages of development. There are holes for me in the text as well as some unresolved character matters.

The piece began with Royce's voice being the dominating one and very little from David. David's voice is now almost overwhelming. I don't want to lessen his but I want to work towards a greater balance so that a reader will appreciate both the differences and the similarities in their inside/outside positions. David is Royce's greatest love and her deepest challenge. This is also true for David but in such different ways.

All of this is to say, please send on your editorial notes. I am looking forward to them. I hope to be finished by the fall.

I want to send you an article I read in *The New York Times Magazine*. The language of the writer reminded me so much of you—the acuity and the seriousness and the music. Let me know the best way for this to get to you.

I like what you wrote in your journal letter to me about your music and writing. I think about it a lot, and the other day, while sitting in the library with a young brother with 200 years, he read a bit of Time and Punishment *aloud and I could hear the music in the long sentences. I have to read aloud more. Thought about all this while watching a documentary on Dos Passos last night, the poetry of his cadence. He was another influence, years ago . . .*

I really don't have much to say other than thanks for your letter and the encouragement.

Be well.

I was called to the package room a little while ago, glad to get out even though it had started to rain a little—they'd just canceled morning rec after I'd put clothes on to go and get some air after being up most of the night and morning trying to get a few pages of a lead written. "Maybe there is a god," I thought wryly, catching the air after trying to get into compositional mode for the last 48 hours. When I get to the mailroom there is the box you sent which I thought they'd returned by now, and the guard asks me where I want it sent to. She opens it and lets me see what it is, and gives me your letter from it. I am overjoyed to see that it is a manuscript, and that they hadn't returned it, as now I can see one of the wardens and make them give it to me, since it technically isn't a "package."

The stack of letters for you/from you has sat on my desk like a pile of explosives in need of detonation.

There is all too often a blurred line between art and insanity, and I am not in position to fuck around but so much, as the saying goes.

I have been stuck at the moment I heard the message from your sister saying your son was dead. I can comprehend his heart failure.

I have wondered what I could write to you that would not sound idiotic. Everything must sound idiotic. What I came up with is this. I hope you can bear it. Much of what is good in me, not lame or escapist is a direct consequence of my daughter. Much of what is determined and flexible is a direct consequence of being a parent. She has transformed me. I have had nightmares of her being suddenly snatched and my standing open-mouthed and disconnected from everything, especially writing. But everything.

As I begin thinking about being out (which I am almost afraid to), I think about the freedom to say what I feel is real.

Also, I needed some remove from the anguish of my past in order to realize the joy of recreating it. Central, tonight, was being able to think about how having a son affected my life. Of course, I was uplifted by his birth, and perhaps it saved me from ruin in California, where things were going sour in the Party.

I was reading *Hurry Home* by Wideman this morning. I have just begun it and I find: "But I did not have a thousand sons; I tempted the number gods in no way. In fact I tried to be humble, wanted only one son, waiting once for one son. Loved all that Esther and I had done together . . . all we would ever do. So when he came and died so soon . . . So when he came and died so soon."

I have struggled to put myself in your place, to not be in your place. What would I do, what would I write if I couldn't touch anyone, if I couldn't drive out the pain with the distractions of sex or sitting alone on a hillside watching the sun or standing out in the rain until words returned to me. I don't know the answer(s). So . . . in sending you this pile of letters, poems, things, what have you, these pages that have been waiting for names, I am saying I don't know what I would write.

Fired at incautious temperatures in the crucibles of our minds—and the smithies of our souls, as Joyce put it. All this is to say I understand, dear sister, I understand. However, if we can hold on and dare as much as we can . . . to borrow again from our Irish cousin.

Got your 6/28 letter today and have put aside other things so that I could respond right away.

Freedom in the Dismal would have never come from me without you. And no, I don't think of myself as an artist. That word is too dangerous. It's so easy to start tripping and to think your life means more than someone else's. That you have license to do or not do. Writing makes the most sense when I think about the everyday nature of it. Writing helps me sort out what I have rolling around inside of me. It helps me make sense of me. I don't know what I'd do without writing because I can confuse the heck out of myself.

Before I close this and run off to chow, I know what you mean about feeling like a collaborator. I often feel that way myself, by not writing, and by holding back when I do write cause I'm under the gun (so to speak).

Questions regarding inspiration (muse, life force, god, deity, ancestor) are too big for me. When I think of them, I see myself trying to carry a huge box on an escalator. I can't see ahead of me and I don't know when to get off.

After he got his book deal ($375,000, plus selling the movie rights to John Singleton), he wrote to tell me that I should shop around a proposal while the door was open. I find myself measuring myself against him instead of enjoying the fact that he's making it. I had to realize I also felt slighted that he had said he was going to come see me so we could do a piece together, but never showed. It's hard to remember that the world doesn't revolve around oneself.

Uncle C. has a radically different and often very funny view of writing. He thinks of it in terms of best sellers, $$$$$$$$$, fame, business. I can't go there, either. Although I do all of the time. I start to feel like a cartoon character with big dollar signs in my eyes. Or like the guy with the hamburger jones in Popeye. What was his name? "I'll gladly pay you Tuesday for a hamburger today." It gets where you can't think of anything else. . . .

How does one deal with oppression overkill and infoglut from pictures of dying children all over the global village? There is a danger of hollering and throwing up both hands, circling back to McCall.

Do I think I have something to say? Yes. Do I think people should care? Yes. Why do I think these things? Because. Do I worry about having something to say? All the time. Does it hold me back? Yes. Does the worrying help? Only to the extent that it makes me work harder at finding fitting words.

I have a character in my play named Naima and she sort of goes on this guilt trip after success in the mainstream, along with a brother (unrelated) who used to be in the Party but turned totally capitalist. The more I worked on it the more I realized that she was similar to you, and he a version of a me who might have been.

All of this is to say, you should think about what you need to think about. Derrell, all of your ideas are good ideas. They always have been. The question is finding something that so engages you that you cannot help but work on it and more importantly, you cannot help but finish it. No matter what it is, if it commands your attention fully, I am sure it will be excellent and passionate and beautifully executed.

And it had me so I had to slack up on writing about imprisonment for a while. One can be thrown off-balance by the rage, as Fanon ran down. And I have already allowed my rage to put me in a rather bad situation. . . .

Did I send you this already? I may have sent it in another incarnation but it has grown and changed and left parts of itself behind.

In the space after that last word, I felt my fingertips almost touching yours.

I didn't proof this, because I might change it. So . . . bear with me.

But the quote from Sanchez in the paper sticks with me: "The time is asking for that." The time is calling out to us for decision. I have been thinking about you a great deal since getting your long letter and journal excerpt. So much about you I don't know, but somehow we seem to be so very much on the same vibe. Like the piece on Foucault, and the common involvement with anthropology. I'll dig out a copy of the verse for you, and maybe share a bit of how it was also inspired by meeting Dennis Brutus and his writing to me later encouraging me to do meter and rhyme. There is so much in this poem of a decade ago that speaks of the man I am and the problems I still face, it is frightening, not to mention the fact of this rather good verse being, like its author, all but lost for ten full years.

And by self-consciousness I really mean self-doubt. Not worrying about the larger world but caring about the world you and I share. This is an intimate enterprise and you probably need to let me know how much you can afford to be yourself on the page. In making this offer, I am saying my love for you is stronger than my fear of feeling too much through you.

I hadn't expected to say that.

Up late, don't quite feel like doing anything significant, tired of working, tired of reading, weary of sleeping . . . my defense against depression. But I had resolved to get this letter off to you tonight, and want to, especially after receiving your poetry manuscript. I am often afraid of bringing too much pain to those I care about. Often I won't call or write because of this. I need to know more than I acknowledge, that people do care about me. Lately, I've become attentive to how I like hearing my name called. My recent work includes more imagery and narrative than before, largely due to the influence of a professor from VCU who works with a creative writing class I direct in here. I didn't keep a copy of this because I'm almost out of paper and my ribbons are gone. So hold on to it if you can. Write.

Our correspondence is, in a sense, part of our autobiography of becoming. It is a conscious attempt to go beyond, at the same time expressing the artistic urge at the heart of the drive to communicate. It is also a reminder of an act that takes place daily between the incarcerated and their families. An act that attempts to transcend much more than genre. It is also emblematic of links in the African diaspora. It presses to look beyond boundaries of genre, time, and distance to address the art of everyday living.

Part IV

Telling Genres
Narratives of Literary History, Rhetoric, and Research

Contributors to this section tell the story of genre in part by telling stories in which genres function as characters of sorts—actors in the plot of discourse. They investigate the role of narrative in criticism and scholarship, and recast narratives of literary history, rhetoric, and research.

Hans Ostrom uses a case study of Countee Cullen, middle-school teacher in Harlem, to enlarge the story literary history has repeated about Countee Cullen, lyric poet. "How Teaching Rewrites the Genre of 'Writer'" also inquires into Cullen's orchestration of genres in the classroom, and into Cullen as "student writer" himself at Harvard. Lynn Miyake generates a theory of genre by retelling the story of literature from Japan's Heian period and in the process shows how much modern and contemporary Western literary theory—including the boundary-dissolving Deconstruction—was anticipated by Japanese notions of genre. Similarly, Allison Giffen examines the interaction between nineteenth-century American women poets and that most venerable of genres, the elegy. She argues, in part, that by "resisting consolation," these poets redefined elegy and gave us productive ways to see literary history as more of a conversation than a master narrative. Giffen also explains how such conversation with genre and history can help student writers.

In "Genre as Relation," Gregory Clark fuses the perspectives of academic writer and scholar of rhetoric, explaining how literal and figurative interactions with Kenneth Burke revealed to him the need for a more ethical, more expansive, more "social" view of himself as theorist. Jane Detweiler "retells the story of telling," as it were, interrogating the several functions of narrative in naturalistic research, asking, for instance, What are the differences and similarities between naturalistic researchers and writers of fiction? How can we productively reveal theories of and assumptions about narrative that are embedded in research-narratives?

Finally, Carol Severino complicates Detweiler's observations by asking us to consider whether Detweiler is not enacting the same rhetorical move she critiques: (over?)valorizing ethnographic accounts that now turn us into "serious storytellers" in a postmodern vein. The questions Severino raises return readers to the subject of antifoundationalism raised by William Lyne and to the concern over genre and its relation to subjectivity raised by Thomas Helscher. Clearly, attending to narrative and story, telling stories, places us quickly onto the professional stage where our most complicated plots unfold.

9

Countee Cullen
How Teaching Rewrites the Genre of "Writer"

Hans Ostrom

I.

More than most literary movements, the Harlem Renaissance continues to resonate and symbolize in our literary and political consciousness. This is so because the movement was at once contrived and spontaneous, potent and blighted, timeless and short-lived—and especially because it either confronted or foreshadowed most of the key conflicts among race, writing, politics, canon-building, gender, and class that were to define American literature and African-American literature during the rest of the century (Lewis; Rampersad).

We are likely to think of Countee Cullen as the conservative poet among that number when the saints came marching in. (Later I'll take pains to define "conservative" poet, as well as to suggest the limitations of the term.) And we are likely to contrast him, not favorably, with Langston Hughes, for instance, whose work seems more various and flexible; more politically charged; less constricted by the tenets of a bourgeois American perspective or a staid Anglo-European literary tradition. The conventional wisdom seems to be that Hughes deserves such continued, multifaceted examination in ways Cullen does not.

I want to use records of Cullen's teaching not just to interrogate the conventional wisdom, but to reverse the practice/theory relationship and use his teaching, his "practice," as a lens, a theoretical screen, through which to reread his aesthetic. Further, I want to show the ways in which genre helps us to understand the interface between his teaching and his writing.

II.

Cullen taught middle-school English for many years in Harlem, and a substantial record of his teaching exists, chiefly at Tulane University (Amistad)
and at the Schomburg Center for Black Culture in Harlem. What does the
teaching have to do with his literary status and his place in the canonical
scheme of things? And what does it have to do with defining genre and
teaching writing in this day and age?

The fact is most writers these days teach, and more teachers than ever
write—poems and stories, I mean. We can bemoan, decry, celebrate, or deny
this condition, but the condition remains (Bishop 1990 and Bishop and Ostrom
1994). However, when we "study" writers, we tend to treat the teaching part
of their lives and careers either as never having existed or as being incidental
to "the real work." Why might we do this? We are convinced that, in fact, the
poems and novels (or whatever) *are* the real work, exclusively, and that
teaching is either play or the unreal work. When it comes to the practice of lit.
crit., who cares if Robert Frost taught? This attitude carries with it New
Criticism's haughty dismissal of biographical criticism, naturally, but it also
carries with it the idea that when Frost (for instance) taught, he was merely
allowing people to be in his presence, his writerly presence. He wasn't really
a "teacher." To play a riff on Archibald MacLeish's infamous edict (in the
poem "Ars Poetica"), a writer should be, not teach.

And of course, when it comes to our own lives as writer-teachers or
teacher-writers, we are just as mightily conflicted—as the awkward, hyphen-
ated terms themselves symptomize. For example, many who live to write,
teach to live: Alienation 101.

More specifically, here are some points I want to pursue in order to
answer the broad questions just outlined:

1. Countee Cullen led a double literary life, the ostensible "nonliter-
   ary" (teaching) part of which we dare not ignore if we are to understand his work, his milieu, his understanding of Harlem, and his
   poetics fully.

2. In allowing his Harlem students certain literary maneuvers he did
   not always allow himself, Cullen dramatized key conflicts within
   the Harlem Renaissance; prefigured important developments in
   composition studies; and gave us a lens through which to (re)read
   his work. One important locus for these maneuvers was genre (see
   point 5). To some extent, my argument here is that the sustained
   teaching career of a writer is in itself an intellectual, critical, epistemological "act"—a working out of ideas about literacy and literature; therefore, what we know about such teaching adds a dimension
   that is as telling as letters, essays, memoirs, diaries, and so forth are
   in the study of writers and their work. Examining the teaching also

enlarges our view of the material conditions out of which writing springs.

3. The case of Countee Cullen can instruct all of us as we make our costume changes from Writer to Teacher to Theorist to Compositionist to Critic to Self-Critic to Master to Apprentice; his case can teach us about our teaching, and about interpreting the costumes into which we madly change in our fragmented one-person shows. If his teaching can be a lens through which to view his work, it can also be a lens through which to view our own.

4. In literal and figurative terms, Cullen was also a student, and a black student in white-supremacist America. In his teaching and writing, he compensated for losses and humiliations suffered as a student—just as we do, even if some of our sufferings are much less considerable, not racial, and so forth. I will not insult you or Cullen by suggesting that we all need to get in touch with our inner student or that all sufferings are equivalent; however, when we focus on power, the hard barriers supposedly separating teaching, learning, and writing evaporate. In significant ways, our "studentness" sticks with us, sometimes in most unhealthy, conflicted ways, especially when we romanticize it, or refuse to analyze it, or both.

5. Crucially, Cullen's teaching helps focus questions of genre, especially questions about appropriate genres and about revealing differences between what writer-teachers assign to their students in the way of genres and what writer-teachers themselves write. Moreover, Cullen cannily used genre to nourish authority in student writers and to help them reaffirm, through writing, the world they knew.

III.

How was Cullen conservative? In relation to other Harlem Renaissance writers, Cullen seems to favor ostensibly universal subject matter, as opposed to writing more explicitly about material conditions, concerns, and predicaments more explicitly African American. Further, he seems less inclined to remake the traditional forms in which he writes—ballad or sonnet, for instance—than Hughes, and here is an obvious place where questions of genre and questions of literary politics converge. Finally, Cullen is more inclined than Hughes to employ formal standard English that sometimes appears even to have more in common with British English than American English. Here I refer to Hughes as but one representative of a more folk-oriented aesthetic numerous writers explored in different ways.

I acknowledge how imprecise the term "conservative" is in this context, but it still seems applicable in the sense that Cullen's work retains many long-standing elements of British lyric poetry, many "genre-characteristics," if you will. Consider Cullen's poem, "From the Dark Tower" (Early, 139). Its message is not meek, the way with words not inconsiderable. But in the company of works by Langston Hughes and Zora Neale Hurston, such writing seems extremely reserved, buttoned down, forced, occasionally antique. Reticence, formality, blandness—these are among the characteristics associated with Cullen's verse and supportive of the term "conservative." Contrast "From the Dark Tower" with Hughes's "Dream Deferred" or even the Madame poems, and you will likely see merit in the characterization. David Lewis writes, "Sometimes Cullen must have set even Harlem's teeth on edge with CRISIS [magazine] throwaways lisping of a 'daisy-decked' Spring with her 'flute and silver lute'" (Lewis, 77). The term "throwaway" implies the idea that Cullen's poetry was weakest when certain poetic manners I have been calling "conservative" became formulaic—easily tossed, thrown, and therefore easily dismissed—tossed out.

The nature and function of Cullen's conservative choices, including choices *of* genre and *within* genre, are more complicated, however, than this basic sketch and the earlier contrast with Hughes reveal. For one thing, not all of his poems are the same—an obvious point but one that's easy to misplace. In "Saturday's Child" (Early, 91), for instance, Cullen seems to inhabit the form—in this case, a ballad—more successfully, finding a way to drive the verse with a more self-possessed diction. By "inhabit," I mean a kind of maneuver in which writers impose power or authority over a genre, as opposed to the maneuver to which Lewis refers in the paragraph above—a detached, unassertive, self-defeating manipulation of stock techniques or genre elements. In "Saturday's Child," for example, Cullen successfully exploits the tension between and among three genres—monologue, ballad, and lyric. In its own way, such a poem is both conservative (attentive to tradition) and improvisational—in the way Wordsworth's most successful "lyrical ballads" are. There are too many pitfalls to count in representing Cullen as the Wordsworth of the Harlem Renaissance, but drawing a momentary parallel between the two writers is instructive, helping to illuminate how Cullen interacted with genres.

The scope and direction of this essay are such that, for more extensive explorations of what I've labeled as Cullen's "conservatism," its complexity, and its limitations, I would refer readers to the work of Avi-Ram, Early, Lomax, and Shucard, and I move now to consider the extent to which the circumstances of Cullen's writerly choices, including choices concerning genre, are perhaps most startlingly complicated by what we know about his teaching.

IV.

When, in the mid-1930s, Cullen joined the faculty of Frederick Douglass Junior High School (P.S. 139) in Manhattan (Harlem), he did so chiefly to make a living. But however economically simple his reasons may have been, to enter that world was to enter a bewilderingly complex matrix of political forces, personal choices, and competing agendas. It was also to enter a public education system that from the vantage point of the late twentieth century looks all too disappointingly familiar.

The Amistad and Schomburg Collections contain school-board and municipal documents that show how underfunded the Harlem schools were in contrast to other New York City districts; how narrowly obsessed the school system was with standardized testing; and how often teachers in such a system had to serve numerous masters: parents, colleagues, principals, board members, educational philosophers, mayors, et al. To this matrix, Cullen brought his own complicated background. He was a poet who had gained renown, but with the coming of the Great Depression and the decline of the Harlem Renaissance, he was—as a black poet—a writer for whom renown did not bring its own momentum.

The teaching materials tell us much about Cullen's adaptability and courage as a teacher, and much about how a writer's and a teacher's choices converge. One remarkable fact, for instance, is that Cullen's English classes enviably integrated literature, composition, and creative writing—even as they had to pretend to satisfy the school board's bizarre demands, which included teaching grammar, academic-essay development, marketable skills, and canonical literature in one fell swoop (sound familiar?).

Cullen's plan books show that he negotiated these almost impossible circumstances and created an integrated writing class using two key pedagogical moves. First, he always adapted—one might even say deconstructed—received curricular edicts. To sift through the materials is to observe a teacher absorbing and transforming exterior strictures of the educational environment, a teacher making the material his (in this case) own. Second, he centered most of his choices on students, their aptitudes, conditions, and interests—a concept that remains radical and threatening to this day partly because of its breathtaking simplicity and practicality and partly because "the subject" is the student. That is, he wanted to make the students' education *their* own—wanted them to "inhabit" it the way Cullen, at his best, inhabited the institution of lyric poetry he chose to join.

For example, a plan book from early in his career (February 1935) shows him struggling to adapt the requirement of teaching "practical" writing. First he decides to have the class write "a letter ordering a magazine." Then he decides to have them write "a friendly letter on 'My Ambition In Life.'" A strange assignment? Well, yes—but the method of Cullen's madness begins to emerge in the adjective "friendly," which the middle-schoolers would have understood, and which would have implicitly introduced ideas of audience and the writer's self. The adjective encodes a deceptively sophisticated rhetorical move, a move allowing entry into a genre.

A month later, faced with the task of teaching such wildly different literary pieces as "The Rime of the Ancient Mariner," *A Midsummer Night's Dream,* and "The Celebrated Jumping Frog of Calaveras County," Cullen becomes even more student-centered: On March 8 he decides to have the students "write a letter to a friend telling what interested you in the A.M. ["Ancient Mariner"]." By December 3, he's having them write "stories my mother and father tell of us children," an assignment that seems to mix narrative, fiction, autobiography, ethnography—perhaps even a little folklore.

For a ninth-grade composition class in the early 1940s, Cullen integrated poetry writing, autobiography, the notion of a "thing poem," the notion of a monologue, reading, speaking, and revision. Here is his note (Box 11, File 13, Amistad):

> Class 9A(2) Composition:
>
> Theme: Original verse: subject: Identify yourself with your favorite toy, and write a poem in which the toy speaks.
>
> Treatment: Class discussion, poems written at home—brought in, read, corrected, re-written.

Naturally, the word "toy" seems a little dated in the context of a ninth-grade class, at least from the vantage point of the late twentieth century, when ninth graders seem more jaded than Philip Marlowe. But otherwise, the assignment seems remarkably current and progressive, using creative writing in a composition class, embodying a student-centered approach, staying attentive to revision, and above all integrating a variety of elements in a rhetorical situation. By emphasizing the topic over the form, Cullen invites the students into the genre of lyric poetry. Here are some lines from student Luke Ramsey's poem, "My Ball Speaks":

> I am the one, who takes the beating,
> Because I'm bounced, all over the place.
> I sometimes can have my revenge on them
> By knocking them right in the face.

What a nice surprise—of a male, middle-school sort—there in the last line. Notice, too, how Luke is working with and hearing the rhythm within the rhythm; his ear tells him to put in commas in the first half of the quatrain to slow down the lines. And it seems that Luke is able to transcend the exercise and inhabit the form by bringing forth an image he knows well: having the basketball bounce unpredictably; the autobiographical element empowers him, one might say—gives him room to maneuver.

Here are lines from Harold Killough's poem, "The Train":

> My name it is Electric Train.
> In the house always, sunshine or rain.
> I don't have a bit of fun.
> All I do is run and run.

An unusual empathetic move here: Harold sees something of Sisyphus in the train, chooses not to see the train as his toy anymore, and—in keeping with the lyric genre!—emphasizes solitude.

Two years later, Cullen puts a historical spin on the assignment, having students write poems on such figures as Lincoln and Douglass. Notice the hint of Rap and Hip-Hop in the lines from James Boffman's "Lincoln and Douglass":

> Lincoln was needy for advice, Douglass' counsel he sought.
> Wisdom and guidance is what Douglass brought.

In such assignments, Cullen offered students an avenue by which they could come to own the poem; he uses the assignment to access issues of voice, revision, precision—and form/genre. Are the assignments too labyrinthine—Rube Goldberg concoctions? A fair question, though Cullen did seem to know what his students could and could not achieve, and he seemed almost always to think through the purposes of assignments, and to construct them in ways that apparently did not bewilder the students. (Would that we had videotapes of his oral, in-class elaborations on the assignments.) All in all, the level of integration and improvisation Cullen achieves remains enviable. After some fifty years, the worth and inherent logic of such assignments endure. Will our teaching materials hold up as well after fifty years?!

Nonetheless, Cullen could not fight City Hall, as it were. He could not make the funding fairer, the classes smaller, racism less monolithic, or educational standards less surreal. But he could and did create productive pedagogical zones for his students. Moreover—and here is a crucial point—he did so through innovative writing assignments, the existence of which one could not have predicted based on the implicit ethos of Cullen's own writing, based on how he himself inhabited lyric form or on how he positioned himself in the Harlem Renaissance. It's too simplistic to say that Cullen the teacher and Cullen the writer were two different entities (a self-defeating reliance on a tired dualism). Better to say that Cullen the writer recognized all too well how marginalized his students were and created pedagogical spaces for them that were rarely if ever created for him. This interpretation assumes a fair amount of empathy on Cullen's part. Like Gerald Early's (3–73) revaluation, it also complicates our view of Cullen's politics.

This is a good place, then, to discuss a telling bit of evidence about Cullen the student, evidence which applies to the "empathy" argument. Among the Amistad Center materials is a graduate paper Cullen wrote for Irving Babbitt during a brief stint at Harvard: "Walter Pater as a Romantic Critic." It is an accomplished piece of criticism, notable in part for the maturity of its argument, its understanding of romantic poetics, and its confident prose style. Professor Babbitt gave it an A–, with this comment:

> A good formulation of Pater from a distinctly modernistic point of view.
> The best corrective of your tendency to overestimate Pater would be to
> build up your background (Aristotle's Poetics, etc.).

This is a quintessentially aloof, unhelpful response to Cullen's essay, of course. Aside from two words ("good formulation"), in fact, it is not a response to Cullen's writing but a kind of express delivery of hidden agendas and coded messages: You like Pater too much. You aren't aloof enough in your rhetorical stance. You have not read what I have read. What about Aristotle, what about Aristotle? Your "background" is lacking. Whereas Cullen's middle-school strategy is to give students power and create pedagogical space, Babbitt's university strategy is to close almost every door along the corridor. His comment isn't exactly mean or bullying; he closes the doors gently. Nonetheless, they are shut and locked. For the strategy of his teacher's discourse (shifting metaphors now) is to circumvent the piece of Cullen's writing before him and, in a way, to force Cullen to fight a rear-guard action concerning excessive enthusiasm, modernist tendencies, and "background," that loaded term. To echo William Lyne's essay elsewhere in this volume, Babbitt was concerned with "white purposes."

After leaving Harvard upon receiving his M.A., after seeing the socio-economic foundation of the Harlem Renaissance get wiped out by the Great Depression, after seeing his early literary fame bear meager fruit, did Cullen rush to Frederick Douglass Middle School determined to become Irving Babbitt's pedagogical opposite? No, it's not that simple, of course. On the other hand, his lack of power as a student and a writer must have been palpable to Cullen in a variety of ways, large and small. And the abundant evidence of how he operated as a teacher tells us that he chose not to visit the sins of the dominant culture on the sons and daughters of a marginalized one.

V.

All well and good, but what does Countee Cullen in Harlem have to do with us—the M.A.s, the M.F.A.s, the Ph.D.s of contemporary North America, the citizens of CCCC, MLA, NCTE, and AWP, the teachers of College Writing in its many forms? Let me count a few of the ways.

First, the example of Cullen gives us a different, more realistic, and therefore more useful model of the writer/teacher from the one that has dominated our professional consciousness since World War II. This dominant model is that of the writer-in-residence, the writer who has "made it" (whatever that means, and it has usually meant a book or a prize or some other cultural anointing) and on the basis of making it is invited to teach at a college, except that the teaching is usually accompanied by a wink and a nod. Cullen, a black writer in Great Depression America, couldn't "make it" in the usual sense. For black writers, early success did not predict later security and status. For Cullen, publishing books and winning prizes and even attending Harvard didn't pay off as it might have if he had been white. Therefore, when he taught, he really did teach: every day, all day, at a school in impoverished Harlem. He taught in ways significantly different from the way most well-published writers-in-residence of his and subsequent generations taught. He taught to a markedly different set of students in a markedly different set of socioeconomic circumstances.

For almost all of the writer-teachers or teacher-writers currently making the transition from M.F.A. or Ph.D. programs to college jobs, Cullen's experience is much closer to academic, economic reality than the experience, for example, of John Ciardi, Randall Jarrell, or Karl Shapiro, to choose writers associated with the 1940s and 1950s; and it is closer to academic, economic reality than that of a shrinking handful of famous writers-in-residence today, such as Rita Dove or Gary Snyder.

Cullen embraced his circumstances with pedagogical creativity, quiet subversiveness, and not a little productive, unsentimental empathy for the disempowered. That is to say, he confronted and made use of a rather brutal fact: he had more in common with the students of Frederick Douglass School than he did with Irving Babbitt or Ernest Hemingway. He did not deny the fact. To reiterate a point made early in the essay, "reading" Cullen's teaching in this way helps us productively complicate our reading of Cullen's poetry; it adds texture and complexity to comparisons between his work and that of Hughes, for instance. It does so not in the usual way biography informs a writer's literary work, but in distinct ways that concern literacy as negotiation, literacy as power, teaching as power. Put another way, seeing how Cullen helped middle-schoolers negotiate writing may well demystify different ways Cullen negotiated his own writing and inscribed himself on traditions of lyric poetry.

Second, Cullen wrestled with the socioeconomic injustice that was killing Harlem and its schools. The literary conservative was, at the very least, an educational progressive, perhaps even a radical. Labels aside, he confronted questions of power and injustice—and he often did so through the use of rhetoric and genre, helping students to situate themselves "inside" a genre and in relation to a subject.

We teacher-writers and writer-teachers should continue to help each other to do the same. How well are M.F.A. programs equipping their graduates for the real work of teaching that these graduates will do? What are M.F.A. and Ph.D. programs doing about the horrendous job market in English? How well is the Associated Writing Programs looking after the interests of students? Why do such hard barriers exist between M.F.A., Ph.D.–literature, and Ph.D.–rhetoric students when almost all of them will end up with jobs that include the teaching of first-year writing?

Third, to paraphrase the bandits in *Treasure of the Sierra Madre,* Cullen didn't need no stinking genre boundaries. Poetry, essays, stories, autobiography, cumulative sentences, sentence combining, letters, prosody exercises, parody exercises: the students of Frederick Douglass school wrote it all. Cullen's class was a great Cajun gumbo of genres. Although virtually all of the theoretical, pedagogical, and practical evidence suggests that our classrooms should be the same, our curricula remain unreflectively genre-bound. Ph.D. students write "papers," M.F.A. students write stories and poems; the deans running the show write memos. Instead, everybody should be writing everything, particularly at the undergraduate level, but also in graduate programs. M.F.A. students should write nonfiction prose about teaching and theory. Ph.D. students (and deans) should write poems and stories. Cullen's maneuvers within a literary tradition are parallel to maneuvers his students made within an educational tradition. Cullen's pedagogical strategies highlight this parallelism for us: Cullen the teacher enables his students to negotiate genres in the same way Cullen the poet negotiates (in "Saturday's Child," for instance) genres of lyric poetry he has received from the Tradition. To put the matter in even broader terms, pedagogy can be seen—ought to be seen— as a vibrant site where writers', students', teachers', and theorists' notions of genre and genre-mastery converge and often collide. Pedagogy "reads" genre and struggles of genre-power in ways we should not neglect—as theorists, as writers, as teachers, as hybrid entities combining all three roles.

Finally, as noted earlier, real and apparent tensions exist between Cullen the writer and Cullen the teacher. Such tensions exist for us all: Perhaps we give ourselves advice about writing that is different from the advice we give students. Perhaps, as M.F.A. students (for example), we take one sort of course in the afternoon and then teach one the next day that is based on different pedagogical assumptions. Just as knowing Cullen's teaching enriches our knowledge of his writing and of issues central to the Harlem Renaissance, exploring the commonalities and conflicts between our own teaching and writing can only enrich us. Probably all graduate students in writing, rhetoric, and literature should keep ethnographic journals or do other sorts of writing that explicitly integrate their experiences as writers, students, teachers, and theorists—as well as parents, workers, spouses, partners, and whatever. That is to say, we need to address not just issues of power but also the insidious compartmentalization of genres, subject matter, and the often alienated, competing roles of writer, student, and teacher.

If teaching rewrites writers, complicating their relationships to genre in general and genres in particular, then studying the teaching of a writer who taught rewrites our notions of the writer, of his or her writing, of his or her maneuvers within traditions of genre. Therefore, we should see teaching as part of the whole, in our lives and work and in the lives and work of writers who came before us—should see that teaching is a site and a text, not just a job. Genre functions significantly on that site because genre enacts theory and exposes contradictions, as Lyne, Helscher, and others in this volume show. These are some of the issues Countee Cullen the teacher raises; maybe the teaching histories of countless other writers can educate us further and become more greatly accepted sites of research for graduate students of creative writing, rhetoric, and literature. By reintegrating teaching histories into ongoing professional inquiry, we are more likely to integrate pedagogy into literary history and genre-theory. Countee Cullen in Harlem was a kind of unwitting beacon for this sort of work.

Also, in English-studies graduate programs, courses should integrate varieties of writing, varieties of genre. Graduate students just embarking on their teaching careers should write about that teaching in a variety of ways, should present that writing or ideas from it in their seminars and workshops, should be encouraged to conduct meta-analysis of their double and triple lives as writers, teachers, and students, tearing down boundaries and dried-up dualisms between theory and practice, "TA-ing" and studying, writing and teaching, and so forth. What was good for Countee Cullen's Harlem ninth-graders could be excellent for our own graduate programs, where issues of power, ownership, masters and apprentices, sexual politics, discourse codes, "background," and hidden agendas are everywhere. As a socio-economic site and as a crucible of competing discourses, pedagogy is every bit as complex and influential as publishing, but mostly it is not treated as such. The same theoretical models that have helped us examine genres in relation to publishing, canon formation, and discourse communities can help us examine genres in relation to pedagogy; in relation to the pedagogical histories of writer-teachers; in relation to ethnographies and self-studies of teachers; and in relation to pedagogy's attendant issues of power, discourse, silence, and reinscription. Elsewhere in this volume, Allison Giffen refers to genre as a "kinetic site." We might profitably depict pedagogy in similar terms—that is, as a place with its own integrity, its own identity; as a place with stories to tell about writers who teach and teachers who write.

Finally, I'd like to echo Gerald Early's insistence that, to "locate" Cullen properly, we must read him "holistically"—by interpreting his mysterious geneaology, his deceptively complex poetry and fiction, and his theology in relation to one another (6–7). One purpose of this essay has been to make Cullen's teaching more central to such a reading, and to make questions of genre central to understanding his teaching. Additionally, we might also productively view Cullen's (and our own) writing and teaching in existential terms, insofar as Lewis R. Gordon has defined *Existential* in his recent book, *Existence In Black:*

> *We can regard existentialism—the popularly named ideology—as a fundamentally European historical phenomenon. It is, in effect, the history of European literature that bears that name. On the other hand, we can regard philosophy of existence [. . .] as philosophical questions premised upon concerns of freedom, anguish, responsibility, embodied agency, sociality, and liberation. [P]hilosophy of existence is marked by a centering of what is often known as the "situation" of questioning or inquiry itself (3).*

Attempting to understand Cullen-the-teacher, then, enlarges our understanding of his *situation,* and observing how Cullen manipulated genres in his teaching—which today we might call liberatory—provides important clues to his own understanding of his students', Harlem's, and his situations.

10

The (Re)making of Genres
The Heian Example

Lynne K. Miyake

Marjorie Perloff, in her "Introduction" to *Postmodern Genres,* writes that "[our postmodern sense of] genre, far from being a normative category, is always culture-specific and, to a high degree, historically determined" (7). The "underlying rationale for genre falls within the larger category of post-Enlightenment culture, [is] a specifically Western project of understanding . . . [and thus, its] manifestations are not hugely generalizable" (Davis and Schleifer, viii). I cannot agree more wholeheartedly. Unfortunately, this "Western project of understanding" often crosses oceans, cultures, and even centuries, "remaking" non-Western textual categories along lines consistent with its own image. As a case in point, in Japanese studies in the United States, the standard of Western genres has been imposed upon Japanese texts, both modern and classical, in the name of describing and introducing them to Euro-American audiences, but in reality regularizing these texts according to contours of Western categorization. Masao Miyoshi labels this process a domestication or a "making familiar" of the exotic or the unfamiliar for Western consumption (9).

In his provocative study, *Complicit Fictions: The Subject in the Modern Japanese Prose Narrative,* James Fujii convincingly argues that Japan's initial encounter with the West has contributed to the persistent conceptualizing of Japan in contrast to the "(Western) hegemonic other." Thus Fujii contends that "[e]ver since the Meiji Restoration of 1868 made Western material and cultural achievements the keystone for nation building . . . the terms for understanding and representing Japan have come in the form of a series of binary categories that reflect these inequalities" (7). This has ensured that modern Japanese literature "be assessed largely through European realist textual conventions by Westerners and Japanese alike" (xi) and be forever "derivative—hence, always lesser than the 'originals'—or . . . exotically different" (8).

If James Fujii has cautioned against using "a form [the nineteenth century realist novel] fixed and given to us from regions far removed in both
geographic and cultural space" (xiv) to describe modern Japanese narratives,
how much more problematic would such genre demarcations be in the
assessment of classical Japanese texts removed not only geographically and
culturally but temporally as well. The first classical works introduced to the
English-speaking West came from the Heian period, historically 795–1185,
but in terms of literature, the tenth through the twelfth centuries, and were
products of an entirely aristocratic, highly educated society of male and
female courtiers and clerics. However, in the name of "making familiar,"
scholars usually described them in terms of genres that were part of the
Western landscape. *The Tale of Genji*,[1] an eleventh century prose narrative
encompassing both prose and poetry, for example, often has been touted as
"the world's earliest novel," despite the fact that it was written centuries
before the novel was created, let alone imported into Japan. A work from the
ensuing period, the *Tale of Heike*, a narrative about a war that was fought
between two great landed, warrior families in the twelfth century, in turn has
been negatively compared to the great Greek tragedies: *Heike* deals with the
likes of tragedy (war and death) but is too aesthetic in orientation and lacks
cathartic depth. Further, although women were among the earliest practitioners of prose in the Heian period and their works are considered the belles
lettres of the period, few novels by modern women writers are translated into
English today. It is as if the late development of women's writing in Europe
(see Gilbert and Gubar), coupled with the Western notion that Japanese
women are docile, submissive, and, therefore, uninteresting, so powerfully
controls the psyche of Western academic circles—both feminist and
nonfeminist—that narratives by Japanese women writers are still being dismissed as unimportant (see Vernon). This despite the fact that some of the
most interesting writing coming out of Japan today is by women.

Much needs to be done to rectify this hegemonic wielding of genre
definitions vis-à-vis both modern and nonmodern Japanese texts. To embark
upon this process, this essay first proposes to examine the contours of the
"genres"/categories[2] of the Heian period, specifically what factors were central
in differentiating Heian texts. It will then show that Western genres, be they
defined as two (literature and nonliterature), three (lyric, epic, and drama), or
four (lyric, epic, drama, or prose fiction), cannot serve as adequate metaphors
of description and assessment of Heian texts. Rather, Heian narratives can
serve as a kind of countercritique of Western genres. From these texts, too,
new strategies of reading—and writing—can be deduced to help our students
realize anew the extent of the "Eurocentric baggage" that they bring to texts
and to their writing, and their need to understand that reading and writing must
be undertaken, always cognizant of the historical, social, economic, literary, to
name a few, contexts that serve as coordinates in their production (see Mani).
Ultimately, our students must be taught to write differently: to reflect in their

writing an awareness of their own positions and groundings in the cultural limits and assumptions of Western culture, especially vis-à-vis non-Western, nonmainstream texts, to take care not to presume to speak for the "other," (Kondo 1991, 2–9) and to be ever vigilant and honest concerning their own ethnocentricity/blind spots.

Even a quick perusal of Heian texts will reveal that post-Enlightenment realist genres are unsuitable for assessing them. To begin, although the so-called binary categories of prose/poetry and fact/fiction[3] were present in the Heian period, these were conceived of very differently from in the West. Poetry (basically *waka*) in Heian Japan was not the metered, rhymed poetry of Coleridge and Wordsworth. The major form of the period, known as the *tanka*, was a mere thirty-one syllables of alternating lines of 5, 7, 5, 7, 7 syllables. Longer poems (*choka*) did exist as well, but these, too, had neither rhyme nor meter and simply alternated lines of five- and seven-syllables concluding with a couplet of sevens. Even the concept of "lines" or "verses" is a misnomer, for Heian poems appear in written manuscripts as single, continuous lines rather than verses of five short lines as they do in most English translations. Thus in its orthographic rendering *waka* did not markedly distinguish itself from prose. The distinction between prose and poetry lay more in the rhythm of alternating five- and seven-syllable lines, although it was not unusual for prose to mimic that aspect to some extent. It is also important to note that poetry was not just an elite art form practiced by professional poets but played a regular part in daily communication and social intercourse. Poetry was central not only to written communication (e.g., letters) but to oral communication as well. Recitation of poetry at the appropriate moment in a conversation was a highly prized and necessary social skill.

Prose (*ji no bun*), in contrast, more closely resembled our expectations of what prose should look like, but it, too, differed in one singular aspect— it incorporated poetry, usually the thirty-one-syllable *waka* but on occasion the longer *choka* as well. To complicate things even further, poetry, even that appearing in the so-called poetic anthologies, was not in "pure" form either. Poems were regularly preceded by prose introductions (*kotobagaki*), contextualizing the particular circumstances, the players, and often the chronological details of the poems.

Thus we can say that a differentiation between poetry and prose was made, but that the demarcation was not rigid and absolute. In fact the boundaries between them were so flexible and permeable that border crossings occurred regularly and often. Under the rubric of poetry then were listed imperially commissioned anthologies (*chokusenshu*), anthologies of poems by multiple writers (*shisenshu*, but this could also be the work of one poet as well), and private anthologies, a collection of poetry by one poet (*kashu*), but all contained not just poetry but extensive prose introductions as well. Some scholars[4] even place certain poetic anthologies under prose, because these

texts include long prose passages and appear very similar to the diary literature (*nikki* or *nikki bungaku*).

At the other end of the spectrum, the prose categories of the diary, the
narrative/tale (*monogatari*), and the miscellany or essay (*zuihitsu*)[5] all contain poetry, some so much so that their very taxonomies have been modified
to reflect the inclusion of poetry—for example, two have been subcatego-
rized as the poem narrative (*uta monogatari*) and the narrative in poetry
(*utagatari*) to name two. From this discussion it becomes clear that not only
was the conceptualization of poetry and prose configured differently in Heian
Japan but that the division between them was never rigidly enforced. In fact,
according to one scenario (see Kikuta), prose narratives and diaries are
thought to have developed from the lengthening of prose introductions to
poems in poetic anthologies.

The "falsehoods and fabrications (*itsuwari soragoto*)"/"real events (*aru
koto*)"[6] dichotomy operative during the Heian period also reveals marked
differences with their Western counterparts, fact and fiction. Heian writers
made a distinction between narratives based on historical persons and events
and those that were not, but this demarcation resulted in two very different
practices in classical Japan. First, as a result of a literary heritage inherited
from China, the Heian period privileged histories and biographies (fact) over
base fiction, thus allowing the predominantly "nonfiction," "actual fact" texts
rather than fiction to take center stage. In effect the diary and the miscellany
(and the nonfictional prose narratives) were accorded the status of so-called
high literature. The *monogatari*, the only category with a subcategory explicitly marked as fiction, actually places three of its four subcategories (the
poem prose narrative [*uta monogatari*], the historical prose narrative [*rekishi
monogatari*], and the later thirteenth-through fifteenth-century war prose narrative [*gunki monogatari*]) under nonfiction. Only one subcategory, the
fictional prose narrative (*tsukuri monogatari*) lives up to its translated name,
"tales," but even it is not entirely "fictional." Although no conclusive evidence can be mounted, historical models for the hero Genji and for the time
period of at least the first half of *The Tale of Genji* have been identified,
thereby blurring the borders between fact and fiction even further.

This permeability of boundaries between fact and fiction (in ways that
did not occur in the post-Enlightenment West until poststructuralism made
moot the artificial division between "real" and fictional events) is the second
distinctive functioning of "fact" and "fiction" during the Heian period. This
practice, however, is not just limited to *The Tale of Genji*, but is evident in
the *nikki* diary as well. Although the recording *nikki* fits the commonly held
definition of the diary as a record of "facts," the fictional or poetic *nikki*
includes "nonhistorical," "fictional" elements, while at the same time operating as a record of the lives of historical personages, usually that of the diarist. It appears then that the creators of Heian *nikki* less stringently adhered

to a black and white demarcation between fact and fiction and allowed for more merging and mixing between the two.

This less well-defined boundary between fact and fiction than is common in the West is very much in keeping with the Heian period's attitude toward the intermixing of prose and poetry and is, in fact, replicated in the border crossings of individual texts. These crossings between prose and poetry categories and among the subcategories therein are reflected in the variant titles of certain works. The multiple titles certainly demonstrate how these texts were received by later audiences and transmitters and reflect the kinds of crossings that occurred. For example, *Ise Monogatari* (*Tales of Ise*) has the alternate titles of *Zaigo ga Monogatari* (*Tales of Zaigo*: Zaigo is an abbreviation for the Ariwara Narihira, the hero of the tale), *Zaigo Chujo no the Nikki* (*The Diary of Zaigo Chujo* = The Diary of Captain Ariwara Narihira), and *Zai Chujo* (*The Ariwara Captain*) and participated in the categories of the prose narrative, the diary, and possibly the individual poetry collection. The variant titles of *Izumi Shikibu Nikki* (*The Diary of Izumi Shikibu*) reflect its membership in three categories: the diary, the narrative/tale, and the poetry collection (Konishi, 251–52).[7]

Simply put, Heian Japan and the periods following appear to have had very different attitudes toward genre categorization. Categorization took place, but it operated in ways very different from the post-Enlightenment, realist tendencies of the nineteenth-century West. Ground rules seem to have been operative, but at the same time much less stringently adhered to. Or perhaps these rules are not discernible to us at this point in time, centuries after the fact. Or it might simply be that for Heian texts strict demarcation between such categories as fact and fiction, prose and poetry was not the issue, and that the blurring and intermingling were the key to the tradition. This does not appear to be an isolated gesture. Rather, interaction between such binaries as orality and textuality, first and third narrative points of view, and the separation of narrator, reader, and text which formed the mainstay of nineteenth-century realist tradition function more fluidly and interactively in Heian texts. *The Tale of Genji*, for instance, appears to have incorporated the recitation aspects of the *waka* poem into its written aspects (Miyake 1994, 77–87). Similar vestiges of orality remain in the thirteenth-century *Tale of Heike*, a text considered to be a written rendition of oral recitations by itinerant monks.

On the issue of first- and third-person narrative points of view, Heian *nikki* challenge the Western notion of diaries' always being in the first person. *The Izumi Shikibu Diary*, for example, is written in the third person, but its usual classification is the *nikki*. The English translation of *The Kagero Diary*[8] is rendered but a much more complex narrative situation appears in Japanese: the work opens with the diarist referring to herself in the third person, but the narration switches to the first person midway through the second sentence. Shifts from first- to third-person narrative and back again occur throughout, often for the space of a phrase or even a single word. Further, narrative points of view can be multiple, and can shift through a series of narrators as they do through different female courtier–like narrators in *The Tale of Genji* and between the male yet female narrator(s) of *The Tosa Diary* (see Miyake, *The Tosa Diary*).[9]

Lastly, the relationship between the narrator, character, and even reader is much more fluid, interactive, and collaborative. In Heian texts the borders between the text and the reader's world are more permeable, allowing the narrator to speak "directly" to the reader and the reader to take a collaborative and performative role in the production of the meaning of the text (Miyake, 1994). A word or phrase from a poem from the poetic tradition, for instance, requires the reader to recognize the allusion and reconstruct the specific poem from his/her stored knowledge, and add that meaning to the text.

Although space constraints preclude me from going into further detail at this time, the phenomena of multiple titles, the collaborative, interactive relationships between reader, narrator, and character, the blurring of the boundaries between prose and poetry, fact and fiction, orality and textuality, first- and third-person narrative points of view in Heian texts show ever more convincingly the extent to which Western post-Enlightenment genres have obscured rather than revealed major aspects of classical Japanese literature. Nonetheless, academia still persists in using the term "diary" for *nikki* when "autobiography" is more accurate. Writing for a nonspecialist Western audience, I, too, am implicated in the perpetuation of these names. Many a time I have been compelled to use the term "diary" instead of the unfamiliar *nikki*, for fear of alienating my audience and being told to explain—yet again. But perhaps it is time, as it was for Donald McQuade in "Composition and Literary Studies," to call for new names and a new language—"name[s] and a language of our[/their] own" (482).

Once we allow *nikki's* existence beyond the limits of diary, perhaps then it can act as a meaningful critique of the rapidly changing and expanding term "autobiography" (cf. Kaplan), which has already profited from the scrutiny of critics working in feminism and ethnic literatures. Perhaps then Heian *nikki* can help to problematize the notions that autobiographies are written in the first person or that these must record the life of an individual and in terms that approximate the life of the diarist. Further, if autobiographies are stories of selves, the entire concept of what constitutes a self must be called into question when dealing with Heian texts like *The Pillow Book of Sei Shonagon*,[10] which is *nikki*-like, records the crafting of not just a self, fully bound and contained within itself, but the many selves of the author, Sei Shonagon, as she moves from one interrelational creation of herself to another. Sei Shonagon's "life story" is not just conveyed through a running prose narrative, but runs the gamut of anecdotes to diarylike entries to lists of what she considers the most despicable, the most aesthetically pleasing, the best moments of each season of the year. Does all this add up to a self? Probably not the essentialized realist subject of the (Romantic) tradition continuous through time, but many selves constantly shifting and crafting themselves in each new relational encounter. (See Dorinne Kondo's *Crafting Selves*.)

From a perspective different from that of the poststructuralists, Heian texts also problematize the meaning of fact and fiction. Because the demarcation between fact and fiction has never been well marked in Heian texts, from the outset historical personages and events have played an integral and crucial role. Even the listing of the name of the poet before a poem in the *utagatari* (narrative in poetry) *Yamato Monogatari* (*The Tales of Yamato*)[11] is not just a designation of the author as we would find it on the title page of a novel. Rather it acts as a signifier, calling up to the Heian reader all the "facts" known about the poet, be it by reputation, personal experience, or even rumor. This exterior, unwritten "text" is incorporated into the narrative and becomes part of the "story" being related.

In similar ways the division between prose and poetry was not as well marked, so these have existed in tandem, blending in and out of each other, pulling their readers into one register and then out into the other. Thus narratives no longer had/have to be entirely in either prose or poetry with beginnings and ends, centering upon the telling of the private individual's psychology and action in logical, chronological sequence. By blending prose and poetry, by privileging nonfictional texts as belles lettres, Heian writers/texts show us that literature includes not just fiction, but nonfiction, and that theory and personal experience play integral roles in the production of literature—in ways that give special significance to the writings of the likes of Gloria Anzaldua and Dorinne Kondo (see Anzaldua 1987; 1990); Anzaldua and Moraga; and Kondo, *About Face*). Ultimately, it is hoped that Heian texts and other non-Western and nonmainstream narratives will expand what we consider to be literature—that people will learn how to deal with the unfamiliar, the non-Western, "ethnic literatures" without exoticizing, trivializing, or domesticating them, truly opening ourselves up to the surprisingly new and different worldviews they offer.

How can Heian texts and genre perspectives help teach genre? I think that they can do that simply by being introduced into our classrooms. As our students attempt to make sense of these texts—and other nonmainstream texts—utilizing the reading strategies and categorizations of poetry, prose, novel as we understand them in English and in a Euro-American context, they will begin to see the gaps and fissures in our definitions. An encounter with Heian texts, then, can reveal the Eurocentric assumptions we hold about how we expect stories to be told, how we unconsciously expect all long prose narratives to be classic realist novels of some kind. As a case in point several years ago when I taught *The Tale of Genji* for the first time, even the most well read of my students did not know what to make of the narrative. There was a beginning, there was a story line of some kind but nothing that he could call a plot, and certainly no ending. All he could conclude was that a young, Don Juan–like figure had a series of affairs with a variety of women. The only "high point" he could identify in an otherwise level plane of no action was the hero's banishment from the capital to the desolate seacoast of Suma after the hero was caught in the rooms of the future consort to the Crown Prince. Nothing else made very much sense—could this be the great work of classical Japanese literature? An encounter with Norma Field's chapter on the heroines of the tale in her informative book, *The Splendor of Longing in the Tale of Genji* (18–85), opened the student's eyes to the complexity of story formation, Heian style— delineated through family lineage, through use of flower metaphors for the names of central women figures, through the intertextuality of images, through the resonance of the prose and poetry in the tale and that of the poetic tradition, to name a few. In this clash of what Catherine Belsey terms competing (ideological) discourses, categories such as the novel, *monogatari,* autobiography, *nikki* collide in untidy and unruly disorder, forcing us to problematize and expand definitions of genre(s).

In other textual moments, the prose in the seventeenth century travel log *The Narrow Road to the Deep North* by Matsuo Basho serves foremost as contextualized occasions for the seventeen-syllable *haikai* or *haiku* poetry, while the format of Santo Kyoden's *Edo mumare uwaki no kabayaki* (*Romantic Embroilments Born in Edo*)[12] from the eighteenth century tempts the reader to conclude that it is the precursor of modern-day *manga* (comic books), replete with line drawings and dialogue and text written within the borders of each frame—what Western taxonomies could adequately encompass such textual performances? Even the 1968 Nobel Prize winner Kawabata Yasunari's *Snow Country* does not comfortably fit into the category of the realist novel: written in three parts and published in three different journals over the course of twelve years, it seems to begin in medias res, ends nowhere, inviting addendum aft, forward, and even in between the three sections. Tsushima Yuko's hauntingly disquieting "stories" from the seventies (e.g., "The Silent Traders," "The Shooting Gallery," "The Shining Light") visit and revisit in one narrative after another the writer's personal experiences: the death of her brother, her existence as a single parent, her continual search for her/a father (figure), who never married her mother and who died when she was very young. We begin these texts unconsciously expecting, desiring, stories that have beginnings, middles, and ends. We want them to be about someone, about something. It would be easiest if they moved along some kind of definable action toward some definable conclusion. We do not want to be stranded in unknown, unknowable landscapes. We want familiar landmarks and guides.

These are not what Heian texts and other nonmainstream writings provide for our students, but it is my belief that encounters—engagements— with these kinds of texts are the key to helping our students write differently.

Writing, according to Belsey, constitutes a kind of reading, so encountering non-Western, nontraditional works—experiencing the clash of discourses—becomes the first step in learning new writing strategies. Engaging the unfamiliar then will help our students confront the Eurocentric biases that they bring to texts. Then and only then will they free themselves of the "common sense," ideological hold on their imaginations and push beyond the parameters that they have been conditioned to believe constitute literature. As products of Western culture, many of our students—and we ourselves—cannot avoid being implicated, but they/we can all learn to forever be(a)ware of "naming" others in terms of our culture-specific categories for the sake of convenience, for the sake of making the unfamiliar familiar. As Dorinne Kondo so eloquently puts it in our encounter with Japan: "Is it possible to avoid the otherness of exoticism and ineffable strangeness, on the one hand, and the cultural imperialism of appropriation—'They are just like us.' or 'What is so Japanese about that?'—on the other?" (1990, 304). It is a difficult task, but by coming to terms with this "dilemma of representation" of the Other, our students can become aware of the positions from which they read, they write, they speak, and only then will they come to terms with the extent to which the hegemonic order of our culture structures and regularizes their/our own stories—remaking personal, oppositional stories into universalized, acceptable narratives that maintain those in power at the expense of "others"/us. Only then can they/we break out a little and write.

Notes

1. *The Tale of Genji* has two translations: one by Edward Seidensticker (New York: Alfred A. Knopf, 1976) and a second by Arthur Waley. *Tale of Heike* also has two translations, but the one by Helen McCullough (Stanford: Stanford University Press, 1988) is the text normally used.

2. Because "genre" is loaded with Western connotations, I have opted to use "category" or "categories" for lack of a better term. I encounter similar problems with the names for genres ("poetry," "prose," "fiction"), but as I will argue later, at this historic moment I am forced to use them, for lack of better terms and for English-speaking audiences' lack of familiarity—tolerance—for non-English terms.

3. These categories and the others that I discuss in the paper seem to be operative during the Heian period, but the earliest records come from later periods. Konishi Jin'ichi argues that most of the titles of texts of the Heian period were not given by the author, for if the original manuscript bore a title, variants would not likely have arisen. He therefore contends that the variant titles "must therefore demonstrate how these texts were received by later audiences and transmitters." *A History of Japanese Literature: Volume Two: The Early Middle Ages,* trans. Aileen Gatten (Princeton, NJ: Princeton University Press, 1986), 252. Although there are problems with Konishi's conservative assessment of Japanese language and literature and there is much that I do not agree with, I feel that this is a fairly accurate assessment of the period to which most scholars would agree.

4. See Konishi, 256. Although as I mentioned above there are some problems with Konishi's assessments, his is one of the few comprehensive histories of classical Japanese literature in English. Earl Miner's *The Princeton Companion to Classical Japanese Literature* (Princeton, NJ: Princeton University Press, 1985) is useful but it is in the format of a handbook, so it provides short definitions and explanations but few extended, contextualized discussions.

5. Another category of prose known as *Setsuwa* (short tales) exists, but for our purposes it can be considered as collections of much shorter, short story–like versions of the nonfictional *mongatari* prose narratives, with several collections based on Buddhist stories from China and India.

6. A quote from the thirteenth-century *Mumyo Soshi (An Untitled Book),* cited in Konishi's history, 225.

7. Izumi Shikibu, *The Izumi Shikibu Diary: A Romance of the Heian Court,* trans. Edwin Cranston (Cambridge: Harvard University Press, 1969).

8. Edwin Seidensticker has translated *The Kagero Diary* as *The Gossamer Years: A Diary by a Noblewoman of Heian Japan* (Tokyo and Rutland, VT: Charles E. Tuttle Co., 1973).

9. The two translations of *The Tosa Diary* are Helen McCullough's *"Tosa Nikki: A Tosa Journal"* in *Kokin Wakashu: The First Imperial Anthology of Japanese Poetry with 'Tosa Nikki' and 'Shinsen Waka'* (Stanford: Stanford University Press. 1985), pp. 263–291, and Earl Miner's "The Tosa Diary" in *Japanese Poetic Diaries* (Berkeley: University of California Press, 1969), pp. 57–91.

10. Sei Shonagon, *The Pillow Book of Sei Shonagon,* 2 vols., trans. Iyan Morris (New York: Columbia UP, 1967).

11. *Tales of Yamato: A Tenth-Century Poem-Tale,* trans. Mildred Tahara (Honolulu: U of Hawaii, 1980).

12. Matsuo Basho, *The Narrow Road to the Deep North and Other Travel Sketches,* trans. Nobuyuki Yuasa (Harmondsworth, England: Penguin Books, 1966); Santo Kyoden, *Edo mumare uwaki no kabayaki,* in *Nihon koten bungaku zenshu,* vol. 46, eds. Hamada Giichiro et al. (Tokyo: Shogakukan, 1971), 136–56—no translation is available. Also Kawabata Yasunari, *Snow Country,* trans. Edward Seidensticker (New York: Alfred A. Knopf, 1956). The first two stories by Tsushima Yuko appear in *Shooting Gallery,* trans. Geraldine Harcourt (New York: Pantheon Books, 1988), 35–44, 91–106, while "The Shining Light" was translated as part of a senior thesis by Carey McIntosh, Pomona College, April 1992.

11

Resisting Consolation
Early American Women Poets and the Elegiac Tradition

Allison Giffen

Most of all, we will refuse to be or become composed or static
. . . we will keep composing, keep opening out to potential ways
of composing ourselves . . . Composing ourselves will call on us to
look closer . . . It will also call on us to "listen closer," to listen to
the voices of the other in each of us and in each other, to listen
closer to the rich and complex diversity our students and classrooms bring to us.

—Andrea Lunsford, "Composing
Ourselves: Politics, Commitment
and the Teaching of Writing"

It is not only in bacchic celebrations that a virtuous woman must
remain uncorrupted, but in sorrow too she must remember that ex-
cess is to be avoided and that transports of emotion require to be
controlled; it is not her love, as the many think that she must fight
against, but the incontinence of her soul.

—Plutarch, "Consolation to His Wife"

I.

On the occasion of the death of a beloved infant daughter, Plutarch writes
what scholars have viewed as a moving and deeply felt epistolary essay to
his wife. Yet Plutarch seems more interested in control than consolation, and
throughout the essay admonishes his wife to *compose* herself. Plutarch
explicitly genders the immoderate expression of grief, associating it with

115

physical promiscuity, an "incontinence of her soul" that is "no less shameful than unbridled voluptuousness." The expression of female grief, that "insatiable yearning for lamentation," like female sexuality, must be mastered, subdued, "bridled." As Plutarch's essay suggests, the expression of grief is especially charged for women, and as any cursory study of women's elegy reveals, grief offers women poets an especially volatile site for creativity. Significantly, women poets diverge most from normative models of consolatory and redemptive elegy by not composing themselves, that is, by resisting the kind of closure the genre typically demonstrates and holding on to their grief.

When writing about grief, American women poets compose themselves by not composing themselves. As my epigraph suggests, I am invoking Andrea Lunsford's opening address to the 1989 CCCC conference, and this allusion is more than a facile play on words. Lunsford suggests that the field of composition and rhetoric is, among other things, "dialogic, multi-voiced, heteroglossic" and as such we aim to open up the classroom into "a site for dialogues and polyphonic choruses." She points to the example of women writers who offer us new discourses by composing themselves, fashioning new narratives appropriate to their specific experience. Exploring a female elegiac tradition contributes to this "polyphonic chorus" by unveiling an alternative approach to the "normative" masculine model of the genre. This alternative approach is compelling both theoretically and practically, offering a more nuanced view of literary history as well as an enabling model for student writing, particularly for women and students of color whose experience is often marginalized in the classroom.

In order to delineate, or to use Lunsford's phrase, to compose a female elegiac tradition, we need to attend to the ways in which a Western literary tradition always privileges male subjectivity as normative. Failing to delineate the gendered contours of this tradition, we cannot frame female elegy as anything *but* divergent, aberrant, ultimately reactive. In one of the most cogent critical surveys of elegy, Peter Sacks relies on classical myths of male desire, both indirectly by relying on a Freudian framework, at the heart of which lies the Oedipal myth, and directly by exploring the paradigmatic roots of elegy in Ovid's parallel stories of Pan and Syrinx and Apollo and Daphne.[1] Sacks finds the genre to be teleological in nature, one that works toward some type of compensatory resolution. As such, he asserts that elegy performs what Freud terms the "work of mourning": "Each elegy is to be regarded, therefore, as a *work*, both in the commonly accepted meaning of a product and in the more dynamic sense of the working through of an impulse or experience" (1). Typically the elegy describes a trajectory from grief and despair to resigned acceptance, often through Christian redemption and resurrection. Milton's *Lycidas* offers perhaps the most celebrated example of this trajectory: by the poem's end the "uncouth swain" becomes reconciled to his loss by reconceiving Lycidas as the "day star" who has "sunk low, but mounted high." The bereaved has worked through his grief and is free to embark "To-morrow to fresh woods, and pastures new."

Sacks looks to the classical roots of elegy to exemplify the relationship of figuration and loss. In Ovid's parallel myths, a male lover pursues a female beloved who changes form—Syrinx becomes the reed and Daphne the laurel tree. The bereft lover then further alters this form, converting the lost beloved into a compensatory sign of poethood, the reed pipes and the laurel wreath. This compensatory sign is at a remove from the actual beloved and thus always inscribes the beloved as absent or lost. Taking his cue from Freud's "Mourning and Melancholia," Sacks identifies Pan and Apollo as "successful" because they have performed the "healthy work of mourning." They have withdrawn their affection from the lost object and have reattached it to a compensatory substitute (6). At stake here is a kind of psychic "survival" achieved by way of a mediating sign. As Freud suggests, grief must be overcome if we are not to regard it as pathological:

> ... although mourning involves grave departures from the normal attitude to life, it never occurs to us to regard it as a pathological condition and to refer it to medical treatment. We rely on its being overcome after a certain lapse of time, and we look upon any interference with it as useless or even harmful. (Freud 243–44)

For Sacks, elegy enacts that "lapse of time": poetic movement, in a sense, overcomes grief.

Freud's observation that "we look upon any interference with [mourning] as useless or even harmful" also suggests that mourning offers the bereaved an unusual kind of freedom. This almost parenthetical remark is highly suggestive for women poets. Since America's first poet, Anne Bradstreet, began writing, the expression of grief has been peculiarly enabling to American women poets. Writing poems about the loss of loved ones, particularly the loss of children, was a congenial enterprise for women because it supported cultural assumptions about woman's role as nurturer and mother. Moreover, audiences find Early American women acceptable as poets as long as they emphasize the importance of their domestic role. In "The Prologue" to Bradstreet's *The Tenth Muse*, rather than requesting the laurels of the (male) poet, Bradstreet claims the homely "Thyme or Parsley wreath," thereby cannily fusing the symbol of poetic achievement with an image of domesticity. In the prefatory material to *The Tenth Muse*, John Woodbridge's eulogistic opening essay suggests that Bradstreet's poetry will be accepted only if she is portrayed as an "honored" and "esteemed" woman. As a paragon of female virtue, she must necessarily subordinate her poetry to domestic duty, and at the conclusion of the essay, Woodbridge assures Bradstreet's audience that "these poems are the fruit but of some few houres, curtailed from her sleep and other refreshments." Bradstreet must appear before her audience as a wife and mother who writes poetry rather than as a poet who has children.

Grieving mothers were permitted, up to a point, an unusual degree of self-absorption. As Freud notes, the experience of loss and grief alienates the bereaved, whose attention is turned away from the community:

> Profound mourning, the reaction to the loss of someone who is loved, contains the same painful frame of mind [as melancholia], the same loss of interest in the outside world—in so far as it does not recall him—the same loss of capacity to adopt any new object of love (which would mean replacing him) and the same turning away from any activity that is not connected with thoughts of him. (244)

Though mourning contains a "painful state of mind," for the woman poet it offers a potentially enabling site for creative activity where she is relieved to some degree of the pressures of social and literary convention. In this marginalized site of grief, she is able to articulate desire for a lost love object and thus define herself as speaking subject. Consequently, to continue to grieve permits women to continue to write.

In the early nineteenth century, despite the fact that literally hundreds of women begin to publish poetry, or perhaps because of it, the need to foreground domestic duties to gain access to the literary world becomes, if anything, greater. As women begin to support themselves and their families through their writing, building careers distinct from domestic roles, the idea of a female poetic identity becomes increasingly bound to prevailing conceptions of femininity. The popular imagination canonizes the True Woman, "the angel of the house," celebrated for her piety, modesty, and submission, for whom domesticity becomes a religious calling. The notion of separate, gendered spheres extends to the literary realm and female poetry assumes the contours of a distinct genre. The poetess becomes a highly recognizable figure.

The elegiac voice emerges as one of the most distinctive features of the poetess, whose fascination with grief, death, and dying reflected a larger national preoccupation with death and its attendant rituals.[2] Characterized as saccharine, pious, and maudlin, the figure of the grieving poetess developed in the national consciousness into a caricature that has obscured a rich tradition of women's poetry.[3] The poetess has been largely scorned in the twentieth century; even great popularity in her own day did not ensure literary status, and in fact, she contributed to an emerging distinction between high and low art. The very qualities for which she was so highly praised also served to subordinate her to the male literati. In the figure of the nineteenth-century poetess, we find the expression of female grief codified, conventionalized, and ultimately trivialized.[4] Yet behind this monolith lies a dazzling variety of women poets who at once participate in and struggle with the construct. The work of reevaluating Early American women poets requires that we both understand how the construct of the poetess developed and explore the particularities of women poets' responses to loss within and against it.

The poems and letters of Ann Eliza Bleecker offer one of the most explicit examples of an Early American woman poet who resists removing herself from the site of grief. During the course of the American Revolution, Bleecker lost her beloved daughter Abella, and her poems dwell compulsively on this loss and her response to it. To give up Abella, to cease grieving, would mean to give up her poetry. Ultimately, in an almost metonymical relationship, Bleecker's poems come to stand in for Abella. But unlike Sacks's model of elegy in which the poem functions as a compensatory substitute for the lost beloved (as, for example, the laurel wreath comes to replace the lost Daphne), Bleecker's poetry seems to depend upon her continued attachment to Abella. Indeed Bleecker's poetry and her attachment to the lost Abella cohere in a dynamic relationship, animating each other. In the involvement that Bleecker displays in her grief, we can discern the ways that she is self-consciously fashioning a poetic identity for herself as bereft mother.[5] In "Lines Written in Retreat from Burgoyne," for example, in which Bleecker tells the story of Abella's death (as she does in a number of poems and letters), she typically struggles with the idea of inconsolable grief while simultaneously demonstrating it. In this poem the bereaved mother seeks ways to justify immoderate grief by rejecting Christian ideals of female submission and resignation and aligning herself with a passionate Christ who weeps over the (soon to be resurrected) figure of Lazarus. The poem concludes in a bold, almost self-righteous tone as the mother vows to grieve forever:

> Yes, tis my boast to harbor in my breast
> The sensibilities by God exprest;
> Nor shall the mollifying hand of time,
> Which wipes off common sorrows cancel mine.
> (ll. 60–63)

Bleecker's elegiac work resists resolution and represents an alternative to the linearity of conventional elegy. She expresses her response to loss from within a kinetic site of grief that offers her access to a poetic identity. Moreover, her resistance to closure calls into question the implications of the resolutions toward which elegy works. What does it mean for a woman poet to be restored to the world? While we must be careful not to diminish her grief as merely strategic, as a woman poet she finds the role of grieving mother in some ways empowering.

II.

In a study focusing primarily on twentieth-century American women poets, Celeste Schenk observes a similar tendency in women poets to hold on to their grief and resist consolation. Schenk offers a gendered conceptual model that stresses elegy as a genre of poetic identity: "The masculine elegy marks a rite of separation that culminates in ascension to stature; it rehearses an act of identity that depends upon rupture. Not so for women poets, who seem unwilling to render up their dead" (15). Schenk delineates her gendered approach in terms of rupture and continuity. Male poets distinguish themselves in elegy in the sense of both proving their poetic ability and setting themselves apart from their literary forebears. Tracing a pastoral elegiac tradition from Theocritus to Virgil to Milton, Schenk implicitly disparages male elegy, a "gesture of aspiring careerism," stressing its focus on "literary succession and poetic potency." While male elegists assume a poetic identity by working through their grief and "rendering up their dead," Schenk finds that women poets resist such violent impulses: "the female elegy is a poem of connectedness; women inheritors seem to achieve poetic identity in relation to ancestresses, in connection to the dead, whereas male initiates need to eliminate the competition to come into their own" (15).

Schenk's oppositional model risks essentializing female poetic expression. While women's elegies suggest an alternative dynamic at work, particularly in the ways they resist "rendering up their dead," to view this work as a poetry of continuity or connectedness is problematic.[6] If we focus our attention on the material lives of Early American women poets rather than on the notion of literary ancestresses, we find that rupture and conflict are at the heart of a female elegiac voice. Certainly Bleecker's willed resistance to consolation creates a profound sense of personal rupture for her within her community. As Bleecker's poems and letters so graphically illustrate, while she wishes to participate in a community of female friends, a community upon whose support she is especially dependent during times of crisis, her immoderate grief alienates her from her circle of women. Her letters reveal an artist consumed with melancholia, struggling for the communal engagement that correspondence yields, yet repeatedly compelled to silence: "The wilderness is within. I muse so long on the dead until I am unfit for the company of the living." Though posed as a complaint, this is also an assertion of self: she is the bereft poet, isolated, alienated, grieving. Indeed a number of her poems and letters take as their subject her anxiety about the tensions engendered by her extended grief. Bleecker finds herself torn between the desire for reintegration into the community and the desire to hold on to her alienating grief, and her elegiac work is powerful because she resists removing herself from this site of orchestrated conflict (Giffen, 224).

Though we can identify such "masculine" qualities as rupture and self-assertion in women's elegies, we should be careful not to dismiss Schenk's perceptive observations. Women poets' "musings" upon the dead *do* look different from those of men in part because the social and cultural conditions of women differ from those of men. Schenk implicitly relies on an Oedipal model against which she defines an alternative female elegiac tradition, but this model overdetermines, perhaps even distorts, the way that she conceives of a female elegiac tradition.

The implications for women poets of an Oedipal model that privileges male subjectivity becomes increasingly clear when we look to Peter Sacks's formulation of the genre. Working from a Lacanian perspective, Sacks finds compelling parallels between early elaborations of the Oedipal resolution (especially the mirror stage and the *fort da* episode) and the work of mourning as he interprets it through classical myth.

> Each procedure or resolution is essentially defensive, requiring a detachment of affection from a prior object followed by a reattachment of the affection elsewhere. At the core of each procedure is the renunciatory experience of loss and the acceptance, not just of a substitute, but of the very means and practice of substitution. In each case such an acceptance is the price of survival; and in each case a successful resolution is not merely deprivatory, but offers a form of compensatory reward. (8)

Sacks focuses on the castrative authority of the father, whose intervention causes the child to take his place in the symbolic order governed by that most powerful of signifiers, the phallus, thus preventing the child from remaining in a "regressive site of undifferentiated union" with the mother. The myths of Apollo and Pan rehearse this procedure, offering specifically male models of desire. In these stories the male lover loses his beloved through a paternal intervention that thwarts his erotic pursuit. The consoling sign (the laurel wreath and the pipes) comes to represent, then, not merely the lost beloved but thwarted sexual desire as well. Sacks suggests that this thwarting represents a castration:

> . . . since in each case it is in the father's territory that the pursuer is forced to check his desires and since Apollo's sign and Pan's new instrument are the pieces of their transformed loves and of their own transformed sexual powers, broken or cut, wreathed or sealed. Each is left grasping the sign of what he lacks, an elegiac token. . . . (7)

These tokens of castration and compensation parallel the child's submission to the law of the father, his entrance into what Lacan terms the symbolic order: "The elegist's reward, especially, resembles or augments that of the child—both often involve inherited legacies and consoling identifications with symbolic, even immortal, figures of power" (8).

Of course this model leads us to question how women might engage in these paternal inherited legacies or identify with these consoling figures of power (that all lead inevitably to the phallus). Sacks is aware of the difficulties that this model poses for understanding women's expressions of loss. In a brief digression he concedes that "[l]ongstanding sexual discrimination has impinged on women's experience of mortal loss; and the difficulty in identifying with predominantly male symbols of consolation greatly complicates the woman's work of mourning" (13). Sacks contributes to an accumulation of disparaging descriptions of female grief that begin as early as Plutarch, who decries the "insatiable yearning for lamentation" as "shameful." This assertion that women's work of mourning is "complicated" implicitly suggests that it is somehow less successful, potentially pathological, certainly not normative. Indeed, given this model, the work of mourning *is* profoundly "complicated" for women.[7] Whether implicitly or explicitly, both Celeste Schenk and Peter Sacks rely on an Oedipal model in their interpretation of elegy that serves to overdetermine the ways in which they conceive of a female elegiac poetry.

Clearly, relying on psychoanalytic theory poses a number of problems for the scholar seeking to explore a female elegiac tradition. Yet its language and interpretive processes are compelling for genre theory, particularly elegy with its concern with loss, desire, and poetic identity. Feminist revisions of this psychoanalytic approach permit us to reconceive mourning and poetic identity in ways more appropriate to women. Most notably, in *The Spectral Mother: Freud, Feminism and Psychoanalysis*, Madelon Sprengnether reconceptualizes ego formation, specifically Freud's notions of the pre-Oedipal and definitions of castration.[8] By looking at the particularities of Freud's cultural moment and exploring his relationship with his own mother, Sprengnether seeks to explore and redress the effacement of the mother as subject. In so doing, she directs our attention away from the Oedipal resolution, emphasizing instead the separation of mother and child. Though Sprengnether does not concern herself with issues of genre, her formulations offer a model in which female elegy, characterized by its persistent and unrelenting embrace of grief, appears neither shameful nor "complicated."

Like Sacks, Sprengnether finds parallels between the work of mourning and ego formation, but by looking to Freud's early work in which he explores castration as a separation between mother and child, she posits the body of the mother as the primary sign of loss rather than the phallus. Sprengnether uncovers the profound difficulties of viewing the mother as the site of ultimate plenitude, that is, the site of undifferentiated union, by realigning our perspective from that of the child to that of the mother, investing the mother with a previously unheard of subjectivity. Further, she suggests that ego formation is predicated on a loss that we can never resolve or truly understand. Comparing this notion of the lost mother to that of the uncanny, she explains this paradox:

> Because the existence of the ego is coincident with the awareness of loss, there is no time at which mother has not been other. As the carnal origin of every human subject, the body of the mother represents at once the dream of plenitude and the recognition of its impossibility. (230)

Sprengnether's model suggests a different way of telling the story. Rather than a linear configuration of male desire, pursuit, loss, and acceptance, perhaps unresolved grief is at the heart of ego formation, what Sprengnether refers to as "a condition of estrangement at the heart of being." This condition of estrangement or loss also lies at the heart of a large number of women's elegies. Rather than working through their grief, women poets work within it, treating it as a kinetic site of poetic production.

My discussion of female elegy is less a plea for inclusion into the literary canon than a renewed call to denaturalize our notions of literary traditions. Practically speaking, by telling more than one story we necessarily change the contours of the narrative: it becomes dialogue rather than monologue. The female elegiac tradition makes available more than one approach not only to literary history but to writing and teaching about writing as well. By opening the genre to multiple possibilities, we create a site for strengthening connections between scholars and teachers of literature, rhetoric, composition, and creative writing. We can readily see the implications in creative writing classes, where we ask students to articulate strong feeling within the prescribed boundaries of a given genre. Understanding the ways in which gender informs our notion of genre by looking to the ways men and women respond differently to loss, we expose the masculinist assumptions that underlie conventional definitions. Consequently, we can offer students more than one model to tell their story, enabling them to compose themselves in ways they find appropriate.

We need not confine this feminine model of grief as a kinetic site for creativity strictly to women and strictly to creative writing. It has practical application in a variety of classroom settings and its implications extend well beyond the walls of the academy. For example, first-year composition students are often called upon to write personal narratives, the purpose of which is to distill meaning from strong emotion, essentially to master and control in order to pass through these feelings. Required of this control is a degree of distancing from one's feelings. Perhaps this distancing, this mastery, is not the appropriate response for all students. Given that racism in America is a social and political reality, perhaps sustained anger is a productive response for African American students. In her collection *Sister Outsider*, Audre Lorde proclaims the creative force of anger, suggesting a response analogous to that of American women poets. In "The Uses of Anger" Lorde makes a compelling case for why she should not harness her anger and "compose" herself. Lorde looks to the constructive dimension of anger. Distinguishing it from hatred, she finds it to be the expression of a sustained and vital grieving for the racial and sexual inequities in American society: "Anger is a grief of distortions between peers, and its object is change" (129). The stakes for Lorde are high. Resisting consolation, and holding on to this "grief of distortions," one can transform emotion into an agent of social and political change.

Lorde tells us, "When we turn from anger we turn from insight" (131). From both a feminist psychoanalytic perspective that posits unresolved grief at the heart of ego formation, or from a sociopolitical perspective that recognizes racial injustice as a fact of life in America today, powerful emotion can be a rich source of creative energy. A female elegiac tradition offers both teachers and writers a model for this approach to writing: women and students of color can compose themselves by not composing themselves.

Notes

1. For work on elegy see for example G. W. Pigman's *Grief and English Renaissance Elegy* and Dennis Kay's *Melodious Tears: The English Funeral Elegy from Spenser to Milton.*

2. See Chapter Six, "The Domestication of Death," in Ann Douglas's *The Feminization of American Culture.*

3. A number of scholars have already begun the work of uncovering this tradition. See especially Cheryl Walker, Emily Stipes Watts, Alicia Ostriker, and Nina Byam.

4. For evidence of the way the poetess had become immediately recognizable to nineteenth-century audiences, see Twain's notoriously satiric portrait of the poetess in *The Adventures of Huckleberry Finn.*

5. For an extended discussion of the ways Bleecker resists consolation in her poems and letters, offering an alternative elegiac model, see my essay " 'Til Grief melodious grow': The Poems and Letters of Ann Eliza Bleecker."

6. In his study of the elegiac poems of Sylvia Plath, " 'Daddy I have had to kill you': Plath, Rage and the Modern Elegy," Jahan Ramazani similarly notes the ways in which Schenk's model admits to essentializing tendencies.

7. Sacks anticipates such objections by relying on Lacanian readings that stress the symbolic dimension of the phallus, then suggests, somewhat unconvincingly, that women may substitue within elegy alternative figures of power such as the fertility goddess. This gesture recalls Schenk's notion that women poets effect a form of continuity with *Ancestresses* when they resist consolation.

8. Juliana Schiesari offers another important contribution to this work in *The Gendering of Melancholia.* Schiesari reveals the ways in which Freud's essay "Mourning and Melancholia" is profoundly influenced by a Renaissance tradition of melancholia that devalues women's grief.

12

Genre as Relation
On Writing and Reading as Ethical Interaction

Gregory Clark

This exploration is prompted by my sense that, in the context of the academy at least, we practice and teach written genres in ways that are more or less ethically impoverished. I have learned to practice and to teach written genres in ways that render my identity and those of the people I read as ideas alone, ways that, consequently, prompt relationships of both autonomy and anonymity. My sense is that these are the major elements of the rationalist ethos that has credibility and authority in our academic and professional culture. I use the term *ethos* here as Nedra Reynolds discusses it, as a socially sanctioned "gathering place" for participation in a public discourse (333).

The culture of this ethos insists that to be credible people must locate themselves in a discourse place where they can interact independent of the attitudes and ends that follow from their disparate histories and experiences, a place where they can assert ideas in a form that appears free from the provisionality that follows personality. I have learned to write and read, and to teach writing and reading, from genres that enact this ethos, one that constitutes discursive relationships in which I both assert my own ideas and read those asserted by others in a way that denies their inherent contextuality in the particular life of a person.

This ethos and its genres came to dominate writing and reading instruction during the formative period of the modern academy in North America. In one history of writing in nineteenth-century colleges and universities, "Personal Writing Assignments," Robert Connors demonstrates that academic writing was defined throughout that period increasingly by a set of genres that bifurcated the identities of writer and reader alike into strictly separate realms of personal and impersonal. By the end of that century, personal writing in the academy had become essentially private writing, and credible public writing was identified as asserting ideas apparently apart from the interests of particular people. This development is a manifestation of the scientism that came to dominate the general public discourse of policy and polity in North America during that period, a discourse that itself asserted the credibility and authority of people who could present their assertions as those of objective and credentialed experts.

A century later, all but the most private genres of writing and reading within the academy as well as without still assert the authoritative autonomy and anonymity of the expert, and so prompt writer and reader to interact as decontextualized, rationalized identities. This remains, as historian Michael Warner puts it, our collective "condition of legitimation" (42). Inside the academy as well as outside, we learn to take seriously only assertions made from what he calls a "posture of negation" (48) that attributes to those who write and read a clear and common freedom from their disparate and particular circumstances, commitments, or purposes.

In our own historical work on rhetorical theory and practice in the United States during the nineteenth century, Michael Halloran and I have described the predominance of this ethos in terms of an identity of the professional. In a rhetorical community where public identity is defined in terms of professional knowledge and affiliation, the most credible and authoritative voice is that of the specialized and credentialed expert whose discourse is located in the apparently impersonal context of a career. And, as Bruce A. Kimball argues, the values that came to dominate public discourse in the United States during the last half of the nineteenth century were those professed by career practitioners of the scientific disciplines that came to be housed in universities. These values, with minor adaptations, persist as authoritative a century later in the academic venues of public discourse that still require the apparent absence of what Connors calls the personal, for we have learned and learned to teach that authority in a text is characterized by the apparent autonomy and anonymity that follow.

Rhetorically and, thus, relationally, texts that enact these values present themselves, using Susan Miller's rendering of this opposition, not as an act of one person intending to persuade another, but, rather, as the presence of an autonomous commodity we call information (1989, 25). In doing so, they misrepresent both people who write them and those who read them by denying the personal relationship that is enacted in the acts of writing and reading a text as they deny the separate and shared relational contexts in which the people who write and read are embedded. This undermines the fundamental purpose of a rhetorical exchange—to enable people to discuss and decide together issues and questions of common concern. An ethical problem emerges when texts prompt writers and readers to interact as decontextualized and thus truncated identities. Genres always prompt some sort of relationship between writer and reader, and that relationship is ethically impoverished when people present themselves to each other as rational identities unconstrained by personal particularity. That is precisely what the act of interaction ensures they are not.

In Context

I was thinking this through the day I learned that Kenneth Burke had died. I had planned to use that day to start an essay for this collection on genre—a theoretical essay that would extend the kind of discussion I began above— but I changed that plan so I could respond to a request on the computer discussion list H-Rhetor for stories of personal encounters with Burke. I wrote about my visit to his home one Saturday in July 1989. After using his major books in my classes for a couple of years, and reading through them systematically for a couple of months, I sat with my friend in Burke's cluttered kitchen late that morning to talk to him about his work. We took turns asking him theoretical questions that he answered roundabout in persistently untheoretical ways. More often than not, he'd respond to a question by reaching for his poetry or his fiction, opening the book to this story or that poem, and then pushing it across the table to us with the question, "You've read this?" He was usually disappointed in our answers. After a series of these exchanges he pushed across a letter he'd just received from Denis Donoghue thanking him for *Towards a Better Life*, and reminding Burke that Donoghue reads Burke's only novel once a year therapeutically to keep himself on course. Neither of us had read it. This was the way Burke wanted to talk with us about his work—as rendered in the narrative contexts of his poetry and fiction. Failing that, he then began to locate our questions in anecdotes about his life and the people who had shared this small farm so far out from Manhattan that had been so long his home. He told us about his grandson, the storytelling singer Harry Chapin—about how Chapin recorded one of Burke's poems as a song on an album, and how Burke's share of the royalties allowed him finally to heat his house, buying him his first winter without chopping wood. He told us about his oldest daughter—he called her Happy, an anthropologist whose summer house was across Amity Road from his, about how he had crossed that road once or twice a week to eat dinner with her, visits he remembered using to complain to and criticize the daughter he would long outlive.

After two hours of storytelling he became distracted, remembered that he had not yet eaten breakfast, and directed me to a bottle of apple juice— his favorite local blend—in the old refrigerator, and to some glasses. He got himself a bowl of Shredded Wheat, advising us as he did that an aging body becomes an ever more demanding landlord. Then, having eaten, Burke, restored, suggested a walking tour of the place. Bent low, he walked with more ease and speed than I had expected, and seemed to speak more clearly while out on the path than he had at the table. The walk was a running narrative of his home. He showed us the old well, the place where the outhouse had been, the place where he had chopped wood every morning—all those places in use not so long ago. Then he led us out along a path skirting the woods that paralleled the road. We walked as far as a place where, to his frustration, someone had made an access road in a right-of-way through his property to cut timber; we crossed the road there to begin a loop back. He showed us the clay tennis court he had built with the help of family and friends, and the dam he'd had built across the creek with money from his *Dial* award, he said, to make a swimming pool for their summers. When we entered a compound of small houses that were across the road and down a hill from his—the summer cottages of his family—children, grandchildren, and great-grandchildren were there, greeting him as "Kenneth!" A little girl's birthday party was about to start, and he was guest of honor. Burke introduced us around, we chatted for a bit and then tried to say good-bye. But he insisted on walking with us back up the path to the road and our car. He invited us to write, warned us that he was slow to respond but that eventually he would, directed us to drive a bit farther down the road before leaving the farm to see where he had lived when he first started writing, and he thanked us for coming. When we drove back past his house he was still waiting there by the side of the road to wave us good-bye.

What I learned that day is that there is more to Burke than the work I had studied and taught, that for him his work was now fully entangled with the experiences of his life. And as he described it to us at ninety-one, that life was constituted not so much of his ideas as of his relationships. His ideas seemed to have been born of those relationships: their joys, their pain, and their confusion. It was what he had learned in relationships, rather than what he had written as theory, that Burke chose to share with us in Andover that day. Indeed, the clearest statement he made to us about his theoretical books was that he had written them only because people—we were not the first— would not read his ideas contextualized in the autobiographical narratives of his poetry and fiction. I learned that day that I needed to read Burke's work in the relational context of his life. What I read in that life as he presented it to us is a refusal to separate relationship and work, personal and impersonal, a refusal to distinguish from private identity. Indeed, more than a decade after his wife's death he wrote to his lifelong friend Malcolm Cowley that he thought he had done all of his work just to please and impress her (Jay, 396). Perhaps this insistence on locating that work in the context of his relational life is why Burke never sought the academic credentials that would make him a marketable expert by institutionalizing his work in a university career, and perhaps that is why his work so persistently resists location in a discipline. The closest he ever came to an academic job was a decade or so of half-year appointments at Bennington, where he was not held accountable to disciplinary definitions.

I left that day with the impression that he had worked to not separate his writing from his wood-chopping, to not isolate his ideas about human relations from his identity as one who enacts them. When he talked ideas that day, he allowed them to surface only briefly from the currents of his personal history on Amity Road. In terms of genre, he turned our talk about theory to fiction and poetry and autobiography. He was clearly disappointed that we knew his ideas only in theory. In this we were like Crassus's interlocutors in Cicero's *De Oratore*, who simply could not understand his insistence that his ideas of good public discourse must be contextualized deeply with the relational life of the community. Clearly, we were not the first to disappoint him. Many people know his ideas in theory, but few know them in the context of his narratives, the writing he told us he valued more, and of his relational life, which he valued most. Narrative, for Burke, is not story so much as it is contextuality. Contextuality embeds ideas and identity alike in the particular and dynamic complexities that develop in relational life, and it denies any possibility of their anonymity or autonomy. Perhaps that is why, as much as he had tried to push the limits of theory, he seemed neither gratified nor comforted by our mastery of his theoretical work. He seemed to think that if we encountered his ideas about the primacy of human relation outside the personal relational contexts in which they had developed, we could not but miss their point.

I had Burke's *The Rhetoric of Religion* (1961) with me that day. I had just finished its epilogue, "Prologue in Heaven," in the motel the night before. This epilogue is the place in his theoretical writing where the necessity of contextuality is suggested most strongly; indeed, it is a place in that writing where he shifts to a contextualizing genre. I read Burke's work as retrospectively summarized there—as Burke did, at least in the early 1970s when he wrote to Malcolm Cowley that "no one is competent to write on boikwoiks in general" who has not read the "Prologue in Heaven," because it embeds Burke's "basic" insights in the necessity that people relate to each other through language in the context of human relation (Jay, 384). Together these insights suggest that it is the inherent ambiguity of language, for better or for worse, that enables human choices, choices for which people are together accountable. And it is accountable choice that is, for Burke, what distinguishes action from motion and, thus, what is human from what is not.

Burke's "Prologue" can read as a version of Plato's *Phaedrus*, or of Cicero's *De Oratore*—a dramatized conversation between a humane master and a self-absorbed novice in which rhetoric is explored as the enactment of human relation. Burke's conversation, however, is before time, and its interlocutors are cast large as "The Lord" and "Satan." In Burke's terms, people are driven beyond their separate "*sheer* bodily purpose" by a desire to establish shared identities that can only be symbolic (274). This is their purpose in language. The paradox in all this, and the source of much pain, is that most of their efforts to use language to do that will force them apart. That is because human idea and identity, interdependent and contextual as they are, are decontextualized by language: they are thus persistently misstated and misread. The problem, then, is that while life in language immerses people in relationships with others, enabling them to influence and be influenced toward the end of communion, language itself leads people to enact that preoccupation—unless they are uncommonly careful—as a struggle for dominance.

Unlike the *Phaedrus*, Burke's dialogue offers no rhetorical ideal method for solving this problem; unlike *De Oratore*, it does not end with a master resigned to provide only the technical lessons in opportunistic living that the novices came for. Rather, "Prologue in Heaven" stops with this complicating contextualization of the problem and leaves its solution to the particular rhetorical occasions encountered by Burke's readers. For him, the problem with language is at the same time the ethical problem with many if not most human relationships: it is that language works to reduce, limit, and contain ideas. It does that, essentially, by decontextualizing ideas, making them discursively manageable because they are conceptually truncated. The difference between "The Lord" and "Satan," as Burke presents them, is that Satan perpetually decontextualizes, making truths into terms that solve problems and resolve contradictions but do so by limiting choices and the responsibilities of those who use those terms for an occasion to relate. Each time Satan does that, The Lord reminds him that "its more complicated than that," and restates the problem in its full relational context. Statements that render ideas and identities accessible by asserting implicitly their autonomy and their anonymity—their decontextuality—function as attempts to limit and control the people who must use them as occasions for their relation. In that sense, they function as prompts to motion rather than action. And *human* relations, by definition, must be characterized by actions whose purpose is to prompt and engage coequal actions-in-response. Such relationships, it seems to me, are not possible without the acknowledgment of each actor that the identities of all reach beyond the extent of their terms.

In Relation

I've written about rhetorical theory for a decade now in a way that is, given what I've described above, decontextualized. The problem is, I don't really know how not to. As a result, I consider what I've written to be ethically impoverished in the sense that it presents my ideas outside the relationally entangled identity within which they developed. For lack of a better method to compensate for that, I want to write here something about that identity.

A few years ago, I was completing my first book, working on a theory of rhetorical ethics that would explain how differences and conflict might be accommodated constructively by people within a rhetorical community. During that time my father was dying. He was dying slowly of successive strokes that gradually disabled him physically and mentally, making him increasingly more dependent upon my mother and—because I was the one of their children in closest proximity to them—upon me. I grew up with my father in a religious tradition that made demands upon me that I had found difficult to accept. Our relationship over the years had been inflected by the tension between my difficulty with these demands and his desire that I accept them. He seemed to me never to have had difficulty accepting them himself, and to have never understood my difficulty. Now he was dying and I was writing about how differences can be addressed constructively—how rhetoric can help people maintain their relationships through their conflicts, a writing process interrupted regularly by his need for my help with his care. Here is some of what I was writing:

> Every rhetorical statement we make necessarily applies the private social ideal that not only defines our own values but also determines our own perception of reality itself to the particular social circumstances we address. That is why rhetoric must present preferences as if they were consensual: from the perspective of the people who make them, these statements state the truth and truth compels the consent of reasonable people. It is in this claim to truth that ideologies demand complete agreement. And it is this demand for ideological consensus that defines for every rhetorical statement its practical purpose: to eliminate among those it addresses the possibility of conflict. That is why ideology is at the root of the ethical problems that rhetoric presents. (1990, 53–54)

Certainly the issues I was addressing here are pertinent and potentially helpful to people whose work involves the teaching of rhetoric and writing. These are the people I was writing to and this the work I was trying to inform. But that is not really why I was addressing these issues. I had chosen these issues to address in an attempt to come to understand my relationship with my religious community and ultimately, though I was unconscious of it at the time, to find a way to *heal* my relationship with the person who represented it most immediately to me. My work on the book was progressively complicated by the concurrent decline of my father—by his increasing dependence upon me that coincided with his increasing inability to listen and speak with me. This is not at all apparent in what I wrote. Indeed, as I remember myself in the act of writing it, this was not on my mind. Writing, I was working to isolate my ideas from my identity, to present myself to my readers as a theorist alone, not as a theorist who is also a son. I wrote on as his ability to relate declined:

> It is the public function of rhetoric to propel that process of transformation within a community of people who consent to the collaborative confrontation and exploration of conflict. Such a consensus must itself be understood as a process, one that requires that writers and readers continually redefine together the changing common ground upon which they can continue to converse. This is the kind of consensus that actually binds us together in communities and defines our social knowledge: our common consent to continue a particular conversation. (58–59)

I remember writing this. I remember identity invading idea as I did so. I remember feeling distracted from my work as I revisited the painful perception that my religious community could not tolerate much conflict, and that my father, whose great hope had always been that I would find myself at peace in that community, could no longer converse.

When I read these passages now they seem hollow. In these passages I presented my readers with theory, I presented myself embodied in idea alone, and in doing so I addressed them as similarly embodied. They prompt a relationship of anonymous, autonomous theorists. They do that because that is the kind of relationship the genre of scholarly monograph enacts. Such relationships are not inherently unethical, but they are, I am suggesting, ethically impoverished and unnecessarily so. Ethics in rhetoric has as much to do with the identities that people assert and impute to each other as it does with the agreed-upon principles they use to guide their interaction. I wonder now what truths are missing from my ideas about ethics in rhetoric that I asserted as decontextualized concerns of a theorist at a time when I was experiencing these concerns as a personal crisis. I wonder now if my abstraction of this experience into theory leaves out something important, or if my insistence upon an ethos of authoritative anonymity and autonomy made it difficult or impossible for some readers who might have found help here to relate to me. I wonder how I might have asserted what I was coming to believe in ways that might have been more accountable to the complications of human relationship than what I wrote is—and still have written a scholarly monograph on the teaching of writing. I wonder what is gained by separating professional ideas from personal identity, and what is lost.

I don't think we need new genres. We do need, however, to consider the value of pushing through the boundaries of the identity that any genre imposes upon both writers and readers. If, as Burke argued in *Counter-Statement*, even form is a matter of human relationships—a matter of connecting a writer and a reader through expectations that are prompted, anticipated, and fulfilled—then almost any genre might be recontextualized by writers and readers who find within them ways to acknowledge the contextuality of their ideas in their identities—in doing so, they might invite readers to relate to them in idea and identity alike. While I have no method in mind for doing this, I can offer an analogue.

A friend I have known since childhood is a sculptor who has carved and displayed his own coffin. He is forty and healthy, and does not expect to die soon, yet he made that coffin and put it at the center of his recent show.[1] I read it there as a text that contextualized his ideas about art and life in an identity that is intricately constituted in relationships. And as a reader I found that the relationship with him that this text enabled made both his ideas and his identity, as well as forgotten aspects of my own, immediately accessible to me. The coffin complicated his aesthetic and philosophical commitments by embedding them in his personal history of relationships, which rendered them as his version of an experience others may share.

Coffins are conventional forms, but he carved into the conventionally blank sides and the lid of his coffin a network of words and images and objects that entangle the identity of the person it will contain with those many others it will not. In doing that, the coffin presents his ideas and his identity as inherently interdependent, an assertion that invites those who see it to establish a relationship with his contextualized identity, and to see their own identity similarly. On the sides he carved names, dates, and places for progenitors three generations before his parents; for his parents and siblings; for the house where he was born and where he now lives; for his birth and baptism. He carved phrases, images, and artifacts that chronicle his life with the woman he loves, and the birth and life of each of their children. And there is blank space yet on the sides, for my friend is still alive. On the lid he carved statements of his guiding ideas, ideas that, because of the way the reader's eye reads the coffin, are read in the context of the relational history from which they came.

He pressed the boundaries of convention not by changing the coffin form but by writing on it where conventionally nothing is written. When he is dead, it will present him to those who survive as neither anonymous nor autonomous, but as a life into which a place for them is written. A coffin is a genre, and my friend used it but pushed through its boundaries a bit by writing a context over its decontextualizing form. Coffins come made of blank hardwood, steel, and brass, with heavy latches and seals that assert to the living the profound separation of the dead. But my friend wrote over that text in a way that would assert that the one who died has lived, entangled with others. Perhaps we can learn to write over written genres in ways that similarly embed ideas in identities that acknowledge and even invite the complicating clutter of living relationships. Perhaps what I did when I wrote a scholarly monograph about rhetorical ethics is something like what we do when we are put into conventional coffins that, closed and sealed, assert both anonymity and autonomy. My friend has told me that he now has requests from other people for coffins that will present them in death in the context of their relational lives. They make those requests, he thinks, from a new awareness of their own contextuality in relationships.

I am writing this essay to suggest that we understand written genres as forms that direct people in conventional acts of relation, and that we look for ways to use them to do the rhetorical work of the academy in ways that enable people to acknowledge more fully not only their own contextuality in relationships, but also the opportunity that the rhetorical relationships of writing and reading afford for transforming both idea and identity, however impersonal the occasion. Such acknowledgment, it seems to me, is ethical because it renders people accountable in their rhetorical interaction, whatever its form or its content, to rhetoric's primary function as a means to the end of bringing people together.

Notes

1. Kurt Knudsen, "Funerary Objects of a Believer," 1994. Brigham Young University, Provo, Utah.

13

Narratives of the Novice
Genres of Naturalistic Research as "Storied Inquiry"

Jane Detweiler

Naturalistic researchers, who have long had to think of their work as a mat-ter of translating narratives into descriptions, have recently begun to describe their work as the making of narratives. That is, writing researchers working in the naturalistic genres are turning their interpretive skills to the study of how our research and textual practices are, like the informant storytelling described with them, ways of "narrating" experience that are culturally situ-ated and inherently rhetorical (Brodkey, "Writing Ethnographic"). With their "storied inquiries," these writers engage narrative discourse in research as a way to blend the "power of self-reflexivity . . . [with] an ethic of care" (Cin-tron, 404).[1]

Storied inquiries address what Clifford Geertz calls the "narratological issue"—how best to get "an honest story honestly told"—from a rhetorical-epistemic perspective (1988, 9). To address the narratological issue, natural-istic inquirers have begun to contend critically with generic considerations similar to those tackled by writers and critics of other serious (if "literary") narratives. However, our commitment to making "honest stories" about lived experience necessarily involves us in complexly interrelated epistemic and ethical considerations: in our research, we attempt to be accountable to our own community and to those whose stories we claim to tell. Naturalistic researchers have thus engaged some of the conventional writerly tactics of narrative representation (e.g. self-representation, characterization, narrative point of view) to invent generic textual "accountabilities" (Bazerman 1988, 60–62) to the intersubjective realities we study and re-create in our case studies and ethnographies.

In our ongoing discussions of naturalistic research genres, we have ex-amined how we populate research stories with self- and other-representations, with an eye for how we might tell about ourselves and others more responsibly. Wendy Bishop and Linda Brodkey, for instance, have taken up the implications of textual self-representation strategies in ethnographies (e.g. authorial voice, stance, tone), pointing out that research writers must consider whether to construct knowledge that hides its connections to them as persons and to our disciplinary motivations.[2] Other scholars and researchers have addressed what might be called tactics of "characterization"; these writers engage critically how participants are represented in naturalistic interpretations.[3] Such discussions have led some researchers to revise current notions of collaborative research by including participants as coresearchers; these naturalistic writers have also experimented with multiple narrative points of view in their reports, arguing that shared narrations or multivocal texts might be used to construct accounts that evoke the relationships upon which research depends, and the messiness of the research process itself. A number of the variously voiced, often conflicted texts that result have been published recently, suggesting the innovations now possible in disciplinary fora (e.g. Anderson et al., Clark and Wiedenhaupt, Kirsch, McCarthy and Fishman). David Bleich and Susan Miller[4] suggest further sharing of authority in research projects: compositionists might encourage those who have been considered "participants" to conduct politically inflected inquiries and construct research stories of their own. In addressing each of these narrative possibilities, researchers have emphasized the *ethical* dimensions of our textual representation, and the need to tell new stories that are more inclusive, and perhaps more tentative.[5]

Only recently, however, has our discussion turned to another central matter of narrative representation: emplotment. While there has been some passing mention of the narrative structure embedded in human-science research report forms, and some more focused examinations of story commonplaces, such as the "arrival stories" that "author-ize" ethnographic accounts (Herndl, 324), the fact that naturalistic research accounts tend to have familiar narrative patterns has gone largely unremarked.

In one notable exception to this relative silence, Thomas Newkirk identifies some common narrative structures used by writers of case studies: what he calls "cultural myths" (136). Where quantitative researchers use statistical analyses to generalize the findings of their studies, Newkirk suggests that naturalistic researchers impose familiar plots on observed details to lend them a broader significance. That is, to make naturalistic accounts that "move beyond the particular and idiographic," a writer frames the details of unique instances with gratifying, familiar narrative structures borrowed from the (Western) culture at large (e.g. "the tragedy of kingship" 136). Accounts that reiterate these seductive story lines appeal to their disciplinary audience by putting us into familiar "moral positions" (149). Since case studies draw upon cultural myths in this way, merely reiterating old plots in new circumstances, Newkirk suggests that such familiarly patterned accounts are "profoundly conservative," and that they subvert the "radically transformative" epistemic potential of the naturalistic genres (136). This rather pessimistic conclusion, it seems to me, follows from the way Newkirk characterizes the narrative structures and research writers' use of them: the "mythic" narrative patterns he describes seem to be relatively stable *types*, forms for the arrangement of data into suitable rhetorical appeals for particular research audiences. Considering our work as "storied inquiry" offers another reading, one that focuses on the ways that generic story lines in naturalistic accounts are intricately and dynamically tied to our current purposes as a group of serious—and disciplined —storytellers.

Like hallway teacher-anecdotes and family kitchen-table tales, "high academic" research plots are at once forms for arrangement and ways of knowing. With plots, as Louis Mink suggests, we "grasp together" meaningful series and wholes out of disparate, temporally separate experiences (547). It is our "sense of an ending" (Kermode), our intentions as tellers and readers of stories that organizes the dynamic unfolding of plots. And, as rhetor-storytellers, we take up and continually refigure characteristic plights to persuade others to share our sense of a desired ending (Bruner 1986, Ricoeur). For academic researchers, this is a political activity, since shared narrative tropes in turn prefigure *what* might be known by framing *how* it might be known—and by *whom*. Conventional stories, research allegories, theoretical metanarratives: these plot out intellectual territory (White).[6]

True, our discipline's narrative genres cannot but resonate with the Western "cultural narratives" in which our academic communities and our work is situated (Journet 1991); true, there are characteristic, conventional story lines that (re)appear to persuade us as academic audiences. But rather than being merely "myths" borrowed from culture and imposed on data, familiar research plots are products of *local* disciplinary rhetorical-epistemic practices, and as such are always under revision by writers. By reflecting on our narrative assumptions and practices, we might change the ways we plot our research accounts. Some research narrators have, in fact, done so. In what follows, I attempt to account for a prevalent thematic pattern—the trope of *affiliation*— that structures some conventional naturalistic research narratives. Although this trope figures in many stories, I have chosen to focus on some narratives of the novice writer, for in them the thematic is prominent. This choice also allows me to show how one research writer inquired into her own storytelling, and how her storied inquiry refigured one of our field's generic plots.

(Let me tell you the story).

The field of Rhetoric and Composition, in its continuing efforts to "emerge" as an academic discipline, has continued to retheorize composing— and to create new narrative premises. Most recently, the community has generated "social-epistemic" (Berlin 1988) theories to construct writers and writing processes. The new theoretical "stories" of writing-to-belong offered some epistemic gains: ways to understand writers in various contexts, and warrants for textualizing our stories in the naturalistic "narrative" genres of case study and ethnography.

In this new narrative space, however, "writing" often became a figure for professionalization, for connection to an academic field. What I call the affiliative trope[7] metonymically inscribes our field's disciplinary commitments onto the academic contexts we study, as we focus our attention on the processes of inscription that take place in those contexts. With its rhetorical gesture, researchers identify the activity of learning to write with that of becoming professional, broadly construed. This gesture is a necessary one, for scholars and researchers must somehow select topics, details, instances that are of interest; our field chooses to examine writing practices. Problems arise, however, when the reduction no longer announces itself as being rhetorical, when the conventional narrative patterns governed by this trope become familiar, their rhetoric invisible, their trajectory seemingly inevitable.

In what I call our conventional "narratives of the novice," the affiliative trope provides both the scene and the impetus for the action. Using this trope, researchers plot out a metaphoric distance between the novice writer and an academic discipline. In this landscape of literate belonging, the novice writer is characterized as moving ever toward a desired "ending": professional affiliation with a chosen discipline. To do so, he or she must be initiated, mentored in the ways of writing appropriate to that disciplinary community. As with any story, this one offers a necessarily partial, conventionalized view of "the study context," foregrounding details that are of interest to an audience in Rhetoric and Composition. As I will suggest in my reading of Lucille McCarthy's "Stranger in Strange Lands," our stories often plot our *discipline's* ongoing affiliation, rather than that of the novice writer. That is, the "ending" that significantly impels many affiliation stories is the novice's acquisition of particular literate practices which the narrator endorses—and which frame a function for our field's future teaching and research. A researcher might, however, acknowledge the partiality of this "ending," and plot more generously the tropic terrain of affiliation by engaging the narrative possibilities of the naturalistic genres. She might, as does McCarthy in her "Boundary Conversations" with Stephen Fishman, conduct a storied inquiry that makes telling changes in the story, opening a new generic narrative space for multiple tales, tellers, and audiences.

In "Stranger," McCarthy constructs a compelling account of one novice writer's struggles to understand the writing folkways of "one strange land after another": the various contexts for writing in an undergraduate program of studies (234). The account details McCarthy's long-term naturalistic study of "writing that was actually being assigned in . . . classrooms . . . how it functioned in each classroom, and what it meant to the people there" (236). For the study, she observed a composition course taught by a colleague, selected three student participants, and followed them to other courses over subsequent semesters. Her intent was to "observe what these students were learning" as they wrote across the curriculum (237). One of these participants, Dave, became the focus of a contextualized case study, presumably because he had a "sensitivity to school writing as a social affair" (233), but also, I think, because he was as patient in trying to provide information as McCarthy was in trying to understand him and portray his experience accurately (the two of them traveled together through numerous, intensive data collections).

Threaded through the conventional research report format is an initiation narrative, wherein McCarthy extensively describes Dave's efforts to learn "new conventions of interpretation and language use" (246) in three academic communities: the composition course, a poetry survey, and finally a biology course. McCarthy offers sketches of Dave's teachers, examining carefully their pedagogical approaches, focusing intently on how each conceives of writing as a professional practice, and on whether these stated goals are expressed in the course contexts. She then relates these features of the course contexts to Dave's experience of relative difficulty or ease, and his level of engagement with writing tasks (e.g. what constituted Gricean "cooperation," what "functions" writing served for Dave, what "roles" he, his teachers, and his texts each played in a course context).

As a researcher, McCarthy uses these intricate comparisons to demonstrate her methodological accountability to her disciplinary audience and to the people she studied in context. As a narrator, she juxtaposes the three scenes of initiation to craft a success story. Using the affiliative trope, McCarthy accounts for Dave's experiences in a narrative that not only foregrounds and tacitly approves his professional aspirations, but also validates a conception of writing to which she herself is professionally committed. Consider, for instance, that Dave feels most motivated as a writer in the composition and biology courses, where the activity of writing served meaningful personal and social functions for him (253–54); these, it turns out, are related to academic belonging, the "ending" of a conventional affiliative narrative. As a premed major, Dave values writing tasks that seem to him connected with his intended "scientific" profession, engaging readily and retaining the rhetorical strategies required for success in his cell biology course (254). Dr. Kelly[8], Dave's mentor at this scene of initiation, promotes such enthusiasm by encouraging the novice to understand writing as integral to his future professional practice (244, 257).

But the real success story appears to "end" in Dave's composition course, from whence he began his journey across the disciplines. At the close of her case study, McCarthy concludes that compositionists might be able to teach transferable methods of rhetorical analysis, or "assessment" of various writing tasks (262–63). This suggestion seems to be based on Dave's continued use of "language," the "process terms" that he learned in his composition course, to describe other writing tasks (255). Since Dave is apparently unconscious that he uses this language—or the strategies of rhetorical analysis it implies—in other contexts, McCarthy is able to frame a narrative that centralizes a role our discipline might play across contexts that appear to be unique in their writing demands. Throughout the report, she draws attention to Dave's failure to note commonalities among writing tasks and to recognize that he is transferring writing approaches[9] that he learned in his composition course to later writing situations (234, 243, 245, 248, 249, 261). In one prominent instance, she uses a table to underscore how likely it is that Dave has drawn from prior experience to assess writing tasks:

> The extent to which Dave drew upon prior experience is difficult to say. In each class he believed he had no prior experience to draw from. However we know he had had related prior experience. (259)

McCarthy continues to assert, over Dave's denials, that he has transferred some writing strategies; she even stages an interview "scene" in which Dave grudgingly admits, after some prodding, that a current task is similar to ones he had done in other contexts (249).

The preoccupation at the center of the narrative is, after all, McCarthy's own affiliative project: she writes this account for an audience of scholars and researchers who share her interest in writing, and in continuing the story of their discipline's "emergence."[10] Thus, Dave's arrival in a disciplinary community is not the ending that impels *this* writing story, although it might have been were he telling the tale. McCarthy's narrative winds up (with) our field's efforts to centralize our research and teaching practices[11] amidst contexts where—as our own theoretical stories suggest—writing practices are unique, situated, best taught by "native-speakers" (241, 262).

McCarthy returns to and revises the scene of (her) academic affiliation in the text she coauthors with Stephen Fishman, a "native-speaker" in a philosophy department. In "Boundary Conversations," the two researchers represent their long-term naturalistic study in a "heteroglossic" or "polyphonic" (Clifford) text that preserves their differences as researchers and empowers them equally as knowers (424). More important for the present study, the researchers' "boundary rhetoric" (Journet 1993) reflects upon—and repositions—our field's affiliative thematic.

The "conversation" mentioned in their title draws attention to the ways that the researchers handle some difficulties that arise from their conflicting conceptions of student initiation, views of authority over the project, and understandings of methodology (459). McCarthy and Fishman offer a reflective, dialogic narrative that recounts their negotiation of such conflicts, to which each researcher contributes a sort of metacomment on the research process, with her or his critical version of significant events and attitudes that led to difficulties.

According to this collaborative account, many of the interpersonal and interdisciplinary conflicts arose because McCarthy entered into the collaborative project with narrative assumptions that Fishman eventually resisted: he felt that her "story" of academic writing inaccurately characterized him as a teacher. True to the theoretical stance that informed her "Stranger" narrative, McCarthy had anticipated finding a scene of disciplinary enculturation, wherein a teacher-mentor trains apprentices in appropriate ways of writing (459). Fishman objects, however, to the "mentor" role that McCarthy's proposed affiliative narrative offers, arguing that her assumptions simultaneously miscast his pedagogy and reductively treat philosophical discourse as one set of writing practices. Rather than teaching students to assimilate themselves into disciplinary ways of knowing, Fishman asserts that he attempts to help them "find themselves and their own voices" (459).

To respond to this fundamental conflict, and to establish a more equitable research relationship, McCarthy places herself, so to speak, within the narrative frame. She acknowledges the disciplinary partiality of her "initiation" account, and with Fishman redefines their respective research responsibilities. The two researchers then negotiate some epistemic points of contact, constructing a multilayered, mutually agreed theoretical frame that they use to understand events in the context. The collaborative narrative reflects (on) this negotiation as a learning process, linking it to the learning experiences of the two student-participants, Ginny and David. Just as the "novice writers" engaged new topics, other points of view, and their personal experiences in a classroom situation that offered them stances of authority, so also did the researchers collaboratively "narrate" new positions: they exchanged views, shared texts that articulated their respective disciplinary and pedagogical commitments, and, finally, connected some of those commitments to their personal educational experiences (458, 461–62).

The narrative turns in interesting ways upon the researchers' personal "narratives of the novice." With a small autobiographical reflection, each writer enlightens the disciplinary initiation narrative that in profound ways underpins his or her pedagogical assumptions. Fishman, ever the "outsider," felt that he had been silenced as a student; he describes his initiation as a difficult process of moving from role to role, of "struggles in the classroom to reach the melody line of the instructor" (461). In contrast, McCarthy moved smoothly into her disciplinary community, "easily understanding her professors' methods and languages and making these her own" (462).

The two researchers thus trace the stories into which they currently cast students—as writers and research subjects—to attitudes they formed during these experiences. And their research narrative shows further evidence of the patterns, with some productive variations that the collaboration enables. At first, Fishman feels that he is not heard, but then he gains a share of control in the research process and in writing the account. Likewise, McCarthy initially assumes that her entrance into Fishman's community should be smooth, that her initial research design would be readily accepted; her experience of conflict moves her to negotiate an innovative approach to research and its recounting.

To underscore the point that they are "novices" at this sort of negotiated research and representation, the two writers also offer telling glimpses of how each of them viewed the other at critical junctures in the study's unfolding process. In a collaborative voice, the writers characterize themselves in ways that depict how each of them negotiated a position that would keep the research going. The two were at first relatively antagonistic, caricaturing one another: McCarthy saw her key informant as "a romantic with very little sensitivity to the social aspects of learning," and Fishman, in turn, saw his collaborator as "following a cookie-cutter view of education" (459). Near the end of the project, the researchers had revised these early impressions: the latter portions of the report tell of how the two matched research responsibilities to their respective disciplinary methodologies and personal inclinations (463). With a contrastive "scene" that depicts how each might have individually approached the conduct of research, the narrators illustrate how they found a blend that suited Fishman's affinity for theory and McCarthy's attention to empirical detail—a blend that is reflected in the generic innovations of their report (463).

The experimental "boundary rhetoric" of this text disrupts McCarthy's disciplined affiliative plot by focusing on tentatively held, emergent positions of narrative authority. With their narrative metacommentary on the process of research, the two authors reflexively describe themselves, fleshing out the theoretical, methodological, and personal "stories" that account for their conflicts.[12] As a representative of our field, McCarthy is willing to juxtapose her "academic writing story" with Fishman's, thus honoring the intentions of both researchers and suggesting new narrative possibilities for her own field. No one implicit ending lends a smooth narrative trajectory, a conclusive wholeness, a satisfying sense of inevitability to the unfolding of the stories: the account contends with, and does not simply reiterate, our field's affiliative troping and plotting. McCarthy and Fishman's plotting is thus more "open," as, in their final accounting, these "novice writers" work out a critical narration that bespeaks its own constructedness, pointing out many of its selections and reductions (Brodkey, "Writing Critical," 74).

In this second study, McCarthy enacts her version of what I have called a storied inquiry, and so opens narrative possibilities for our naturalistic genres. The text she coauthors with Fishman casts McCarthy as a serious storyteller who collaboratively, continuously develops an ensemble of research practices that will allow her to be both responsive and responsible to a context populated with other potential narrators. McCarthy is thus able to position our field's "affiliative plot" as but one story in the midst of multiple, divergent story lines, and our disciplinary genres of storytelling as but one set of narrative commitments among the many possible.

Such reflexive narrations mark an ongoing rhetorical, political, and epistemic "refiguration" of naturalistic research that anthropologist Barbara Tedlock has described as a move "from participant observation to observation of participation." Truly *narrative* research genres are emerging, Tedlock suggests, as communities of naturalistic inquirers reimagine their relationships with people "in context" (82). When researchers recognize that they write for and about two potential audiences—the "other" communities under study, and their own academic community—they produce narrative, "engaged writing [that centers] on the ongoing dialectical political-personal relationship between self and other" (81).

In my own narration here, I have described McCarthy as an innovative storyteller to draw attention to the ways storied inquiries might address the crucial matter of our shared conventional plots, the narrative premises on which we work as professionals. My story has foregrounded the ways that, as a community of research storytellers, we are creating narrative genres—habits of telling—that query our own shared stories. Though these narratives do "discipline" us by framing what (ac)counts as acceptable knowledge, I hope to have shown that we serious storytellers do more than simply follow their familiar plot turns. For the satisfying, coherent wholes that our narrative thematics make of experience are not myths, beyond the reach of our revisionary telling; these stories are political realities, alive and vibrant, susceptible to our reflection on their effects and transformation of their uses.

Notes

1. Cintron draws the notion of an "ethic of care" from Schweikart.

2. See also Kleine, Cintron, Sullivan (1992), and Kirsch.

3. See Sullivan on North; Jarratt, Lunsford and Ede on Clark and Doheny-Farina; Schilb on Berkenkotter et al.

4. Miller participates in such an effort with five student-researchers: Worth Anderson, Cynthia Best, Alycia Black, John Hurst, and Brandt Miller (Anderson et al.).

5. See Cintron, Kirsch, and Sullivan.

6. See Gould, Haraway, Hrdy, Journet (1991), Landau, Myers, in addition to White, ch. 3, for discussions of how disciplinary narrative-interpretive practices enable and constrain what might be known.

7. My discussion of "affiliation" here draws upon some resonances of Edward Said's critical examination of a thematic that has figured in Western intellectual history: the passage from filiation to affiliation (21–23). In academe, this pattern has vested cultural authority in disciplinary affiliation; it is manifested at a practical level in increasing specialization, which in turn dictates practices with which researchers signify their disciplinary membership (e.g. adherence to theories, objects and methods of inquiry, genres of research) (22). He also suggests that texts show "affiliations" with

broader cultural patterns, and the political work of those patterns that their writers undertook and/or resisted (16 passim).

8. McCarthy also cites Dr. Kelly as providing the most direct statement of what I might call an affiliative pedagogy, one which ties the writing students undertake in class to "real-world" professional writing (244).

9. E.g. prewriting, drafting, revision (255).

10. This figurative dynamic also plays itself out in other research narratives that focus on processes of (usually advanced) disciplinary learning. I will just mention two other salient examples. Paul Prior constructs a narrative that implicitly concludes that the social processes it is ostensibly "about" are figuratively identified with, if not identical to, the writing process itself: the process of enculturation is "recursive and nonlinear" (306 n.3). And Berkenkotter et al. depict "Nate" as moving toward professional status by adopting the writing practices of the community he aspires to join.

11. See also Susan Miller's discussion of our "centralizing" narrative strategies. Anderson et al., 27–32.

12. McCarthy and Fishman continue their collaboration; they published another article on their study (Fishman and McCarthy) and presented papers in a panel at CCCC 1994 in Nashville.

Response to Jane Detweiler, by Carol Severino

Employing the lexicon and metaphors of "story" as Jane Detweiler does so skillfully, I will characterize her essay as "an arrival story" of the composition profession represented by the professional stories of Lucille McCarthy and, to a lesser extent, Stephen Fishman. Detweiler's laudatory, almost "victorious" reading of McCarthy and Fishman's self-reflexive ethnographic account "Boundary Rhetoric" constitutes a climactic episode in the story of the composition profession—contrasting markedly with earlier plot-thickening episodes of critique: Linda Brodkey's (1987) and Ralph Cintron's (1993) critiques of Shirley Brice Heath's *Ways with Words*; John Schilb's (1988) critique of Berkenkotter, Huckin, and Ackerman's "Conventions, Conversations, and the Writer"; and Carl Herndl's (1991) and Cintron's (1993) critiques of Stephen Doheney-Farina's "Writing in an Emergent Organization."

Brodkey, Schilb, Herndl, and Cintron had rigorously exposed the assumptions, narratives, and tropes that lay buried in those researchers' discourses; they criticized the researchers' unquestioning stances and their lack of reflective metadiscourse, urging that future researchers engage in self-conscious reflexivity in their fieldwork and reporting of results. Detweiler adds another episode of critique; she contrasts the McCarthy and Fishman piece, which indeed did self-consciously and reflexively "bespeak its own constructedness" (Brodkey, 74) and "reconfigure one of our field's generic plots" (xx), with McCarthy's earlier study indicatively titled "Stranger in a Strange Land," which had failed in these respects, unconsciously assuming and imposing a plot of initiation into disciplines ("the narrative of the novice") on its subjects and subject matter.

Continuing with the same narrative framework and rephrasing Susan Sontag's "anthropologist as hero" as "compositionist as heroine," I see Detweiler's story characterizing McCarthy as a postmodern heroine—"an innovative story-teller" (xx). McCarthy is a pioneering naturalistic researcher, who like the desired target genre of the postmodern ethnography is self-reflexive, and admitting of "multiple and divergent story lines," (xx) including Fishman's. In effect then, Detweiler's essay is also a success story, its message to the profession via McCarthy: "You've come a long way, (postmodern, naturalistic compositionist) baby."

As Detweiler points out, the McCarthy-Fishman narrative possesses all the desired features of the "new" postmodern ethnography of writing according to the paradigm of humanist anthropologists Clifford Geertz, James Clifford, and George Marcus. The McCarthy-Fishman narrative is, as Detweiler says, storied inquiry that critically reflects on the process of doing the research while at the same time presenting the results of the research. Instead of the cool, falsely objective, dispassionate, author-evacuated prose of the (pseudo) scientific ethnography, Detweiler demonstrates in McCarthy and Fishman's research the desirable features Wendy Bishop outlined for naturalistic write-ups: the warm, admittedly subjective, author(s)-involved, voiced, or, even better, multivoiced discourse and metadiscourse of the humanistic ethnography.

Detweiler's project—pointing out, praising, and thereby arguing for and solidifying the position of inclusive, self-reflexive genres for writing research—is exceedingly worthy. Research stories that unmask the role of the researcher in the research and write-up are a long-awaited, positive development and should be included, in fact, highlighted in what counts as "acceptable knowledge" in the profession. However, in my role as amplifier of Detweiler's text, I have two "yes, buts" to add. The first, also discussed in anthropology, has to do with the possible eclipsing of subject matter that occurs with the increased presence in a final text of the researchers and their concerns about their research and writing processes. My second "yes, but" involves my doubts about the claims of the new generic paradigm to include multiple and divergent story lines.

First, just how far does "storied inquiry" go before it reaches reductio ad absurdum? My response is, after all, Severino's story about Detweiler's story about McCarthy and Fishman's stories of themselves and their stories of Fishman's students, all of which also represent the story of the composition profession. And how do we prevent the stories of the composition profession and the personal and professional stories of the researchers from dominating accounts that are ostensibly about students' language learning and writing experiences? When do we decide that the ethos of the ethnographer has taken over the text? In other words, when does self-reflexivity become self-aggrandizement? I assume that most of us read composition literature such as McCarthy and Fishman's "Boundary Rhetoric" mainly because we are interested in research and teaching issues, not because we view the biographies of the authors or the direction of composition studies as crystal balls or measuring sticks to predict and assess our own careers. Indeed, "Boundary Rhetoric," with its intimate view of Fishman's class and his students, has a lot to say to writing teachers about the ways they can move a class from the experiential to the philosophical level as Fishman did. Yet for Detweiler, the authors' stories and their collaborative difficulties are more compelling than the students'; that is, she seems more interested in the story of Lucille and Steve than she is in the story of Ginny and Dave, Steve's philosophy students.

As rhetoricians, we are always aware that the presentation of any research involves ethical appeals and the "rhetoric of display" (Carter), but inherent in the postmodern ethnographic paradigm, with its emphasis on the writerly concerns of characterization, plot, and point of view and the need (compulsion?) to bring these out in the open is the danger of overplaying and overexposing the authors, their own writing, and their own writing processes at the expense of their subject matter—issues in language-learning and language-teaching, in short, the students' writing and writing processes. Anthropologists Nicole Polier and William Roseberry warn us about the possibilities of authorial narcissism in their article appropriately titled "Tristes Tropes: Post-Modern Anthropologists Encounter the Other and Discover Themselves." They quote from Clifford Geertz's "Thick Description":

> A good interpretation of anything—a poem, a person, a history, a ritual, an institution, a society—takes us into the heart of that of which it is—an interpretation. When it does not do that, but leads us instead somewhere else—into an admiration of its own elegance, of its author's cleverness, or of the beauties of Euclidean order—it may have its intrinsic charms, but it is something else than what the task at hand . . . calls for. (245)

I am not so naive as to deny that what Detweiler calls the "affiliative trope" applies to the connected trajectories of our individual careers and the composition profession, as well as to the students and teachers in our research narratives. However, I wonder how much we should *want to* write and read about the former concerns. For me, the characterization, in terms of the trope of affiliation, of "writing to belong" in the "landscape of literate belonging" (137) could easily and more comfortably be replaced by the less reflexive (less self-involved, less insecure?) "writing to learn" in the "landscape of literate learning."

My second question is about how inclusive the new generic paradigm is. Will it truly admit "multiple" and "divergent" stories? What will happen to tellers of more traditional stories in more traditional styles—for example, those coming from an expressionist perspective or those coming from a perspective of controlled experimental research with data in the form of short-answer questionnaire results or holistic essay ratings? Will they have an audience for their stories or will they have to fight to be heard? How much will they have to conform in order to be "affiliated"? What about research narratives that are not obviously and openly self-reflexive? Will they be returned to the authors so that they can incorporate self-reflexive metadiscourse and metacommentary about their research and writing processes? Is the new paradigm then "Anything you can do, I can do meta"?

Another cautionary note: James Berlin's taxonomy opposing expressivist and social constructionist rhetoric has had a lasting impact on the profession. It has labeled and indicted any teachers, like Fishman and Peter Elbow, who speak about helping students find their own voices, as apolitical and naive hippies who deny issues of power and social class. It is indicative that in the episode of the Fishman and McCarthy collaboration that follows "Boundary Rhetoric," the authors feel it necessary to defend expressivism as having social goals in agreement with social constructionist rhetoric ("Is Expressivism Dead?"). Indeed, both expressivism and social constructionism acknowledge the constructedness of texts and the role of writing processes. If new genres are truly inclusive, then the good guy/bad guy plots and polemics that have characterized episodes in composition, for example, process versus product and expressivism versus social constructionism, must also be continually interrogated and eventually eliminated.

I join Detweiler in celebrating an arrival story for the composition profession—the self-reflexive genre represented by McCarthy and "Boundary Rhetoric"; but I believe our enthusiasm must be tempered with concerns about an overpowering authorial and professional ethos, and about which story lines will be included under the categories "multiple" and "divergent."

Part V

The Intersection of Politics Within a Genre
Autobiography, Feminism, and Teaching

The two essays and response in this intersection allow readers to focus on a single genre, moving from the historical and professional overview provided by Lynn Bloom to the more particular consideration of feminist issues in autobiography provided by Wendy Hesford. In her response, as she fine-tunes Hesford's discussion, Eileen Schell reminds us of the implications feminist investigations of autobiography have for our pedagogy.

The genre we call "autobiographical writing" provides an open field for discussing the social construction of forms. We know this type of writing exists, but—as Lynn Bloom points out—autobiography provides us with a "contested, slippery, protean" writing space. For a long time the genre was reserved exclusively for telling the lives of the rich and famous—heroes, statesmen, or military leaders—though it was challenged at the margins by contesting, nonmainstream narratives, diaries, letters, confessions, often those penned by women. Bloom charts the increased interest in autobiography since the 1980s (an increase that can be compared with Bishop's discussion of the increase of interest in alternate forms of professional discourse in composition). Bloom claims autobiography is always a statement of individual politics—an idea complicated by Helscher's earlier consideration of the ways genres constitute our subjectivities (and hence our politics).

Similarly, Wendy Hesford alerts us to the dangers of championing feminist autobiographical writing, a genre of choice for many women scholars, for in doing so, we may be simply reinvoking liberal ideologies of gender and family. And, as Lyne points out earlier in this collection, such invocations may support rather than disrupt, may reassert middle-class white ways of thinking and silence alternate voices, may depoliticize what Bloom has claimed as the quintessentially most political of genres. To make her case, Hesford looks at riot grrl 'zines and focuses on agency rather than difference. In her response to Hesford, Eileen Schell cautions against a wholesale importation of autobiographical writing—even liberatory, feminist-influenced autobiographical writing—into our writing classrooms.

These authors raise important concerns that arise from our developing conceptions of genre as social action. Autobiography no longer raises the single question—who is writing?—but the more complicated questions of how do the practices of autobiographical writings produce cultural criticisms, helping writers make and remake their selves in and across societies?

14

American Autobiography and the Politics of Genre

Lynn Z. Bloom

Every day, year round, I swim laps at the university pool. Seven years ago, when I was new to the campus, all the bodies were blurred, streaked figures in or out of water.

That the personal is political is never truer than in relation to autobiography. American autobiography, what we write, read, teach, study, and critique, is inseparably intertwined with political concerns. Indeed, autobiography has throughout our national history been a conspicuously political genre. Political concerns strongly influence who writes (or tells) their stories, as well as the themes and masterplots of these stories. Politics influence which works are published and circulated, which are canonized, and consequently, which are read and studied in the schools. The last section of this paper will deal with issues of teaching autobiography in literature and in composition courses.

I try to avert my glance, but it is hard to ignore the presence of people who share the shower day after day, naked.

Definitions

But first, because autobiography is even today, at the height of popular and critical interest, a contested genre, slippery and protean, definitions are in order. In the old days, before 1970, autobiography was defined as the true story of a person's whole life, artistically shaped as the result "of an interpenetration and collusion of inner and outer life, of the person and society" (Pascal, 185). There was no debate, no disagreement; readers knew an autobiography when they saw one—most likely, the public life of a Great White Older Man—statesman, military leader, or self-made man in the mold of Benjamin Franklin. Critics paid scant attention to the genre, and except for canonical works by Augustine, Franklin, Henry Adams, and occasionally that rascal, Rousseau, the subject was seldom taught at any level in the American educational system.

But by 1980 the universe of American autobiography had changed, utterly. The definition of autobiography has changed, and changed again, to encompass the multiple and diverse variations of the genre—many in existence from the settlement of the country. These include not only partial as well as full-length self-portraits, but diaries, collections of letters, oral histories, personal essays, childhoods, spiritual autobiographies, confessions, and hybrid forms—dual portraits; family or group histories (combining biography and autobiography, as in Pauli Murray's *Proud Shoes*); personal travel narratives; and blends of fiction, myth, and personal narrative (as in Maxine Hong Kingston's *Woman Warrior*). We could also add films, videotapes, and political, legal, ethnographic, educational, critical, or other treatises in which the author's personal narrative is embedded, such as Mike Rose's *Lives on the Boundary* or Patricia Williams's *The Alchemy of Race and Rights*. Despite this diversity of form, critics and common readers alike agree on two central points of definition: that the autobiography's author, the story's narrator, and "the character who is being talked about" all have the same name (Lejeune, 12); and that the autobiographer is (or purports to be) telling the truth (see Bruss, 10–11), rhetorical and aesthetic strategies that combine "tell it slant" notwithstanding (see Andrews, 2–3).

Why Is Autobiography So Prominent Now?

I silently compare my body to theirs. Fatter than me. Thinner. Breasts bigger than mine, they could scarcely be smaller. Is she pregnant, or just flabby? Older than me. Younger. The spraying water makes us innocent, washing away makeup, hairdos, neutralizing skin color. Only the tattoos remain—a discreet butterfly poised on an ankle. A rosebud amidst cleavage. Numbers ragged on a forearm, indelible. And scars.

Since 1980, in the space of about a decade, this most democratic and diverse of literary genres moved from the margin to the mainstream, where it remains to this day. Autobiographical literature of all sorts is read, discussed, and taught across the educational spectrum, from classes in beginning literacy to graduate seminars in the genre. There is a literary theory to accommodate whatever textual politics the critic or teacher wants to employ, for autobiography—much closer in form and technique to fiction than to biography—is hospitable to diverse schools of contemporary criticism: postmodern, poststructuralist, reader-response, rhetorical (whether Bakhtinian, feminist, deconstructionist, social constructionist, or other). Between 1950 and 1970, only nine books on autobiography as a genre were published in English, not including book-length studies of individual works or authors.

Since the publication in 1972 of Olney's conceptually revolutionary *Metaphors of Self,* there has been a 2,500 percent increase in critical books alone—nearly 250 in English, as well as innumerable articles. Between 1970–74 and 1985–89 the number of critical articles on the twenty-one most frequently studied autobiographers cited in the *MLA Bibliography* had risen from 100 to 382, a nearly 400 percent increase (Bloom and Yu, 183). Since 1991 MLA has had a Division of Life Writing; entire journals are devoted to *Biography* (b. 1981) and *Auto/Biography* (b. 1985) and *Creative Nonfiction* (b. 1993), all of which encompass autobiography. Moreover, numerous articles on this versatile genre appear in a wide range of other publications.

A major reason for the current prominence of autobiography is the legitimation of the genre by the impact of various contemporary political and social movements that gave power and voice to people previously suppressed or subdued in the dominant white male culture: women, African Americans, Native Americans, Asian Americans, Hispanic Americans, recent immigrants, gays, and people with disabilities. Gertrude Stein says at the beginning of *Everybody's Autobiography,* "Alice [B. Toklas] did hers and now everybody will do theirs" (3). In this most democratic of genres, even people who can't write can tell their life story through collaboration with an oral historian or a coauthor.

The stories they tell, by and large, have comic (in the cosmic sense) masterplots that validate the movements that enabled them to speak—testaments to endurance, survival, triumphs over adversity. The parallel white and black exemplary lives of Benjamin Franklin and Frederick Douglass are cases in point, providing, as Bercovitch observes of Franklin's *Autobiography,* "'the pattern American,' both for 'a rising people' and (later) for the entire genre of the American success story" (141). Such works chart and indeed celebrate the protagonists' movement from bondage to freedom, outcasts to insiders, rags to riches, powerlessness to power—including the power of the self-presentation that manifests these triumphs. Although life isn't necessarily fair—Andre Dubus will never again walk, Stanley Elkin and Nancy Mairs will continue to deteriorate from MS, Zora Neale Hurston will die penniless and forgotten—autobiography can right the balance. Works such as *Broken Vessels, Pieces of Soap, Ordinary Time*, and *Dust Tracks on a Road* represent the existential triumph of art over existence, endowing even the most difficult and problematic lives with significance.

The newly acknowledged value of these works diverse in mode and authorship has contributed to the explosion of the literary and critical canon, as well: Franklin, Adams, Thoreau, and Augustine now share the critical shelf with Stein, Kingston, Douglass, Jacobs, and Rodrigues. Barbara Herrnstein Smith explains that all canonical texts reflect "contingencies of value," i.e. that all evaluations of literary texts are actually reflections of how well any particular work satisfies the ever-changing needs (the implied criteria) of the individual and society (52).

Indeed, from 1970 to 1990 critical interest in women's autobiography expanded elevenfold, dropping the man:woman ratio from 9:1 in 1970 to 2:1 in 1990 and changing the canon to include, in addition to Stein and Nin among the top twenty in 1970, Kingston, Angelou, Hellman, Dillard, Antin, Jacobs, and Hurston in 1990. During the same period critical attention to minorities and people of underclass origins (Wright, Kingston, Angelou, Antin, Hurston, Black Elk, Malcolm X) increased by 40 percent (Bloom and Yu, 154–57). These works are widely taught, not only in literature classes, but in courses in history, sociology, psychology, anthropology, women's studies, African-American studies, and a host of other disciplines.

Contemporary political and social movements have also created a revolution in the way we study our culture—for example, our history, our society, and our literature. History no longer has a top-down, kings-and-battles focus; society is not just plantation owners and captains of industry; the literary canon has expanded widely beyond its elitist orientation. These disciplines, among others, are now eclectic in philosophy, choice of subject, and research methodology. An abundance of primary autobiographical documents written by common, as well as uncommon, women and men, minorities and majorities offer compelling views from the grassroots. Three examples among many possibilities illustrate this point. "The Female World of Love and Ritual" (1975) is Carroll Smith-Rosenberg's landmark study of nineteenth-century women's "long-lived, intimate, loving friendships," derived from an analysis of the "correspondence and diaries" of thirty-five ordinary American middle class families (54–55). Elizabeth Fox-Genovese's *Within the Plantation Household: Black and White Women of the Old South* (1988) draws extensively on collections of southern family papers—authors' commentaries on their own works, account books, and especially letters, diaries (notably Mary Chesnut's), and autobiographies (notably Harriet Jacobs's). Annette Kolodny's *The Lay of the Land* (1975) uses comparable documents to dispute and reinterpret Henry Nash Smith's analysis of the American West in *Virgin Land* (1950).

Autobiography as a Genre of Political Empowerment

We move in concert when the toilets are flushed in the adjacent room, dance or be scalded. Gradually we begin to talk, under the streaming water. Where to get good maple syrup. Sightings of bluebirds, coyotes, a red fox. Peace Corps work in the Peruvian Andes. RN training in hospitals vs. college nursing programs. When to plant tomatoes so they won't freeze.

In one sense every autobiography, marginal or mainstream, could be considered a statement of individual politics, for its subject embodies the argument that Joan Didion says all writers make, "listen to me, see it my way, change your mind." Autobiography has remained a perennially popular genre among common readers, in part because it lets them look at life through others' eyes, providing a host of vicarious experiences, and models to marvel at, if not to emulate, as is evident in the best-selling *Lives* of the repentant, the rapscallious, and the rich.

Yet entire categories of autobiography have always had political agendas; these works aim not just to affect the individual reader, but to revolutionize society. Every political autobiography is a form of witnessing, as Elie Wiesel explains in "Why I Write." Every political autobiography uses the "power of the word" not only to convey the profundity of human experience but to move readers to action. "Not to transmit an experience," says Wiesel, talking of the life and death of the Holocaust, "is to betray it" (41). A disproportionate number of political autobiographies place the subject in what Mary Louise Pratt calls "contact zones," "social spaces where cultures meet, clash, and grapple with each other, often in contexts of highly asymmetrical relations of power, such as colonialism, slavery, or their aftermaths" (1991, 34).

In our country's history, the most conspicuous examples of such manifestly political autobiographies are captivity narratives and slave narratives. All use personal stories to promote political ends, allegedly in the national or regional interest, which may or may not be in the subject's best interest. Such narratives are never unmediated works; oral historians, ethnographers, or other amanuenses (since many of the subjects couldn't write), translators, editors, and publishers all serve as gatekeepers, permitting as well as denying the subject access to an audience—and on their terms, rather than the subject's. As Andrews has observed of the "large number of dictated, edited, and ghostwritten narratives that appeared under the ostensible authorship of blacks," 1760–1865, "Editors . . . assumed the right to do everything to a dictation from 'improving' its grammar, style, and diction, to selecting, arranging, and assigning significance to its factual substance" (20)—exactly what literate authors, such as Frederick Douglass and Harriet Jacobs, could do for themselves.

Thus the title page of the first (1861) edition of Jacobs's *Incidents in the Life of a Slave Girl* bears a political message: Northerners " 'have no conception of the depth of *degradation* involved in that word, SLAVERY; if they had, they would never cease their efforts until so horrible a system was overthrown.' " As Sharon Harris has observed, in Mary Rowlandson's *The Soveraignty and Goodness of GOD, Together With the Faithfulness of His Promises Displayed; Being a Narrative of the Captivity and Restauration of Mrs. Mary Rowlandson* (1682), "one woman's trauma-ridden experience of captivity became an icon of national ideology." Rowlandson's depictions of the Native Americans as "barbarians," "savages" who inhabited Satan's domain, fueled the colonists' arguments that "the removal of the Algonkians and other native tribes" from regions where the whites wanted to settle "was in the 'national' interest" (340, 42). Space does not permit elaboration here on the fact that not only slave narratives, but African-American autobiographies of any era, are documents of social protest and social critique, from

Olaudah Equiano (1789) to Frederick Douglass (1845, 1855, 1888, 1892) to
W. E. B. Du Bois (1968), Zora Neale Hurston (1942), Richard Wright
(1945), Malcolm X (1963), Mamie Fields (1983), and Pauli Murray (1987).

The Politics of Teaching Autobiography

*Sometimes we talk now when we swim laps, with pauses for the turns. The
Met's pre-Impressionism show ("Don't go"). Dissertation research—
astrophysics, patiently explained, but most of us still don't understand. How
children can learn three foreign languages simultaneously, with impeccable
accents, and never mix them up. Problems closer to home. Day care, policies and possibilities. Health care, ditto. Helping aged parents live, and die,
with dignity. I tell people whose names I do not know things I have never told
my own sister.*

The personal is compellingly political. Readers of all races must applaud
Frederick Douglass's declaration of freedom, "You have seen how a man
was made a slave; you shall see how a slave was made a man," as he fights
his cruel overseer, wins, and experiences "a glorious resurrection, from the
tomb of slavery to the heaven of freedom" (75, 81). Whether monocultural,
bicultural, or multicultural, readers must share Maxine Hong Kingston's
painful introduction to American kindergarten, where because she spoke only
Chinese, she couldn't say anything in English, "spoke to no one at school
. . . and flunked kindergarten" (192). However patriotic, however sympathetic to federal policies, readers must sympathize with Sioux Zitkala-Sa's
critique of the white practice of sending Native American children away
from their families to white boarding schools: "I was . . . neither a wild
Indian nor a tame one . . . among a cold race whose hearts were frozen hard
with prejudice" (93). No matter what their health or linguistic preferences,
readers must applaud Nancy Mairs's feisty decision to label herself, an MS
victim, as a "cripple . . . one to whom the fates/gods/viruses have not been
kind, but who can face the brutal truth of her existence squarely. As a cripple, I swagger" (9). And so on.

Teaching Autobiography in Literature Courses

The expanded literary canon has expanded the teaching canon as well. Autobiography is a natural subject for curricula designed to include women,
minorities, people of diverse cultures, and other previously marginalized
people. Because autobiography is so diverse and eclectic, a literature curriculum that incorporates it can be fine-tuned to emphasize whatever agenda(s)
the teacher, institution, or system desires—with (despite the insistence of the
other Blooms—Allan and Harold—and E. D. Hirsch on the superior quality
of the traditional canon) no diminution of quality. Specialized genre courses
can, and do, focus on particular aspects of autobiography. These include: the

historical or generic survey (say, from Augustine's *Confessions* to Gertrude Stein's *The Autobiography of Alice B. Toklas*); works of a particular culture or region (Asian Americans, the American West or South); explorations of a significant stage in one's life (childhood—e.g. Frank Conroy's *Stop-Time*); or development as a writer or other professional (such as Eudora Welty's *One Writer's Beginnings*); works emphasizing a journey (physical or psychological, crisis, or watershed—Jill Ker Conway's *The Road from Coorain*; Paul Monette's *Becoming a Man*); and a host of other possibilities.

However, students are more likely to encounter autobiography-by-anthology in literature survey courses. The widely used *Heath Anthology of American Literature*, for instance, was a leader in remapping the landscape of American literature to include numerous autobiographical works: from literature of exploration (Christopher Columbus to Samuel Purchas) to literature of American selfhood, including excerpts from the autobiographies of Booker T. Washington, Zitkala-Sa, Mary Chesnut, Mary Antin, N. Scott Momaday, and Aurora Levins Morales. Paul Lauter's preface to the first edition (1990, reprinted in the second edition of 1994) articulates as its editorial principles all of the reasons I've given above for the current prominence of autobiography in American culture (I, xxxiii–xxxviii), which he summarizes in "Reconstructing American Literature":

> Many of today's [college] courses regularly use more diaries, letters, and other "discontinuous" forms tha[n] traditional curricula might, and they probably make greater use of autobiographical writing, at least by minority writers and white women. In part, such curricular broadening is a consequence of new feminist and minority scholarship. (111)

Teaching Autobiography in Freshman Composition

Freshman Composition, in many schools the only course required of all undergraduates, is the site of numerous agendas, social, political, cultural, intellectual, acknowledged and unacknowledged. Freshman Composition has, among other tasks of socialization, initiation, and indoctrination, the job of making first year students aware of their college's prevailing political philosophy. This is often accomplished by requiring the students to read anthologies of essays on contemporary topics, to which they respond with essays of their own. It would be hard—perhaps impossible—today to find a commercially published anthology that does not give equal representation to women, men, and writers of diverse ethnic, racial, religious, and class backgrounds. Much of their writing is autobiographical—personal essays or chapters of autobiographies—elegant, eloquent testaments of both personal witness and social reform. The canon of familiar essays by Henry Thoreau, George Orwell, E. B. White, Joan Didion, James Baldwin, and Mary McCarthy is now expanded by equally canonical pieces by autobiographers Frederick

Douglass, Maxine Hong Kingston, Richard Rodriguez, Alice Walker, and N. Scott Momaday, augmented by personal essays of Gary Soto, Amy Tan, Linda Hogan, Judith Ortiz Cofer, Nancy Mairs, Scott Russell Sanders, and the late Jeffery Schmalz.

The teaching of such autobiographical writings, like other texts, is amenable to a variety of prevailing literary theories and pedagogical philosophies. These range from expressivism (Murray 1968, 1985, Bloom 1990), to feminism (see Flynn and Schweickart, Gannett, Nancy Miller), to social constructivism (Bruffee, Berlin 1988), to Freire's liberatory pedagogy translated into such works as different as Elbow's *Writing Without Teachers*, Rose's *Lives on the Boundary*, Spellmeyer's *Common Ground*, and Scholes's *Textual Power* and *Text Book*, which theorize and demonstrate how students can construct texts of their own to respond to the texts they read. Personal writing requires the same tough-minded analytic capability that academic discourse involves (see Behar 1994); it is only that the personal-sounding writer appears to be cruising on overdrive instead of grinding gears on the uphill climb. Students can as easily learn how to read and think critically and to understand a variety of discourse communities from reading and analyzing autobiographies as any other kinds of literary texts.

In addition to being theoretically sophisticated readers, many composition teachers are experienced writers, of poetry, fiction, belletristic essays, autobiographical literary criticism (see Diane Freedman et al., Jane Tompkins 1990, Cathy Davidson, Marianna Torogovnick). Such teachers are well positioned to give autobiographical writing assignments that will enable their students to learn what they themselves come to understand as they write and rewrite and rewrite: the innumerable versions in which a particular experience can be rendered; the relation of style to substance, style to self; the significance of emphasis, deemphasis, omissions, gaps, erasures; the difficulties, ethical, intellectual, and aesthetic, of dishonesty; the importance of each word, each syntactic structure, each punctuation mark, in every text; the critical rigor that undergirds writing well for an external audience; the necessity, aesthetic and personal, of rewriting. Moreover, writing and revising autobiography reinforces the importance of reading literature with an understanding of the writer's craft, the writer's art (see Scholes 1985; Bloom 1995).

In brief, through writing autobiography (or other forms of belletristic personal essays), composition teachers can teach their students how hard it is to write well—and how exhilarating. Because, as Behar notes, "personal writing represents a sustained effort to democratize the academy," teachers and students alike can experience the power that comes from treating a meaningful subject, as Behar says, "in plain language that will be understood by a large audience . . . that resonates more than jargon-laden analyses do with readers" (B2). It is not sentimentality but a desire to engage understanding at "the deep heart's core" that leads teachers and their students who become writers to lay their lives on the line.

A Mexican linguist lends me literature on good places to learn Spanish, "But it's really easy anywhere with an interactive computer program." A fiber artist designs and makes me the perfect dress, simple, comfortable, distinctive—"I've never done this for anyone before." I give another swimmer, a Thai microbiologist who moonlights as a caterer, copies of my books. We share recipes. We will cook together soon, in her house and mine. The community we have negotiated, interpreted, is the community we have become.

15

Autobiography and Feminist Writing Pedagogy

Wendy S. Hesford

In the late twentieth century, a time when our classrooms are becoming increasingly diverse, liberal notions of the private and public spheres and expressivist conceptualizations of autobiography are no longer pedagogically feasible. A new conceptualization of the genre of autobiography and its pedagogical role in the academy, particularly its use in feminist writing classrooms, is required to salvage its potential as oppositional discourse. Through the use of spatial concepts such as borderlands, contact zones, and coalition building, feminists have recently begun to explore the paradoxical nature of doing autobiographical work in the academy; feminist writing classrooms are themselves paradoxical in that they are situated in spaces made available by larger patriarchal structures. This survey of various conceptualizations of autobiography in feminist writing pedagogy over the last decade will, I hope, give readers a fuller understanding of why autobiographical acts are important in the academic environment and a more complicated understanding of their pedagogical potential and risks. My exploration will be guided by two key questions: How have feminist teachers in composition within the last decade used autobiographical spaces to challenge traditional pedagogies? How has the genre of autobiography become feminized in writing pedagogy? In considering these questions, I focus on both strategic uses of autobiography and its limitations. Also important to this essay is the recent interest in and return to autobiography in multicultural writing pedagogy.

Pedagogical "Blind Spots"

One of the first anthologies to attempt to define a feminist approach to composition is *Teaching Writing: Pedagogy, Gender, and Equity* (1987), edited by Cynthia L. Caywood and Gillian R. Overing. Many contributors to *Teaching Writing* position the personal voices of women and the genre of autobiography as alternatives to traditionally and institutionally imposed masculine voices and genres. For example, Olivia Frey argues in "Equity and Peace in the New Writing Class," "The teacher no longer has the Truth about writing. The student has the truth as she makes the writing her own" (97). Frey continues,

> the new writing class encourages a woman to develop her inner resources. She must make choices, discover her purpose as a writer, shape her writing according to her own needs [. . .] As the student makes small choices, then important ones, she discovers her rhetorical voice along with her personal female voice [. . .] the new writing class recovers the authority of the writer's own experience [. . .] in this case prescriptive rhetoric and grammar, no longer "intervene between herself and herself," between the image in the mirror that society has created, and the genuine self behind the mask. (101–2)

The pedagogical assumption here is that if women would only write about their own experiences, then patriarchal constraints of the academy would gradually cease to intervene. The autobiographical subject is constructed as if she were a fixed referent, as if social prescriptions and discourses could somehow be transcended and the "genuine self behind the mask" revealed. Sexual difference is presented as a given and the relationship between representation and identity is construed as mimetic—as if language were a mirror of reality. It is significant that the autobiographical subject is repositioned in a way that disrupts the bourgeois male subject by redefining this subject as female and giving her qualities historically awarded to men; these qualities include the ability to discover a "unified core essence" or "true self." In Frey's repositioning of women's voices, however, she reinscribes an oppositional logic based upon liberal notions of gender and space, where "masculine" is associated with the political and public and "feminine" with the personal and private. I am not suggesting that it is false to recognize that women are silenced by the academy or that many women have been confined to the "private" sphere. However, I am arguing that a pedagogy that focuses solely on making women's voices present without framing these voices as socially produced and situated within the structural and literary parameters of the academy will not enable women to confront the system and its discourses or to recognize asymmetrical power relations among themselves.

Numerous feminists in composition reinscribe liberal ideologies of gender and the family by invoking maternal metaphors for reconceptualizing relations between students and teachers, and by cultivating abilities in women students that researchers such as Carol Gilligan (1982) and Mary Field Belenky et al., (1986), have found characteristic of "women's ways of knowing." In "Sexual Politics of the One-to-One Tutorial Approach" (1987), another example from *Teaching Writing*, Carol Stranger argues for a pedagogy that privileges collaboration and consensus building. Drawing upon Nancy Chodorow's theory of pre-Oedipal development in *The Reproduction of Mothering*, Stranger proposes that "successful collaboration in the class-room" can create "oceanic feeling[s]" in the woman writer and reproduce "a perfect sense of oneness" associated with the primary identification with the mother (40). "In the sense that collaborative learning taps learners' early experiences with their mothers," she claims, "it is a feminist pedagogy" (40). This image-metaphor of the feminist teacher as maternal figure, and the pro-jection of a holistic unified nonconflictual self, however, does not account for political struggles in the "private" sphere or for the experiences of working women who are also mothers. Not only does this ideology of motherhood work toward creating classroom climates that maximize the comfort level for white upper- and middle-class women by buffering critical intrusions from white working-class women and women of color, but it does not expose the fragmenting qualities of most middle-class white women's lives. To define the maternal and the "feminine" as harmonic, fluid, and nonconflictual can serve to reinforce traditional gender distinctions and a discourse of class- and color-blindness.

It is possible, however, for maternal metaphors to assume a subversive function. Indeed, one of the fundamental claims in pedagogical appropria-tions of French feminist discourse has been the link between the maternal and the subversive (Worsham), between the "feminine" and experimental writing (Bridwell-Bowles 1992). Maternal metaphors of female empower-ment may nevertheless end up silencing women by rendering some women invisible. The problem is not so much that cooperative and nurturing rela-tions are privileged over conflict, but that these relations are rooted in a logic that locates these characteristics on the bodies of white heterosexual women. Another troubling aspect of the invocation of the "feminine" as a metaphor for resistant language is that language of resistance is often linked to the experimental discourses of the modernist literary avant-garde—a movement that is not necessarily synonymous with the social marginalization of women (Felski). The interruption of dominant discourses and the affirmation of "unofficial" discourses are important aspects of feminist approaches to writ-ing. But to simply associate the genre of autobiography only with the "pri-vate" or "feminine" is to remain trapped in a model with intrinsic limitations, namely that the experiences of white, middle-class women stand for the whole. Thus, although metaphorical reformulations have had enormous influence within feminist pedagogy, I am concerned about their capacity to configure women into limiting categories by enshrining traditional ideologies of gender that confine women to traditional roles by reinscribing polarities such as passion/reason, personal/political, private/public, and body/mind.

Feminist research on autobiography in composition has not fully chal-lenged the primacy of gender analysis over other modes of difference. For example, in "Composing as a Woman" (1988), Elizabeth Flynn uses Carol Gilligan's theory about gender differences in moral and intellectual develop-ment to interpret patterns in the autobiographical narratives of four first year college men and women. Flynn found that the narratives of the first year college men stressed separation over connection, whereas the college women wrote stories of connection or frustrated connection (428–29). While both Flynn and Gilligan acknowledge that these patterns are socially constructed, both researchers nevertheless tend to essentialize gender differences. Janis Tedesco in "Women's Ways of Knowing/Women's Ways of Composing" (1991) wisely points out that the findings of Belenky et al. and Gilligan are descriptive; that is, they are mediated through the speaker's languages. She argues that these works "summarize how women themselves perceive their experiences and attitudes" (253). While Tedesco acknowledges that language shapes identity, neither she nor Flynn questions the naturalizing power of women's descriptions or consider how gender is discursively displayed, displaced, and/or essentialized. Neither theorist fully accounts for the fluidity of identity categories themselves or the complexities of women's and men's discursive and spatial movement between and among them. The problem with pedagogical appropriations of the work of Belenky et al., Chodorow, and Gilligan to date lies in many feminists' resistance to account sufficiently for ways that both women and men negotiate cultural scripts and how they challenge developmental schemas by constructing multiple speaking positions as they move from one context and genre to another.

A more recent pedagogical piece that centrally positions autobiography but fails to acknowledge how writers struggle with inherited narratives of the self is Maxine Hairston's controversial essay "Diversity, Ideology, and Teaching Writing" (1992). Hairston, a self-defined liberal, positions herself in an adversarial relationship to a generation of composition teacher-scholars who, informed by social constructionism, put "ideology and radical politics at the center of their teaching" (180). According to Hairston, the cultural left has taken over; deconstruction, poststructuralism, and Marxist theory have "trickled down to the lower floors of English departments where freshman English dwells" (183). It is interesting to me that Hairston recognizes the spatial segregation of composition programs through verticality metaphors and her image of leaky basement plumbing, yet reinforces this marginalized position through her association of English departments with the theoretical and composition programs with the pedagogical. Not only does Hairston refuse to acknowledge the political nature of all pedagogical situations, but she strategically dismisses or ignores altogether the scholarly work of writing teachers who focus precisely on the ways in which inequities are pedagogically inscribed and structurally reinforced. Hairston recognizes the increasing linguistic and cultural diversity of the student population in American higher education, and thus argues that our students are our "greatest multicultural resource" (190). "Real diversity," she claims, "emerges from the students themselves and flourishes in a collaborative classroom" (191). She continues, "The beauty of such an approach is that it's *organic*. It grows out of resources available in each classroom, and it allows students to make choices" (191). I agree with Hairston that writing courses should be student-centered, but I do not find her description of student-centered approaches as "organic" (as in "natural" or apolitical) accurate; these approaches are just as political as any other. Equally problematic is Hairston's portrayal of the writing class as a safe space for the "free exchange of ideas" (188). Hairston constructs the writing classroom as a neutral public site wherein autobiographical experiences can be shared without invoking differences shaped by gender, race, and/or social position. The assumption here is that all students present are equally empowered. As Nina Chordas points out in "Classrooms, Pedagogies, and the Rhetoric of Equality" (1992), "the blind spots in pedagogies that presume open and equitable writing spaces derive partly from idealistic notions about the unconditioned individual and myths about America as a classless egalitarian society" (217–23).[1]

I do not quarrel with the feminist hope for developing pedagogies that recognize the shared struggles of college women or for student-centered multicultural pedagogies; *Teaching Writing*, "Composing as a Woman," and "Women's Ways of Knowing/Women's Ways of Composing" have played an important role in challenging patriarchal academic conventions and traditions. However, pedagogical projects that do not enable both women and men to recognize how societal structures have shaped their voices can act to reinforce the status quo. The pedagogical positions of autobiography discussed thus far tend to privatize and depoliticize the personal voice, and in so doing uncritically reproduce cultural values that reinforce inequities already present in the academy. Feminists must step outside such narrow definitions of autobiography. We must take down the curtain that perpetuates the illusion that private and public spheres are fundamentally separate and applicable across different populations. We must expose the ideology of selfhood associated with the genre of autobiography, which in Western societies has been defined as a universal, disembodied subject marked as masculine (S. Smith, *Subjectivity*, 5–11). Thus, it is not so much a question of dismissing the autobiographical but rather of locating it in a different historical, theoretical, and pedagogical context. As bell hooks suggests, the discourse of memory can be used to "shift the focus away from the mere naming of one's experience [. . .] to talk about identity in relation to culture, history, and politics" (1989, 110). Autobiography can no longer be positioned in feminist writing pedagogy simply in terms of gender differences. The privileging of gender analysis over other forms of difference has been challenged by the diverse experiences of working class women, lesbians, gay men, and people of color, who argue that a whole range of social relations constituted by sexuality, class, and race are experienced simultaneously. In order to acknowledge the power of dominant discourse in shaping a writer's voice and to recognize the possibility of resisting these shaping forces, feminists must better understand the paradoxical nature of doing autobiographical work in the academy and the paradoxical qualities of feminist writing spaces.

Paradoxical Writing Spaces

Riot grrrl 'zines are particularly interesting to study as paradoxical feminist writing spaces. Riot grrrl 'zines are "homemade" magazines (copied and stapled or sewn together) that offer a discursive space for young women to express themselves without using the tools of the mainstream media to do it. They serve a function similar to that of the nineteenth century women's literary societies, except that the exchanges among women are in print. The term "grrrls" is used strategically by creators of 'zines and their contributors to deny identification with the "adult" academic and patriarchal world of status, hierarchies, and standards. Although riot grrrl press offers some young women a "safe space" in which to share personal experiences, to express anger against the academy, and to critique mainstream patriarchal society and technology, as Irene Chien points out, they are also exclusionary. Produced by women at private high schools and elite colleges, many 'zines reinforce the privileges of the upper white middle class even as they challenge other conventions and boundaries. What I find particularly interesting about riot grrrl 'zines is the way their contributors negotiate with and appropriate the discourses of dominant culture and liberal feminism. Consider the enactment of the social spaces of writing and gender in the following excerpt written by an Oberlin student for an Ohio feminist riot grrrls 'zine, *Real Hot Spit* (1993):

I am in a cafe. There are tables here, where I am, and more outside, under an awning, with a glass wall in between. Two longhaired older men are outside at tables, watching me write. They make me nervous. Every time I look up to see if they are still watching, I meet their gaze. This, of course, encourages them. I feel very self-conscious. Maybe I should do something. Make a sign. "STOP WATCHING ME" but that would probably make them or one of them come over. Any excuse to say something to me. If I look to check if they're still watching, they'll take it as a come on. Go away! I can feel eyes on me now. I hate feeling self-conscious. [. . .] I've written the sign. Big letters in the back of my notebook. I wonder what would happen if I held it up for them to see. Perhaps we'll see. I held it up. They laughed. Why do people not realize the power they have? My heart is thumping but at least I let them know. I don't need to share my feelings with them—someone's tapping on the glass. I'm not looking up. I showed them that I didn't want them to watch me anymore, so now they shouldn't be. I don't have to check. More tapping. Someone comes up to me, "excuse me, those guys over there want you to look at them." I'm sure they do. Should I? I look up to see, written on a napkin held up to the window: ENTRAPMENT! [. . .] Does that mean that in order not to be watched I must put on a sweater? Leave the room? Why the hell is it MY goddamn responsibility? What do I have to do NOT to "entrap?" What did I do to lead them on? It's not all for me to think about—shouldn't they have to? They don't *have* to because there's no danger involved. For me, as a grrrl, my status (according to American culture) DEPENDS on those looks. They are suppose to vindicate me as feminine, fill—temporarily—the void of insecurity that the fashion and 'beauty' industry has ripped open in me. Part of being "feminine" is being seductive, entrapping. But if a man rapes me, then femininity becomes incrimination. [. . .] LA

What fascinates me about this piece of prose is how the writer articulates her feelings about the paradox of watching her watchers. She is literally watching herself being watched; the writer is aware of her position as "Other"—the one being watched by men. Although she is separated from her onlookers by a pane of glass—a transparent curtain divides the "outside" public from the "enclosed" public—the glass does not protect her. In an attempt to interrupt the male gaze and its threatening presence, she holds up a sign that says, "STOP WATCHING ME," which, paradoxically enough, reasserts to the two men that she is paying attention. Instead of breaking the male gaze or claiming a sense of agency, her action serves to reinforce the men's prerogative. She becomes even more self-conscious of her position as one who is watched. What power she claims is constantly called into question: the men laugh at her, they continue to watch, they even engage in her "game" of sign writing. She recognizes the impossibility of fully staying outside or escaping the power of the male gaze and the way it positions her as other: "What can I do not to entrap?" She asks, "in order not to be watched [must I] put on a sweater?" Unable to reverse the power of the male gaze, she detours through it to see herself. She is forced to concede that, at least in part, her status "DEPENDS on those looks." Clearly, power lies on the side of the one who looks. The image of the writer displayed here, then, is not only the subjectivity of the woman seen but the desire of the men looking. The gaze will not let go—not even of her text. Since the writer cannot free herself from the language of the gaze, she writes from within it. In this sense, the writer is literally and figuratively caught inside the space from which she writes. What constitutes the writer's agency is not the reporting of the event, but her ability to situate herself as a medium of the testimony— her self-consciousness about how she has internalized the male gaze psychologically and discursively.

While women's personal testimonies may disrupt traditional values, genres, and discursive conventions of the academy, they do not automatically result in alterations of dominant ways of organizing and understanding identity and difference. As this 'zine excerpt demonstrates, although the writer is aware of how dominant discourses shape her identity, to a certain extent, she ends up reinforcing them by perpetuating some of their essential binarisms. She does this by presenting unified discursive identity categories—women and men—unmarked by race or class. Race and class are not explicitly figured in the written text; the author does not write from a racially identified body. However, superimposed over the text are two images. One is of a woman of color in an skimpy bodysuit and the other is of a white male in a power business suit. Unlike the text, here femininity and masculinity are explicitly racialized. One might also argue that these images enact cultural stereotypes by depicting white men as predators and controllers of black women's sexuality. Whether these images were created by the author or spliced in by an editor later is unknown. However, what is clear is that the way these images and the text depict race is linked to larger social trends toward relying upon visible differences. When differences are based solely upon the color of one's skin, ethnic, sexual, and class differences within the white population and among people of color are ignored.

I can imagine this text and its particular feminism emerging from a pedagogy that does not focus on women's agency or negotiations with dominant narratives and cultural scripts, but that locates women, unmarked by difference, solely as passive victims of patriarchal structures and discourses. The pedagogical challenge that this 'zine excerpt poses to feminist teachers is to find ways to enable students to recognize how their constructions of self are shaped by feminist discourses and ideologies, and to enable them to consciously engage these discourses. If, as feminist writing teachers, we are to transform pedagogies of domination, and the essentializing differences that some feminist pedagogies produce, then we cannot afford to dispense with a critique of the struggles and invisibilities within our own and our students' work. This means listening for the silences as well as recognizing how what was previously unspoken is newly encoded; as bell hooks puts it, " 'the politics of location' necessarily calls those of us who would participate in the formation of counter-hegemonic cultural practice to identify the spaces where we begin the process of re-vision" (1990, 145). Unlike the feminism displayed in the 'zine excerpt, which privileges visibility politics by focusing on skin-color and by framing difference through an us/them construction of power, imagining oneself in a counter-hegemonic autobiographical space is a much more complex project. The 'zine excerpt provides, then, a pedagogical opportunity to consider how feminist autobiographical spaces are critical sites for the construction of social identities and how they may be marked paradoxically by the interplay of dominant and counterhegemonic discourses.

The concept of paradoxical spaces has been put forth by numerous feminists, namely feminists of color and lesbian critics whose notions of location imply "contradictory spatialities" and "heterogeneous geometries" (G. Rose, 140–41). For example, Aida Hurtado, in "Relating to Privilege: Seduction and Rejection in the Subordination of White Women and Women of Color" (1991), profoundly challenges the spatial division of the world into a male public and female private. She suggests that the autobiographical work of women of color is not so much a projection of the private into the public but rather an enactment of how the "public is personally political" (849). Patricia

Hill Collins has also articulated the paradoxical positions of working-class black women in American culture. She describes the position of black domestic women workers in white homes as an "outsider within–stance" (Rose, 152). Diana Fuss suggests an equally doubled position common to lesbian and gay men who may be simultaneously inside and outside. Fuss points out the paradox of being out: "to be out, in common gay parlance . . . is really to be in—inside the realm of the visible, the speakable, the culturally intelligible . . . [but] to come out can also work not to situate one on the inside but to jettison one from it" (Fuss, quoted in Rose, 151).

Additionally, numerous feminists contest and blur the boundaries between the public and private by mapping the terrain of autobiography differently and by explicitly bringing autobiography into their scholarship (e.g., Anzaldua, Bannerju et al., Behar, N. Miller, and P. Williams, among others). Sidonie Smith in her discussion of feminist autobiographical manifestos shows how such texts challenge the hegemony of white liberal feminism and the nostalgia of the pastoral tradition wherein the speaker travels away from the metropolis to a more "natural" space that promises "reinvigoration" and access to "truer selves" (*Subjectivity,* 170). Autobiographical manifestos, according to Smith, unqualifiedly assert "the politicization of the private and the personalization of the public, effectively troubling the binary complacencies of the *ancien regime* of selfhood with its easy dichotomization of private and public" (160). In her analysis of Gloria Anzaldua's *Borderlands/La Frontera: The New Mestiza* (1987), for example, Smith points out that the "topography of the borderland is simultaneously the suturing space of multiple oppressions and the potentially liberatory space through which to migrate toward a new subject position" (169). Anzaldua embraces this paradox by adopting multiple positions in her negotiations with the predominant cultural and linguistic identities of her borderlands experience: "I will no longer be made to feel ashamed of existing. I will have my voice: Indian, Spanish, white. I will have my serpent's tongue—my woman's voice, my sexual voice, my poet's voice. I will overcome the tradition of silence" (59). The concept of borderlands, then, moves between centers and margins— dismantling traditional notions of singular selves and stable places of origin. Border residents assume a fluid positionality, one that is neither completely inside nor powerlessly outside dominant cultures.

One might argue that the great binary metanarratives of sexual difference and its division of the world into male public and female private are in decline, being replaced with an awareness of heterogenous differences and contradictory spatialities. Although the inadequacies of expressivist feminist projects are becoming clear, it is important to recognize the perpetuation of binarisms and essentializing practices in public institutions and their presence as structuring devices in feminist pedagogy and our students' writing.[2] With few exceptions, namely the work of Susan Jarratt, Min-Zhan Lu, and Lynn Worsham, feminist composition teacher-scholars have not fully explored these contrary impulses and paradoxical positions. What I find particularly striking about Lu's pedagogical scholarship is that she blurs disciplinary boundaries and blends autobiographical and academic discourse in ways that highlight negotiations among them. Lu approaches composition pedagogy dialogically, by placing "different orders of experience—each of whose languages claims authority on the basis of its ability to exclude others—into dialogue with each other" (Holquist, 87).

Crossing Borders: Pedagogical Tourism or Coalition Building?

In "Conflict and Struggle" (1992), Lu applies Gloria Anzaldua's metaphorical concept of the borderlands to composition in order to foreground the complexities of social, personal, and textual relations among students and teachers. While the concept of borderlands and its attention to the heterogenous nature of spatial and discursive positions offers feminists new ways to conceptualize the dynamics of autobiographical discourse, one has to be careful to consider whether a writer has chosen to reposition herself on the borderlands, or whether such repositionings have been imposed or chosen for her. Students and teachers do not have the same freedom of movement to cross into or out of the borderlands. For example, which borderlands are inaccessible to Lu? Since many students and teachers have not been cast out of their home or language as have Anzaldua or Lu (1987), is their movement into the borderlands or margins a form of pedagogical tourism?

Caren Kaplan cautions first world white feminists, like myself, to ask such questions in her compelling essay, "Deterritorializations: The Rewriting of Home and Exile in Western Feminist Discourse" (1989). It is worth quoting her at some length:

> For the first world feminist critic, therefore, the challenge at this particular time is to develop a discourse that responds to the power relations of the world system, that is, to examine her location in the dynamic of centers and margins. Any other strategy merely consolidates the illusion of marginality while glossing over or refusing to acknowledge centralities. Thus, the first world feminist critics may be marginal *vis a vis* the literary establishment or the academy that employs her, yet she may also be more closely linked to these institutions than a non-western or third world feminist critic. (189)

I invoke Kaplan's warning precisely because of the apparent reluctance on the part of liberal feminists in composition to fully contextualize their identity positions and theoretical appropriations of and alliances with the borderlands. Kaplan points out, "Oppositional consciousness can not simply be put on like a cloak, it is shaped by experiences of oppression" (191). There is a danger inherent in movement from one cultural space to another, a potential for reenactment of domination—a kind of representational colonialism that constructs the feminist teacher-scholar as having a panoramic worldview and an ability to move through historical geographical terrains unnoticed.

I am particularly concerned about the potential of metaphoric reconfigurations within multicultural pedagogies that position feminist teachers as innocent wanderers or neutral cartographers of the experiences of the oppressed. Lu refers to this pedagogical tendency as "cultural tourism," wherein "teachers and students approach cultural diversity by assuming that they themselves are somehow outside of rather than implicated in the cultures *about* which they read and write" (1994, 1–2). Along with Lu, I would suggest that it would be far more useful for feminists to think about the writing classroom as potential "contact zones" (Pratt). In "Arts of the Contact Zone" (1991), Mary Louise Pratt defines "contact zones" as "space[s] in which peoples geographically and historically separated come into contact with each other and establish ongoing relations, usually involving conditions of coercion, radical inequality, and intractable conflict" (441). Framing the feminist writing classroom as a "contact zone" can help us to understand the perils and paradoxes of writing autobiography and doing feminist work in the academy.

One of the results of this view of the feminist classroom as a "contact zone" is the reconceptualization of the relationship between the self and language. "Life on the contact zone rejects the notion of an authentic self." As Lu suggests, "instead of affirming the belief that there is some kind of stable essence within each of us called 'me,' . . . the concept of the contact zone teaches us to perceive one's self . . . as made and changed through interaction with others, in the process of negotiating with those with less as well as more privilege than oneself" (1994, 6). This is not to diminish the very real oppressions that composition teachers face, particularly women, but rather to call upon ourselves to consider if and when we have concealed our own privileges and mobility.

It is not my intention to commodify the metaphor of the "contact zone" as yet another ideal form into which feminists should pour all their pedagogical questions. Instead, I would suggest that as a conceptual model it enables us to understand the power of language as action, and to recognize how the genre of autobiography and the social languages and conventions that a writer uses to construct the self may reproduce, as the 'zine excerpt demonstrates, the very conditions that subjugate the writer in the first place and/or obstruct the writer's ability to focus on her own position and power relations. The writer of the 'zine excerpt literally wrote *in* the contact zone, using a language that was trying to overcome itself; she questioned the male gaze by invoking the very language and values that it privileged. Thus, the feminist repositioning of autobiography demands creation of writing and reading spaces where subjectivities can be examined with respect to their historical, cultural, and rhetorical configurations.

While the concept of the "contact zone" deconstructs the pedagogical fantasy of discourse utopias and universal sisterhoods associated with expressivist feminist pedagogies, I could imagine its potential misuse. As feminists embrace the paradigm of conflict and its critiques of liberal strategies such as collaboration and classroom decentering, we have to be careful not to construct new pedagogical situations that silence students who are uncomfortable writing about personal experiences or who are less "intellectually combative." A pedagogy based on the concept of the "contact zone" does not demand the creation of combative or confessional classrooms, but rather requires the construction of writing and reading spaces that enable writers to experiment with a wider range of points of view (Lu 1994, 7). This will involve challenging students' ideas about autobiography and questioning the kind of self-making marked by slogans such as "Just do it" or "Become whatever you want to be," which treat autobiographical positions as if they were simply a matter of individual choice.

As long as we remain aware of the problematics of both self-representation and representing others, then there is some hope for the liberatory use of autobiography in feminist writing instruction and research. The challenge, as I see it, is the constant struggle to situate oneself in the position of a questioning subject—to develop an antagonism in oneself. This involves, as the work of Paulo Freire suggests, identification with positions that allow one to critique one's "own" subject position (JanMohamed, 246). Unlearning one's "own" position, however, does not result in the attainment of a historically transcendent point of view, but rather involves repositioning oneself within the cultural production of knowledge (Spivak [1990], 42). The concept of the "contact zone" can help us to recognize how various groups in the academy "delineate their discursive boundaries, name and expel the Other, express and reinforce their bonds, their sense of being 'at home' with each other" (Altman, 504). In this sense, the metaphor may also help us to better understand the difficulties involved in building feminist pedagogical coalitions. The metaphor captures well the complex position of autobiography within the geographical imagery of feminist writing pedagogy—a pedagogical terrain comprised of contesting social languages, histories, and identities—heterogenous, contradictory, and in process.

Notes

1. Centrist approaches to diversity are becoming more prevalent in composition through the inclusion of multicultural readers, which are produced by large publishing corporations that reap enormous economic benefits through this commodification of difference. Although a small number of multicultural readers do historically and socially contextualize autobiographical acts, many perpetuate the myth of America as

a cultural melting pot by simply stressing greater visibility of historically underrepresented groups without including a critique of the unequal power relations of those who are looked at and those who look.

2. In "Essentialism and Experience," hooks reminds us of the ways in which essentialism is expressed from locations of privilege. Yet others remind us of how essentialism is often used as a contingent strategy of empowerment and resistance. Joy Ritchie, for example, in "Confronting the Essential Problem," highlights the ways in which students in a feminist literature course shifted from naive essentialist positions to strategic essentialist positions as the semester progressed. I argue in "Writing Identities" for an understanding of the double-discourse of essentialism and its strategic use by the disempowered.

Response to Wendy Hesford, by Eileen E. Schell

In "Autobiography and Feminist Writing Pedagogy," Wendy Hesford convincingly argues that we need to reconstruct liberal feminist theories of autobiography in composition studies. I share Hesford's critique of theories of feminist expressivist autobiography that are based upon "authentic voice." The theory of "self" forwarded in many of the essays in feminist expressionist work such as *Teaching Writing: Pedagogy, Gender, Equity*[1] proves troubling to those of us who do not subscribe to the view that the female subject is a coherent, rational, unique "individual" who can achieve self-discovery and self-actualization through autobiographical writing (Faigley 1992, 15; see also Faigley 1989). The ideology of selfhood embedded in feminist expressionist theories often constructs autobiography as a self-disclosing narrative account where the writer's authoritative self is called to witness about a significant past event (Benstock, 1047). In this autobiographical tradition, there is a double referent in the "I" who writes—the "I" who is constructed as the Subject in the current narration of events, and the "I" who remembers the past events and reconstructs them. As Shari Benstock notes, the "gaps in the temporal and spatial dimensions of the text itself are often successfully hidden from reader and writer, so that the fabric of the narrative appears seamless, spun of whole cloth" (1047). This "seamless" autobiographical writing is magical, "the self appears organic," and the writer appears to have control over her subject matter (1047).

Conversely, feminists who are compelled by social constructionist theories of subjectivity contest the ideology of selfhood presented in feminist expressivist theories of autobiography, contending that we need to be more self-critical of the ways in which we deploy autobiographical student writing. Like Hesford, I believe we need to shift the main focus of feminist autobiography from the act of urging women students to narrate or "tell" their stories to urging them to tell their stories *and* to examine the discourses, narratives, and "cultural" scripts that shape those stories. This shift from the act of telling stories to understanding the act of constructing stories is symptomatic of a larger critical shift in composition theory toward social constructionist notions of identity.[2] Social constructionist thought establishes that the subject who "writes" herself is being written by a "plethora of discourses—a rich variety of texts inscribed in the persona of the individual. The subject is thus a construction of the play of discourses that a culture provides" (Berlin, 108).

In order to reinvigorate the oppositional potential of autobiography and to account for social constructionist views of identity and experience in the feminist classroom, we need to heed Hesford's call to relocate autobiography in a "different historical, theoretical, and pedagogical context" (11). She suggests that feminists need to "re-imagine" autobiography through new spatial configurations such as "borderlands," "contact zones," and "coalition building" (4). These spatial configurations relocate autobiography as "cultural criticism," a genre of writing that examines the signifying practices of living cultures. Feminist cultural criticism, then, examines what Sidonie Smith (1993) refers to as the hermeneutics of self-representation, "which cannot be divorced from cultural representations of women that delimit the nature of her access to the word and the articulation of her own desire" (1059). Instead of framing "experience" in narrative form, a linear, chronological progression toward a definitive conclusion, autobiography can be refigured as an "act"—a self-conscious performance, dramatization, and self-figuration— where the storyteller critically considers the cultural scripts by which she makes sense of "personal" experiences. Thus, autobiography becomes an act of struggle where the writer must grapple with her constructions of self in light of the cultural constructions of race, class, gender, sexuality, family, and nation.

An example of autobiographical struggle with self-representation can be found in Gloria Anzaldua's *Borderlands/La Frontera*. Anzaldua enacts autobiographical discourse as a clash of conflicting discourses and identities that "results in mental and emotional states of perplexity," contradiction, and paradox (49). Anzaldua as a mestiza—half Indian, half Chicano, living in Anglo-American culture—straddles three cultures and their value systems, undergoing "a struggle of flesh, a struggle of borders, an inner war" (50). To enact this struggle politically and rhetorically, Anzaldua mixes genres in her autobiographical writing, moving between poetry and prose, narrative and drama, polemic and cultural criticism. Moreover, she dramatizes her multiple ethnicity by juxtaposing conflicting discourses and languages: Standard English, Standard Spanish, North Mexican Spanish dialect, Chicano Spanish, Tex-Mex, and Pachuco (Calo). Acknowledging difference and ambiguity, contradictory information, and conflicting cultural points of view, Anzaldua does not enframe her autobiography as a quest plot to "find the self," rather she examines the "borderlands" between competing cultural discourses, ethnic identities, and her personal/cultural experiences.

Anzaldua's work participates in the "autobiographical wave" sweeping feminist theorizing, a wave that blends feminist theory, autobiographical writing, and cultural criticism. Despite differences in style and tone, identity politics and positionality, Carolyn Heilbrun, bell hooks, Jane Gallop, Adrienne Rich, Gayatri Spivak, Jane Tompkins, and Alice Walker are just a few of the many feminist critics who write what Nancy Miller refers to as "autobiographical cultural criticism," a genre where self-narrative is woven into critical argument and where self-representation functions as political representation (2). Autobiographical cultural criticism also has been referred to as "personal criticism" or "an explicitly autobiographical performance within the act of criticism" (1).

My brief discussion of autobiography as feminist cultural criticism is meant to further reiterate Hesford's call for a reconsideration of autobiography in feminist composition studies; however, I do not intend to issue a "call to action" for all writing teachers to assimilate this strategy into their classrooms and for textbook publishers to begin manufacturing composition readers and assignment sequences devoted to this practice of autobiography. As Nancy Miller contends, autobiographical cultural criticism poses the problem of becoming a "congealed genre" in the academic world, an intellectual fashion of the worst kind in which tenured academic "insiders" indulge and divulge their personal experiences (3). Indeed, a similar danger lurks in touting experimental genres for first-year writing courses. Feminist writing teachers must be careful not to treat this autobiographical practice as the latest composition commodity available for easy distribution and consumption; I can, for instance, imagine dozens of my white, middle-class students at Virginia Tech striving to imitate Gloria Anzaldua as they once imitated E. B. White's "Once More to the Lake." Some teachers might rightly argue that the shift from imitating White to imitating Anzaldua would be an improvement, but we must acknowledge the political implications of autobiography as cultural criticism. Feminist teachers must treat writing in experimental modes as a process of unlearning, a process Lynn Worsham refers to as a "defamiliarization vis-à-vis unquestioned forms of knowledge" (101–2). Thus, reimagining autobiography as cultural criticism necessitates a two-way process of negotiation; students need to critically examine how they are compelled to represent their experience through images and metaphors drawn from larger cultural narratives, myths, and archetypes, thus studying their process of self-signification. Likewise, teachers need to question their expectations for autobiographical writing and examine their modes of reading and evaluating these student texts.

The following questions may serve as a starting point for reconsidering how teachers "interpellate" students as autobiographical subjects: What are ways that students have been disciplined and stylized to produce narratives of personal experience? What sorts of "personal" experiences are "institutionally" sanctioned writing topics? Is autobiographical writing really "liberatory"? What about students who feel oppressed rather than liberated by personal writing, who convolute their experiences, twisting them to suit what they think the teacher wants? What are ways to avoid voyeurism in reading students' "personal" writing? By what criteria does the teacher judge the "honesty" and "authenticity" of the student voice and experience presented in an autobiographical narrative?

While some of us may feel comfortable with evaluating the veracity of students' experiences, others recognize that students may feel obliged to falsely present a singular, essential, authentic self, masking the confusions, contradictions, and partialities of their subjectivities. Indeed, we should not forget that celebrity autobiographies, television movies, and childhood books that present the "rags to riches" story of individual achievement often serve as narrative framing devices for many of our students' "personal stories."

In enacting autobiography as feminist cultural criticism, students must be allowed the pedagogical and linguistic space to see their experiences differently—in larger cultural contexts rather than in individualistic, privatized terms. If autobiography is to work as a form of cultural criticism, writers need to "remain aware of the problematics of both self-representation and representing others" (Hesford, 22), and in doing so, they "may discover ways to make something of what has been made of them" (Worsham, 102). Instead of closing down ambiguity and contradiction in student autobiographies or tuning out voices or experiences we do not understand, feminist writing teachers may have to listen differently, in a different key—a process that asks us to shed some of the more familiar, comfortable pedagogical practices we wear as a second skin.

Notes

1. *Teaching Writing: Pedagogy, Gender, Equity* draws upon two main strands of feminist thought: liberal feminism and cultural feminism. Advocates of liberal feminism wish to achieve gender equity in all aspects of life without radically transforming the social and political system. Liberal feminism foregrounds similarities rather than differences between men and women, emphasizing initiatives that will assist women in achieving equity in the socioeconomic sphere (Flynn 1995, 202). Cultural feminism, according to Linda Alcoff, is "the ideology of a female nature or female essence reappropriated by feminists themselves in an effort to revalidate undervalued female attributes" (408).

2. The shift in composition theory toward social constructionist theories of identity and experience has caused many feminists in composition studies to question the commonly circulated notion that women share common ways of knowing and composing (see Elizabeth Flynn, 1988). Critiques of essentialism in feminist composition studies have begun to appear with increasing frequency, for instance, see Devoney Looser's "Composing as an 'Essentialist'? New Directions for Feminist Composition Theories." Also, see Linda Alcoff and Diana Fuss for a history of the feminist debate over essentialism/constructionism.

Part VI

Genre on Academic Sites
Students, Teachers, and Technologies

Collaborating as editors, as authors in several genres, and with other colleagues in English studies has taught us that our students, in a similar way, need to "write themselves." They need to write about writing, about themselves as newcomers and scared tender souls thrown into the flux of university life and university genres to brazen it out. They have lives. Those lives continually burst through boundaries and dams of English-studies control, to mention just one discipline. In *Howard's End*, E. M. Forster said, "Life demands that we connect the prose and the poetry" (quoted in O'Reilley, 53). For us, considering the classroom as genre and genres of classroom means being drawn into what we teach and residing there more ethically. We do this by helping writing students *situate* themselves and *situate genres*, to borrow from Aviva Freedman. In fact, all the authors in this section share research, teacher-observation, and/or student voices from actual classrooms in ways that ask us to compare the definitional and theoretical discussions in earlier essays with the lived experience of committed teachers in actual classrooms.

Aviva Freedman, for instance, focuses on student success (rather than the unfortunate normal default of student failure), considering how students write in social science and financial analysis classes. Her research finds that writers' success rests on the richness of the discursive contexts and the degree of active learning orchestrated by their classroom instructors. Ruth

Mirtz takes up the territorial metaphor to propose that the "ground" of student writing is not as familiar as we think. She argues against viewing this
textual territory as writings of and by uninitiated, inexperienced, or juvenile
individuals; she recasts student writing as a genre that needs to be studied
and explored—a metagenre—wherein these writers make their meanings.

Brad Peters and Robert Brooke and Dale Jacobs, in two further essays,
return the metaphor of genre and grammar raised by Amy Devitt to classroom locations. Peters shows us students reading the grammars of autobiography and biography. He argues for teaching genre literacy and shows us one
example of how it might be done, and with what results. Brooke and Jacobs
see genre as a social grammar that informs our developing identities as writers. In their classrooms, students tend to explore several genres and to produce reflective writing that is important to their developing sense of self-as-
writer. Michael Kuhne's response to Brooke and Jacobs reminds us that
genres are not a developmental issue—can students master this one or that
one, is this one or that one harder or easier? Instead, genre study provides
the classroom, the teacher, the writers, with a paradoxical richness, a way of
thinking about thinking.

Thus, Michael Spooner and Kathleen Yancey show that classroom
genres, student writing as genre, are all being complicated *by our students,*
whose computer sophistication often outpaces that of their instructors. Their
fluency and fluidity within the complex discursive spaces of the Internet once
again raises the question at its deepest level—what is a text? Is email a
genre? Is email the genre, the ideal location of student writing as metagenre
proposed by Mirtz? Or the place to learn and contest genre grammars as proposed by Peters, by Brooke and Jacobs? Does email tumble us into textual,
intellectual chaos or provide a democratic arena for testing all the definitions
that have plagued and interested the scholar/teachers in this volume? Of
course, Spooner and Yancey don't themselves agree on these issues, but they
do take us into the dialogue, put us into the ether and the action on these
issues. Like all the authors in this section, they ask us to reexamine
definitions, issues, arguments—our practices—in the important light of our
own classrooms.

16

Situating "Genre" and Situated Genres
Understanding Student Writing from a Genre Perspective

Aviva Freedman

Recent reconceptualizations of genre as social action have provided powerful ways of laying open the nature of what is achieved in linguistic transactions whose complexity and sophistication have been occluded because of the tacitness of the processes and the ostensible "normalcy" of the undertakings.

Like the early researchers into language acquisition who unpacked the extraordinary complexity of what and how children learn when they acquire language, recent genre scholars have begun to open our eyes to what is achieved, say, by our own students—who, over the course of a semester or a year, with almost no explicit instruction and with the minimum of fuss, somehow learn to produce written genres whose textual features can be described by linguists as distinct and specialized, although neither our students nor we as teachers have explicit access to the rules according to which these new genres can be parsed. (See, for example, the complex rules governing "novelty" in student writing laid out by Kaufer and Geisler, or Giltrow and Valiquette on discipline-specific criteria for "shared" background knowledge.)

Carl Bereiter pointed out years ago that, as teachers, we are mostly concerned with how our students fall short, while as researchers, the more we uncover the more awed we are by the complexity and sophistication involved in what we deem commonplace. Over a number of years, I have been trying to find a theoretic frame for understanding that remarkable linguistic feat that most of us notice only in its failures. Recent genre studies have provided just such a frame—one that offers insights into both *what* is accomplished through writing "school genres" as well as *how* that feat is accomplished. In this essay, I draw on genre theory to illuminate these two aspects of learning to write new genres (especially school genres): what is learned when the new genres are acquired; and how that learning takes place.

Theoretic Reconceptions of Genre

In a seminal article entitled "Genre as Social Action," Carolyn Miller reconceptualized genre: picking up on notions suggested in the work of Lloyd Bitzer and Kenneth Burke, Miller made the following point: "a rhetorically sound definition of genre must be created not in the substance or the form of discourse but in the *action* it is used to accomplish" (emphasis mine, 152). Genres thus are "typified social actions."

Action implies both situation and motive. Using Bitzer's definition, Miller describes situation as a "complex of persons, events, objects, and relations presenting an exigence that can be allayed through the mediation of discourse" (152). Miller, however, redefines Bitzer's "exigence" by denying its material aspects. She focuses instead on the role of interpretation; exigence is socially constructed, and recurrent situations are those which are socially interpreted as typical. Genres are typified rhetorical actions in response to recurrent situations or situation-types. As to motive, Miller makes an interesting distinction: she distinguishes the social motive of the rhetor in writing the genre, from her private intentions, which may be ill formed or dissembling.

Equally important for the discussion here is Bakhtin's work, naturally. For Bakhtin as linguist, the primary unit of analysis in language is the utterance, rather than the word or sentence; his focus is on language in use in context. Building on the notion of the utterance, his conclusions concur with those of Miller: while "each separate utterance is individual . . . each sphere in which language is used develops its own *relatively stable types* of these utterances. . . . Genres correspond to typical situations of speech communication, typical themes, and consequently also to particular contacts between the *meanings* of words and actual concrete reality under certain typical circumstances" ("Problem," 87).

Bakhtin's discussion extends that of Miller in a number of ways that are particularly productive for understanding school genres. First, he focuses on the textual or linguistic dimensions of the typified situations that form the context of genres: "any utterance is a link in a very complexly organised chain of other utterances." That is, texts are dialogic and intertextual. Second, he acknowledges not only the active and constructive role of the listener/reader, but also the corresponding recognition by the writer/speaker of this fact: "the entire utterance is constructed . . . in anticipation of encountering this response" (94). Interaction is at the heart of the genre. Finally, Bakhtin notes repeatedly that generic forms are "more flexible, plastic, and free" (79) than other forms of language.

One further notion provides crucial theoretic background. In a recent article, Berkenkotter and Huckin develop a model of genre knowledge based, in part, on current notions of situated learning. This set of notions has particularly powerful explanatory force and is discussed in detail in the section "How They Learn."

Research

Because of my involvement in a university writing center, I have been exposed to a wide range of writing elicited in courses across the disciplinary spectrum and have consequently been struck, at an impressionistic level, by two phenomena: the variation in types of writing (depending upon the discipline, and sometimes upon the specific course) as well as the general uniformity among the specific student texts for each context. (Other researchers, such as Herrington, McCarthy, McCarthy and Fishman, Schryer, and Giltrow and Valiquette, have found this same kind of variation.) These impressions led to my involvement in a series of research projects aimed at teasing out the distinctive nature of what was expected in different disciplines/courses and at understanding the processes by which students acquire the knowledge necessary to perform appropriately (see Freedman, "Learning," "Reconceiving," and "Argument," and Freedman, Adam, and Smart).

My research has always entailed at least these two dimensions: close textual analyses of student texts written in response to essay prompts (and where possible, all such texts were analyzed) as well as naturalistic observations of students and classes. The text analyses involved analyses of syntax, lexicon, rhetorical strategies, overall rhetorical structure, and mode of arguing (using Toulmin et al.'s categorizations). The naturalistic research included close observation (and where possible, tape recordings) of classes, observation of seminars and student presentations, extensive interviews with students before, during, and after their composing, regular interviews with professors including think-aloud protocols of instructors responding to student texts, and tape recordings of student collaborative composing sessions (where such collaboration was a natural part of the composing).

For this discussion, I will focus in particular on research conducted on a year-long first year undergraduate social science course (in law), where students were required to write four essays over the year (see also Freedman, "Learning," "Reconceiving," and "Argument"), and an upper-year semester course in financial analysis, where students wrote in response to case studies (Freedman et al. 1994).

The social science course was a year-long course introducing students to basic principles of legal thinking. The 1,500 or so students involved were divided into six large lecture sections for three hours a week, and each lecture session was further divided into seminar groups of twenty students for an additional hour a week of discussion. We audiotaped and observed all the lectures over the course of the academic year, and focused on one seminar group of twenty students, all of whose work was collected. In addition, six student volunteers (four females and two males) were interviewed by us weekly, for an hour or so, about their processes of learning, composing, etc.

The upper-level course was, in contrast, a small seminar class of some thirty-five students, conducted entirely by the course professor for one semester. The classes were similarly observed, the work of all students collected, and a group of three students (two males and a female) was selected for focused interviewing. The course was generally seen as the most difficult in a selective program at the upper levels. The two courses represent two extremes in terms of the Carleton University student body. Canada has a much lower participation rate in postsecondary education than does the United States, and all our institutions are publicly funded, so that there is less differentiation by institution here. On the other hand, Carleton University is committed to a policy of wider accessibility than other institutions, and so our students represent a range of ability levels.

What Was Accomplished Through the Writing

In each case, textual analyses revealed the distinctiveness of the genres elicited in each course (as compared to the writing the same students were doing for other classes over the same year) and pointed as well to the significance of the writing for the learners. Margaret Himley discusses the acquisition of specific genres in the following terms. "We discover new ways to mean, and thus how to participate more fully in the actions of the community. To learn how to write most fundamentally requires learning a social role in an interpretive community" (139–140).

Social Motive

For both the law essays and the case studies written for financial analysis, the social motive was *epistemic*—not in the sense of producing knowledge new to the reader, but rather in the specialized sense of enabling its writer to see and interpret reality in new ways (and, of course, of demonstrating that knowing to the reader, so that the writer might be evaluated on that basis in comparison to other students). Furthermore in that these ways are the ways of currently constituted communities of scholars, the purpose of, and the action undertaken in, such writing is social and cultural as well.

Law Essays

By comparing these essays to all other academic essays written by the same students over the same year, we found that the lexicon was discipline-specific (both in its use of specialized terminology and its use of common words in specialized ways); that its syntax was more complex (more words per T-unit, more clauses per T-unit, more clauses of concession and condition); that its modal use was distinctive; and that the rhetorical structure was characterized by a contrapuntal movement at both micro and macro levels.

Furthermore, the nature of the argumentation was distinct, not only in the nature of the claims and evidence, but in the careful elaboration of the connections among grounds, warrants, and backing, using the categorization specified by Toulmin, Rieke, and Janik. Using such a frame of reference to illuminate the distinctiveness of the law writing, it was apparent that, whereas for most of the other academic writing undertaken by our students, emphasis was laid on presenting a claim and clarifying its implications by pointing extensively to the grounds or specific facts relied on (with the warrants, or the principles for connecting the claims to the grounds, often tacit), the primary focus in the law papers was on specifying the warrants and their backing (or authority) in detail, and on showing how these warrants applied to the grounds. In the end, it mattered less what claim one made as long as the relationship between the various warrants possible to the grounds, accompanied by the appropriate backing, was all laid out.

Also, the warrants drawn on were far more highly formalized, precise, and exact than those in other academic essays. There are precise rules or principles for statute interpretation, and these must be specified in each instance of their use. The following excerpt reveals on the micro level the kind of argumentation that persists through the whole.

> The defence in this case would presumably argue that the wall is not a building by definition. Using *eiusdem generis* (of the same kind) canon of interpretation, it is evident that "building" as seen in section 4 refers to the list in section 3: a house, shed, barn, or other structure, which infers the membership of those structures that can be occupied. Therefore, the exclusion of members of the class, fence and wall, imply that they are not included under the meaning of "building." The elements listed that infer building all imply that one can occupy them. Since one cannot occupy (in the sense that one cannot enter into it and take shelter) a wall, Brown's boundary marker is therefore not applicable for prosecution under this statute.

Traditional analyses might have begun and ended with the articulation of such textual regularities, but recent work on genre studies has broadened our understanding of what is accomplished through such writing. In writing these law essays, the students began to share the stance of, and consequently to affiliate with, those associated with a certain discourse community or argument field: the community of legal scholars or students of law. In their writing, the students not only looked at the kind of phenomena typically analyzed by the discipline; they also used the same lenses. The specialized lexicon reveals that specific phenomena are being examined, classified, and organized according to the classificatory principles involved in the discipline of law studies. As to the increased complexity of the syntax, the longer T-units and the greater number of clauses per T-unit suggest a more intense interest in the hierarchical interrelationships among propositions: specific propositions are seen in the context of others (with relationships of cause, effect, condition, and concession highlighted). This complexity was the syntactic instantiation of the instructor's goal—to get the students "to see the forest rather than just the trees." The law essays were also characterized by a distinctive mode of argumentation involving highly formalized and specialized modes of reasoning. Without suggesting that such modes of reasoning replicated the students' original discovery processes, I am arguing that, at the stage of drafting, the students needed to enact in writing certain modes of reasoning that differed from the modes enacted for other disciplines. In other words, the students' attention was oriented to specific kinds of human activities, and these were addressed in highly specialized ways: not through the analysis of the psychological or social dynamics involved, nor from the perspective of ethics, politics, or aesthetics, but rather from the point of view of the relevance of certain specialized legal principles. Charles Willard has pointed to the social dimensions of such interpretive stances. To use Willard's language, through their writing, these students began "to construe certain phenomena in roughly the same way that other actors in the field [i.e., legal scholars or students of law] construe them" (34).

Finance Papers

Similarly, for the papers in financial analysis, one of the goals for assigning the writing was to have the students affiliate with members of a specific community. Consider the instructor's comments about a flawed paper:

> Here the problem is he's making statements which have no meaning in finance. For example, well it's more English [i.e. English literature]— "keep the dream alive" "faltering economy" "playing havoc with the economy" "its already fragile credit rating." So, it's not the type of thing a chief financial officer would like to read because he has to almost say, "Tell me, what do you mean by 'faltering'? Show me the ratio which tells me this company's faltering. If you cannot show it, don't say that." If he says something like, "For example, looking at the current ratio (x) and the liquidity ratio (y) and interest calculations (z), it seems as if the company would be unable to continue in its present course." Unless he says that, I wouldn't put any faith in his statement "in his faltering company" because he hasn't proved to me it's faltering.

Note the invocation of a figure from the workplace, "a chief financial officer," and the way that the professor slips naturally from what that officer would say to what he, the professor, says.

Textually, obvious features of form and format differentiated these case studies from other academic writing: the first page was an executive summary, there were headings and subheadings, and the text included an appendix consisting of a number of charts that summarized the numerical data. These papers looked like workplace writing. More significant, perhaps, were other more subtle differences. To focus on one, the case studies in the financial analysis course differed from other academic papers in *that* they used numbers and in *how* they used numbers—i.e., in ways that differed from those in accounting and economics courses. "In accounting cases," according to the professor, "you simply have to consolidate a balance sheet," whereas "the quantitative stuff [in the financial analysis course] requires some judgement. . . . Here there is a lot of interpretation." And the interpretation is always expressed verbally. In other words, the case studies always involved verbal interpretations of numeric phenomena. As to economics, the writing assignments for that discipline were characterized by an alternation in the text between verbal discourse and mathematical discourse: that is, between sentences and equations. In the case studies, numbers occur *within* sentences— generally as part of subject or object noun-phrases: i.e., the numbers are expressed in a *linguistic*, not a mathematical syntax. As we have argued elsewhere (Freedman et al. 1994), when numbers are absorbed into verbal syntax—within sentences rather than equations—the numbers become assimilated to the commonsense version of reality associated with verbal discourse, while the representation of reality thus entailed is correspondingly imbued with an illusion of greater precision and factuality.

The categorization of the elements of argument developed by Toulmin, Janik, and Rieke proved equally revealing in differentiating the case studies. Particularly distinctive were the kinds of claims made, and the ways of justifying such claims—that is, in the latter case, both the nature of the grounds or evidence adduced as well as the kinds of warrants connecting the grounds to the claims. The claims, warrants, grounds, and the interrelationships among them were all consistent with the economic model of human behavior—a model based on rational expectation and utility maximization. The various textual features already cited—the numbers assimilated into the verbal syntax, the stripping away of emotive and noneconomic values, the specific warrants entailed—derive from and re-create value systems and ideologies that focus on the profit motive and market forces. Further, they valorize a rational self-interest model of human behavior, on the one hand, and technicorational processes, on the other. In writing these texts, students assumed certain stances to reality that were privileged in the discipline of finance and in the related financial worlds.

How They Learned

How did the students learn these new genres? In our research, the negative evidence was clear-cut. They certainly did not imitate models. In neither course were the course texts appropriate models for their writing: in the law course, one course text consisted of documents (like the Magna Carta), and the second presented an introductory overview to legal studies, whose rhetorical organization and purpose was distinct from that of the student essays, and whose language and syntax proved to be far *less* complex than any that the students used. (See Freedman, "Argument," for precise comparisons.) As to the course in finance, the textbook consisted entirely of case histories. In addition, the students consulted no examples of successful student writing to guide their work, even when they knew such examples were available (see Freedman, "Argument").

Furthermore, there was no explication of rules or discussions of the nature of the genre by course instructors or teaching assistants—except with reference to gross features of format, like the need to include an executive summary or tables.

Situated Learning

A powerful model for understanding how this learning is achieved is provided by the literature on situated learning—a literature that Carol Berkenkotter and Thomas Huckin have already pointed to as consonant with genre theory.

A key point in this literature, and one that is consistent with our observations, is that what is entailed for the teacher is "not giving a discrete body of abstract knowledge ... [but rather] the skill to perform by *actively engaging* in the process" (Thomas Hanks). To be more specific, central to this literature are the notions that learning (and knowing) are context-specific, that learning is accomplished through processes of coparticipation, and that cognition is socially shared. Social sharing is understood in two senses: as Hanks writes, "human minds develop in social situations" and they "use the tools and presentational media that culture provides to support, extend, and reorganise mental functioning."

For our purposes, two key dimensions of such learning can be presented as a) collaborative performance by a guide and learner and b) mediation of this learning through cultural tools (and especially language).

The literature on children's language acquisition is rich with examples of collaborative performance. The mother sits with the young child to look at a storybook, and they read the book together. Over time, the child takes over more and more of the activity—from initially simply holding the book jointly; to turning the pages; to pointing to "relevant" parts of the picture (and learning what is relevant is important); to learning how to make a relevant comment about the picture—until the child, perhaps at the age of three, is able to sit alone and turn the pages of a book on her own, pointing and commenting appropriately as she goes. Barbara Rogoff describes the nature of the interaction as "guided participation," while Jerome Bruner (1978) and Courtney Cazden have used the term "scaffolding" to get at the way in which the adult collaborates with and supports the child's learning, gradually giving over more and more of the task to the child until autonomy is achieved.

In many ways, what goes on at university is very much like what goes on when mother and child sit to read storybooks together, where the mother plays a delicately staged supportive role that gradually enables the child to read alone. To a large extent, it was this kind of guidance and scaffolding that was offered by the instructor in the courses we observed. The "guide" in both cases, caretaker and teacher, is oriented entirely to the "learner" and to the learner's learning. In fact, the activity is being undertaken primarily for the sake of the learner. Not only is the guide's attention focused on the learner, but the whole social context is shaped and organized by the guide for the sake of the learner (recognizing that each such context is itself located in some larger institution whose goals are also at play—Family, University, Capitalist Society, etc.). The caretaker has organized the story-time experience, and the instructor orchestrates the course (within certain temporal, spatial, organizational constraints): readings are assigned, lectures are delivered, seminars may be organized, working groups may be set up, assignments are specified—all geared toward enabling the learners to learn certain material.

An illustrative example is the course in financial analysis. At the beginning of the course, the instructor assigned cases to be written up at home and then he himself modeled in class appropriate approaches to the data, identifying key issues and specifying possible recommendations for action. As they attempted to write up the cases themselves at home, the students were "extremely frustrated" because "you have to do a case before you have the tools to know how to do it." "It's like banging your head against a wall." However, the modeling in class—especially *in the context of their struggles to find meaning in the data themselves*—gradually enabled them to make such intellectual moves themselves. At the beginning, "when he would tell us the real issue, we're like—'where did that come from?'" Then, "When you're done and he takes it up in class, you finally know how to do it!"

Like the mother with the storybook, the instructor showed the students first where to look and then what to say. He picked out the relevant data from the information in the case. He constructed arguments, using the warrants and based on the values and ideology valorized in the discipline. Later in the course, he provided corrective feedback to students making oral presentations. Gradually students were inducted into the ways of thinking, that is, the ways of construing and interpreting phenomena, valued in that discipline.

These processes of collaborative performance offer part of the answer to how the students learned to write the genres expected of them. There is, in addition, an essential second dimension: situated learning involves cultural mediation—especially through use of semiotic tools such as language. Thus each instructor sets up a rich discursive context—through lectures and through readings—and through the mediation of these signs, the students learn to engage appropriately in the assigned activities. James Wertsch, drawing on Mikhail Bakhtin, talks of the power of dialogism, and of echoing (or ventriloquating) social languages and speech genres. In all the classes that we observed, the students responded—ventriloquistically—to the readings and classroom discourse, in that they picked up (and transformed in the context of their preexistent conversational patterns) the social language or register they heard. Here are oral samples culled from the students' conversational interchanges as they worked together producing their report.

> I guess the biggest thing is the debt-to-equity ratio. Notice that? X has way more equity. If you look at Y, their equity compared to their debts is nowhere near, it's not even in the ballpark.

In writing their papers, the conversational syntax and lexicon disappeared, as the social language of the finance class was absorbed into the register of formal academic written language that the students had already mastered, modified of course in crucial ways in each course—for example, by the kinds of modalities in operation, the lines of reasoning, and the syntactic operations entailed.

Teaching Implications

I began this chapter by referring to Carl Bereiter's observations about the different stances taken by researchers and teachers viewing the same acts: the former are filled with awe at what learners have accomplished, the latter with chagrin at how far short many still fall.

Most of us play dual roles, as teachers and researchers, and in deference to our roles as teachers, I will add the following comments. First, if my stance, for most of this chapter, has been like that of Bereiter's researcher, my motive for taking on this perspective has been equally affected by teacherly concerns: it behooves us as teachers to remind ourselves from time to time of the complexity and the extraordinary sophistication of what our students do, even those who fall short. In addition, I would argue that this socially oriented model of student writing is of more than theoretic interest: that is, it has implications for teaching, and in particular it can help to account for both success and failure. (For more detailed discussion of the pedagogic implications, see Freedman, "Show," "The What.")

The good news is that evidence from the many research studies cited seems to suggest that we are doing something right, however unconsciously —at least in the context of discipline-specific writing. (See Freedman and Pringle, Freedman, "Argument" for a critique of composition class writing.) The success of these teaching events seems to depend on two things: the richness of the discursive context established by each instructor (through reading, lecturing, talking, and writing); and the degree to which the instructor is able to engage the learner actively in carefully orchestrated, cued, and subtly directed processes.

At the same time, of course, there are failures—whose importance may be exaggerated by the teacher as evaluator, but whose existence cannot be denied. A possible reason for such failures is lack of sufficient exposure to the relevant context. The degree of necessary exposure varies by individual of course, but students already familiar with similar discursive contexts will be at an advantage. Issues of cultural proximity are thus highlighted, where cultural distance is created by socioeconomic factors, gender differences, minority status, or cross-cultural differences. Some of this may be compensated for by enriching the context further, and by more extensive intervention through collaborative performance by student and instructor.

In addition, genre studies recognize both the power and responsibility of the learner as well as the political and ideological issues often at play. Issues of identity, resistance, subversion, and power are foregrounded. The learner must want to take on this identity—however temporarily—and must feel that in doing so, there is no betrayal of other allegiances. Some students learn to resist and others to subvert the genres valorized and elicited in their contexts (see Green and Lee).

Conclusion

Both the processes and products of acquiring new genres then, are profoundly social. Through processes of social participation and cultural mediation, students are enabled to take on new perspectives, associated with the ways of being and knowing within specific communities. Through the writing the students take on new subject-positions, and in that respect, even new identities. But we must not make too much of this. The identities and subject-positions are best understood as "personae" or masks. Perhaps the best metaphor for the university, especially in this postmodern age, is that of the shopping mall, where students don and doff the clothes available—to see which they are prepared to buy; whether they will wear these clothes, when, how often, and for how long is yet to be determined.

17

The Territorial Demands of Form and Process
The Case for Student Writing as a Genre

Ruth M. Mirtz

Current writing instruction often preaches the good news of student writing as a legitimate form of discourse which should be foregrounded in writing classrooms as models and celebrated as meaningful to a wide audience. However, we writing instructors have difficulty thinking about how student texts as a form or genre could or should entail other changes in how we teach writing. The fact that several of my students each semester call their journals (informal personal, exploratory writing) "papers" and their papers (essays, research reports, letters) "journals" tells me that I'm not always conveying even the simplest of distinctions about products or genres.

This vagueness about genre in writing classrooms is partly the result of a territorial battle of pedagogies: products, genres, and modes are seen as the domain of teacher-centered, formula-oriented teaching, while process, substance, and experience are seen as the domain of student-centered, process-oriented teaching. Form-finding and genre-knowledge are bound to be at war within writing instruction until we see the genre of student writing not as contested territory but as unexplored territory.

The difficulty that process pedagogy has in defining student writing as a legitimate, rather than illegitimate, genre has several sources. Competing definitions of genre and process cause one of the tensions. The question of genre assumes the need to know conventions, style, formats, and products, or a kind of "knowing-that." Amy Devitt points out that "whether called genres, subgenres, or modes, whether comprehensive or selective, whether generally accepted or disputed, these systems for classifying texts focus attention on static products.... Traditional genre study has meant study of textual features that mark a genre: the meter, the layout, the organization, the level of diction, and so on" (1993, 574–75). In addition, James Slevin argues that the "literary appropriation of rhetoric" has made the study of genre a kind of text or product analysis and not an analysis of how writers use genre as they write (6–7). This emphasis on immovable, insoluble conventions in the history of traditional genre studies keeps most teachers at a distance, even though questions of genre at all levels (sentence structure, paragraph organization, essay formats) should naturally fit into the writing process as part of rhetorical awareness or part of the conventions of literate and/or academic discourse, as a kind of "knowing-how."

In my own writing courses, generic choices largely rest in the authority of my self as the teacher, as part of the "assignment," instead of as part of the writing process. For instance, I ask my first-year students to develop their own subjects, explore what they have to say, but I assign a personal essay. I reason that I need to emphasize a range of writerly roles, student-teacher relationships, collaboration, and the recursiveness of invention and revision (all important goals), and that I need to avoid the overemphasis on product and performance that previous (current traditional) writing instruction in genre produced. So I may teach organization and structure as one part of the writing process or the rhetorical situation, but I do not consistently help students with the fight between self-expression and the demands of form that will likely engage most students as they write that personal essay.

Part of the problem lies with our unexamined belief that genre is merely a set of textual conventions. Unlike grammatical conventions with which our students have extensive sophisticated experience on a daily basis, generic conventions (so we believe) have to be "taught," correct and incorrect formats must be presented, a list of essential parts checked off as accomplished. I have heard myself argue that my students will learn about genres when they have a job and have a reason to learn them: the appropriate purpose and structure of an interoffice memo will be apparent to them when their job requires them to write one, because it's just a matter of following the format and formula. Another approach toward genre in college courses is to teach the "essay," its history, variations, and special advantages and disadvantages in the hope that advanced knowledge about one genre will transfer to all other genres (see Haefner for a more effective version of this approach). Neither of these rationalizations, however, nor the traditional definitions of genres, is complex enough to deal with the levels of form-finding going on in student writing.

The peculiar competition between genre and process is absolutely concrete when I work to remove any traces of mode-generated course design in any of the courses I teach while not replacing it with any genre-oriented instruction. Since I agree with Robert J. Connors that the "describe-narrate-define-compare-argue" sequence is "divorced from the composition process," bears no relationship to what writers do, how thinkers think, or how writing is produced in the world outside of the classroom (1981, 20), I do my best to devise assignments that don't depend on this sequence. I design assignments that depend more on a sequence of questions about language, investigations into what writers do and how language works, individual and collaborative inquiry into the values and struggles of postadolescents and/or the human condition.

However, in my enthusiasm to eradicate leftover modes from an increasingly process-oriented pedagogy, nothing in what remains deals with form or genre. As "current" as I'd like to think my ideal pedagogy is, I also know that I've eliminated what was ineffective without replacing it with a sufficiently radical pedagogy of genre. In other words, while I'm convinced that modal instruction does not own the territory of genre, I've refused to let process pedagogy own that territory either. Countless new texts are published each year with the modes as the organizing principle for student writing and reading rather than genres, forms, or formats, despite Connors's prediction in 1981 that "the only teachers still making real classroom use of the modes are those out of touch with current theory" (1981, 19). Without rethinking the place of questions and practices about genre and the larger forms and formats of language, we will continue to teach format and formula (or ignore both), instead of teaching form-finding.

Devitt claims that genre needs a closer association with form, so that aim and context, purpose and situation are as important as format and formula (1993, 576). A new definition of genre may help us rethink our questions about that closer association. If we define genre as Aviva Freedman and Peter Medway do, as "typical ways of engaging rhetorically with recurring situations" and believe that part of the act of writing is "using generic resources to act effectively on a situation through a text" (*Learning,* 2, 11), we are led to ask our students the question "Does your solution for this problem require a letter or a feature article in your hometown paper or a postcard to your senator in Washington, D.C., or a story for children?" But that question is difficult to ask when we see questions of genre as a matter of forms dictated rather than forms to be found and when we see student writing as a nongenre itself in a field where genre is not an important issue.

The potential for systematically teaching genre as a writing issue, as a part of the form-finding process of meaning-making, is enormous. Form-finding is a verb, a process, which holds all the recursiveness and inventiveness that process pedagogy seeks to emphasize. And yet critics have noticed the lack of attention to genre or forms of any kind in process pedagogy (see Berthoff 1981, and Slevin, for instance). I believe how we view student writing keeps us from merging form-finding into the writing processes we teach.

Why Viewing Student Writing as a Genre Might Change How We Teach Genre

While current writing instruction pays lip service to student writing as a legitimate form of discourse, our research and scholarship assumes that student writing, especially that of first-year writers, is either a) "uninitiated," which implies a need for rules and insider information; b) "inexperienced," which implies that time, practice, and apprenticeship are mostly the answer to writing problems; or c) "juvenilia," which assumes that immature students become masterful writers when they are older and have more to say. And unfortunately, if a student is not an English major or does not continue to graduate school, these models result in stunted growth when no "adult" or "experienced" texts are forthcoming.

One premise of my argument here is that current traditional and literary critical theory still hold us to a view of student writing as an inferior genre of nongeneric novice writing. Student papers are considered an outside kind of writing, a nongenre. Robert Scholes pointed out a decade ago that composition is considered a "pseudo-non-literature," denigrated because it is not interpreted and because its production is sweat and revision and procrastination rather than divine visits from the muse. Student writing is teachable but not consumable (1985, 5–7).

What if we regard student writing as "experimental" or "knowledge-making" to characterize the *need* to learn through the production of this discourse, the emphasis on change (in the writer and the text) rather than stability and performance, and the exploratory nature of both form and content for student writing? Among the characteristics of "knowledge-making" (student) writing, which I have heard called "think-pieces," are these: it always has a language-learning purpose or aim at its inception; it always has an effect on the writer in terms of learning something new about the writer's self or experiences or beliefs; it is always attached to a process dialogue (metawriting about how the text came about and was responded to, what the writer learned from the text); it is not always well polished at the sentences and editing level, perhaps not even finished in the strict sense; it may include handwritten notations, and therefore is not easily typeset. (Some texts written by people who are normally considered "professional" writers might or might not fit this description.) The most thoughtful student writing I see (and ask for) has exactly those characteristics. One advantage to viewing student writing as a separate, new genre is that writing-in-progress is then elevated to a legitimate product in itself. More assignments in writing classes can be directed toward learning and less toward finishing or coming to closure, exactly the goals of process pedagogy. Textbooks for students could be filled with these "think-pieces" and the accompanying process narratives. Instruction might move away from the undefined, unauthored form of writing that is so much of student writing. By only redefining the product, however, we allow ourselves to continue our neglect of form-finding and the questions that writers ask themselves about form. We can continue to assign and accept the amorphous or unconstructed kind of student writing that students call their "papers."

We need, therefore, to go further; we need to think of student writing as a "metagenre," a kind of experimental, knowledge-building writing which contains many other kinds of writing. M. M. Bakhtin describes primary and secondary genres in "The Problem of Speech Genres" as simple and spoken forms of language and complex and primarily written (literary) forms of language, respectively (61–62). Student writing contains both of these levels of genres, but has institutional requirements (such as the "mastery of academic discourse") and extrainstitutional resistance (such as collection of a whole dormitory floor's papers on one hard drive to facilitate borrowing of text) that move it to a tertiary genre. Student writing has overarching purposes that mediate and influence and construct genre choices for students in ways different from professional writers. This is partly what I mean, then, by "metagenre."

If students' attempts at letters, short stories, personal essays, etc., as a metagenre are specially characterized by experiment and change in ways that regular genres are not, then form-finding necessarily remains a central issue in the classroom, a means for form to become process and process to become form. For instance, the question of "how I might say this" becomes a helpful part of the drafting process instead of a question to avoid until after drafting. The forms we use to create knowledge (such as metaphor, emotion, and story) become part of the writing process. Established genres such as a lab report, a short story, and the personal essay become part of an array of choices contained in each writing process. Genre choices are generated by the student, rather than by a curriculum, an artificial sequence of activities, or the requirement of an assignment.

Process pedagogy, then, offers a way to transform the nongenre of student writing, not just into a genre, but into a metagenre. It can turn powerful and power-enacting language experiences into form-finding and reveal the form-finding generic resources that exist within a repertoire of writing processes. Teaching form-finding requires new metaphors, and new questions, and courage. In a plea for "curricular courage" many years ago, James Murphy described what it takes to reexamine the past and ask the "shocking" questions: it means thinking the unthinkable (10–11). One way to think the presumably unthinkable is with new metaphors. Ann E. Berthoff suggests several metaphors for reconceptualizing form—from organic processes such as gardening, from observation and seeing ("the logic of the eye"), and from craft (patterning, designing, whittling, darning) (103–105). These new metaphors force new constructions on us as we think about form: "Construing and constructing: at the heart of both reading and writing is interpretation, which is a matter of seeing what goes with what, how this goes with that" (168).

The language of craftsmen and craftswomen may be particularly well suited to questions of genre since crafts are characterized by well-known and recognizable forms, always accompanied by the craftsperson's special interpretation or variation (quilts, for example). Berthoff's suggestions reassure and encourage us: we don't have to start from scratch as we change our questions, our metaphors, and our conception of student writing.

In summary, if we continue to see student writing as a nongenre or as only genre practice, then form-finding will not become a part of the writing processes we want our students to experience and to think though in powerful ways. If, however, we see student writing as a metagenre of writing based both on "learning-how" and "learning-that," and if we investigate the genuine forms of student-oriented writing that already exist, then we don't have to "teach" genre as a set of conventions. We can set our students to investigating real-world or "naturalistic" genres as an organic part of many kinds of form-finding in writing processes.

Student Writing as Metagenre: Implications

With a definition of student writing that highlights its special characteristics, teaching form-finding becomes more than presenting models or prompts: it means changing the way we look at student writing, what we ask for, and how we ask questions. Following are some lines of inquiry for writing instructors, researchers, and theorists to consider. The list is by no means exhaustive, but it suggests some implications of viewing student writing as metagenre.

1. We can learn more about form and genre. We can study more knowledge-making genres and the forces that create subgenres. For example, we can further explore Carol Berkenkotter and Thomas Huckin's notion of "activity-based" genre knowledge (1993), as well as James Slevin's, Peter Elbow's (1991), and David Bartholomae's (1985) diverging concepts of academic discourse as genre knowledge. We can explore the conflict between Bakhtinian conceptions of genre as a response to language situations and Foucaultian conceptions of genre as "institutional constraints." Form-finding requires asking the questions these thinkers are asking: Do we learn about genre from writing or from reading or from acting? What genres do students use in academic discourse? How do the genres of academic discourse relate to nonacademic discourse genres? How do the expectations of audience and assumptions about conventions affect a writer's behavior? How does genre generate and/or limit language? Much has been done already in these areas, but viewing student writing as metagenre opens up additional avenues.

   In addition to learning from other academics, we can learn about genre by asking students what they know and believe about forms and forming. For instance, a student's description of her writing process for a class assignment shows a certain engagement with form:

I first made a cluster of everything I could say or knew about P&G [Procter and Gamble]. Then I sat down and wrote a draft about why P&G should be boycotted and then I thought about narrowing it down to three main reasons and wrote a section for each of these. I then revised it and put in a list of P&G products that should be boycotted. Then I wrote a letter to Governor Chiles, thereby changing my focus from consumer to politician and narrowed my topic to concentrate on the problem in Perry Cause by P&G. The letter probably took the most energy because I had to go back and remember the format for a business letter. I deleted from the paper some of the technical details that only confused people and included only the details that were completely relevant to the paper and of course the paper changed formats when I wrote the letter and it changed its focus point. . . .

This student clearly discusses issues of genre that arose as she narrowed her focus, clarified her envisioned audience, and recalled the standard format for a business letter. These rare occasions when a standard writing assignment is complicated and questioned by genre issues convince me that we can engage student writing as/in generic choices. But as we do so, we will have further questions: What knowledge about genre and form do students come to college with? What writing activities and experiences will provoke their learning? Does the student's response above show what we want students to be able to describe about forming language? Does most students' lack of concern about genre indicate a lack of generic resources, an indifference to issues of forms, or something else?

3. We can develop a philosophy of writing that includes the writing our students do as worthwhile in its own right; that is, stop assigning the amorphous "student essay" with no expectations of form-related struggles and start asking students what kind of product would be most appropriate to get their message or meaning across to someone else or what would be most useful to them as thinkers. We've made great strides in understanding how writers compose and don't compose, but we've paid too little attention to questions of genre, probably because in the universities we feel forced or may actually be forced to rush to questions of mechanics and editing as soon as a draft takes shape. We need to create space and time for students to explore form-finding.

Susan Miller damns composition programs that teach "process for its own sake," programs in which "expectations within . . . courses or of . . . students are not clearly linked to writing the students do for themselves in other settings" and serve to replicate traditional literary subjectivities rather than "the full, highly political experience of an external world" (1991, 94). We may be able to answer Miller's condemnation with three changes. First, we can ask for self-consciously exploratory writing or "think-pieces" and develop those texts as legitimate writerly texts. Second, we can ask students to collect, analyze, and practice peculiarly student-oriented forms of discourse, such as the written portion of teacher evaluations, the essay question on exams, letters to the editor in the campus newspaper, and protest manifestos. Certainly as a starting place for asking questions about products, these student-genres make student writing practical and purposeful beyond the grade and the course credit. And third, we can perceive our students' attempts at real-world genres as a kind of metagenre with its own goals and needs.

3. We can stop rejecting the teaching of genre as another version of teaching the modes and develop a more coherent pedagogy of genre. We'd have to truly invest in process teaching, emotionally, financially, and politically. Part of that investment requires admitting that we're afraid to talk about products and that form and genre make us think of products rather than process. As Ken Macrorie writes, "It's not enough to talk about *process* without bringing the *product*, or evidence, to the courtroom" (1994, 69).

    Sending students to investigate a form of writing like the five-paragraph academic personal statement for job applications, or a lab report for biology, or a letter asking for a refund on a defective appliance teaches them about genre while not teaching them conventional forms. I'm not advocating that we go back to writing "cases" for students or giving them models to imitate, but I do think we must ask questions about products within the writing process. Instead of devising assignments that specify the murky genre of "student essay," ask students to conduct what James Slevin calls for: "a critical study of academic genres, a study that questions them as well as masters them, indeed masters them by both writing within them and contextualizing them" (16). For example, what are the explicit and implicit purposes of a personal statement? How and why do writers deal with one-draft texts? How do you learn to write letters to the editor when you receive no feedback? What cultural and rhetorical assumptions do five-paragraph themes encourage? Slevin says this kind of study is necessary because it's "consistent with how we really learn" and because students "need not so much to be told about and practice *our* understanding of academic genres . . . as to participate in their making, examining critically, on their own, the nature of those genres and the generic basis for thinking, reading and writing . . ." (16). Students themselves can think through what form might reach the audience they want to change through their writing.

Conclusion: Mapping the Metagenre

Our scholarship on genre, as this book attests, far outstrips our teaching; that is, most of us pretend first-year students don't need to study genre as a helpful concept or as part of a writing process. Not confronting the tension between form and process (either in our classrooms or in our curriculum or in our educational goals) devalues the concept of genre, confuses students, and continues our separation of (genre) theory from (genre) practice. Our less thoughtful classroom practices result in mixed messages to students about what and why they are writing. Ann Berthoff's call to define meaning-making as "form finding form" (1981, 168) and James Slevin's invitation to engage our students in critical challenges of forms of discourse (14) need to be heeded as writing instructors continue to stake out a greater territory for process pedagogy. If our metaphors for describing the dispute between form and process change, then our roles as teachers and students change, too. We can become readers of the "lay of the land" of genre and student writing while we record like map makers what we learn.

18

Genre, Antigenre, and Reinventing the Forms of Conceptualization

Brad Peters

I. Two Responses to an Exam

For three weeks, students in a college sophomore composition class had joined me in reading *The U.S. Invasion of Panama*. *Invasion* is a collaboratively written book that largely analyzes the December 20, 1989 military assault from a Panamanian perspective. They had discussed and written about the book's apparently anti-U.S. stance. They'd investigated U.S. media coverage, conducted interviews, and listened to an army sergeant from ROTC recount his participation in the venture. No one had responded passively. Some rejected the book's message out of hand. Others accepted it reluctantly. Still others didn't know exactly what to think: the issues surrounding it sounded too complex.

Time had arrived for the midterm exam. Students knew the focus of the exam beforehand. Each had prepared four chapters to explicate in terms of argumentative techniques. They had a specific format to follow: How might the book's techniques persuade a Latin American reader? How might such a reader summarize the overall argument of the text? What three points in any chosen chapter might this Latin American reader find most compelling? What three points might seem fallacious? How would such a reader's reaction compare to the students' own, as they'd discussed those reactions in class?

A young woman I shall call Brenda—one of two Black students in the class—included the following passage in her response:

> First of all I would like to share something that was said during one of my interviews [with a male relative who'd served in the armed forces] concerning *The Invasion of Panama*. "You have a lot of prejudiced whites that have guns in their hands. Hey, this is their chance to blow them off a nigger!"

199

> ... In trying to think as a Latin American, I would believe excerpts
> [from the chapter "Racism Was Central to the Invasion"] by Albert Barrow
> the most persuasive. ... Back in 1907, the U.S. went as far as to "structure
> a gold and silver payroll system. White laborers [on the Canal] were paid
> in gold currency, non-whites ... silver. They both drank from different
> water fountains, lived in separate barracks ..." (Barrow 81). This identifies
> that the U.S. as a whole system has brought prejudiced acts into Panama
> before. Who's to say that isn't what they did in the war? ... "U.S. troops
> carried out five major raids in the Republic of Panama ... Those five neigh-
> borhoods are inhabited by hundreds of thousands of Blacks, Mestizos and
> Mulattos" (Barrow 82). Everyone in the world pretty much knows about the
> racism that has always trailed the United States. It is only probable cause to
> believe that the U.S. is bringing racism to Panama ... when the U.S.
> brought someone in to take the place of Noriega. ...

Brenda had earlier remained silent while most of the others in class
vehemently protested Barrow's chapter as an example of extensive fallacious
reasoning. Not before the exam, it seems, did she have a format for framing
and expressing the dissent that her silence represented. The exam enabled her
to organize her understanding of the chapter, the protests of her classmates,
and the implications of her interviewee's comments. Just so, the exam took
her beyond her classroom experience and beyond the personal awareness that
her interview had heightened, to a sharper, more disturbing conceptualization
of how racism might shape and direct international relations.

Bill Cope and Mary Kalantzis agree that writers such as Brenda can use
"a knowledge of genre and grammar to find [their] own voice" (89). By
"genre," Cope and Kalantzis mean "a category that describes the relation of
the social purpose of text to language structure" (2). By "grammar," they
mean the conventions that identify a specific genre for its readers. For
instance, I identify the midterm exam as a genre whose instructions delineated its grammar, so as to "provide the tools for discourse critique, for
understanding the ideological loadings in language" (85). Consequently, the
genre approach that the exam represented gave Brenda a more effective
gauge to assess what she'd learned. She recognized the grammar of the exam
as a way to critique the book. But more important, it was a way to critique
her classmates' predominating discourse about the book, from a position that
had otherwise marginalized and silenced her. That position coincidentally put
her in allegiance with the Latin American reader whom the exam had
required her to imagine.

Actually, I was a bit surprised that such a traditional and frequently
unnerving genre as an exam had invited such results from Brenda. But maybe
it did because it did not decontextualize the site of conflict: the classroom.
Instead, it kept Brenda in mind of the social situation where her dissent-
ing insights about the book would have been panned or ignored. Moreover,

without the immediate grammatical support and exigencies which the exam presented to her, she might have dismissed the more global problems of race and empire, which her own experience in discussion had reflected in a small and personal, but very telling, fashion.

This study explores ways in which knowledge of genres and their attendant grammars helps students to form concepts about issues they deem important. However, the study also examines how such knowledge helps students to conceptualize not only "within genres, but across, between and around genres," because oftentimes, "Those who are really innovative and really powerful are those who break conventions, not those who reproduce them" (Cope and Kalantzis, 89, 15). Another student's response to the *Invasion of Panama* exam will illustrate.

Rita tailored the format of the exam to meet slightly different needs. She began with a statement of purpose: "I want to introduce you as the reader to my close friend, Maria . . . a native Latin American. . . . Due to her differing views from my own, I will allow her to explain her viewpoints personally." Rita went on to write from "Maria's" fictional perspective:

> The U.S. government claims to have been performing a "Just Cause" of wiping out drug trafficking; however, there is little support behind the indictments made, and the tragedies and devastation they left behind are not comparable to the drug problem that was previously and currently occurring. The U.S. is a selfish country which hides behind an admirable façade.

Once Rita completed the rhetorical analysis required by the exam, she dropped the "Maria" persona and took up her own in the form of a letter to Maria. She wrote:

> Dear Maria,
>   I appreciate your viewpoint. . . . Unfortunately, it was the [U.S. government's] motives that the American people were ignorant of . . . drugs were definitely a façade for the true motives. . . . I will be more careful in the future to look closely into the media for such "demonization" tactics as were used during the invasion.

Rita's response to the exam format is what I identify as an "antigenre." An antigenre often reconstitutes the voice of the writer and reinvents a grammar that functionally satisfies the social purpose of the genre it resists. Antigenres may appear in student writing when the student associates an assigned genre with a particular ideology or rhetorical technique that makes her uneasy. Or it may occur when the writer feels a need to conceptualize and articulate what she knows about a topic in a new way. In Rita's case, the exam format might have seemed too prescriptive to help her make sense of a Panamanian's perception of North Americans and the uncomfortable perception she had of herself as a result. Her response to the exam resonated with her contributions to class discussions, and clearly entailed an evolving concept of literacy—one that called upon her to discern when information might be withheld from her, and when it might be manipulated to misrepresent or mask the truth.

If we accept Cope's and Kalantzis's assertion that a grammar must be functional so that students may construct genres as social acts and conceptualize issues more profoundly, how do we go about helping them to acquire—rather than acquiesce to—the grammar of a genre? From this perspective, most effective writing assignments would not occur under the peculiar circumstances of exams. Even exams don't always provide an explicit grammar, but usually rely on the students' apprehensions of what the teacher-as-examiner expects. A. L. Becker says a functional grammar of any genre needs to be developed from the premise that "The real *a prioris* of language are not underlying structures, but prior language, prior texts" (see Swales, 86). The acquisition—*not* the prescription—of a grammar ought to be based upon ". . . a set of differentiated, sequenceable goal-directed activities drawing upon a range of cognitive and communicative procedures" (Swales, 76).

In the account to come, I review certain goal-directed activities that occurred during two semesters—one of freshman and one of sophomore composition. These activities represent key moments in the acquisition of rudimentary grammars for three different, but interrelated genres: autobiography and cultural critique for the freshmen, and biography for the sophomores. Student commentary will supplement my review of activities, as well as my brief analyses of writing samples. I hope to address a number of questions that I think are pertinent to the cognitive effects of a genre approach in writing instruction.

II. Constructing a Dialectic of Self

Perhaps the most useful approach to autobiography is one that initially defines the genre as a form of exploratory discourse that examines a writer's highly subjective assertions about her world, "a dialectic of the self with self" which leads to "the examined life—the objectivized life—consisting only of those assertions that can withstand the critique of others" (Crusius, 73, 28). Yet every semester, freshmen remind me that they entertain their own notions of autobiography. One student described it as "a bunch of facts in chronological order . . . boring to read and boring to write." How was I to coax such a student to shed his idea of the chronological strait-jacket, so as to put on the nether garments of dialectic?

The class activities began with a series of reading responses to anthologized essays that contained autobiographical elements. The students chose their own reading selections according to topics such as self-image, family, gender education, and social/political values. We conducted what I call prewriting discussions, organized around voluntarily shared, impromptu writing on questions relevant to the more structured reading responses. The prewriting discussions—which suggested a grammatical principle for comparing or contrasting personal experiences with those of others as well as the authors they selected—thus helped the students to pool together the influences of their similar and dissimilar backgrounds. Combined with the workshopping activities they carried out when they shared their drafted reading responses, this approach got them beyond the often narcissistic attention autobiography can place upon the self.

The students' personal connections to what the anthology authors had to say frequently led to surprising insights. For instance, one young woman realized:

> The essays inspired me to experiment with role playing. I had been several different women. I was the career woman that needed no man. I was the family woman that needed no career. Neither of these positions fit me to a tee so I thought of a woman that does it all. The "Renaissance Woman."

The student's perception of the autobiographer as role-player rather than chronicler of events helped her to understand, quite literally, how a grammar of that genre names the self and categorizes it. She found that naming and categorizing situates the writer in a larger world and shapes her stance toward it—an exciting discovery that inevitably projects its effect on others in that world, as she learned in composing her letter.

In reflecting upon his experiential connection to one of the reading selections, another student sagely observed: "Spoken English and written English are totally different. Even if it is a story that you have told a thousand times, when you go to put it on paper and try to incorporate details that you take for granted, it is tough. . . ."

Details of autobiographical writing—whether descriptive, psychological, emotive, informative, or other—require a complexity of governing rules that are best acquired from actual oral and written practice among listeners and readers who will offer feedback. Of course, workshopping helped, because it included classmates hearing as well as reading their written work to each other.

But the students needed other activities to help them formulate principles dealing with the disparate *and* interrelated links between writing and speaking. One such activity seemed particularly useful. Students visualized a place that was important to them. They used the eye of their memory to reconstruct the physical details. They also recalled emotional and experiential details that they associated with the place. Then, after practicing this meditation, they were invited to write what their memories had retrieved. Upon doing so for twenty minutes, they joined partners who listened actively—stopping the writers whenever they had a question or wanted more detail. The exercise ended with the writers commenting on what they could have added, omitted, developed.

The students performed other activities that integrated speaking and writing. Most notably, these activities helped them when they had difficulty discovering patterns and themes in their autobiographical writing. Two five-minute talks were especially helpful in getting them past the chronological dictum. They did the first talk three weeks into the semester. It required them to assemble stories through which they could create an image that they wanted other college freshmen to have of them. The second talk occurred four weeks later, shortly before they drafted a seven-page version of their autobiography. It required them to interview and gather material about themselves from someone who knew them well over an extended period of time. They could perform each talk from notes rather than a written essay. But they had to write summaries and reflections upon what they discovered from each talk, afterward.

Not surprisingly, the second speaking assignment caused a considerable amount of revised thinking about the first. As one student put it:

> Many things that I found, realized, and discovered, shocked me; things that I was not aware of in the past. Through the interview with my father, I not only discovered feelings that my father had not shared with me before, but I believe that because of the interview my father and I are closer. . . . I received better understanding of my place in this world and to what extent my existence is viewed. . . . Some of the ways I saw myself were confirmed by my father, and secondly by your comments on the [summary and reflection] paper.

So far, I have briefly suggested only three exercises contributing to students' acquisition of an autobiographical grammar. The grammatical principles are important ones—naming the self, contextualizing the self, detecting thematic patterns in the development of self. Others surely merit equal consideration. But these three led to a student's essay that emerged as an antigenre.

Rob came to a writing conference excited by what he planned to do with his autobiography. He had read several sample autobiographies that I'd brought to class one day. He especially liked one by a Japanese woman, who had composed a series of testimonies by people who had influenced her. The testimonies implied a narrator whose self could only be discovered through the words of others. Rob paid particular attention to the way she had a friend—a rock singer—state a major theme in her life: ". . . she was always struggling with her identity as a Japanese. She said that she was a foreigner outside when she was in the States, but she felt foreign inside when she was in Japan."

"I don't want my essay to sound as negative," Rob told me. "I want to say some good stuff about how people affected me." He decided that his testimonies would consist of three people: his father, (mentioned in an anecdote about football below) a former golf coach, a close friend. "I used to act kind of down on myself, like that Japanese girl," he added, "but I want to show how my male role models helped me not to."

Rob's autobiography contained definitive examples of the grammar that he and his class had acquired. His father's voice named him in a story about an unsuccessful football game:

Later that evening, Rob came home from the game looking very disappointed and broken-hearted. For about two or three hours we did not speak to each other. Finally, Rob looked up at me and asked, "Dad, why are you not talking to me?" I said, "Well Rob, I want you to know that I love you and I accept you totally. I love you whether you are the football hero or whether you play terrible. I love you because you are Rob and my son, not because you are number ten on the football squad."

His golf coach's voice contextualized him in a specific human and athletic environment: "The fact that his parents and relatives showed up added pressure on Rob. Although he had been very anxious to play that day, he shot the worst round of his life. . . . I was disappointed in his performance, but I could not let him know that. Instead, I congratulated him on the positive aspects of his round. . . . I told him to be proud and to hold his head high."

And his friend's voice demonstrated a particular thematic development —the necessity of people taking care of each other: "Rob, being worried, left during the concert and took me immediately to the nearest hospital . . . they took me in and pumped my stomach because I had alcohol poisoning. After I recovered, the doctors told me that I would have died if I had arrived five minutes later. . . . He never reminds me how he saved my life. . . ."

M. M. Bakhtin suggests that a person acquires accountability—becomes a *supraperson*, or his own witness and judge—only through the autobiographical project. "Authenticity and truth inhere not in existence itself," he notes, "but only in an existence that is acknowledged and uttered" (137–38). The objectivity accompanying this concept does not occur solitarily: "a person's consciousness awakens wrapped in another's consciousness" (138). Just so, Rob mimicked a dialectic of different voices to articulate how he'd learned to look after his friend, somewhat as his dad and coach had looked after him. Implicitly, his autobiography demonstrated how he'd met the expectations he'd been prepared to meet. Robert Graham affirms that in instances such as these, "A sense of worldliness, of social consciousness is built into the very foundations of the autobiographical urge" (42). But why did Rob compose an antigenre of testimonies to convey his message? He seemed to sense that encomium belongs in the mouths of others. It risks inauthenticity and untruthfulness in the first-person narrative of conventional autobiography. He therefore embraced the trope of self-effacement that so attracted him to the Japanese model.

III. Narrating Cultures

When I first became interested in getting students to work with cultural critique, I knew little more than they about the grammar of the genre—or even if it could be called a genre. To complicate the matter, "the number of genres current in any society is indeterminate and depends upon the complexity and diversity of the society" (Miller, 163). However, I found that the tools and arguments of narratology can apply—and in cultural critique, "various forms of knowledge legitimate themselves through narration" (Prince, 527). Students often concur. For instance, one student examined three essays on families from different cultures, which he chose from the anthology *Ourselves Among Others*. He then thought about how he'd summarized the essays and tried "to capture, on paper, what family means to me. . . . From that paper I learned a lot about how to better bring my points across and make connections by use of a narrative voice."

"Use of a narrative voice," as the student put it, encompasses two principles: succession and transformation (Todorov 1990, 30). Yet guiding students toward a grammar of cultural critique requires more, because some students may perceive this genre to be overly laden with an ideology that challenges their own. Another student examined the same cross-cultural approach to the idea of family and protested:

> We all know about the American dream: white picket fence, pink house, Mom and Dad happily married, the dog out in the back yard. Three authors, Gyanranjan, Mehta, and Duras, totally disassemble the "pink house" concept. What is wrong with stable family life? I know that foreigners dislike Americans, but there is nothing to hate about American lifestyles. . . . My point is, the American Dream still exists. My Dad pays for my brother's college education and my Mom pays for mine. They work 45 hour weeks and see each other an average of 3 hours a day. They love each other and treat one another as equal . . . and that's okay in the U.S.A. . . .

Despite his more obvious misperceptions about the usefulness of other cultural perspectives, this student illustrated an important point which Tzvetan Todorov also observes: "Ideological organization seems to possess a weak formative power: narratives that do not frame the actions that result from this organization with another order, adding a second organization to the first, are hard to find" (37). In the presence of such substantiated resistance, I felt challenged to clarify a grammar of cultural critique that negotiated rather than polarized ideologies. I also needed to find a way to distinguish for such students the difference between cultural critique and cultural chauvinism. Mary Crow Dog's *Lakota Woman* provided students with an example of how such grammar might function. It is a narrative that draws a fine bead on the American Indian Movement's [AIM] active recovery of native culture, leading up to and beyond the 1973 reoccupation of Wounded Knee.

Many of the students resided in a state of comfortable assumptions regarding Native American culture. "I haven't given much more thought to Indians than what I learned in high school about the different tribes and such," a young woman said. However, upon completing two assignments that compared how the media portrays Indians and how Native American poetry speaks its culture, she said:

> I never realized how awful their ordeal was. My article [on the Indians vs.
> the U.S. government] made me think about this, as did *Lakota Woman* ...
> I don't think there's ever been a time when I have been more embarrassed
> of my own country. Why did I not know all of this information? I have
> become curious as to what is hidden from the public by the government.

In comparison, another student was especially attracted to the poetry
"about the American Indians having identity problems, sadness, feelings
about nature. . . . My great aunt and uncle once lived on or near a reserva-
tion, so I can't wait to discuss this with them." A grammar of cultural critique, as the students implied, might consequently start with a function of
negation, which somehow unsettles the equilibrium of assumptions they
entertain about their own culture. It can therefore encourage dialogue. Yet
the students' equilibrium cannot be so challenged that they are cut off—or
cut themselves off—from that very dialogue. Still another student observed
in retrospect: "I really came down on my own people hard. I blamed everyone for what some people did to the Native Americans. I think we shouldn't
blame, but instead find a solution to what is happening on the reservations."

The succession and transformation that occurred as students sought sup-
plemental sources carried over to the class reading of *Lakota Woman*. Students
began to see that Crow Dog strongly indicts mainstream American culture, but
she doesn't advocate separatism over coexistence. Either reaction might develop at its proper, most useful moment—contingent upon the other. In groups,
the students then took up topics found in *Lakota Woman* that offered possibilities for closer examination of where cultures came together in their own
lives. For instance, one young man had worked with his parents in various soup
kitchens. After recalling the experience in an interview with his mother, he
revisited one of the soup kitchens. Then he reported to the class:

> ... alcohol and [Mary Crow Dog's] dysfunctional [childhood] family con-
> tributed to her wild roaming. . . . I have two real life examples that pertain
> to Mary's situation. . . . [Martha] lives in an alley between two large build-
> ings. She has tuberculosis and needs to be institutionalized. . . . She refuses
> to go pick up food anymore from soup kitchens, so volunteers . . . travel to
> the alley where she lives and try their best to help her. . . . [Maria] had no
> real home, the projects acted as temporary shelter. . . . she went to [a soup
> kitchen] for food to feed her large family. During that time, she became
> pregnant once again. The social workers . . . introduced her to a Mother-to-
> Mother program. . . . She herself became a volunteer. . . . Maria obtained a
> GED through a different program at the center. She is now working to be
> a nurse at a trade school.

Narrative principles of succession and transformation are certainly evident in this passage. But a far more significant permutation of these grammatical functions emerged when the student considered his report and asked:

"... what would it be like if I could not get into a car and drive away from [Martha or Maria's] hardship? I can leave the cold, hunger, and frustration of poverty in my rear view mirror, not having to look back unless I choose to do so." He successfully noticed that a grammar of cultural critique must account for—and challenge—the concept of distance: technologies and intellectual abstractions can and do tempt people to place those whom they perceive as other at a comforting, insidious remove.

The exercises recounted here suggest that a genre such as cultural critique requires a substantial degree of invention. Narrative succession and transformation transpire on a number of epistemological levels, including negating easy assumptions, negotiating differences, and recognizing distance. From this point, the students went on to compose an essay on a topic that combined perspectives from *Lakota Woman*, some other source, and personal experience. Their mission was to identify and examine cultural differences and similarities in a way they hadn't fully realized before.

Katie hadn't mentioned it previously, but she was half Navajo. She used the assignment to look again at her cultural roots, beginning with an unexpected application of the negation principle: "My mother is a full Navajo. . . . I questioned [why] she went off to make something of herself in school. To my surprise she answered [that she was] . . . prejudiced against her own people. . . ." Katie then pondered how to negotiate with Crow Dog's contrasting experience. Finally, Katie thought about her own position, and the distance she'd encountered:

> I have seen both worlds. . . . When we went to visit grandma in Arizona, we had to use an outhouse for the bathroom. . . . I can remember being served a bowl of mutton stew and looking over toward the sheep pen. My mother received a pathetic look from me, begging her not to [make me] eat it. At night I had to dust my feet before getting into bed because the floor was dirt. . . . What was it that the Indians did to deserve to be shut away in the bottom drawer? Why weren't they a part of my U.S. history course this semester? . . . Where did their pride and nobility vanish to? . . . Being ethnically aware is now a task I have to set myself to . . . we are each individuals with different backgrounds that vary as much as the fingerprints found at the tips of our hands.

Todorov finds that the narrative logic of succession and transformations brings about the most effective kind of learning when "the event itself is less important than our perception of it, and degree of knowledge we have of it" (31). The structure of Katie's narrative verifies as much. Her last passage recounts a primary experience of Navajo culture, which provided her with unsophisticated criteria to critique it, even though those criteria caused her to claim stronger allegiance to mainstream American culture. On the other hand, her mother's narrative impinges upon hers with much more specific and disturbingly overlapping criteria: lack of educational opportunities, maltreatment of women, alcohol abuse, infant mortality. Yet reading Crow Dog's oppositional narrative reveals aspects of Indian culture that neither Katie's narrative nor her mother's accounts for—spiritual knowledge; political identity; a "model of the natural, rooted wholeness of an 'organic community'" (Graff and Robbins, 420–21). These latter criteria add up to resisting the idea of oppression when one culture deems itself superior to another. The narrative of Katie's primary experience appears last because it represents her—and *she* has become the site of a new, unwritten narrative, one that can only exist if she sets herself the task of becoming more ethnically aware.

IV. Historicizing Biography

A genre approach to biography might derive its *modus operandi* from Thomas Carlyle's famous assertion: "History is the essence of innumerable biographies." Notwithstanding occasional criticism that Carlyle favors an elitist and reactionary emphasis, I think it is safe to say that biographical writing transforms students into historians. Consequently, writing biographies should probably involve "the transformation of a *text* into an open, changing, and contradictory *discourse* that is cumulatively produced . . ." (Montrose, 406). Under this definition of collaborative practice, it's the transformation of text into discourse which enables students to acquire a grammar of biography.

Having a common historical text provides the place for the process to begin. The same sophomores who had read about the Panamanian invasion moved on to *I, Rigoberta Menchú*, the Guatemalan Nobel Prize winner's story edited by Elisabeth Burgos-Debray. Their initial impressions of *I, Rigoberta* focused on what important generalizations about history might come from a study of one person's life and how Menchú could claim: "This is my testimony . . . [but] I'd like to stress that it's not only *my* life, it's also the testimony of my people" (1). Next they considered whom to study in their own biographies. They had to choose a person who had exerted a direct influence upon them. It had to be someone whose story would not be told if the students did not become historians. They had to consider what that person represented in a larger sense.

As we discussed the stories Menchú tells about her family, her community, and Indian culture, the students started conducting interviews on their own subject. They drafted and shared the anecdotal information they found. Then, they reflected on what they were learning about the aims of epideictic prose. One student wrote:

> . . . the "life writing" exercise you gave us in class helped me discover more about Menchú's purpose and [Burgos-Debray's] techniques for writing a biographical study. Menchú strove for equality and respect [for] . . . Indian lifestyle . . . all her stories are directed to prove it. This helped me . . . so

that my study wouldn't be a random assortment of memories but show
some purpose in organization. . . . [My grandmother MamaBea] was
southern-bred proper, a female in a man's world, a woman of wealth married to a man of poverty, a strict [religionist], a leader in the community, a
helping hand, a disciplinarian, and a role model. . . . I will never know all
the intricate complexities that made her, instead I can only grasp the nature
of "MamaBea-ism."

This student suggests that a biographer must not only represent a person,
but also raise questions about how cultural practices and social codes are
reproduced in that person. MamaBea proved problematic, because she "believed in the role of a woman as it pertained to . . . the biblical role of fe-
maleness"; she "was a southern woman complete with all the racial
preferences." As much as she admired MamaBea, the student didn't want
readers to think she endorsed her grandmother wholeheartedly. So, as a biographer she found herself relating stories in which she challenged the woman,
such as when she once asked MamaBea what she would do if her grand-
daughter married a Black man. "I'd disown you," the woman answered. The
student explained: "I was going to see to it that she verbalized her opinion. . . ."

But as with the other genre approaches, the beginnings of the biographical project did not occur without some student resistance. Writers are not
always willing to create a critically balanced representation of their subject.
At the root of students' resistance to biographical writing is often the need to
see *how* to transform text into shared discourse, and then how to convert that
discourse back into a text that accurately reflects the person they want to
represent—without doing violence to their motives for studying that person
in the first place. Yet they find that the ethos of biography includes a critique
of the person's life, which requires them to square their perceptions with the
potential misperceptions or reasonable expectations of their readers. Accordingly, they must ask themselves how others' demands for historical accuracy
and their own sense of personal exigencies make peace with one another.
This is an eminently rhetorical conundrum which I knew all students would
have to confront.

The second step in the project came when the class examined their subjects' worlds more closely. In preparation, they first examined the political
context of Menchú's life and the struggle for human rights in Guatemala.
They shared their library findings. One woman observed: "it was exciting to
see that we weren't just reading an obscure book discovered by a professor.
Rigoberta is a very real person with a very important life in relation to her
country and our own." This exercise led to an annotated bibliography which
the students compiled on sources reflecting important issues impinging on
their subjects' lives. After using the bibliography as a basis for a talk about
their subjects, a young man from China noticed—as with the library research
on Menchú—

> Trying to write the annotated bibliography . . . helped me to understand my father's life during some special historical periods of China . . . just two months before his graduation from university . . . the Cultural Revolution broke out. . . . Scholars in the universities were thrown into prison or sent to the remote areas. . . .
>
> [My father] made his choice to serve in the Army, the only place which was still kept in order and separated from the outside environment. There, he served as an information translator. . . . [Ten years later] my father left the Army and settled [in] his job in Shanghai University. . . .

As the Chinese student shows, a biographer will probably reveal, on one hand, the way a person reacts to any combination of psychological, social, or political circumstances. On the other hand, he must demonstrate how a person—despite the human capacity for choice and action—still submits to those very circumstances. It is a process of "subjectification," which may turn biography into a text that implicitly critiques the world of the person it portrays, even when the biographer is trying to convey just the facts (see Cadzow, 536).

Next, students began to think about reliability and appropriateness of sources. They read a startling book review of *I, Rigoberta,* by Stephen Schwartz. One student responded: "[Schwartz] points out that Menchú's book is not of her own views. Burgos-Debray is the editor and the transcriber that . . . is projecting her own feminist and radical views." He and the class rejected Schwartz's generalizations as hasty, and his argument as *ad hominem.* Then they discussed the sources they'd gathered for their own biographical projects. How might unreliable or inappropriate sources affect an interpretation of their subjects' lives? When dissonances—or gaps of silence—occur among the sources which the biographer has chosen to help him interpret a person's life, he arrives at a point where he has to become a theorist.

If a student acquires a biographical grammar that at least generates these three conventions—a critically balanced representation of a person, evidence of how that person subjectified his world, and an assessment of historical sources that help critique that person's subjectification—she has a tool for elucidating rather than clouding the rich complexities and inconsistencies of human character. She may also find that such complexities and inconsistencies form a gestalt rather than a narration, which derives from the plurality of voices, social codes, and historical contingencies which constitute a person's life.

Norma arranged an extra writing conference with me during the drafting of a study on her boyfriend, Allen. "I want to do it differently," she said. "But it's not coming together." She had collected excerpts from his letters, anecdotes from his family and best friend, poetry he'd written. She had interviewed his grandparents, Polish Holocaust survivors, who had influenced her boyfriend's sense of ethnic identity powerfully. I glanced over her draft and remarked that visually, it almost looked like a play. She smiled and told me that Allen wanted to be an actor. When I asked her if she had put her material in the form of a play, to help herself and the reader explore Allen's life as a dramatic presentation, she replied: "No. But I could." For the rest of the conference, we discussed the possibilities of doing so.

Norma's resulting biography, an antigenre, contained a stunning mélange of voices in monologue and dialogue. There were three "acts." They took place during a series of Sunday family dinners. The acts focused on Allen's childhood and ethnic background, his best friend's reminiscences, and his relationship with her.

She first represented Allen this way, the critical balance coming from a glimpse into how he came to perceive himself as an actor:

> *"That you are here, that you exist . . . That the powerful play goes on and you contribute a verse. . . ." Walt Whitman ["O Me, O Life"]*
>> From the ashes, a life arises to contribute a verse. I know a man who descends from a heritage of hardships. . . . His philosophy is captivating. . . .
>>> "I believe in fate and destiny. . . . I believe everybody has a final destination in life . . . how you get there is, of course, your own choosing. . . ."
>>> **"When I was a kid, I used to act a lot. . . . "**

Characters:
> Allen Koslowsky
> Elene Koslowsky, his mother
> Mr. Dorman, his grandfather . . .
> Enoch Brunski, his friend . . .
> Norma Sorrentino, his friend/love interest

Scene
> The action of the play occurs over many different years, starting with 1982 and going to 1994. ACT 1: The upstairs bathroom and the kitchen of the Koslowsky house in Creve Coeur, Missouri, an upper middle-class part of St. Louis. . . .

ACT 1
A little boy wraps his waist in a dark green towel after climbing out of the bath tub . . . he eagerly pulls the footstool out from under the sink and stands on it to view his reflection in the mirror . . . he twists his face into a resemblance of his idol, Jackie Gleason. . . . "Allen, the chicken's ready!" calls his mother.

Subjectification entered Norma's study of Allen this way:

> My grandparents were in the Holocaust. . . . I know my grandfather's entire family was killed. . . . My grandmother hid her religion for three years . . . [her] only living relative . . . is her brother. . . .
> I don't believe I've ever been discriminated against, but I have been the first Jewish person that some people have met. . . .

> I am bitter about the Holocaust. I think it does affect my relationships.
> I am now living in Indiana, and the Ku Klux Klan is very large here . . . in
> a place like this, where people have never met Jewish individuals, [I feel]
> . . . a little hesitancy sometimes to form a relationship with them.

And Norma incorporated an assessment of sources this way:

> Mrs. Koslowsky began speaking about *Schindler's List*. "I got published in
> *Time Magazine!* Can you believe it? . . . they cut a lot of what I wrote. This
> is how it reads, 'Spielberg has brought humor, tears, joy, pain, love, and
> every other conceivable emotion to audiences . . . and he has sent a mes-
> sage. . . .' What do you think of it, Enoch?"
>
> "Well," replied Enoch, "I think Spielberg has done a wonderful
> job. . . . [The movie reminded me that] my grandfather hid in a closet for
> half a year and was not found. He also saved about 40 to 80 people in his
> house by hiding all of them. . . ."
>
> I could tell that Allen's grandparents felt strained and so did their
> daughter, so she said, "I think the dinner is ready. . . ."

Amy Devitt reminds us: "Individuals may . . . combine different genres
or may 'violate' the norms of an existing genre" because "genre is both the
product and the process that creates it" (579–80). Norma indeed stipulated
that her reasons for "violating" biographical norms were not aesthetic or
experimental when she composed her biography. They were conceptual. She
wrote: "It is difficult to sum up an individual's life. . . . I synthesized this
mess of *ideas*, with the help of the unifying dinner scenes, into a collaborative genre of sorts, which I feel has come to represent Allen's existence
rather well." Her interesting reference to genre as a collaborative and unifying device indicated an unusual sensitivity to how genres dynamically
respond to specific situations. The problems of representation—which Devitt
identifies as essentially semiotic—caused Norma to perceive (even before
she consciously realized it) that the task of writing a play and writing a biography were similar, because of the exigency she felt to replicate Allen's
presence and the effects she wanted his replicated presence to exert upon her
readers. She seems to sense that writing and reading biography are ways of
participating in, as well as reconstructing, history. The result is phoenixlike,
above all in her insights about new generations rising from the ashes of the
Holocaust—but not forgetting what those ashes mean.

V. Why a Genre Approach to Writing Instruction?

In this review, I hope I have provided classroom-based evidence that contributes to a conversation about dealing with what Cope and Kalantzis identify as
the accretive influences of current traditionalism, modernist progressivism,
and postmodernism on the writing curriculum. Whereas we writing instructors
have become wary enough of prescriptiveness to practice process-oriented,

student-centered strategies, we are now wondering—quite rightly—about the needs of students whose backgrounds haven't provided them with either the ethos or the conceptual apparatus for self-directed learning. Many of us are also concerned about the political implications of such learning in relation to how it may hinder, rather than promote, social change.

Cope and Kalantzis emphasize that a pedagogy of genre literacy begins to address these problems. They claim it can set up a dialogue between a student's culture and academic discourse communities, for instance. It can accommodate rather than suppress cultural otherness; it can affirm the teacher's position as authoritative but not authoritarian; it can scaffold learning at the same time that it brings the recursiveness of learning to the fore. It can juxtapose, alternate among, and synthesize different kinds of thinking, language functions, learning styles, and knowledge-making (17–18).

Rob, Katie, Norma, and their classmates adequately attest—in their own words and work—how a genre approach to writing enabled them to discover new insights about themselves, to examine texts more closely, to probe life-affecting issues, and to ponder the nature of their social relationships.

But this foray into teaching genre literacy has also made me more conscious of pedagogical guidelines that teachers might want to keep in mind. Here are a few of the more obvious ones: It's necessary to have a dynamic, not a static, definition of the genre we invite students to write. Activities and assignments should aim for the acquisition of a functional grammar—and we need to have a clear notion of what the most valuable grammatical principles might be. We have to allow sufficient time for students to acquire and practice those grammatical principles. Since sometimes we may be overlooking an especially important principle, we should ask students to engage in metalingual reflection upon what their assignments are teaching them; in this way, they'll teach us. We have to be alert when antigenres emerge in student writing and ask ourselves what sort of conceptualization is taking place and why it's useful to the student. *Accordingly, we have to allow students to develop those antigenres, helping them rather than resisting their experiments.* Just so, ultimately, we also need to question why we may privilege certain genres over others, and to assess how the functional grammars of those genres might complement, contrast, or interlink with ones that students are expected to write in other disciplines. This last guideline requires a long view—and in my opinion, a residually humanistic one—that dwells upon the holistic development of student writers.

Note

Many thanks to the students who allowed me to cite their written work anonymously or pseudonymously, including: Myla Brigance, Kelly Carver, Marla Cotten, Jennifer Duncan, Kim Haught, Robert Howington, Melissa Kelly, Judy King, Greg Sands, Kathryn Sasina, Amy Stark, Brad Skiles, and Zhibin Zhang.

19

Genre in Writing Workshops
Identity Negotiation and Student-Centered Writing

Robert Brooke and Dale Jacobs

You have to give yourself the space to write a lot without a destination. I've had students who said they decided to write the great American novel and haven't written a line since.
—Natalie Goldberg

Genre kills. We all know this. It's the end of the semester, and we dread writing that one more recommendation letter for a student we've worked with all year. We know the genre we must write, the conventional phrases. We know the uses of these genres. But, as writers, part of us resists these writing acts. Our teacher-student relationship with this student isn't containable in these conventions. We chafe at the artificial boundaries, the fact that the genre of recommendation letter assigns us only a narrow way of seeing Susan, an incomplete way. We don't want to write Susan in this genre.

Genre kills. It restricts, it reduces, it mutilates, it limits what our lived experience might say if we could choose how to present it.

But of course we're lying. Genre doesn't kill. It also gives birth, it midwives, it makes possible. It leads us on as writers into new discoveries, new worlds, new interpretations. This is partly why we write. It's why so many of Donald Murray's quotations from practicing writers (1978) use metaphors of discovery for writing: writing as journey, as mining for deep ore, as search, as magic. To follow out the implied structures of your idea or your presentation strategy, to give yourself over to the internal requirements of your piece, is to be a mobile subject modifiable by the words that you write.

Genre kills, but it also gives birth. A paradox. Genre both limits and enriches the writing self. That's the paradox: as writers, our relationship with genre is one of negotiation. How do we turn the paradox of genre into something usable by real writers (students in college, first-year students frightened of college, high school teachers and students, the two of us working on this article)?

As we each sit down to write, we have some vague ideas of what to write and how we want it to proceed ("I want to write a poem about my mother," says Shannon, a student in Robert's advanced writing class), but as we get into the writing we find the structure of the ideas themselves have some say in how we go about proceeding ("I kept comparing my mother now with how she was when I was ten," says Shannon), and these structures may or may not fit with the conventions we know as a reader of this genre ("It didn't work to make it rhyme," says Shannon). We're endlessly in negotiation with the internal structures of the ideas we're building and the external structures that come from what we know of this genre. In the process of this negotiation, our ideas are transforming themselves. So are the ways we think of ourselves as writers, the roles we use to describe ourselves. ("I learned something about my mother and myself writing this," says Shannon, "I learned how much I carry from her even though I'm so different. I also learned I'm not a poet yet—the piece felt so much better when I shifted it away from poetry into what you called a collage essay. I could write a lot more of those. Maybe someday I'll do poetry.")

Such negotiation of internal and external structures is a feature of many writers' experience with genre, and isn't limited to so-called creative genres like poetry and the collage. Todd, a student in Dale's fall 1994 introductory composition class, for example, began the term by writing a straight argumentative piece about gays in the military, using a form familiar to him from his high school writing experience. Over the course of the next few weeks, he moved away from this type of familiar genre structure in the examination of his personal reaction to Nebraska's first execution in thirty years—a reaction that led him to reassess his position on the issue of capital punishment. Through this introspective type of writing, Todd combined a personal essay form with social argumentation, negotiating a new position at the intersection of these two genres. As Todd's example illustrates, a writer's negotiation of the internal and external structures of genre can occur in many types of writing.

We see writing instruction as about role negotiation, about identity negotiation (Brooke 1991). For us, the burning experience in writing classes isn't learning a set of strategies for text production or a set of conventions for genres of academic or business prose—the burning experience in writing classes is the negotiation of writers' roles, of whether or not (or to what degree) each individual can make the role of writer one that fits into the roles she already attaches to herself. We negotiate how we interact with the genres we write, even when they are assigned to us, because we need to 1) discover what, if anything, the experience of using those genres makes possible for us, 2) explore how, if at all, we will adapt our roles and selves to the possibilities and limits these genres supply, and 3) use the experience inside the genres to clarify and reinterpret what we already know about ourselves and what we already know how to do. In these ways, genre is a site of identity negotiation.

Our relationship to genre as writers, thus, follows the same logic as our relationship to social roles as individuals. In the same way we create a self by negotiating our stance toward the social roles we inhabit (teacher, friend, spouse, white male, gay, evangelical Christian, Midwesterner, immigrant), so we create our self *as writer* by negotiating our stance toward the genres we use. Here's some basic Erving Goffman sociology:

> [Let us define] the individual, for sociological purposes, as a stance-taking entity, a something that takes up a position somewhere between identification with an organization and opposition to it, and is ready at the slightest pressure to regain its balance by shifting involvement in either direction. It is thus *against something* that the self can emerge. . . . Our sense of being a person can come from being drawn into a wider social unit; our sense of selfhood can arise through the little ways in which we resist the pull. (319–20; his italics)

As writers, our use of genre provides the social grammar that allows us to negotiate a self. The limitations of genre, the conventions, the "that which is expected," serve the same function for us as the similar limitations and conventions of social roles; the possibilities of genre, the discursive events that lead us onward, the opportunities for shifting or breaking the conventions to make a point, provide the same function for us as the similar possibilities in our behavior in our roles.

So let's apply all this to teaching, to writing instruction, to the experience of our students as they learn about themselves as writers.

In spring and fall semesters 1994, we began paying close attention to the genres students choose—and their uses of those genres—in our writing workshop classes at the University of Nebraska–Lincoln. Both semesters, Dale taught in the centrally important first-year writing courses. In spring 1994, Robert taught in the junior-senior level writing course in addition to English methods courses for precertification Teachers College students; fall 1994, Robert also taught in the first-year writing courses.

Our writing program at Nebraska provides a fertile ground for examining the negotiation of genre, because in our courses students are encouraged to choose their own genres and purposes for their writing. Drawing on our department's long involvement in the Nebraska Writing Project (NWP) and kindergarten-college curriculum planning, we've organized our courses as writing workshops in the tradition of NWP, Lucy Calkins, Nancie Atwell, Linda Rief, Peter Elbow, and Donald Murray. In our first year writing courses, students are invited to write frequently, to choose their own topics and genres, and to reflect on the many purposes, strategies, and uses of writing throughout their lives. Furthermore, since students respond weekly to their peers' writing in small groups, they become aware of themselves as audience and of the construction and choice of audience in their own writing. By requiring students to reflect on their own writing processes, group responses, and audiences throughout the semester, our program challenges students to become reflective about the ways genre and community interact, the ways individuals and community interact, and the ways in which individual and community inform and even construct each other. We see our program, thus, as situated at the intersection between social constructionist and expressionist approaches to literacy, as described in the field's recent debates. Like Kurt Spellmeyer in *Common Ground* and Lester Faigley in *Fragments of Rationality*, we believe the most provocative questions about writing instruction circle around the investigation of agency or subjectivity and its relation to community. We see writing workshops as an important pedagogical method for investigating subjectivity and community.

In our program, we assume that students already operate (or can operate) as writers in a number of discourse communities, most of which are located outside of the academy. We seek to help students grow more flexible in the ways they can use writing within any of their communities, an aim that requires an adaptable approach to genre. It seems to us that most writers who operate in several communities have two places where they can focus their efforts to become more flexible as writers: material and form. For some writers, development comes through examining new kinds of material, usually with the aid of genres about which they already know a good deal. For example, this fall in both our classes several students are writing seriously about their confusion over the death penalty (in response to Nebraska's first execution in decades), and most of these students are using familiar personal narrative genres in order to focus their attention on the difficulty of the issue. For other writers, development comes from exploring new genres and forms while maintaining a focus on a familiar sort of material. For example, this fall, after reading Gretel Ehrlich's essay on rodeo in *The Solace of Open Spaces*, one of Dale's students explicitly tried to write a descriptive essay like hers, but about his long-standing experience as an offensive lineman in the Nebraska football system. Since students in our program are encouraged to explore new *material* through genres familiar to them, but also encouraged to explore new *genres* using material familiar to them, our program immerses students in both sides of the paradox of genre.

Dale's and Robert's writing classes (four first year, one junior-senior level) exemplify our program's principles. No specific writing assignments were given in these classes, nor were students asked to write on any particular topic or within any particular genre. Students came up with their own topics, writing or substantially revising a new draft every week throughout the semester (three to four pages per week in Dale's classes; whatever was produced in a minimum of six hours of out-of-class writing in Robert's). Students were helped to find topics, when they had need, by a series of very general invention activities, such as drawing a timeline representing the span of one's life on which are marked important people, events, places, and changes. In addition, each student kept a writing journal (Dale's spring class) or writer's log (Robert's classes) which included some mix of ongoing reflections on their own writing, reactions to class readings and discussions, records of small group responses to writing, goal setting, reflections on writing processes, and in-class writing activities. One day each week, students shared their writing with each other within a group of peers, selected by the students and fixed for the duration of the semester.

What we've found from these courses is interesting. First, when given the choice, many college students write in a wide number of genres, from fiction and poetry to argument, editorial, analysis, and reflection, from private journals to public announcements. Second, the reflective writing students complete about their writing (in learning letters, author's notes, process logs, and responses to each other's writing) is easily as important in their experience as the "writing" itself, for in this reflective writing they often label and articulate the personal significance of what they write and the learning they feel it prompts. And third, while students in any class choose a wide number of genres, and most students experiment with more than one genre each semester, in any given week a significant number of students' pieces (especially in the first-year courses) take the form of a related set of personal experience genres: the personal experience narrative, the reflective essay, the travel essay, the character essay, and the opinion essay using personal narrative as the main expository method.

We find the patterns of genre choice in these classes interesting for two reasons. First, these patterns support the claims of other teachers of writing workshops that developing writers normally will choose to explore a wide range of genres. At the middle school level (sixth to eighth grades), for example, where students have a full year in writing/reading workshop and are choosing their own texts for both, Nancie Atwell reports a list of forty-six different student-selected genres that students select to write, including such diverse items as reports of current events, advertisements, field journals, petitions, scripts, eulogies, rules and regulations, correspondence, and awards. About this list, she writes:

> The list goes well beyond the ubiquitous personal experience narrative. When students have chances to read different kinds of writing and when teachers introduce new genres in conferences and mini-lessons, writers begin to identify and explore many purposes for their writing. Writing becomes a sensible activity appropriate to a wide range of real-life situations, and teaching and learning about genre take on new significance as we help writers begin to make sophisticated decisions about the requirements

of particular genres as well as the appropriateness of particular genres for
particular concepts. (269–70)

Robert's experience teaching semester-long writing workshops at the junior-
senior level in college has suggested a similar range of student choice of
genre. In one representative group that Robert reported on more fully in
Small Groups in Writing Workshops, the four individuals wrote in the following genres in the course of a semester: psychology research articles,
impersonal essays on the Nature of Mind, private journals, poetry, cross-
generational family chapbooks, personal opinion essays, personal experience
narratives, nature writing, and lesbian issue pieces. Apparently, given ownership of their writing, time, and support, most writing students will experiment widely with genre.

But, at the same time, given this general pattern of wide experimentation from elementary to advanced college writing, we find ourselves needing
to look more carefully at the place of personal experience writing, especially
at the first year college level. Nancie Atwell's reference to the "ubiquitous
personal narrative" in her prelude to her list of middle school genres suggests
that many seventh graders choose these genres, among others. In Robert's
advanced writing workshops, the average student writes in four to five different genres during the semester, but most students choose personal experience as one of the genres for at least some of their work. In first year college
classes the two of us have taught, this pattern is even more pronounced.

In the courses we have taught at the first-year level, the easy majority of
student writing was in personal experience genres. In Dale's spring 1994
course, *almost all* of the student self-selected pieces fit into three personal
experience genres: of seventy-one different papers, thirty-one were straight
personal experience narrative, thirteen were reflective essays based on personal experience, and twenty-five were hybrid pieces (three reflection on
graduation pieces, six profiles of significant people, five travel pieces, etc.).
The only completed texts not in these genres were one book report and one
editorial. In our fall 1994 classes, the dominance of personal experience pieces
still exists, though in less pronounced form. In any given week, each of us is
receiving two-thirds of the submitted papers in these genres and one third other
genres (including poetry, fiction, social argument, news stories, meditations,
and Christian apologetics). While most of our first-year students have tried
more than one genre in the first six weeks of classes, almost all of them have
also written in personal experience genres for at least one of their pieces.

The prevalence of personal experience genres at the first-year level merits reflection and explanation. Some teachers may assume first-year students
choose personal experience genres because they are easier, but we think this
assumption actually begs the question rather than supplies an explanation.
The *form* of personal experience pieces may be familiar to students, and initially the *material* of such pieces seems more familiar because they know

more about their experiences than, say, the causes of the French Revolution or legal arguments for and against animal rights. However, as they begin working on their pieces the very richness of what they know about their experience brings up contradictions, unanswered questions, unaddressed feelings, and a host of other complexities. And it's often exactly these *new complexities* that students write about as they develop their personal experience pieces.

If writers, as we've suggested, can extend their writing by working either on form or material, using their familiarity with one as a way to develop the other, then we would expect growing writers who choose to write in familiar forms to be using this work to explore material new to them. And this is, in fact, what we find in the personal experience writing of our first-year students. Students seem to use the texts they write as ongoing explorations of the roles that surround them (especially, for first year students, the new roles of college and the abandoned roles of high school). Part of this exploration involves trying to find roles as writers that might connect to the roles they have already adopted, might clarify other roles to which they hope to adapt, and might provide new roles that integrate the two.

When students leave high school and enter college, they are faced with a major turning point in their lives; their previous experience will not account for the new roles that they see for themselves (or have thrust upon them), nor will it provide them with a relationship between past roles and new roles. Students in English 150, who are often in their first year of university, are thus at a point where they are concerned with their identities. How will I fit in? How does this new life and these new roles fit with my past life and past roles? Will I be able to make it here? How will I change? How will I stay the same?

Narrative theorist Anthony Paul Kerby suggests a reason, perhaps, for the prevalence of personal experience genres at this point in students' lives. "[T]he self is given content, is delineated and embodied, primarily in narrative constructions or stories" (1). Narrative-based genres, like personal experience pieces, provide a way for us to reorder our experiences and to write ourselves and our life stories from the prenarrative experiences of our lives. Normally, Kerby claims, such self narration takes the form of oral stories we tell others (and ourselves) about past events in our lives, and normally we don't need to structure such narratives in writing. Overt concern with our life narratives is a rare occurrence, since each person almost always believes that she or he has a constant, unchanging (or at least very incrementally changing) identity. It is only at times of rapid change or crisis that self-conscious examination of our life narratives occurs: "Questions of identity and self-understanding arise primarily in crisis situations and at certain turning points in our routine behavior" (6). At such points in time, individuals become more conscious of the construction of their life stories, and often turn to writing as well as oral narratives in order to focus this construction. Personal experience genres allow writers what Charlotte Linde calls "narrative reflexivity": a way to both inhabit and step back from the roles that comprise our lives, narrating a self as other and evaluating the self as they perceive others evaluating them (120–21).

The first year of college is exactly such a period of self-conscious examination of life stories and life roles. Students are moving from high school to college, from their hometowns and parental houses to semi-independent living in a large city, and are involved in career and romance choices with long-term consequences. It seems sensible that first-year students would thus gravitate toward personal experience genres. In comparison, junior and senior level students in Robert's advanced classes seem far more willing to experiment with other genres—genres such as article writing in their chosen profession; poetry and fiction, which they felt had been ignored in their school experience; or editorial pieces that took a public stand on public issues. The range of genres advanced students choose thus seems greater than the range first-year students choose, perhaps because they are more secure in their roles as college people and feel instead greater need to explore roles outside themselves (professional roles, roles put aside for a while, etc.). Interestingly, first-year and advanced students choose these various genres despite being given in class virtually the same invention prompts: in both Robert's and Dale's classes, lifelines and authority lists are used as the core invention exercises. Life stage, more than a teacher's prompts, thus seems to determine the majority of the genre choices writers make.

Since first-year composition is often the only small class that students have and the only class in which they are in close contact and interaction with other students and the instructor, it provides a safe space for them within the chaos of change that is the first year of the university. Also, since they choose their own topics and genres, it is a natural space within which to explore the life narratives that comprise the self they feel changing and growing around them. Adding a writer's role to the self, confronting the learning that personal experience genres engage them in, would thus seem a normal and natural occurrence for students on the cusp of college's first year. The processes of identity negotiation—and genre as a site for that negotiation—are the essential processes that lead to student texts like these:

> It's been over a year now since that day on the hill. I've moved from home and am on my own. I've grown up a bit and changed a little too, but as I left the state of Montana I had a tugging at my heart. I'm not really sure where I will end up in the end. I do know that no matter where I go or what I become, I will always keep a piece of the ranch inside of me. ("The Ranch: My Home")

> For the rest of my life I will continue to go under the needle. Maybe I will achieve full cover some day, I don't know. Every time that I have a new piece done, I am filled with a power beyond my physical self. The pain of the

needle is like a cleansing and healing process for me, and I come a little bit closer to the true independent spirit that I want to become. ("Tattoos")

Given free choice of topic and genre, students negotiate their identities by writing about experiences of both past and present, moving between pre-existing and emergent roles, seeing how each fits, and seeing how all these roles relate to one another. "One of the best exercises we did at the very beginning," wrote one student to Dale, "was the timeline. It was very appropriate because it made us think of significant times in our lives, which we could use as topics later." "With college comes a lot of changes," wrote another student. "Sometimes I might not want to share them with anyone, yet I need to express them in some way. By writing them down, it is as though I have shared them without actually having to do so." In the act of sharing their writing with others, students move from an internal process of role exploration to an external modeling among their peers in which they can see which roles will be successfully operative within this new social context.

The entry into the new context (and new roles) of college, we suggest, creates a heightened awareness of the issues of role choice and identity negotiation. The reflective writing we ask students to do about their writing provides a place for students to make these connections. Given their heightened awareness of issues of role choice and the place provided by reflective writing, it isn't surprising to find student writers circling back through their past experience in their writing, searching for coherence across past and current contexts, seeking to find out if the role of personal experience writer might help them combine past and present into an experiential whole. However, asking students to write about their writing processes over the course of a term doesn't *necessarily* lead to the connections first-year students often make with identity-negotiation issues. Students in Robert's junior-senior level courses, for example, tend to write more about newly developed writing strategies in the reflective writing they do.

At midterms and finals in his spring 1994 first-year course, Dale asked his students to write descriptively about their term's writing and about themselves as writers. When we examined this reflective writing, we found that the three main topics students wrote about in summarizing their experience all pointed to uses of writing—and genre as a named or unnamed feature of writing—as role negotiation.

First, they wrote about growth in their writing process, especially in developing a new awareness of what they could write about and of their readers' interests. "I learned that I do have subjects to write about and can now better describe what I want to relate to the reader," one student wrote. Another wrote, "I have also learned that you just write and don't worry about perfecting it right away. Another thing . . . is that there are many different styles of writing and many different things to write about." All of Dale's students wrote about enriched awareness of writing processes, suggesting that to some degree all his students were exploring what the role of practicing writer might offer them at this point in their lives. Students were clearly aware that the added strategies and possibilities they discovered for writing provided them with inviting options for future work. Several students wrote explicitly that the strategies they'd learned through working on their personal experience pieces were already transferring to college papers required in other courses. "I feel that this class has given me the opportunity to acknowledge that writing takes time and a lot of effort," one student summed up. "Each time I revise a paper and focus on what changes need to occur to make the paper more interesting, I begin to feel more confident about my writing."

Second, they wrote about personal uses of writing they had discovered or developed during the semester, explicitly naming the internal importance of what they'd done. "This class has made me realize more than anything that writing is important to me and that I do have a lot to write about," wrote one student. "Writing is a way for me to truly express myself and I like having it as an outlet . . . I think that my journey as a writer has just begun and I'm curious to see where else it will take me." Another student wrote, "[The course] has taught me how to become a better writer and in some ways even a better person. It has shown me how to express my feelings more openly on paper and in talking with other people in general." Within the conventions of the end-of-term letter, students claimed for themselves the (often new) role of writer and identified a set of uses of writing they wished to continue.

Finally, students wrote about the context of their writing class, the small size, small groups, the chance to share their experiences with someone else going through what they're going through. They wrote of the social support the class provided for their developing roles. One student wrote, "I feel at ease and comfortable with expressing my views and opinions. I think that one of the reasons that I have come to feel this way is because of the fact that by sharing your writing with people, you are sharing a big part of yourself. . . . I have come to feel safe in my surroundings with the class." Another student wrote, "As I told you at conferences, [this class] is an escape from my other classes which all have over 150 students. I like working with the people in my group; they are all very easy to talk to." The chance to share their writing with peers, to explore with them the new roles college presented, the old roles they had left behind, and the uses of writers' roles to negotiate between the two, created for these entering college writers an important, safe space for their own identity development.

Process, personal uses of writing, community support for developing roles: these are the themes students identify from their experience in first-year college writing workshops, and they all point to the role negotiations surrounding the act of writing. For these students, the genres that were the site of this growth were mainly personal experience pieces, as if surrounding themselves with the stories and reflections of what had happened to them (and what was about to happen) could engage them in a process that might guide and inform the self.

As they write personal experience pieces, students explore the places they have been, the roles they have adopted, and the roles they wish to take on in college. Genre, for these writers, becomes a facilitating site of identity negotiation, a process through which they can explore who they already are and who they are becoming. Seen as process, genre opens possibilities, births, shows us what writers are choosing (and why) as they develop their own reasons for writing; seen as product, genre restricts, reduces, shows us what writers aren't choosing (and why) as they distance themselves from some of the social roles around them. In writing workshops, the paradox of genre is experienced individually, within the choices students make, within the wider identity negotiations that match individuals' stages in college and life. In writing workshops, genre becomes a fruitful site for identity negotiation. This is genre's strength, and its possibility.

Response to Robert Brooke and Dale Jacobs by Michael C. Kuhne

Like Robert Brooke and Dale Jacobs, I, too, employ a writing workshop design for my first-year writing courses, so it is not surprising that much of what they have written here resonates with my own perspectives on genre and writing. In electronic mail exchanges with the authors, I confessed that I liked personal writing from students, and (more important) what the students do with their personal experience writing over time. And yet, we who defend the writing of personal experience narratives by students are confronted by those who argue for the abolishment of personal writing assignments (some of them, ironically, written as persuasive, convincing *first-person narratives* of pedagogical reflection). In light of this debate, I am particularly interested in the argument Brooke and Jacobs present regarding the prevailing assumed motives for students who, when provided a choice of genres, select personal experience narratives. I am particularly intrigued with their rebuttal to those who argue that students select personal experience narratives because that genre is somehow "easier" than other genres.

Granted, the personal experience genre might be an easier place for students *to begin* writing, since there is a familiarity with one's life (at least at *some* level), but to produce intelligent, thoughtful texts about personal experience is anything but easy. After all, the beginnings of personal experience narratives tend to be little more than an account of some particular event, place, or person. The writer's first draft is the record of a memory, always incomplete or imperfect, but something about the event, place, or person has prompted its retention. And, no doubt, the first drafts of personal experience narratives will be messy. Students will mimic other personal experience narratives. They will inadvertently mix genres and consider their personal experience narrative a fable, with the attendant moral tacked onto the end. And they will select topics that are intensely personal, even painful, in spite of repeated cautions from the instructor that what they write has as its intended audience the rest of the class.

Perhaps the trouble many students have in discerning private/public boundaries is the main reason so many writing instructors have difficulty with the personal experience narrative genre. In numerous composition training sessions, the topic of disturbing confessional student writing is broached by new instructors with comments such as "I am not a therapist," or "I am very uncomfortable reading that type of writing," or "Students will never need to write personal experience essays in any class other than in first-year composition, so wouldn't we be better served teaching academic genres?" It is true that composition instructors are not therapists, but consider for a moment all of the terms that are part of the composition studies discourse that are borrowed from psychology or possess psychological overtones: writing *growth*, the focus on students' *voices*, the emphasis on *process* and the attendant attention to *reflective writing* about the writing process. Like it or not, students and instructors are part of a larger social web of interaction; instructors touch the lives of students and students touch the lives of instructors. No doubt personal experience narratives highlight this engagement in ways that argumentation, op/ed pieces, or research essays might not—or at least not quite so directly. But the personal experience narrative as a genre is not the problem in and of itself; it seems to me that the problem (if there is one) has to do with what is done with the genre by the students and the instructor. What follows are three examples of students and instructor using personal experience narratives with varying degrees of success. (All student names are pseudonyms and writings are cited with their permission.)

Jane was a nineteen-year-old first-year student, attending her first college classes after taking a year off after graduating from high school. Because she had been writing in a journal since she was six, and because she had assiduously saved all of her journals (some forty notebooks in all!), Jane was in many ways a composition instructor's dream student. Early in the course, she began writing about the journals, what prompted her to write and keep them, and what they meant to her. The personal experience narrative that she wrote for the class, especially in the early drafts, was fragmented and disorganized, but it was chock full of wonderfully reflective, thoughtful material. During small group response conferences, Jane's group was able to draw attention to the sections of her personal narrative that they wanted her to expand. As her instructor, I talked with Jane about the ongoing theme of growth and identity that seemed to run throughout both her journal writings and her writing for class. By the time she submitted her final portfolio, the original personal experience narrative had all but disappeared. In its place, Jane submitted an excellent first-person essay about the media's portrayal of Generation X, a short story about a trip to New York with high school classmates, and an essay—written in the third person—about alternative music. Her original personal experience narrative contained snippets of all three works, but through conferences with other students and the instructor, Jane developed three excellent pieces of writing based on personal experience, but more in keeping with the genres that are traditionally more palatable in academic circles: the essay, the short story, and a journalistic article. For Jane, beginning with personal experience narratives allowed her the writing space to organize material for other, related topics. She decided to write about those topics in genres other than the personal experience narrative, but I suspect (and her end-of-the-course narrative evaluation corroborated this) that this genre served as an effective catalyst for Jane's other writings.

Shee's early writings in the course were amazing accounts of his family's escape from Laos to the United States in the mid-1970s. His conference group did not spend much time on the second language issues evident in Shee's writings; instead, they spent much of the time talking with Shee, asking for more information about the escape, his family, and Hmong culture. Because his small group and instructor were interested by his story, Shee devoted considerable revision time to polishing and editing the escape story so that it would please not only his audience but himself as well, and his personal experience narrative submitted in the final portfolio was quite moving. In addition, Shee had been able to negotiate the second language issues that were so prevalent in the early drafts. Shee's final portfolio also contained a fine research essay about Hmong migration to St. Paul, Minnesota, drawing from a series of local agencies for his source material, and another personal experience narrative about his difficulties in dealing with his parents and their traditional Hmong values. It was a thoughtful essay, one that challenged Shee to consider honestly his parents' values, their concerns and worries, and his resistance to their guidance. I am not sure how anyone could read Shee's essay and say that it was *easier* to write because it was personal. If anything, Shee selected one of the most difficult topics (and genres) he could have when he decided to write about his parents and Hmong culture. For Shee, the personal experience narrative was a genre that gave voice to his story, a story that was successful both in interesting its audience and in producing responses that led Shee to write in other genres. In this example, the personal experience narrative was crucial, because it connected the personal with the public in a series of intersecting ideas that pleasantly surprised both the writer and his readers. This is when the personal experience narrative works best: when the personal narrative provokes a *public* perspective. Each instructor, however, could find success stories to support a particular assignment, and I do not pretend that every student finds the personal experience narrative genre useful. Nor do I pretend that every student is able to see the genre as a catalyst for exploring other genres. The next example is a case in point.

Linda was a high school senior taking her first-year composition course through an extension night class. She was a devoutly religious person, and very early in the class, she wrote that most of the writing she had done previously had been argumentative pieces wherein she tried to present the reasoning for her faith and for her stance on controversial issues such as abortion. Her early writings focused on her birth to a teenage woman who gave Linda up for adoption, her adoptive parents, and her recent search for her birth mother. There was some resistance to her religious stance within her small group, but Linda was a strong, likable individual, and by the third week of the class, her small group had found a way to talk about Linda's writing constructively and critically so that all members of the group felt at ease. Her group was especially interested in Linda's African-American brother, who was also adopted by Linda's adoptive white parents. At one point in her early writings, Linda wrote that, because she, as a white person, had an African-American brother, she had been "saved . . . from having to deal with feelings of racism," and yet she also wrote about the difficulties her brother was experiencing with her parents. Her small group wanted to know more about her brother and his battles with her parents. They challenged (more indirectly than directly) Linda's statement that she had been saved from "feelings of racism." In short, Linda's group was cajoling her to try some different approaches, topics, and genres so that her arguments, faith, and stories might be presented in a more convincing manner. But in the final portfolio, Linda submitted a personal experience narrative about her family with only minor revisions from earlier drafts and an essay arguing against abortion and for adoption in which she used her experience as proof for her argument. Although Linda was encouraged to explore a variety of genres, she seemed hesitant to change her writing approach. The result was a portfolio of writing that hadn't shown much variation or growth over the duration of the course.

What I find interesting about Linda's example is that her peer group was encouraging her to explore other approaches and genres for her topic matter, but, for whatever reason, Linda did not pursue their advice. This seems to support Brooke and Jacobs's argument that first-year students are less willing and/or capable of exploring other genres. Perhaps in her later years of college, Linda would have been more willing to adopt some of their suggestions.

Genre is indeed paradoxical: in Brooke and Jacobs's words, "genre both limits and enriches the writing self." This is true of the personal experience narrative as much as it is of any other genre. It is important that instructors and students discuss this paradox, that they understand the contextuality of genre. The advantage of the personal experience narrative genre, however, is its richness both in and of itself and as a springboard to other genres. When thoughtfully taught and learned, the personal experience narrative is anything but "easy." Instead, it promotes the critical thinking, reading, and writing skills so highly treasured by all academic discourses.

20

Postings on a Genre of Email

Myka

Kathleen, How does this grab you for the opening? <mspooner>

I was talking with a novelist recently about various kinds of writing—nothing special, just happy-hour talk—and I found my earnest self assuring him that, oh yes, academic writing nowadays will tolerate a number of different styles and voices. (I should know, right? I'm in academic publishing.) He choked; he slapped my arm; he laughed out loud. I don't remember if he spit his drink back in the glass. Silly me, I was serious. And, among other things, I was thinking about this essay/dialogue, in which we're turning discourse conventions of the net—often a rather casual medium—to some fairly stuffy academic purposes.

Interesting that you call it an essay/dialogue (nice slide, that one). But many readers will expect a "real" essay here—or, betterworse, an academic essay. And we know what that means: a single voice, a single point (to which all the others are handmaidens), a coherence that's hierarchically anchored.

We couldn't say this in one voice. We—Griffin, Sabine, and Georgia notwithstanding—aren't one; we don't have identical points of view. This could have been an epistolary novel, were we novelists; it could have been a Platonic dialogue, except that most of Plato is single-minded essay in dialogic dress. This text takes the form of dialogue and is a dialogue.

Not just our own two voices here, either. Others interrupt us with commentary, obiter dicta, humor. All writers hear voices, but here we've made the convention/al choice to amplify those voices that inform us (or contradict us). It's different from essay, article, paper, dialogue, because this convention allows more juxtaposition with less predication. On the other hand, it's very like discourse on the net, but more coherent, more pre/pared. This has been done before, even in the academic world. It reminds one of Winston Weathers's "Grammar B" discussions (1980), though we're not being as artistic as the authors he has in mind. But there is something about email that brings this out, and I'm predicting it will be commonplace within a very short time.

It's too much to claim that it's Bakhtin uncovered, but that's its tenor. Email seems to make this aspect of language more obvious. The point is that reading this piece is in some way like emailing, feeling the staccato effect of jumbled messages, the sense of the incoherent ready to envelop you, the quick as well as the sustained. Voices always populate; the transmission of them on email is just more obvious—flagrant, almost—celebratory.

To use the tropes and gestures of the net seemed an obvious decision in an article about the discourse of the net. Natural, too, because we've composed it entirely from email exchanges. (In fact, I don't remember the last time I actually saw you: 1993?) Then there's the fact that we don't agree about the topic.

Our disagreement makes the blender-voice of many co-authored pieces virtually ;-) impossible for this one. Besides, the disagreement is part of the content. It's important to show that, while we do work toward each other, we finish feeling that there is still room for two separate soapboxes at the end. At least two.

I don't think we have an argument with each other so much, even though we do have more than a single point of view. But we write in different voices, and this is a problem if one insists on proper genres. Can't we just call it a text?

What is the difference between an article and an essay? A dialogue and a paper? Between hard copy and email? Between what we are submitting and what certain readers expect? Those questions all center on genre—a central thread woven here. The essay genre becomes a place where genre itself is the topic of inquiry, even of dispute.

One thing we do agree about is that email offers new ways of representing intellectual life. This is one way.

> :) This post has been smiley-captioned for the irony-impaired. :)<skeevers>

The Digitized Word

Email is a floating signifier of the worst sort—whether it's called E-discourse, or VAX conferences, or whatever. So the first task is to narrow the focus. Let's look at these few dimensions.

- *Email simple. Much like writing a letter, it is signaled by greetings, emoticons, closings, and other conventions; sometimes the author composes online, sometimes uploads a prepared text; author and topic are not unique, but audience is (as in letters). In its affective dimension, it feels like a hybrid form, combining elements one would expect in letters, on the phone, or in face-to-face conversation.*

- *Email on "lists"—electronic discussion groups. These groups have developed a new lexicon to cover unique rhetorical or technical functions online (e.g., flame wars, FTPs, lurkers, emoticons). Within the lists that I know, there is an evident territoriality (we who use the list, those who don't—benighted souls), but also an effort to democratize interaction. Some explicit conventions of interaction ("netiquettes") are established, others are in process, others implicit.*

- *Email in the classroom. Cooper and Selfe (1991) argue that democracy is closer in the computerized classroom. I wonder. I think a number of the features that seem to define lists do not obtain in the classroom—mostly authorial authority. But it does offer another kind of interaction, a chance to write differently, a different *opportunity* to learn.*

- *Email as resource. This is the networking function that Moran (1992) mentions—the thinking together that creates "a corporate, collaborative, collective 'self' that is more social and therefore more knowledgeable than the old."*

- *Email as mode of collaboration. As we write together/to (each) other, the author and audience elide; how does one represent that— in a single voice? in multiple voices? in CAPS? in multiple typefaces?*

It's easier to see these as discrete categories in theory than in practice. For example, we've both taught students in at least the first four of these five dimensions, overlapping freely. In many classrooms, they use the fifth one, too.

It is also worth pointing out that merely *composing* on a computer does *not* make your list here. It is clearly electronic writing, but these days it has been absorbed into the normal. Not so long ago, using a computer at all to teach writing was considered so novel that many teachers bought books to help them do it (e.g., Rodrigues and Rodrigues, 1986). Now, many (I'd guess *most*) writing teachers and students compose with computers routinely. And, while electronic writing in the classroom offers some unique opportunities that progressive teachers are exploring, it hasn't *required* a shift in any single teacher's pedagogical values: while some classes are models of social constructivism, others are still cranking out those five-paragraph themes. That is, the machine will serve the most progressive and the most traditional practice with equal indifference.

On both counts, agreed. The second, first: the fact that a pedagogy seems innovative or uses new technology does not prevent it from simply reproducing the prior paradigm. Aviva Freedman and Peter Medway (1994) make this point when talking about journals, which they see, all claims notwithstanding, not as a new genre, but as another and unacknowledged kind of test—a replication of the same game:

Although the writer's focus was now claimed to be solely on thinking about the topic, the rhetorical demands had not disappeared; they had simply taken a new form. Journals were, in our experience, still judged as *writing* and not just for the assistance they provided to the students' learning. The generic criteria were not made explicit, but, as Barnes and his colleagues found, clever students knew they were there (18).

As to the first point about classroom email practice *incorporating* many of the features articulated in the list above, again, agreed. But classroom email is different in kind. Janet Eldred and Ron Fortune (1992) use classroom policy as the lens allowing us to see email as its own type. Consider the case of the email listserv group: subscribers presumably elect to subscribe, and there's no rule or convention or folkway that says they *must* participate. They may choose the Bartelby route, preferring not: they can lurk. But if an email "discussion" group is a requirement of the course, lurking is not an option; it's forbidden.

The point? Classroom email has a different set of conventions from other emails; precisely because it takes place in a different context, it inscribes a different ideology.

Vignette 1

They're mighty white, I think, as I wander into the IBM classroom. There are eighteen of them, methods students and prospective teachers, and they're mighty female, too. On a second take, I see: they are all white, all women, and all anxious as they pose at keyboards, studiously avoiding them, carefully *not* touching them, collectively praying that our meeting in *this* classroom is a function of computer error. Computer error, after all, can be fixed.

Several tasks we have, I say. Write to Purdue's On-Line Writing Lab and secure some handouts that will help you. You are in groups, I say; here are the IDs. Read the Ednet discussions on grading, I tell them, as I hand out thirteen pages of listserv discussions on grading.

Mimi says we shouldn't have to do this; we don't have any *real* students so we can't develop a grading philosophy *now*. Angie writes me an email begging me to stop this exercise; it's too frustrating, and they already have too much to do.

They write, they cc to me. One group decides to number their posts to each other, in order to get a sense of chronology. They all greet each other as in a letter, and they all close: "See ya's!" and "Later's" predictably end the screen. They reassure each other that everyone is frustrated; they respond to each other's points, with varying detail. They share news. Kim writes, addressing me more as a friend than a teacher, remarking on the orange juice I might be drinking as I read her post. Through the opaque window of email, she sees teacher as person. We begin to see each other a little differently, a little more fully. If the medium is the message, then affect is the medium.

Two weeks later a set of papers come in. Sam's paper is among the best, and, to be honest, I'm a bit surprised at the quality of her work. Not that I thought she was incompetent, but she's the sort of student who's easy to overlook: compliant, not terribly vocal, older than the others—a "returning student." (And I admit: I'm troubled when she tells me, early on, that teaching will be *convenient,* easily slotted among motherhood, wifehood, the PTA, and Sunday school teaching.) More to the point perhaps, she's new to computers.

> Sitting at the computer the first day of class was more stress and agony than I had imagined. I had never used a computer before, and now I was expected to write with one. When our class did a SneakerNet as an opening exercise, I did not know how to scroll the screen and there wasn't time to ask for help . . . .

Sam chooses to take her midterm on computer, earns the highest A in the class. During our fourteen-day email cycle, she posts among the highest number of messages (ten of them) in the class and writes on various topics— including appropriate uses for technology in the classroom. After the email cycle is over, she continues to post. Always, she is aware of how the computer is changing her world, changing her.

> **Hi, I saw something interesting in the Observer today. There was an article on computer-user language and do you know what "snail-mail" is? It refers to slower mail or any mail that is not email! That meant something to me today but one week ago I wouldn't have understood that description.**

Sam uses the occasion of composing her portfolio to look back—"Putting together the portfolio was actually a review of the course"—and to anticipate what she will do next—take more coursework in computer technology, with specific application to teaching and to using writing with the computer.

At the end of the term, I attempt to distribute the collections I have maintained, in my closet of an office, to trashcans and bookshelves and file cabinets, as students drop by to collect their portfolios. Sam arrives; we talk. She regrets that her email has been cancelled. Oh, yes, they do that fast, I say, once the term is over. I can cosign for you if you'd like to have another account, I say. Well, maybe next fall, she says. See you soon, we say.

Thirty minutes later, she's back, asking me to cosign.

Welcome to the net. ;)

Virtually Yours

The emotional boundaries of our encounter seemed to have been much expanded by the email that preceded it. — John Seabrook

If you have been in love, if your lover could write, you know what I mean: it appears every day. It's transactive—not plain exposition, not pure narrative. It's a letter, but then, not the sort of letter you get from the bank or university. It's more like conversation. It's not conversation: it's one-way, and it's written. And it's written in the knowledge that days may pass between the writing and the reading—that in fact (though heaven forbid) it may be lost before it reaches you. As you read it, it speaks in the familiar voice of news, disappointments, and desires. It's affectionate—full of affect. Sometimes it's telegraphic, sometimes oblique, sometimes it includes a sort of lover's code: silly abbreviations, smiley faces :), Xs and Os.

> loved your smiley run over by a truck: ..-_ <lffunkhouser>

I want to argue that what email writers are doing on the net does not in essence or in genre differ from what writers do off line. In some cases, it looks like a business letter. Sometimes it's a bulletin, sometimes a broadside, sometimes a joke, a memo, a grafitto, a book. In many one-to-one postings, email shows all the features of the lovers' correspondence you used to read (or did you write it?) every day.

So email is like a letter, a personal letter that allows both cognition and affect: is that it?

Often, yes. But often otherwise. I send and receive formal letters (a different genre, by most accounts) via email, too. Also announcements, assignments, essays, one-liners, poems, and dirty jokes. Just like paper and ink, this technology allows a wide range of genres. *That's* the point.

So it's not a genre, you say. Well. There are several ways to look at this question: we could try older, more literary definitions of genre, grounded in form; we could include more recent rhetorically-based definitions, more oriented to the social dimension; and we could speak from the vantage point of literary theory so dominated by interest in the ideological workings of genre. Or we could simply listen in on the thing itself:

>**I found myself writing to a friend last night . . . and thinking how there *is* a difference between writing and this spontaneous posting that we do.<mullanne>**

>**. . . our conversations seem much more like oral conversation than like written correspondence.<newmann>**

>**. . . there is an element of spontaneity. And the essentials of conversation (as opposed to letter-writing) are there: a topic**

focus, a variety of voices, and statement-response structure. But unlike conversation, each of us can 1) edit and 2) speak without interruption. ⟨csjhs⟩

>... we all adopt a light, informal tone (and some real wit too) that is too often missing from letters typed on university letterhead. <harrism>

>If writing on the net is a hybrid, what shall we call it? Well, it seems ... to be kinda in between expressive writing ... and transactional. ... Maybe we could call it expractional? Or transpressive? Then, again, it gets downright poetic at times. <ccrmitta>

These writers or speakers—or what shall we call them?—seem to share common perceptions about email, about its friendliness, about its use for play as well as for thinking, about its novelty, about its inability to be categorized into any of the conventionalized schemes. I think this last point may serve as a place to start.

I don't seriously disagree with the consensus expressed by these folks, but there's something in it that troubles me: I wonder if we've truly come far enough in theorizing the electronic conference (whether one-on-one or in a group) to decide what these folks are deciding.

The consensus is not limited to this group, of course; it's repeated throughout the literature on computers and composition. And the consensus claims a great deal more than the comments above reveal. For example, we're told that the net is inherently non-hierarchical, "intrinsically communal," and that it is challenging the "hegemony of the teacher" (respectively: Zamierowski; Barker and Kemp; Cooper and Selfe). There's a fervor about this body of opinion.

> The Internet's glorious egalitarianism is one of its chief attractions for me. ⟨csjhs⟩

But these community-enhancing qualities of the net seem more *assumed* in the work on computers and composition than demonstrated, and I'm not sure we have examined our assumptions. Consider these few comments, selected from a single discussion thread on a single list (Cybermind).

>... however much I may like these identity-erasing facilities of the Net, my actual feelings of community are predicated on, and arise only with the revelation of, identities. <malgosia>

>... my virtual communities are very dependent on gender and sexualities. ⟨lysana⟩

>Not everybody came here to form a community (maybe no one did; it wasn't on the agenda), and not everybody wants one. ⟨marius⟩

In Hawisher and LeBlanc's *Re-Imagining Computers and Composition: Teaching and Research in the Virtual Age* (1992), Gail Hawisher acknowledges that "... as yet there are only a few studies of the electronic conference that have been conducted within composition studies" (84). She alludes to research in fields like distance education and information science, and she suggests that it supports the current heady consensus about computers in composition. In other publications, Hawisher has been careful not to overlook potential misuses of technology in pedagogy (e.g., 1991), and I don't necessarily doubt her here. There is surely research underway now specifically on issues in computers and composition, but in the meantime, should we rely on inference and extrapolation from other fields to give us the grounds for declaring utopia-at-hand in *writing*?

*But is this *writing*?*

Isn't it?

In the same collection, Paul Taylor effectively summarizes the consensus when he says "computer conferencing is evolving into a new genre, a new form of communication that has not been possible before now" (145). Not to single out Taylor, but, when he (as momentary speaker for all this enthusiasm) applies Carolyn Miller's (1984) criteria for genre identification to computer conferencing, immediately he has to fudge.

> First, the associated texts must exhibit similarity in form. Although computer-based messages are not yet exceptionally uniform, they do display several common features . . . Second, Miller states that the genre must be based on all the rhetorical elements in recurring situations. Do computer conferences arise from a genuine exigence relative to a specific audience? Only if we begin to narrow the terms somewhat—if we begin to see computer conferencing not as a single genre, but as a collection of related genres. (145)

A genre of genres? Wishful thinking. And I wish he'd bluffed—held out for a vision of one E-Genre. After all, if we equivocate on any of Miller's criteria, the whole case caves in. And he has to equivocate on two.

The facts are, on the one hand, that computer-based messages (whether in conference or not) come in a *very* wide variety of forms and, on the other hand, that they have common features with a zillion forms of *non*-computer-based writing: e.g., the memo, the report, the bulletin, the note, the list, the valentine. One could argue that the *only* distinctive feature of online writing is that it is transmitted via computer. And further, if we see computer conferencing "not as a single genre, but as a collection of genres," we're tripped again. Why gather them generically here? Why not let them individually stand where they were—with the memo, the report, the bulletin, and the others—where they have both formal and rhetorical commonality? Just because we send them over the net? It seems to boil down to that.

I can't see why the technology associated with a text is enough to warrant the claim of a distinctive genre. To my mind, we have to think of genres of writing as logically larger than the technologies through which we convey them.

I agree that today's technology shows much of the wonder and potential that these writers see in it. Perhaps the most careful, thorough exploration of this potential that I have read to date is in Richard Lanham's *The Electronic Word* (1993)—a portion of which I actually received via email from the publisher. This is the hopeful claim of the rhetorician that the computer is intrinsically a rhetorical device, and that through digitization it will invevitably democratize education in the liberal arts. Again, I don't much disagree about the computer's potential here—until we start using words like "intrinsic." Because it is quite clear that the same technology that stirs hopes like Lanham's for a postmodern avatar of the Rhetorical Paideia even now serves pedagogies of drill-and-skill, of Great Books, and other rigid traditional paradigms. The same technology.

My point is simply this: we are seeing a transition in the technology that delivers our written genres, not an innovation in genres themselves. And, in our enthusiasm for the (mere) technology, we are mistaking transition for innovation.

Vignette 2

These days *nothing stays buried*. . . . Particularly not on a computer. (Gail Colins)

"Do you mind if we take notes on the computer?" asks Tara (a pseudonym). "It's easier for us, but I know the clattering distracts some teachers."

These students are computer-literate—twenty-three seniors in the Tech Writing program. They are also white, most of them are women, middle-class, and they're from predominantly religious, politically conservative, semi-rural communities in the West. All right: they're Mormon kids.

The computers are high-grade for the times (and for anywhere in the college of humanities): twenty workstations outfitted with network software and several industry-standard programs. There's email with an uplink to Internet, and, oh yes, a couple of games. When I boot up, my machine plays a clip from Pink Floyd. "Hey! Teacher! Leave them kids alone!" Like the others, Tara has never used the Internet, and she has only a general concept of a listserv or newsgroup. But she shrugs. It's just another network like the classroom LAN or the campus VMS. After minimal instruction from me, she attacks the subscribe routine through her workstation; she's an Internet list-member within five minutes.

I ask the students to comment on the Internet discussions as well as other matters in their online journals. They are used to the idea—both writing such things and the process of saving their entries to a common area on the network. They know how to check back later for my replies. In one entry, Tara complains about how tedious the listserv of copyeditors can be.

I mean, it's interesting to see the comments on [whether to use] one space or two after a period, but is it really worth 25 postings?

In another, she reflects on the topic of obscenity on email—someone used the F-word in a realtime electronic conference in another class.

Since the letter was sent to the entire class as instructed, everyone got the message. Some people were offended, others were not. One general argument was that if you don't want to read that kind of thing, don't— delete it! The other argument was: even if you decide to immediately delete it, you have already been offended the instance [sic] the word hit your eyes.

In her journal, Tara didn't make any comments about the difference between online writing and writing to a printed page. Where she referred to online issues at all, she was concerned not with the writing, but with matters of propriety—the choices and judgment of individuals in relation to others— as in the two quotations above.

In other words, the technology was transparent to her. And, ironically, this is best illustrated by an amusing twist from the end of the quarter. Finals were over, students were gone, and I was clearing the journal directory. There I found a long letter from Tara to one of her classmates—evidently dropped into my space by mistake. Suddenly, I was a teacher picking up folded notes from the virtual classroom floor, somewhat stunned to see my best student write:

Well, I gotta go! Class is over! As you can see I find ways to entertain myself in class since I don't get anything out of the lectures! Welcome to the net. ;)

A Virtual Genre

If email represents the renaissance of prose, why is so much of it so awful? (Philip Elmer-DeWitt)

"Conceptual or substantive identity" and "procedural identity" are key terms that Larson (1982) used in arguing that the research paper as currently taught in freshman comp isn't a real paper. I liked the terms, and I thought they might help me think about genre—as having these kinds of identity.

Several articles composed via email collaboration have been published by now; how did the authors know how to write them? How do we know what we're doing here? When I use email in my class this term, I want the students to write *this way*—but what *is* this way? And what conventions should I point out to them as accepted? Students have enough trouble trying to navigate through "regular writing," yet if I want to extend the class and show them how we are working (e.g., in this paper), I have to help them do this. But *this* is still undefined.

>I just got a beep from you. Let me send this now, and I'll read you, then finish. <mspooner>

If you want to argue therefore that *this* is not a genre, that's fine with me, but it doesn't absolve you of the need to show students how to put such a piece together. There is still a lot to be learned here about composing.

And the medium allows us to claim what is ours—as it makes the audience real. The fictionalized audience itself becomes a fiction, and the concept of the author becomes more collective. In other words, the rhetorical situation is different—not theoretically so much as really, practically. According to a definition of genre that is oriented to purpose or to social action, this should make a difference.

I'm in accord with you on the need for a social or purpose-oriented approach to genre. I'll accept Swales's (1990) claim that "the principal criterial feature that turns a collection of communicative events into a genre is some shared set of communicative purposes" (51).

However, the mere fact that we can discover the several different dimensions to electronic writing you described earlier is evidence to me that we are not in the realm of a single rhetorical situation. Among the five dimensions you listed are family resemblances, but they do not represent a coherent set of communicative purposes, let alone a coherent set of formal conventions. By the logic of the social/purposive approach to genre, electronic writing is no more one genre than writing on clay tablets is one genre (cf. Swales on correspondence, 53). At best, we have a random clutch of communicative purposes and an enthusiasm for tech novelty.

According to Swales, a genre is "a class of communicative events, the members of which share some set of communicative purposes" (58), and which can vary along three dimensions (at least): complexity of rhetorical purpose; degree of advanced preparation or construction; and medium or mode (62). Swales also talks about pre-genres and multi-genres: the former too persuasive and fundamental to be generic, a place of "life" from which other genres may emerge; and the latter, the multi-genre, a larger category including several genres, as in letters vs letters-of-condolence (58–61).

Could I get back to you by email? I'm not comfortable dealing with you in voice mode. (Anon.)

*Bakhtin seems to make the same distinction between pre-generic and generic communications when he talks about primary and secondary genres: secondary genres "absorb and digest primary (simple) genres that have taken form in unmediated speech communication" (946). And as we might expect, he describes secondary genres as arising "in more complex and comparatively highly developed and organized cultural communication (primarily written) that is artistic, scientific, sociopolitical, and so on" (946). But what Bakhtin has done in his formulation is to validate as genre what Swales calls pre-genre, by classifying *all utterances* as participating in genre, the distinction resting on the same features later identified by Swales, especially organized communication.*

Others have made contributions to the definition that will help us. Lloyd Bitzer (1968) discusses rhetorical situations, like genres, and the role that recurrence plays: "The situations recur and, because we experience situations and the rhetorical responses to them, a form of discourse is not only established but comes to have a power of its own—the tradition itself tends to function as a constraint upon any new response in the form" (13). And, as Vincent Leitch (1991) says, the constraints—the conventions—helping to define genre act "as political instruments insuring order, effecting exclusions, and carrying out programs" (94). Genre is never innocent, he reminds us. Carolyn Miller (1984) makes the same point, but with greater attention to the role of social action in genre. Despite its ideological authority, however, genre is neither completely stable nor fixed. As Catherine Schryer (1993) observes, "Genres come from somewhere and are transforming into something else" (208).

> To be able to create discourse that will count as a certain kind of action, one has to be able to produce a text with the features that distinguish it as belonging to a certain genre. One has to know that form to be able to perform. (Fahnestock 1993)

The English novel as developing genre helps illustrate the concept. Its beginnings, most literary historians agree, took place during the seventeenth and eighteenth centuries. According to Walter Allen (1954), this was in part a function of literary history. Elizabethan drama, with both tragedy and comedy, with realistic characters and plots, with audiences of ordinary people, played an unwitting role in preparing for a new genre. History itself, the recorded variety, played another; written accounts of events and people and places, buttressed by diaries and autobiographies—the latter genre also evolving at this time—provided material and context for the novel, as well as a kind of preparation for the acceptance of the realistic as opposed to the fantastic/romantic.

But it was during the nineteenth century that the novel in England flourished. Why? History and the pre-generic "novels" no doubt played their parts, but a critical factor was simply the material conditions of the time, particularly as they affected a possible audience. Given the rise of the middle class in the nineteenth century, the celebration of a middle-class conception of family, the opportunity for leisure and some resources to fund it, the novel easily found a home within the lives of a large group of people. And of course the novel itself was delivered in various forms—through the penny papers and through single editions (which often became different versions of the novel), through the silent reading of an adult, through the performative reading of a mother to spouse and children.

The episodic quality of the Victorian novel resulted, at least in part, from the penny paper distribution schedule. As important, the material conditions of the audience had everything to do with those forms. The point here is that the genre "novel" took more than one form, and the form had everything to do with the means of delivery.

We would say now that this blurred Romantic conceptions of writer and reader. And didn't the audience influence both form and content, in effect pressing the author and publisher to reproduce middle-class ideologies?

Yes. In fact, arguably, both author and audience were influenced by merchants, publishers, and schools, too.

As they are today, as well, or why are we writing this?

So how is literary history relevant to our discussion? As a class of utterances, one could say, email is "pre-genre"—i.e., in the process of becoming genre. We can see analogies between this process and the process that gave us the novel:

- *The material conditions of the late 20th century have enabled a group of generally well-educated, relatively affluent people to communicate in a new medium.*

- *Many of these people believe that this form of communication is new, is different, and that it enacts new relationships between authors and readers. There is, in other words, an ideology already at work here, and it entails social action.*

- *Email seems currently, however, to function as a primary utterance. The conventions that its advocates cite as defining it seem closer to those "constraining" a phone conversation, which is itself not a genre. And a lack of consensus governing this "netiquette" suggests that it doesn't yet exert the conserving force characteristic of genre. Through recurrence, however, these conventions will become more stabilized, and will in turn define more clearly what is acceptable, what the boundaries will be.*

- *Email does also, however, seem to be challenging what we have taken to be both the role/authority of the author as well as the relationship between author and audience. As Jay David Bolter (1991) suggests,*

The electronic medium now threatens to reverse the attitudes fostered by the [printing] press, by breaking down the barrier between author and reader. . . . Anyone can become an author and send his merest thoughts over one of the networks to hundreds of unwilling readers. His act of "publication" is neither an economic nor a social event. (101)

If this observation is correct, then the rhetorical situation of email is indeed different—something beyond and apart from other genres. Moreover, as it becomes more stabilized, particularly with reference to rhetorical intent, we should see more clearly the features defining it.

All of which leads me to suggest that email may be a genre-in-the-making.

I'm of two minds about this. In the first place, though Bolter's book, *Writing Space* (1991), is stunning, sometimes I think he is plain wrong about one thing; the "publication" he mentions is indeed a social event, and it may be an economic one as well (as, obviously, in the case of the many merest advertisements on line). I would suggest further that such phenomena as flaming and "cancelling" (censoring) are evidence that the "barrier between reader and author" is still intact, if it ever was. Besides, "Anyone" has always been an author (i.e., anyone with the means—just like today), and has always been considered important or not at the discretion of the reader.

There's yet one more factor. In a recent piece on writing-in-geography as genre, Bill Green and Allison Lee (1994) focus, if implicitly, on the identity a genre requires of its authors. They locate school writing and curriculum as special contexts with special rhetorical situations producing school genres.

According to this formulation, curriculum work, as the provision of appropriate training in subject-disciplinary knowledge, has as part of its effect the projection and production of particular forms of student identity. This production is necessarily tied up with other major identity formations, such as gender, and connected to broader social power dynamics. For us, rhetoric is as much concerned with the formation of identities as the construction of texts (210).

Another commentator on this scene, speaking of using email in his own classes, also locates the identity issue as central. Russell Hunt (1994) sees email as a device for forging and maintaining social relationships as well as for carrying on an intellectual discussion. The politics of email, then, in the larger context are certainly those of the bourgeoisie, who—like other classes—seek to replicate their own ideology. Yes. But the politics are also those of the classroom, where identity formation is chief among its priorities.

I don't argue with the idea that rhetorical situations project and produce forms of identity—aside from my instinct that, for the sake of our postmodern anguish, we overstate this sort of thing. In any case, this doesn't establish that email is a new rhetorical situation or genre; I believe Hunt could perceive the same identity effects by assigning a pen-pal unit. Exchange would be slower, but that has merely to do with the mechanics of the process. It's un-hip, I know, but I tend to believe that rhetorical situations are *not* defined by the mechanical process through which they travel, so much as by the social purposes of the rhetors. According to your sketch of the English novel, different media (penny papers, single editions) delivered a single genre. In that case, then (and I think in almost all cases), the genre is logically prior to the means of delivery. I don't doubt that new mechanics make new purposes possible (more about that in a minute), but I insist that we're overstating this effect. The purpose that an extant genre serves very rarely disappears at the appearance of a new mechanical device. More likely, the new device is bent to the old rhetorical purpose.

I think that's why most electronic communications are simply reproducing extant genres of writing instead of creating new ones. And for the same reason, I predict that we will see discourse communities on line arrange themselves in terms of very familiar hierarchies and conventions. The page, the phone, the monitor is neither the utterance nor the context; it is merely the ground for them.

In fact, I see plenty of evidence on the net that this is true. The material conditions you mention fit here, I believe. One could argue that computer literacy lives within an even more elite socioeconomic hierarchy than does print literacy. But this is often quite forgotten by the users.

>Distributed technology is the antithesis of the totalitarian apparatus, seems to me. Freedom of speech for anybody who owns a modem. ⟨johnmc⟩

Leaving merely 90 percent of Americans disenfranchised. And how many Mexicans? How many Somalis and Burmese? In what may be a watershed article, even Selfe and Selfe, who have often led the optimism in the field of computers and composition, are now sounding a much-needed sobering note: "The rhetoric of technology obscures the fact that [computers] are not necessarily serving democratic ends" (1994).

We need to think of cyberspace as the commodity that it is, manufactured and marketed by today's captains of industry for the benefit of those who can afford it. So much of the "university view" of cyberspace seems naive on this point; we seem almost to believe in magic. As if this virtual reality we love were not constructed hammer-and-tongs by grunts in computer factories, packaged and sold by slick marketeers. As if Bill Gates got richer than God by magic. Perhaps this is because we in the university usually don't have to pay our way—access is our caste privilege. Perhaps it's because Bill Gates looks like us: he's a baby boomer, and very very smart.

But the cold gray truth is that cyberspace and its equipment are created in the real world by the same socioeconomic structures that gave us the railroad, the automobile, and the petroleum industry. It is merely our place in the hierarchy that conceals the hierarchy from us. "Let them use modems," we say, in all earnest charity.

Even within the online world, true democracy is a polite fiction. Zamierowski (1994) argues that power on lists (electronic conferences) is not hierarchical; it gravitates merely toward wit and erudition, he says, as if those were the great equalizers. But aren't these plain old bourgeois values, revealing their source in our larger social structures? Besides, even this is a weak version of the truth. Perhaps *especially* on academic/professional lists, power gravitates toward prestige—prestige in written dialect and opinion at least (common surrogates for wit and erudition); and where user addresses include institutional identifiers, power gravitates toward prestige institutions. Some users even perceive a hierarchy among different lists and networks:

>**Subscription requests are not automatic for this list. Your request has been forwarded to ykfok@ttacs.ttu.edu for approval. <listproc>**

>**In my experience, most of the regular post-ers on *interesting* lists are not academics. <artsxnet>**

>**Anti-AOL rantings routed to temp\trash\bigot\internet. ⟨lysana⟩**

On less formal lists, power moves toward the most verbal and assertive users—whether they're witty and erudite or not. In other words, when people go on line, they do not leave their biases behind. And, circling back, that's also why the "old" genres are being reproduced on the net instead of being replaced with new ones. If electronic communication is pre-generic, this is not because it's still young, but because it's indifferent: it is raw and mutable enough to handle the conflicted array of current genres just fine, thank you. And if you want to try a new one, that's fine, too.

When a new element such as email enters the system that is our profession, it changes every element in that system. (Hawisher and Moran, 1993)

*Among other things, postmodernism has concerned itself with the role of context in meaning. The strong position is that context *is* meaning, or that meaning is so context-bound that we cannot ascertain it apart from context. The literal sentence has become, quite literally, a dinosaur. We see the influence of this line of thinking on genre as well. Because genre occurs in context, it too derives meaning from the context, but—just as quickly—it shapes the context. (They are in dialogue.) As Freedman (1993) puts it: "genres themselves form part of the discursive context to which rhetors respond in their writing and, as such, shape and enable the writing; it is in this way that form is generative" (272). I think, then, that in order to declare something a genre, we'd have to describe the context in which it is likely to occur. How fixed is the context? How particularized? How quickly changing?*

A Genre of Chaos

To most users of the Internet, unbridled freedom, even anarchy, are guiding
principles. (Peter Lewis)

In my second mind, I'm beginning to think that, insofar as email can be said
to make new approaches possible, it might offer most advantage to the anar-
chic. In many ways, the TV with a remote controller is analogous. If we
think of the remote controller as keyboard, and the TV hour as text to be
created, then the channel-surfing teenager may be the most creative artist yet
undiscovered.

Armed with a remote control, stocked with a cableful of channels, the
home viewer creates montages of unspeakable originality, editing parallel
transmissions into an individual blend. This art form is rhythmic, improvisational, and ironic (Wittig 1994). You get the idea. "Surrealism Triumphant,"
Wittig calls it (90), and it is founded in what is essentially a hermeneutic—
or at least an aesthetic—of anarchy. Of course, it is worth noting that the TV
artiste is improvising within a narrow range; he or she can only create from
the very homogeneous values that TV offers. But at least the principle of
random montage is evident.

When we recognize that the computer makes an analogous montaging
potential available for the writer, we see some interesting new takes indeed
on the scene of writing.

**>Moments in MOOspace where multithread conversations become
recombinant and seem to take on a life of their own. Part of one thread
responding with amazing aptness to part of another. A kind of gift.
<swilbur>**

Eventually—perhaps within a decade—electronic writing and publication will be boringly normal. Predictions about what will then be possible
abound: multimedia and hypertext figure prominently; information transfer
and storage beyond our wildest dreams. Our technology even now can
accommodate not only combined media (e.g., the "publications" on CD-
ROM), but combined voices, epistemologies, even intelligences, juxtaposed
into densely populated canvasses of electronic text. We may be seeing, in
other words, a collapse of written and visual and aural genres back into the
collage of raw experience. Only this time, it would be a prepared rhetoric of
chaos, a genre of chaos, perhaps, designed to exploit more of our native ability to process many channels of information simultaneously.

But even this doesn't represent a raw new frontier of human communication; it only brings our technology closer to a capacity for what we already
do daily, unassisted, in spades. What dinner-table parent isn't all too familiar with multi-tasking? What child isn't alive to two worlds at once? (I return
to my student Tara, who does fine work in my class while sending notes
online to her girlfriend. The sneak.)

One issue, then, in this kind of discourse, is how to manage the multi-vocality and at the same time create enough coherence that a spectating conversationist can enter the fray, can discern what the fray is. *This* is what we need to teach our students.

> The period we are entering . . . will see the ascendance of a new aesthetic animated by the vision of the cultural world as composed of mobile, *interchangeable* fragments—common property—messages constantly in motion, ready to be linked into new constellations. . . . A perfume, a broken muffler, the texture of a boot, two bird calls, and an electronic message will be understood to form an inseparable and organic whole. (Wittig 95)

Instead of hailing a brand-new genre, or speculating on pre-generic stases, perhaps we should reread your reference to Schryer: written forms have never been seamless wholes—they come from and point to many directions *at once.* And maybe we should acknowledge that in the postmodern age, the reader, not the writer, is the real tyrant: multitasking, channel-surfing, capricious and fickle, free to interpret, misread, manipulate, and (horrors) apply. We're all guilty; we start at the end, in the middle, we don't finish, we joyously juxtapose bits of what we read with other readings, other experiences. But the point is that this is our most natural process. Both reader and writer are engaged constantly in making knowledge from a very random world.

As our technology enables us to present multi-tasking in more and more tangible form, maybe we should be predicting not new genres, but the end of genre.

>Communities in cyberspace are "real"—but it's important to keep in mind that they are only rhetorical; they have no other dimension. <baldwine>

Last winter someone told me that on email, when we argue in words, we argue. (Decades ago, Scott Momaday said that we are constructed of words.) Words are, apparently, all we have. But we are production editors now, as well as writers, changing fonts and adding borders and lines, managing a rhetoric of the document to energize the text. Through the technology, we can more easily than ever make the multilayered "postmodern" dimension of writing evident.

Which brings us round to the beginning again. The technologies through which this dialogue/text (and I sense we are no closer to an answer, but do we need one?) is composed has made possible (or made convenient–for all but Joe perhaps) the performative stances we're taking in it. It allows us to use unfamiliar conventions in the familiar context of academic publishing, and in so doing it highlights the joints and seams in the process of making meaning through writing.

To call it the end of genre was flippant and extreme, of course (and very Net—they'd love this on Cybermind), and it doesn't address all kinds of cognitive theory about our need for schemata in processing information. Implicit in my argument all along has been that extant genres are functional mental frames, and the rise of email doesn't eliminate the need for them. I see email as merely a kind of tablet with courier attached. As such, it serves only to deliver extant genres more efficiently than we could deliver them before, and hence I think email itself doesn't destabilize current genres of writing.

But I still think emailing isn't writing—or not the discursive variety we're used to reading in academe. Our expectations will not the centre hold. This is the start of another kind of e-speech-that-is-writing: montage-like, quick, unpredictable in form and substance and tenor. That unpredictability, that flexibility, is its charm and thread. The linear and hierarchical, the neatly categorized, seen under erasure.

Well, yes. Where I wasn't being flip was in the sense that one can see email as symbolic—I think you see it this way—as a harbinger, and multi-media as what it heralds. In that case, our tablet expands in many directions, and we see possibilities for combining text with graphics, with sound, with motion, in a wonderful stage-managed chaos of virtual communication. We become not only the production editors you mention, but the stars and directors of our own movies, or more likely (heaven help us) our own commercials.

Of course, montage and pastiche are increasingly chic now, partly as a function of a society that celebrates its difference by fragmentation. But it's also partly done in defense—to deconstruct before being deconstructed, partly to alleviate the anxiety of influence. In writing, electronic technology is the ideal medium for this. That is an important point, but it's one I think we don't fully comprehend yet. And it's one that is affecting us even as we write this, in ways we can't yet articulate. In other words, working on email—constructing the messages within a pregenre that is still being shaped itself—is constructing us, too.

We don't care. We have each other, on the Internet. (Dave Barry)

Note

Several people not explicitly noted in this conversation were crucial to its development. Our thanks to Wendy Bishop and Hans Ostrom, without whom nothing. Thanks also to Joe Harris for his several readings, his tolerance, even his resistance on certain matters, and to Carolyn Miller, Nedra Reynolds, and Jeff Sommers for very helpful criticisms and encouragement. Finally, a general word of acknowledgment to the several hundred writers who contribute to genres of chaos on the following listservs: Cybermind, Megabyte University, WAC-L and WCENTER—interface wit' ya later.

Part VII

The Intersection of Politics and Genre
Shares and Futures for Graduate Education

Because our focus has been on students, on the dynamics of genre, on the relation of genre to society, on the means and conditions of genre-production, it is no surprise that we look at last to the academic sites of genre in our final Intersection. This movement is foreshadowed in Ostrom's discussion of Countee Cullen, whose "case" shows a student/writer/teacher navigating a complicated educational system. In addition, the autobiographical impulse of many authors in this collection—our own included—has been to say who we are and where we have been, and now it is time to consider where we should be going. What does our developing understanding of the social nature of genres predict for the ways we organize writing programs and programs of English studies? How might we best teach genre and writing within or without English departments?

At the end of the twentieth century, contributors to this volume seem to agree that genre-study is no longer about the forms of the story, poem, and novel, preexisting categories of politically assigned textual quality. Nor will we any longer view the classroom as an uncontested site for inculcating good grammars of forms. Instead, genre-theory calls us to consider the social and political conditions of textual production. We have looked at how we have taught, how we might teach, on a teacher-by-teacher basis. The last two contributors look at graduate education: perhaps the most socially significant site of our profession and certainly a very political place.

Stephen North and his colleagues (and we're glad to be able to include such a number of voices on such a critical topic) found themselves questioning the fragmented nature of graduate course instruction where learning in one area rarely amplified or connected to learning in another area; where writing—in courses and in the dissertation—is constrained and stylized, part of an initiation process into a community that does not yet, even now, agree about its goals. They use the instance of curricular change at SUNY Albany to show how a new understanding of the work of genres might usefully alter the politics of English departments. Their discussion of nexus-based classrooms might usefully be read in tandem with Journet's earlier discussion of boundary rhetorics. Their essay begins in a curricular description and plays out in a case-study illustration, showing how one student negotiated a series of classrooms, each with a sponsoring discourse, each that allowed him to enter that discussion while retaining the discourse he was most involved with, in this case, fiction writing.

North and his colleagues provide a program-wide vision of curricular revision while JoAnn Campbell, in our final chapter, critiques the genre of graduate-student writing as a mimetic paradigm, intended to initiate newcomers into their profession. Campbell rethinks the processes, purposes, and products of graduate student writing; she argues at the graduate level what the authors in the preceding section were arguing at the undergraduate level: that we need to multiply our discourses as well as broaden and complicate our understanding of genres. Indeed we need to make genre the center of many of our discussions, so that "rather than reproduce the diseases of the profession, graduate studies can be a site and graduate writing a source for creative alternatives." Campbell, like all the contributors to this volume, predicts that genre-theory, genre and writing, the territories of our discourses, will provide the most exciting venues for change in English studies today.

21

The Role of Writing in English Graduate Education and the "Nexus of Discourses"

Stephen M. North with Lori Anderson, Barbara Chepaitis, David Coogan, Lale Davidson, Ron Maclean, Cindy Parrish, Jonathan Post, Amy Schoch, and Beth Weatherby

Graduate training in English, as in most disciplines in the American academy, is generally understood to be a form of professionalization, making each graduate student into "one of us." On the one hand, it has demanded what usually gets called coverage: that students read what we have read, and (thereby) come to know what we know. On the other, it has required initiating students into the discipline's modes of inquiry: once they know enough of what we know, they can begin to do what we do. What actually happens in courses—the lectures, Socratic dialogues, student presentations, or whatever—may have been discussed in faculty lounges or TA offices, but rarely in the pages of *PMLA* or *College English*.

And so it has gone with the *writing* students do in such courses. Again, the logic of professionalization is straightforward enough. To become one of us, graduate students must learn to write what we write. The measure of such learning might be called publishability: students become one of us when what they write is judged to be publishable (or is published, which is sometimes another matter). For programmatic purposes, this teleology is emblematized in the form of the thesis or dissertation. Generally characterized as "an original contribution to knowledge," these texts are in effect "publishable" by definition—are so, that is, whether they are actually published in any usual sense or not. Thus *The MLA Style Manual* declares not only that such texts should "make a substantial contribution to your field" (237), but that they "qualify as forms of publication in themselves" (238). In curricular terms, therefore, it follows that the primary professionalizing function of the

251

course-based writing that precedes this final project would be to prepare for it. In other words, the purpose of the fifteen or twenty courses's worth of annotated bibliographies, editing exercises, and abstracts, as well as the more full-fledged "critical" or "seminar" papers is to school students in the rudiments of research methods, say, or to give them credit-bearing time to get the dissertation under way. As with graduate classroom practices in general, though, detailed accounts of such writing within specific courses—what forms it takes, who reads it, how it is responded to—these are rare indeed. (For a key and noteworthy exception, see Sullivan 1988, 1991).

Over the past two decades or so, however, this long-standing, largely unarticulated logic of professionalization has become less and less workable as the basis for graduate training in English. Over that span, the field has had to struggle to maintain its disciplinary identity as perhaps never before— struggled so hard, indeed, that we have taken to calling it, in what often seems a strained effort at inclusivity, English *Studies*. To be sure, English has faced challenges along related lines in the past. So, for example, Wellek and Warren's "The Study of Literature in the Graduate School" (1949) answers the question "What is the matter with our 'higher study' of literature?" by attacking the "provincial" reductivism, the "personal compoundings of pedantry and dilettantism" (298) which the authors claim characterized much of the field at the time. And it points the way toward disciplinary reform by identifying, among other things, some "hopeful signs" in "the world of professional magazines." Not only have the "'learned journals,' including the *PMLA* . . . increasingly admitted articles (theory, literary criticism, studies of contemporary writers like Joyce, Proust, and T. S. Eliot) which, before, would either have been rejected or never received"; but "our magazines of 'literary scholarship' include also, and centrally, the critical or critical and creative quarterlies—the late *Criterion* and *Southern Review*, the current *Scrutiny, Sewanee Review, Kenyon Review, Partisan Review,* and *Accent*" (289). Moreover, they are ready to extend this broader range of discipline-sanctioned writing to "the doctoral thesis," which "should be conceived of as flexibly as we conceive of professional literary distinction" (294).

Writing twenty years later, Don Cameron Allen (1968) takes an even more pointed look at his contemporary "we" and offers an even less flattering portrait of graduate training:

> The whole system brought across the Atlantic by Americans of the last century has become fossilized, and like all fossils is dead and stone cold. We have only infrequently asked ourselves what we are doing or why we are doing it. The heroes who taught the heroes who taught us invented an American version of the methods they learned at Leipzig or Berlin. They endured it; we endured it; and, by all that's holy, our students shall endure it! . . . We have unquestioningly followed these primitive customs, but we regard them as high acts of civility. (109)

It is not surprising, therefore, that like Wellek and Warren he should favor broadening the range of acceptable disciplinary discourse. And indeed, if Wellek and Warren are not entirely clear about how flexible they might be in conceiving of "professional literary distinction" as a measure for dissertations, Allen leaves no doubt whatever:

> If good sense suggests that the thesis be greatly shortened and made more to the point, does not good sense also suggest that something other than the traditional dissertation is sufficient evidence of a candidate's literary ability? Many theses of a so-called critical nature would have been turned down coldly before 1935. May we not go further and, granting that the student follows the usual doctoral program, accept an original work of literary merit? We cannot say we are unable to judge this merit. If we do, we should give up our profession. (115–16)

Nevertheless, while such proposals for reform are radical enough that they would still be controversial in some circles, the most recent set of challenges to who we are and what we write appear to be of a significantly different order and to have raised, therefore, even more far-reaching questions about the purposes and forms of English graduate education. It is significant, we think, that neither Wellek and Warren nor Allen follow their proposed reforms in dissertation practices very far back toward any curricular implications. This omission is particularly telling in Allen's case. Earlier in the section we have been quoting (Chapter 9, "Some Suggestions by Way of a Conclusion"), he argues that if graduate courses absolutely must be taught, then "the best means of graduate training" would be "a properly conducted seminar with a true expert at the head of the table." Such a seminar "should result in an interesting final essay that all liberal students of the topic will want to read. [The seminar] produces at its best a dissertation in embryo or a chapter or two of what will eventually be the dissertation" (111).

You can see the curricular challenge posed by the line of inquiry Allen thus *fails* to pursue. That is, although he very clearly endorses the "original work of literary merit" as a viable dissertation option, he also makes it clear that the writer who chooses such an option must follow "the usual doctoral program"—an imperative that would include, presumably, doing that program's "usual" writing, particularly in those seminars he values so highly. But there's an obvious problem here. What happens if the dissertation turns out to be a novel? Would the seminar paper, the "dissertation in embryo," therefore be a couple of chapters, a draft, a novella . . . as opposed, that is, to "an interesting final *essay*" (our emphasis)? If so, what would be the announced topic of the seminar? That is, what sort of disciplinary inquiry would lead English graduate students to produce fiction? What would be the credentials of the "true expert" at the head of such a seminar? And in what version of the "usual doctoral program" could such a seminar be considered the paradigmatic course, an example, as he puts it, of the "best means of graduate training"?

The forces driving the current refiguring of English Studies would be unlikely to produce a single set of answers to questions like these, but it is absolutely certain that they would not leave them, or a host of others, unasked. They would not, in short, fail to follow through on such a curricular challenge, nor would they stop outside the classroom door in pursuing it. Moreover, whatever labels we use to designate the forms such forces have taken—creative writing, feminism(s), postmodernism(s), rhetoric and composition, cultural studies, and so on—they have moved us beyond wondering only what sort of dissertation might demonstrate "professional literary distinction" to consider as well what such a notion might even *mean*, and whether or why it should constitute so unequivocally the goal of graduate study in English: to question, in short, what English Studies as a discipline is or should be and, in terms of graduate study, how other possible goals might change not only what dissertation writers might do, but what sorts of work such writers ought to be (free to be) doing in English graduate courses.

The Ph.D. Program at SUNY Albany: "Writing, Teaching, Criticism"

The graduate curriculum at SUNY Albany, entitled "Writing, Teaching, Criticism," was initiated in 1990, and it represents one response to these forces for change in the discipline. In the words of the Program Proposal (1991) that serves as its charter, this curriculum is designed to explore "the interrelatedness of several branches of English studies: writing, rhetoric, criticism, pedagogy, language study, and literary history" (1) and, by means of such exploration, to foment the formation of a notably different whole. At the heart of this enterprise, the feature that "distinguishes it most sharply from the traditional Ph.D." is

> the way [the] curriculum gains coherence not primarily from period courses but from the integrated interests of those who teach and take the classes. Every course, whatever its focus, explores its subject from the perspectives which creative writers, students of rhetoric and composition, and literary critics bring to bear on it. (2)

As the second sentence of this passage makes very clear, it is crucial that this exploration of interrelatedness be carried out on a class-by-class basis. It would not be enough, for example, to organize these branches of English Studies in parallel, creating separate but equal "tracks" within the program, and then to establish distribution requirements that forced students to sample specializations other than their own. However much such an arrangement might depart from traditional practice, it would subvert our commitment to exploring *interrelatedness* by moving that exploration outside the curriculum: banishing it to the hallways, coffee shops, and TA offices where students have always gathered to make sense of the department's offerings. In addition, and more serious in the long run, it would effectively remove the faculty from the process. Under such circumstances, the exploration of interrelatedness, and any consequent reimagining of the discipline, would have to be done in the absence (and even in spite) of the teachers who were ostensibly sponsoring it.

Clearly, then, our courses have to be the occasion, and our classrooms the location, for the program's major work of disciplinary refiguring. Just as clearly, such a commitment requires a shift in the way we understand the classroom roles of professor and graduate student. The traditional pattern in English Studies has been for faculty to derive their authority from work in specialized areas of study, with mastery usually demonstrated by publication. And in keeping with the logic of professionalization, faculty members are by and large assigned to teach graduate classes in these areas on the basis of such mastery.

The traditional student counterpart to this specialty-based mastery is what amounts to a specialty-based apprenticeship. Students are generally expected to conform themselves to the peculiar trajectory of each course they take, a conformity both most visible and most important in what they (are assigned to) write. So, for example, in the fairly standard period-based curriculum that preceded our current system, three students whose own eventual "professional literary distinction" might be based on such divergent specializations as Milton's prose, the contemporary reception of *Uncle Tom's Cabin*, and the fiction of John Hawkes could all quite easily have found themselves in a Chaucer seminar writing on *The Legend of Good Women*, or in a course on "The Transcendentalists" preparing an essay on *The Dial*. In other words, the mastery that licenses the faculty for graduate teaching determines not only what courses are offered but also each course's discursive *raison d'etre*—including, of course, the professionalizing "what we write" students are enrolled to master for themselves.

However, a program in which every course "explores its subject from the perspectives which creative writers, students of rhetoric and composition, and literary critics bring to bear on it" necessarily alters both this configuration of authority and these discursive *raisons*. We do not want to exaggerate the magnitude of this shift. Each course still features an instructor's sponsoring perspective. Moreover, it is essential for students to engage that perspective and its corresponding professional discourse much as they always have: reading texts that represent it, responding to it, writing from it themselves.

Nevertheless, each class also faces the challenge of fulfilling, on a day-by-day basis, the program's promise to make meaningful room for these other perspectives. At least some of the time, then, the course's explorations must invite a disciplinary angle of vision that the faculty member cannot provide. Creating such occasions is in part a matter of course design: course subjects conceived in ways amenable to approach from multiple perspectives, reading lists that feature texts representative of those perspectives, classroom practices that invite a variety of response, and so on. Above all, though, they require changes in the relationship among teacher, students, and subject matter. Thus, instead of being *the* master of *the* perspective the course exists to explore, the teacher must learn not merely to include but to negotiate, and negotiate with, other perspectives. Correspondingly, the students obviously cannot afford to be simply apprentices. If these other perspectives are indeed to be represented, students must represent them. Instead of conforming more or less exclusively to some dominant perspective in every individual class, then, each student must adopt, even if only provisionally, a disciplinary perspective, a professional identity—theorist, poet, rhetorician, literary historian, etc.—with the concomitant right and responsibility to "bring [that perspective] to bear" on the subject area of the course.

And it is crucial that this happen with regard to the courses' *writing*. Writing is, after all, the primary medium of power in the discipline. From the dissertation to the book to the article—and, following the teleology we traced earlier, from the annotated bibliography to the seminar paper to the dissertation proposal—the coin of the realm is the written text. Therefore, any serious exploration of the interrelationships among the discipline's various branches entails working in and through their various forms of writing. Moreover, this is a programmatic imperative students help enforce. That is, given the relationship between writing and evaluation in the credit-based economy of graduate school, students are unlikely to take very seriously invitations to represent alternative perspectives if that representation does not extend to the writing on which they will be evaluated. In short, for at least some of the writing in every course, students *must* (be free to) exercise their particular disciplinary perspectives in the texts they produce: poets enrolled in "The History of Rhetoric," say, must be encouraged not only to talk and read and think about the course matter from that perspective, but to approach it in and through their ongoing composing of poetry; students who would see themselves as theorists enrolled in "Poetics and Literary Practice" must be encouraged not only to think and talk and read about their classmates' writings in the context of their ongoing work, but to theorize about that writing in the prose characteristic of *Critical Inquiry* or *Works and Days*, and so on.

Writing at the "Nexus of Discourses": Genre and the "Work" of English Studies

As our subheading indicates, we refer to this initiative as writing at the "nexus of discourses," a label borrowed from Eugene Garber's "Every Classroom a Nexus of Discourses." Garber argues that "the most exciting prospect of the new graduate curriculum" is the opportunity it offers "to foster the disturbing but, I think, uniquely constructive mixing of discourses in our classes." And in the first four years of the curriculum's operation this initiative has had, at least in a broad sense, the desired effect. Despite occasional breakdowns—courses in which negotiations over discursive possibilities have failed, so that students have been forced either to opt for the mode determined by the teacher or to drop the class—we really have altered the traffic patterns, if you will, in our curricular universe of discourse: poetry appears in courses where the sponsoring discourse is one brand or another of critical prose, critical prose in courses where the sponsoring discourse is fiction, and so on.

As these new patterns have emerged, however, they have also begun to reveal what the relentlessly egalitarian rhetoric of the Program Proposal and our departmental deliberations had rather effectively, and perhaps necessarily, obscured: that this effort turns out to be terrifically asymmetrical in its impact on the program's various constituencies. For reasons deeply rooted in its institutional history, the disciplinary bias in English Studies has been overwhelmingly in favor of what might be labeled, albeit somewhat sweepingly, the argumentative academic prose essay, and with it a rather restricted range of what are now most often called (disciplinary) subjectivities. Other forms, and other subjectivities, when they have been recognized at all, have served almost exclusively as objects of study. The curricular result of this bias has been a disciplinary hegemony that can most conveniently be characterized in this context as *generic*, but with the crucial proviso that that term carry connections to the more complex issue of sanctioned disciplinary subjectivities. That is, it is not only (in the sense of "merely") that students have been constrained in terms of the modes or forms or genres they could write in to satisfy the requirements of graduate academic coursework, although they generally have been. It is also that such strictures have played a substantial and conservative role in determining who they could "be" as disciplinary inquirers, and how that inquiry could be constituted.

This hegemony is most visibly at work, perhaps, in the simple quantitative realities of course offerings. In our previous curriculum, for instance, only three of the sixteen courses offered per semester featured anything other than argumentative academic prose as their proprietary discourse: one workshop each in fiction, poetry, and (so-called) nonfiction writing. This ratio looks to be fairly standard for graduate programs (when, indeed, courses like these are available at all). But the dominance of argumentative academic prose shows up in other ways, too. Consider, for example, inequities in what might be called discursive mobility. "Critical" discourses cast in argumentative academic prose have always claimed at least some space in graduate writing workshops. Responses to texts in such courses are nearly always in something approximating that form and not, say, other versions of (what would usually be characterized as) poetic or fictive forms. By contrast, however, there is no traditional reciprocal space in the more usual topically defined courses (the Shakespeare seminar, say, or History of the English Language) for poetic or fictive forms, or for much of anything that would likely (and tellingly) be labeled an "alternative" discourse. Moreover, even *in* the workshops, student writings in such alternative forms are generally understood to function in a way quite different from their counterparts in more topical courses. By and large, that is, each submission is seen less as contributing to the discipline-driven, course-based exploration of some agreed-upon subject than to the development of its author and/or that author's *oeuvre*—constructs which, whatever their value elsewhere, have traditionally had very little professional standing in either the graduate curriculum or English Studies overall. In short, while there have been a few sanctioned curricular uses in English Studies for forms other than argumentative academic prose, these have very rarely included service in what the larger field, as traditionally constituted, would be likely to regard as disciplin*ed* or disciplin*ary* inquiry.

Consequently, important as the license for work in alternative forms is to the program's "interplay of responses," it is extending that license to include forms *other* than the argumentative academic prose essay that may turn out to be the initiative's most radical innovation. The challenge lies in establishing new relationships between such forms and the courses that sponsor them. Under the curricular model we called the specialty-based apprenticeship, and the concomitant hegemony of the argumentative academic prose essay, the relationship between writing and course has never been much at issue. To invoke our earlier image, each course is imagined to have a particular discursive trajectory, and student writings are expected to conform to it—to run not only parallel to but, in effect, coterminous with it, connected to that trajectory not only formally but topically and methodologically. That is, it is not only that student writings are expected to take the form of the argumentative academic prose essay, following the textual conventions spelled out in such sources as *The MLA Style Manual*. They are also expected to be on topics—"about" something in a fairly narrow sense— approved as falling within the boundaries of a given course. And they are to be investigated in accordance with sanctioned *methods* of scholarly inquiry, not only in the discipline's usual sense of that term, where it refers with varying degrees of specificity to what are understood to be "reading practices" and their attendant rhetorics of interpretation; but also in a more overtly behavioral sense, whereby the students' research and composing activities—the "scene" of scholarly writing—are regulated as well. (It has always been possible, of course, for students to satisfy these formal, topical, and broader methodological requirements without following the attendant behavioral strictures. A savvy academic writer can construct a plausible "paper" both "about" and "from" entirely nonexistent sources. In our experience, though, nearly all students do follow them. And it is quite common for instructors to enforce such strictures by requiring annotated bibliographies, outlines, and the like.)

The nexus-based classroom, of course, represents by definition a different kind of discursive juncture. The course will likely have, as we indicated, a sponsoring discourse, and some of the time students might well conform to it. Just as often, though, and sometimes more often, students will not thus conform. Rather, they would be better understood as seeking ways to inter-sect or—to make sure that we do not lose the sense of a dynamic at work—interact with that sponsoring discourse, sending them and ultimately (although in much finer increments) it off in directions neither might have taken without such contact.

One way to illustrate the nature of these connections is to trace the work of one student on a single, albeit evolving, project as he moves through a series of courses (in this case, three). The student is Ron Maclean, who identifies himself primarily as a writer of fiction. The project in question begins in a course called "Theories and Practice of Creativity" (Fall 1990, team-taught by Judith Johnson and Harry Staley). As a part of the course students were given a two-part assignment designing and carrying out a ran-dom writing experiment drawing on the methods of, among others, John Cage and Ethel Schwabacher. For the first part of the assignment, Maclean composed a poem called "The Source of Streets," which included these lines: "It was a wrong number, a grid of/scorching streets, ringing/three times in the dead of night." The second stage of the assignment required students to expand upon an image produced for their initial compositions in an alterna-tive form. Maclean chose this image of a grid of streets, and produced a narrative—also entitled "The Source of Streets"—that imagined what such a grid would look like, and where it would have come from. An excerpt:

> Montiel explained to us, as we watched in awe, how there were exactly seven routes from any one point in the city to any other, the shortest always exactly three blocks, the longest several hundred miles, so that you could vary the length of your trip according to how eager you were to reach your destination; he explained, his face lit in a broad grin, that in addition to the aesthetic and engineering beauty of the grid, this maze, there was a very practical beauty. And with a flourish of his arms he lifted a cloth of the same color as his handkerchief to reveal a giant iron lever of the sort once used for trains at switching yards. This, he said, was to be our city's defense against attack for, when pulled, it would change the pattern of the outer sector of streets so that they would all lead into one another, but none of them would enter the city proper. Montiel demonstrated, receiving help from both Edward Bears on the awkward lever, and we watched with amazement as the grid shifted and the city became protected by countless dead ends, surrounded by what seemed to be one endlessly meandering road that went all around us but never led anywhere.

In the context of the specialty-based curricular model we outlined above, "Theories and Practice of Creativity" (were it offered at all) would almost certainly require argumentative academic prose research papers on some topic concerning creativity ("Gender-Based Differences in Paradigms for

Creativity: John Cage and Virginia Woolf," say)—writing, in short, that conformed formally, topically, and methodologically to a fairly standard "academic" trajectory. In this instance, though, the creativity course and Maclean's writing obviously intersect rather differently. Not in terms of form, since neither the initial experiment nor the subsequent expansion imposed any major formal constraints; nor in terms of topic, since neither his poem nor the later narrative are "about" creativity in any usual sense of that term. Instead, their intersection—their *interaction*—is methodological, particularly in what we labeled that term's more behavioral sense.

A semester later (Spring 1991), Maclean enrolled in "Models of History in Literary Criticism," taught by Don Byrd. For his writing project, Maclean continued to work on the narrative that had begun with "The Source of Streets," and which by this time had evolved into a novel-in-progress called *The Beet City Chronicles*. Maclean now sees the constitutive chapters as representing

> a series of fragmentary manuscripts unearthed in archaeological digs around what was once the citadel of a ruler of that part of the world, called Khan. These manuscripts present varied, ultimately incomplete, and often contradictory versions of events of a world that had seemingly succeeded in writing itself out of existence. This book is an effort to piece together and present the history of this lost city, its development and ultimate conflict with the Khan's empire, and an attempt to understand the desire of its residents to remove themselves from history.

Byrd's course, therefore, presents him with an interesting opportunity:

> I had a fairly definite agenda. I wanted to work on my novel, and get feedback on it. Since the novel is the attempt to recount the history of a mythical city, pieced together from fragmentary and contradictory accounts of this lost civilization, reading and talking about how literature has perceived history seemed relevant. I hoped the class would stimulate my thinking about literary constructions of history, and provide an opportunity for reactions to my novel—are the historical themes coming through? are they "working"—from people who were reading and talking about the things I was writing about.

Consider, in keeping with that agenda, this excerpt from a chapter called "Letter from the Khan":

> My rule has become dominated by an aesthetic, my judgment and decisions guided by the colors and shapes of the movement beneath me, the panorama of human activity that reaches me only as a shifting of color and shape, patterns of fluidity that are more, or less, appealing to the eye. I lead based on these patterns of fluid motion. I make my decisions based on the shifting shapes below me, removed from considerations of individual humanity,

of budgets and timetables and lunch hours. I watch out the small square window of my uppermost room for hours every day. You'd be surprised at the consistency of the movement, at the familiarity of the patterns. . . .

How would I serve my people by going down among them? How could I better govern from seeing their problems, so many, so varied, so mutually contradictory, so that to help one group is to harm another? (2–3)

In this case, then, course and writing intersect in a way that, given our rubric, would be called topical. In a reasonably defensible way *The Beet City Chronicles* is a novel that, like the course, can be said to be "about" models of history, about the "problem" of history—or at least is so in a way in which its earlier manifestations were *not* "about" creativity. Probably a more accurate (and, in terms of future course designs, useful) label for this sort of connection would be something like "thematic," with the understanding that such a term allows for the often very different kinds of "about-ness" that our constituent disciplinary perspectives entail. Maclean explains his experience of that license this way:

The class provided me with a healthy balance of freedom and constraint. The freedom not to have to make explicit connections every week between the reading and my responses allowed me to assimilate material that was significant to me at my own pace and in my own way, which tends to be intuitive, relying more on pursuing a thread of emotional and subconscious connections than on "rational" argument, where connection must always be evident. The useful constraint came from knowing that I would be asked, "what does this have to do with the reading?"

Finally, Maclean established still a third relationship between course and writing the following semester (Fall 1991) in Eng 616, "Revisionary Poetics and Literary Practice." The catalog copy for Eng 616 calls for a "study of the ways in which our notions of textuality, both within and beyond western cultures, have been challenged and refigured by, for instance, aleatory and performative practices, post-narrative conventions, and the ethnographic study of oral traditions" (13). Working within those general parameters, the version of the course Maclean took (taught by Eugene Garber) focused on fairly recent developments in American fiction. The reading list included both fiction (e.g. Djuna Barnes, Ishmael Reed) and criticism (e.g. Maurice Blanchot, Shoshana Felman), but the course also depended very heavily on student writing.

Such a course allows plenty of room for the more familiar forms of graduate school writing—i.e., for any number of argumentative academic prose studies of such fiction: a comparison between Robert Coover and Clarence Major, say, or a study of the influence of H.D. on Djuna Barnes. But it also allows, indeed very specifically invites, "fictions" as inquiries, fictions understood as fully legitimate explorations of the subject area. Maclean's response to the required substantial project was in two closely related parts. First and primarily, he continued work on *The Beet City Chronicles*. By the end of this course, he had completed drafts for some ten chapters—"Letter from the Khan," "Montiel's Revenge," "The Khan in the City of Streets," "Coming of Age," and so on. In addition to his ongoing work on specific chapters, though, Maclean intersperses his narratives with a series of commentaries on how he is working out the novel's overall structure. This commentary is the first (in a series of seven) under the heading "*The Models*":

1. The Mirror Model

In which the structure would mirror the grid of streets; a maze which, from within, at various moments seems to be leading somewhere, only to come to a dead end, or to a shift which leads somewhere entirely different, which eternally denies access to its center. The streets of Beet City are designed to keep the heart of the community protected; to defend against penetration. They allow access to the outskirts, to various supplementary roads toward the city, but a shift of the lever keeps those roads from leading to the center, and keeps the Khan always wandering a perimeter, convinced he is getting closer to the core. His desire sustains in him the hope which the structure of the system categorically frustrates: there is no way in.

So with the novel. Each story strand would progress for a time, moving toward a moment of revelation, toward Montiel's kitchen, toward the knowledge of what happened there, who died in the straight-backed hardwood chair, who won the war, why the story of this conflict and of these civilizations disappeared from world history—and then, in turn, each strand would be walled off by the impossibility of knowing, whether because of a myriad of contradictory possibilities, or due to an information gap where something is simply unaccounted for.

In an already complicated novel, however, I fear that such a structure, while true to the principles the book grows from, may render it incomprehensible. No, that's not entirely it. This approach leans too far to the side of deconstruction; it lacks sufficient drive of the desire to tell a story.

The relationship between course and writing in this third instance, then, can be characterized as primarily *formal*, with some traces of a topical connection. That is, Maclean explores the subject of avant-garde fiction mostly by working at length in a *form* that falls under that rubric, while his commentaries, although focused specifically on his own project, are—by virtue of that project's formal status—therefore also on the course's *topic*, "about" (an) avant-garde American fiction (his own).

Graduate (School) Writing and Disciplinary Change

As we hope our presentation makes clear, the extended example we have offered here might legitimately be characterized as illustrative of the writing

Albany's program allows, but it is not "representative" or "typical" for at least three reasons. First, students' interest in and/or ability at sustaining projects across courses in the way Ron Maclean does varies a good deal, as does their success at making good on Allen's ambition that course writing lead directly to dissertation writing. On both fronts, some do more, some less. (Indeed, it is worth noting that Maclean's dissertation turned out to be an entirely different fiction project—albeit one indebted to *The Beet City Chronicles*—entitled "Who We Are.")

Second, our method of representing the course-to-writing relationship tends to make influence appear to be entirely one way: the writer is affected by something loosely designated as "the course," without any discernible reciprocal influence on, say, his fellow students or his instructors. While we are admittedly not in a position to trace such influence with equal authority, we are convinced that it is both a very real presence in the program and central to its long term success.

Third, we have been limited by space, and in particular by our commitment to offering relatively long excerpts of the writing we have sought to account for, in terms of the *variety* we could present. Except for Maclean's poem in the creativity course, all our excerpts are in fairly standard prose forms. A more representative sampling—and we are at work on this—would have to include a broader range of prose, everything from correspondence to extended riffs in (Gertrude) Steinian mode to prose collages. Moreover, it would have to feature a rich variety of poetic forms; dialogue-based work, including both stage-oriented drama and a variety of performance materials; electronic compositions of all sorts; and, last but hardly least, work that combines or challenges these and other forms and their attendant conventions.

Despite these limitations, however, the writings we have featured here represent quite well the *spirit* of the curricular experiment that sponsored their production. It is an experiment about which we confess to having somewhat mixed feelings. In our headiest moments, we find ourselves talking about writings like these as documents from the future of English Studies. Not documents *about* that future, like the Program Proposal or the catalog copy, but *from* it: texts sent back, as it were, from discursive places that the discipline itself has not necessarily gone yet. That is why they sometimes seem quite alien: the context in which these writings "make sense"—a context framed, as it were, by the outer edges of the boundaries we are used to honoring from the inside, out there on the frontier of interrelationships—is not one most of us know. Understood in that way, our program's collective work is not simply or even mostly about how writing is best deployed in the education of English graduate students. It is not, in other words, about new means to an old end, but about new ends; not about refiguring these texts to suit English Studies, but about refiguring English Studies to suit these texts.

At other times—more sober moments—we recognize that that is a pretty tall order for what are also, in some sense, "school" writings. Consider, by way of commentary on their professional status, the irony of our having to explore these alternatives to the hegemony of the argumentative academic prose essay in—what else?—an argumentative academic prose essay. At the very least, then, we should talk only about futures for English Studies, and *possible* futures at that.

For the most part, though, our faith in this curricular enterprise lies somewhere between those extremes. We are convinced that our classrooms at their best do promote very different and very valuable possibilities for English Studies. Even more important, the students in those classrooms literally embody the discipline's future. Not all of it, obviously—there are lots of other graduate programs in the world—but still, a not insignificant portion of it. They will go to their own classrooms and their own programs, impelled by a vision of English Studies that none of their teachers could ever have fully shared, let alone realized. It is by such means, and in such increments, that disciplinary changes are made.

22

Alternative Genres for Graduate Student Writing

JoAnn Campbell

I recently received a memo from two graduate students in my department
who want to compile a bibliography of theoretical and critical texts that faculty and advanced graduate students consider important.[1] The opening paragraph describes the rationale for this project:

> As you know, the transition from undergraduate to graduate study can be a
> difficult one. First year graduate students must confront many new
> approaches to literary study and must begin to familiarize themselves with
> that mysterious body of knowledge called "theory."

What new graduate students might *do* with the texts is unstated, but the
assumption seems to be that they first consume a dominant or privileged
body of knowledge. Only after students have immersed themselves in the
reading currently privileged, it seems, might they find their own project of
inquiry that theory might support, expand, or examine.[2]

To a degree, the assumptions embedded in the graduate students' seemingly straightforward memo reflect the prevalence and the limitations of the
mimetic function of most graduate studies, studies in which incoming students read what their professors value in order to eventually produce the kind
of writing the professor publishes, writing that is presumably of value itself.
In labeling the dominant genre of graduate student writing mimetic, I draw
upon Carolyn R. Miller's point that "a rhetorically sound definition of genre
must be centered not on the substance or the form of discourse but on the
action it is used to accomplish" (151). In "Genre as Social Action," Miller
argues that genre as *discourse situated around action* reveals cultural and
historical currents that illuminate more than individual motives for writing:

> What we learn when we learn a genre is not just a pattern of forms or even
> a method of achieving our own ends. We learn, more importantly, what

ends we may have . . . [F]or the critic, genres can serve both as an index to
cultural patterns and as tools for exploring the achievements of particular
speakers and writers; for the student, genres serve as keys to understanding
how to participate in the actions of a community. (165)

Miller's metaphor of genre as key indicates an opening or entrance into
a community but also suggests that genre may lock a door as well. Most
significant to Miller's definition of genre as action is Patricia Sullivan's
finding that the writing done by graduate students was "not valued for what
it contributed to the course and to other students' understanding of the issues
. . . [but] for its evaluative properties as an academic exercise, as the basis for
a grade" (1991, 287). The action of graduate student writing was less to create new knowledge or develop critiques than to represent a mastery of given
knowledge and information.

Is it likely, in such a system, that this entering class will be asked to
compile a bibliography of recommended readings for the faculty as well? In
order to answer "yes," graduate study in English will need to become multi-
directional; that is, in addition to a traditional model of faculty teaching students, students would more routinely teach faculty, faculty and students
would teach members of communities not in the university, and those in the
community would teach students and faculty. Certainly some of this goes on
already, but it's not institutionalized, at least as the practice might be
revealed through the most common genres of graduate student writing. While
students may not yet be experts in the genres of professional academe, their
knowledges and experiences in other arenas can situate academic knowledges and literacies in ways that challenge and integrate what have been
called public/private, personal/academic, or university/community dichotomies. I believe that as we approach the next century, our institutions must
change to more effectively create knowledge that works to solve our global
problems of living. We can and should include graduate students to help create a new academic path, one that uses the authority intellectuals already
have to work for a cause larger than an individual career or a department's
or college's reputation.

Current State of Graduate Student Writing

Richard Boyd argues that a mimetic composing model lies at the center of a
number of approaches to teaching writing, including that expressed in David
Bartholomae's influential essay "Inventing the University." Boyd urges composition scholars to examine the "good" of mimetic ends:

If these students are perceptive enough to recognize that we are also saying
that they cannot and should not ever perfectly emulate us because we must
always remain their superiors, qualitatively different by virtue of our superior power and prestige, then the result can only be frustration and finally

struggle and conflict as they seek to possess what the model holds out with one hand but takes away with the other. (341)

Boyd refers only to undergraduate writing, and Bartholomae's essay focuses on entering college undergraduates, yet the mimetic model dominates graduate student writing as well. While completing writing assignments successfully is essential to the advancement of a graduate student's career, it seems faculty devote little instructional time to sharing their own writing, or working individually with students through a series of drafts to improve an individual's writing. In her study of graduate student writing at six institutions, Patricia Sullivan found that most professors expected graduate students to already know how to write, and the *process* of writing thus "assumes a secondary and often marginal role in graduate education" (1991, 285). Without specific guidance as to what separates undergraduate from graduate student writing, beginning graduate students must rely on earlier training and practices that may not be highly valued at a more advanced level. As one woman at my university remarked, "I thought that graduate student writing was just long," and so for her first seminar paper, she researched everything about the topic and put it into a fifty-page paper, "like the classic data dumping that we tell our students not to do" (Welsh-Huggins). Written forms most frequently assigned at the graduate level include short papers and a long term paper, which Sullivan describes as a "discursive training ground" where students practice research and writing skills in preparation for journal articles they'll be expected to write later.

Certainly a model of professorial apprenticeship is held out as one ideal for graduate student life. At a material level, graduate student salaries are in proportion to what they can expect to earn as English academics, just as the stipend of a biology or a chemical engineering graduate student is relative to her or his later earning power. Graduate students read books from lists drawn up by professors, answer examination questions deemed important to professors, and use course writing to practice for later professional tasks, with term papers a precursor to journal articles and dissertations precursors to books. Less encouraged to be radical and use alternate forms than to learn and reproduce existing traditions and genres, graduate students work in a world with fairly clear boundaries (and hoops to pass through) because a main assumption is that there is plenty of time for alternative ways of thinking, being, and writing once the student has become a more established member of the community.

While this model of writing may serve to initiate newcomers into their chosen profession, I see three main problems with an exclusively mimetic genre for all graduate student writing. On a practical level, in the current job market many graduate students will not become professors, and therefore writing for only academic publications may offer too narrow an experience for their needs. Cary Nelson and Michael Berube observe that "the collapse of the job market makes the logic of graduate apprenticeship morally corrupt" (B1).

A second problem with a mimetic paradigm stems from the professional writing it models. The convention of separating parts of the writer's experience and ideas from what is sanctioned as academic subject matter and academic treatment of a topic has come under discussion from a number of perspectives. Patricia Bizzell, in a study of academic writing and critical consciousness, argues for a critique of academic conventions from the inside, *after* one has become fully initiated into an academic discourse community. Bizzell acknowledges that academic literacy "exerts hegemony over other ways of knowing," but she believes that "the abstracting, formalizing power of academic work enables us to understand our experience in ways not made available by common sense or folk wisdom" (125). "Abstract" and "formal" both imply a critical distance from an idea or experience, an act requiring separation in order to see more "clearly" or in superior ways what others only know through "common sense."

Such distancing is not problematic in itself, yet we need to understand just what we require when we ask students to remove their lives from their writing. In her book *The Alchemy of Race and Rights*, Patricia Williams insists upon bringing the life she lives as an African American woman into contact with her life as a law professor; indeed they are inseparable, and while Williams's critique is of law education and legal theories in the United States, her understanding of the relationship of a "world of real others" present in all academic prose illuminates my point that such practices, perhaps seemingly necessary for initiation into academic discourse, contain ways of seeing that may undermine the effective work academics can do. Better than any writer I know of, Williams expresses the stakes of mimicking a "neutral" academic voice:

> What is 'impersonal' writing but denial of self? If withholding is an ideology worth teaching, we should be clearer about that as the bottom line of the enterprise. We should also acknowledge the extent to which denial of one's authority in authorship is not the same as elimination of oneself; it is ruse, not reality. And the object of such ruse is to empower still further; to empower beyond the self, by appealing to neutral, shared, even universal understandings. In a vacuum, I suppose there's nothing wrong with that attempt to empower: it generates respect and distance and a certain obeisance to the sleekness of a product that has been skinned of its personalized complication. But in a world of real others, the cost of such exclusive forms of discourse is empowerment at the expense of one's relation to those others; empowerment without communion. And as the comfort of such false power becomes habitual, it is easy to forget that the source of one's power is quite limited, not the fiat of a heavenly mandate. It is easy to forget how much that grandiosity of power depends on the courtesy and restraint of a society of others no less equally endowed than you. (93)

In asking any writer to "skin" her writing of its "personal complications" and comply with forms of academic discourse where autobiography may frame a piece but is not central to an inquiry, teachers can cut students off from a powerful source of insight, not to mention a primary motive for writing. A growing body of writing by academics indicates that the traditional forms and purposes of academic writing, such as to pass along information from a distanced or detached perspective, no longer serve all readers, writers, or purposes in the academy. Responding to a need to reach a wider audience and include more of their lives in their writing, a number of writers such as Gloria Anzaldua, Helene Cixous, Samuel Delany, bell hooks, Nancy Miller, Trinh Minh-ha, Mike Rose, Nancy Sommers, Jane Tompkins, and Victor Villanueva weave experiences from their lives outside the academy into issues raised by and important to academics. Many of these writers hold positions of power within institutions, having already proven their academic socialization with more traditional forms of writing. Lillian Bridwell-Bowles, for instance, acknowledges being able to ". . . afford the luxury of experimentation because I am a tenured and reasonably secure member of the profession" (1992, 366)

Yet the problems these established scholars name and ameliorate with their writing may be equally pressing to those just entering a discipline. This version of the genre of academic writing as a separation of what Peter Elbow labels "personal" and "academic" concerns is reinforced at the graduate level because graduate students *embody* the place where boundaries break down. As writers of dissertations, graduate students must make "original" contributions to knowledge but are not rewarded for simultaneously challenging conventions of the dissertation genre. Yet because they straddle at least two worlds—professional in training and student, teacher of undergraduates and apprentice to a master—alternate genres of writing must be opened to them. Otherwise they are caught in the conflicted struggle that Boyd detailed above, trying to be like the professor and reminded at every turn of the ways they are not. Always, then, they are inadequate or inferior, which is a difficult state of mind in which to write anything, let alone something designed to illustrate one's intelligence.

Finally, mimetic work may be insufficient to do the work demanded of today's academy. A mimetic model in which graduate student writing primarily demonstrates the individual's ability to fit into existing academic structures and conversations works to contain the potential contribution of the graduate student writer who wants to go beyond fluency in theory to create what Nicholas Maxwell calls a philosophy of wisdom. Maxwell suggests that the problems of living in the late twentieth century require all the resources of university communities and he argues that academic work should consist of "articulating problems of living and proposing possible solutions" (3). Certainly state legislators around the country are questioning the ability of traditional academic discourse to serve larger communities, and academics might be proactive in their work to bridge university and community interests. Alternative genres of learning and writing are one way to accommodate those who end up outside academe and to support those who might remain in a transformed institution of higher education.

Rethinking Graduate Student Writing

Increasing the subjectivity of a piece of writing is one way to stretch the boundaries of the genre of academic writing. Terry Caesar argues that there is so little discourse about dissertations—the kind of graduate student writing presumably most like that produced by professionals—because the writing as a process matters more than the final product. By definition, the subjectivity of this genre requires writers to submerge theirs in order to occupy what might be considered a universal student subject position. According to Caesar:

> (Like any ritual, it [a dissertation] purges subjectivity and renders what must be undergone as something impersonal.) And when at last completed, a dissertation must be immediately abandoned *as such*: 'no unrevised dissertations considered' publishers caution. Why the caution? Is it because, in addition, a dissertation is ultimately nothing but the sum of its discipline, ceremony, and form? (130)

This process of certification cannot be accomplished with a model other than mimetic if the only definition of academic is someone who can reproduce a text recognizably *academic* by its conventions, subjectivity, subject matter, and approach. Because a dissertation is required to offer something new to a given field of study, the mimicry is not exact; it can't be. If the writing announces itself as esoteric and reveals the learning of the writer, then it has performed its function of certifying the importance of the field of study as well as the writer's existence, and thus justifies a program of study that has grown to a national average of nine years. By keeping the work of graduate student writing within a specialized community of academics, a larger community is cut off from the scholarly inquiry, and these scholars learn that they don't have to be accountable or accessible (and I think those concepts are intricately connected) to those outside a narrow sphere.

What if dissertations took a variety of forms, depending on the work the writer hoped it would do? Then collaboratively written dissertations might be as acceptable as individual scholarship on archival materials; projects that met community literacy needs would be as rewarded as studies of university practices. Thinking of alternative genres for graduate student writing means thinking beyond the confines of the academy to ask, What kinds of social actions are required by the community in which the writer lives? By articulating problems of living throughout a semester, students can collectively create projects and sites that require the expertise they already have. That collective enterprise might result in coauthoring or sharing individual papers on a regular basis to facilitate a common vocabulary and focus of inquiry. Having an exigency for one's writing as fulfilling community needs and thus going beyond the pressures of producing it for a grade may alleviate some of the anxiety associated with the performance aspect of writing. Sullivan found that because writing *instruction* holds such a marginalized place in graduate study, any writing problems were frequently "attributed to personal deficiency, not institutional *praxis*" (1991, 288). If fostered in graduate school, the practice of writing for readers inside *and* outside the academy could help produce scholars who saw that making their expertise available to a larger community and drawing their research problems from it was important, even necessary, work.

This task of helping students find the best form for their messages or questions positions the graduate student teacher as a facilitator for students' ideas and projects, a kind of midwife or coexplorer rather than expert or "master" writer. In my own teaching, I've felt most comfortable and been most effective in classes where my expertise was named, my limitations acknowledged, and our joint project articulated by the entire class. To illustrate briefly, in the fall semester of 1993, eight women enrolled in my graduate seminar, Academic Writing as Social Practice. I borrowed the course title from Linda Brodkey's ethnographic study of academic writing communities because I wanted to examine the conditions of writing most frequently valued, taught, and produced in universities today. The course was conceived out of my own frustration with the limits of academic knowledge and writing practices. I felt we had to create an environment in which we would regularly talk about our own writing and reading experiences and strategies and examine the dynamics of the class itself, the ways in which the academy shaped the questions we asked, and the avenues of inquiry we pursued. I drew up a reading list, ordered textbooks, and created assignments before the class met, but the pace of the class, the nature of the assignments, and at least two of the texts changed over the course of the semester to meet the direction in which we were heading as a group. We compared samples of nineteenth-century academic writing by students and professionals with writing today, examined "alternative" prose currently being produced by a number of people in composition and literary studies, and read theories of academic discourse and teaching. All of us duplicated and distributed a one-page response to the readings each week, so that the nine essays by the participants became a text that we also studied. Students did a rhetorical analysis of an academic journal of their choice and reported on its conventions, hot topics, and the people who populated it; at midpoint they wrote a draft of their longer, final project which we workshopped in the class, and their final paper was described in the syllabus as a

> Seminar paper on a topic of your choice, perhaps a revision of the earlier paper (15–20 pages). This paper may embrace a traditional academic style

or stretch those boundaries. I invite you to think creatively about the shape
of your inquiry and the genre that will best reflect your concerns.

Because the course was an upper-level seminar, I did assume that students had successfully written in a "traditional academic style," and also that
by the end of a course devoted to its study we would have arrived at a shared
understanding of said style. Two students constructed final products that
appeared alternative or experimental; that is, they used genres not frequently
submitted in advanced seminars: a maze produced and read on the Macintosh
program Hypercard, and an illustrated written text with an accompanying
cassette tape of the writer reading the text.

The two students who elected to write in a "nontraditional" form said
later that they wanted to create an experience for their audience that would
expand the questions they asked and the points they made, and they wanted
to produce an interactive text that challenged the conventions of academic
literacy we had been studying all semester. Pam Welsh-Huggins had
described her typical graduate student writing as "largely unsuccessful," at
least in longer projects. An earlier attempt at nontraditional, multivocal writing was not received well by her professor, and she "divorced" herself from
the project and cranked out something more traditional that she wasn't
"invested" in. She described herself as needing to be engaged in the process
of writing the paper to be proud of the results, and described many papers as
feeling like hers only because she recognized "some goofy turn of phrase."
Pam created a Hypercard maze which she labeled "a metaphor for graduate
school," and she described it as "theorized play" in that the form itself drew
attention to the points she was making. There were excerpts from class readings and members' response papers, pictures of her daughter and grandmother, an extended meditation on sewing as a kind of literacy, musings on
academia and graduate school, and the "blank wall," a space for readers to
write. Her goal for the project was:

> ... to have the person enter in and determine their own path within the
> confines of the maze, and see how you make sense of the path you take and
> the texts available at the different turns. What do you as a reader bring to
> make the texts cohere or how do you read them against each other? (Per-
> sonal interview)

Pam designed this project to help her learn a new technology and found
that the technology and genre of a maze suited her life as the mother of a
three year old; although she needed *some* sustained time, "doing the Hypercard I could do a little bit and then go away and come back. Fragmentation
was allowed here." Pam concluded that the Hypercard maze wedded process
and product in a way we often read about in composition but seldom experience: "as a process that is also a product that is also a process it allowed
me to feel a sense of ownership and engagement with the project that has

been very rare for me in graduate school." In Miller's terms of the social action of this genre, Pam's project invited others in as equals and situated her writing as competent, individual, and connected to her life. She didn't have to be an expert on Hypercard or on academic literacy but could raise questions, encourage discussion, and point out connections that readers hadn't noticed or considered. By using a form that stretched traditional reader/writer relationships, Welsh-Huggins stepped into a space occupied by professionals without mimicking how professionals occupy that space.

Kathryn Wooten Sobel's project was a thirty-three page collage that contained drawings, poetry, a meditation on graduate student writing, a survey for the department on graduate student writing, and two explications of poems that analyzed her reading strategies. She read the text onto two cassette tapes, sometimes adding material not found on the text, sometimes skipping past some of the language of the collage. In an interview, Sobel said she wanted to do "something like performance poetry [because] I've been unable to be creative in form even if I can be creative in content, and I wanted to bring those things together somehow in the project." Given the constraints of a fifteen-week course, she felt that this project might best reflect her thinking as still in process. By foregrounding reading and writing connections and making this reading event unfamiliar to the reader, she constructed a project that seemed to her "holistic" rather than a more traditional graduate student writing, which she characterized as "Here's my idea, I've read everyone else's ideas on this, I've processed them, here's what's good about this, this is what's bad about them, here's mine, this is how it solves all of the problems, it's brand new, and aren't I smart?" Kathryn said, "I didn't feel like I had to be so smart with you," which I chose to interpret as a compliment.

One of the vignettes Kathryn included in her collage was a day when her composition class complained about the textbook; she admitted she didn't like it much either but told them she hadn't selected it, and she told her students they had to use it. In her collage she asks, "What power/authority/subjectivity do my students gain or lose through my simultaneous admission of powerlessness and my exercise of power over them?" Voicing these tensions may not resolve them, but their articulation can challenge and test theories of composition, rhetoric, or cultural studies in ways necessary for graduate education. When asked if she would do such a project again, Kathryn replied that it depended on who was teaching the class and whether or not they specifically invited students to try experimental forms; Pam added that such a reply "is a recognition that the site in which we construct these projects is very much determined by the person who's standing at the door. Whether they have a spear in their hand or a bunch of posies makes a big difference."

As their teacher, how did I decide to pick up posies rather than a spear? How did I convince these students that a posy really was a posy? And are posies really lighter to carry than spears? Offering posies at the door of the classroom seemed the easiest thing to do. In a move similar to the one Jane Tompkins describes in "Pedagogy of the Distressed," I was exhausted from trying to be an expert, so I took risks, shared my own uneasiness with academic writing, challenged definitions of intelligence that seem to be valued by academe, and reframed one role of teacher in a graduate course. During our first meeting we spent most of the three hours introducing ourselves, telling why we were drawn to the course, what our relationship to academic discourse seemed to be at that moment, where we wanted to go, what we hoped to learn. Our reading was also manageable, so that we really did have time to focus on the participants' writing, including mine. Perhaps by doing the work with them, sharing my responses, I helped to demystify the teacher's reading. I certainly found their responses just as thoughtful and provocative as mine.

Yet I don't want to indicate that the ideal graduate student teacher is simply one of the class. Clearly I was being paid to guide this seminar, and certainly I had thought about the issues longer, written about them, placed my own experience within the context of these theories, so that I had something unique to offer. But so did everyone else. The woman from Japan told us of the elite nature of "personal" writing in Japanese scholarship and checked my tendency to universalize it as a necessary remedy to academic discourse; the former high school teacher helped us articulate the hermeneutics of working with less flexible institutions, thus contextualizing the complaints we raised about our own; the woman interested in Blake raised issues of belief and discipleship in literary criticism in ways that helped us examine what we believed and how those beliefs were expressed by our favorite theorists. I don't expect graduate students to resolve the paradoxes and contradictions of their positions. I also don't expect them to write from the perspective of someone who has taught for fifteen years and written three books. Nor can I. As we let go of the idea that a graduate student can produce a journal article in fifteen weeks and thus turn to new genres, we might suggest that they highlight and explore the sometimes painful tensions of their status. Rather than participate in what Sheree Meyer has called the "confidence game" of academic writing that requires students to pretend they have more authority than they do and often creates feelings of fraud, graduate writers can produce a form that functions in tandem with their lives. Pam's comment that the Hypercard maze fit her fragmented life as a mother, wife, teacher, and student and Kathryn's observation that a collage permitted her to display her thinking at its present state and not to be as "smart" as traditional essays required indicate the ways alternative genres can make a difference in the lived experience of graduate student writers.

Graduate students are in an important position to criticize the academy, but they may too often be silenced by the perception of a single model of professional discourse. Rather than reproduce the diseases of the profession, graduate studies can be a site and graduate writing a source of healthy alternatives. Teachers of graduate studies in English can construct graduate courses with an aim other than to professionalize students, direct dissertations that acknowledge the writer's life inside and outside academe, and suggest graduate writing assignments that allow a writer to know what she currently knows, to ask what he most needs to ask, and to acknowledge the connections and contradictions that make up life in graduate school. These changes, of course, will ripple through other institutionalized rituals of education, shaking them up, perhaps for the better.

Notes

1. I'd like to thank Janice Brown, Kate DeGroot, Laura Lovasz, Linda Sneed, Kathryn Sobel, Sharon Sperry, Naoko Sugiyami, and Pam Welsh-Huggins for creating the environment that gave rise to the seed idea.

2. The process of initiation implied in this request raises questions as well. Do the memo writers still find theory "mysterious" or are they now positioned to demystify the field for the next group of initiates? At what point is initiation completed? The fact that graduate students plan to initiate new students indicates to some extent at least that the current curriculum of graduate education in the department needs improvement, or perhaps that peers can initiate in ways professors cannot.

Works Cited

Achtert, Walter S., and Joseph Gibaldi. *The MLA Style Manual*. New York: MLA, 1985.

Alcoff, Linda. "Cultural Feminism Versus Post-structuralism: The Identity Crisis in Feminist Theory." *Signs* 13.3 (Spring 1988): 405–36.

Allen, Don Cameron. *The Ph.D. in English and American Literature*. New York: Holt, 1968.

Allen, Walter. *The English Novel: A Short Critical History*. New York: E. P. Dutton, 1954.

Altman, Meryl. "What Not to Do with Metaphors We Live By." *College English* 52 (1990): 495–506.

Amistad Research Center, Tulane University, New Orleans, Louisiana. [The teaching materials are contained in Box 11 of the Cullen papers, which are organized according to correspondence, literary manuscripts, etc. Whole plan books have survived, as have many samples of students' writing.]

Anderson, Worth, Cynthia Best, Alycia Black, John Hurst, Brandt Miller, and Susan Miller. "Cross-Curricular Underlife: A Collaborative Report on Ways with Academic Worlds." *College Composition and Communication* 41 (1990): 11–36.

Andrews, William L. *To Tell a Free Story: The First Century of Afro-American Autobiography, 1760–1865*. Urbana: University of Illinois Press, 1986.

Anzaldua, Gloria. *Borderlands/La Frontera: The New Mestiza*. San Francisco: Aunt Lute Books, 1987.

———. "Haciendo caras, una entrada." *Making Face, Making Soul/Haciendo Caras: Creative and Critical Perspectives by Women of Color*. Ed. Gloria Anzaldua. San Francisco: Aunt Lute Books, 1990, xv–xxviii.

Anzaldua, Gloria, and Cheri Moraga, ed. *This Bridge Called My Back: Writing by Radical Women of Color*. New York: Kitchen Table, 1983.

<artsxnet>. "Hillbilly in Cyberspace." Cybermind Discussion List [online]. Available email: CYBERMIND <LISTSERV@WORLD.STD.COM>. 6 Jul. 1994.

Atkinson, Dwight. "A Historical Discourse Analysis of Scientific Writing." Dissertation, University of Southern California, 1993.

Atkinson, Paul. *Understanding Ethnographic Texts*. Newbury Park, CA: Sage, 1992.

Atwell, Nancie. *In the Middle: Writing, Reading and Learning with Adolescents*. Portsmouth, NH: Boynton/Cook-Heinemann, 1987.

Auslander, Bonnie. "In Search of Mr. Write." Editor's Choice. *College English* 5S.5 (Sept. 1993): 531–32.

———. "Lip-Synching with Your Dog." *Writing on the Edge* 5.2 (Spring 1994): 53–54.

Austin, J. L. *How to Do Things with Words*. Oxford: Oxford University Press, 1962.

Avi-Ram, Amitai. "The Unreadable Black Body: 'Conventional' Poetic Form in the Harlem Renaissance." *Genders* (March 1990): 7, 32–46.

Bakhtin, Mikhail. *The Dialogic Imagination*. Trans. Michael Holquist and Caryl Emerson. Austin: University of Texas Press, 1981.

——— . "The Problem of Speech Genres." *Speech Genres and Other Late Essays*. Trans. Vern W. McGee. Ed. Caryl Emerson and Michael Holquist. Austin: University of Texas Press, 1986, 60–102.

——— . *Speech Genres and Other Late Essays*. Austin: University of Texas Press, 1986.

<baldwine>. "Define cybermind." Cybermind Discussion List [online]. Available email: CYBERMIND <LISTSERV@WORLD.STD.COM>. 6 Jul. 1994.

Bannerju, Himani, Linda Carty, Kari Dehli, Susan Heald, and Kate McKenna. *UnSettling Relations: The University as a Site of Feminist Struggles*. Boston: South End Press, 1991.

Barker, Thomas, and Fred Kemp. "A Postmodern Pedagogy for the Writing Classroom." *Computers and Community*. Ed. Carolyn Handa. Portsmouth, NH: Boynton/Cook-Heinemann, 1990.

Barrow, Alberto. "Racism Was Central to the Invasion." *The U.S. Invasion of Panama: The Truth Behind Operation "Just Cause."* Ed. The Independent Commission of Inquiry on the U.S. Invasion of Panama. Boston: South End Press: 1991, 81–83.

Barry, Dave. "Through Internet, 'cybermuffin' shares intimate computer secrets." *The Columbus Dispatch*, 6 Feb. 1994.

Bartholomae, David. "Inventing the University." *When a Writer Can't Write: Studies in Writer's Block and Other Composing Problems*. Ed. Mike Rose. New York: Guilford, 1985, 134–65.

——— . "Writing with Teachers: A Conversation with Peter Elbow." *College Composition and Communication* 46.1 (Feb. 1995): 62–71.

Bartholomae, David, and Anthony Petrosky. *Facts, Artifacts, and Counterfacts: Theory and Method for a Reading and Writing Course*. Portsmouth, NH: Boynton/Cook, 1986.

Bartholomae, David, Peter Elbow, Don H. Bialostosky, Wendy Bishop, and Susan Welsh. "Interchanges: Responses to Bartholomae and Elbow." *College Composition and Communication* 46.1 (Feb. 1995): 184–203.

Bauman, Richard. *Story, Performance, and Event*. Cambridge: Cambridge University Press, 1986.

Baym, Nina. *Feminism and American Literary History: Essays*. New Brunswick, NJ: Rutgers University Press, 1992.

Bazerman, Charles. *Shaping Written Knowledge: The Genre and Activity of the Experimental Articles in Science*. Madison: University of Wisconsin Press, 1988.

————. "Systems of Genre and the Enactment of Social Intentions." *Rethinking Genre*. Eds. Aviva Freedman and Peter Medway. London: Taylor & Francis, 1994.

————. "Whose Moment?: The Kairotics of Intersubjectivity." *Constructing Experience*. Carbondale: Southern Illinois University Press, 1994.

Bazerman, Charles, and James Paradis, eds. *Textual Dynamics of the Professions: Historical and Contemporary Studies of Writing in Professional Communities.* Madison: University of Wisconsin Press, 1991.

Beale, Walter. *A Pragmatic Theory of Rhetoric*. Carbondale: Southern Illinois University Press, 1987.

Beebe, Thomas O. The Ideology of Genre: A Comparative Study of Generic Instability. University Park, PA: Penn State University Press, 1994.

Behar, Ruth. "The Body of the Woman, the Story in the Woman: A Book Review and Personal Essay." *The Female Body: Figures, Styles, Speculations.* Ed. Lawrence Goldstein. Ann Arbor: Michigan University Press, 1992.

————. "Dare We Say 'I'? Bringing the Personal into Scholarship." *Chronicle of Higher Education* 29 June 1994: B1–2.

Belenky, Catherine. *Women's Ways of Knowing: The Development of Self, Voice and Mind.* New York: Basic Books, 1986.

Belsey, Catherine. *John Milton: Language, Gender, Power*. New York: Oxford University Press, 1988.

Benstock, Shari. "Authorizing the Autobiographical." *Feminisms: An Anthology of Literary Theory and Criticism.* Ed. Robyn R. Warhol and Diane Price Herndl. New Brunswick, NJ: Rutgers University Press, 1993, 1040–57.

Bercovitch, Sacvan. "The Ritual of American Autobiography: Edwards, Franklin, Thoreau." *Revue Française d'Etudes Americaines* 14 (1982): 139–50.

Bereiter, Carl. "Does Learning to Write Have to Be So Difficult?" Paper delivered to the Learning to Write Conference, sponsored by the Canadian Council of Teachers of English, Ottawa, Canada, 1979.

Berkenkotter, Carol. "Paradigm Debates, Turf Wars and the Conduct of Sociocognitive Inquiry in Composition." *College Composition and Communication* 42 (1991): 151–69.

————. "A 'Rhetoric for Naturalistic Inquiry' and the Question of Genre." *Research in the Teaching of English* 27 (1993): 293–304.

Berkenkotter, Carol, and Thomas Huckin. *Genre Knowledge in Disciplinary Communication: Cognition/Culture/Power.* Hillsdale, NJ: Erlbaum, 1994.

————. "Rethinking Genre from a Sociocognitive Perspective." *Written Communication* 10 (1993): 475–509.

Berkenkotter, Carol, et al. "Conventions, Conversations, and the Writer: Case Study of a Student in a Rhetoric Ph.D. Program." *Research in the Teaching of English* 22.1 (1988): 9–44.

Berlin, James. "Composition Studies and Cultural Studies: Collapsing Boundaries." *Into the Field: Sites of Composition Studies.* Ed. Anne Ruggles Gere. New York: Modern Language Association, 1993.

————. "Rhetoric and Ideology in the Writing Class." *College English* 50.5 (Sept. 1988): 477–94.

————. *Rhetoric and Reality: Writing Instruction in American Colleges, 1900–1985.* Carbondale: Southern Illinois University Press, 1987.

Berthoff, Ann E. *The Making of Meaning: Metaphors, Models, and Maxims for Writing Teachers.* Montclair, NJ: Boynton/Cook, 1981.

Bhatia, Vijay. *Genre Analysis.* London: Methuen, 1994.

Biber, Douglas. *Variation Across Speech and Writing.* Cambridge: Cambridge University Press, 1988.

Bishop, Wendy. "Co-authoring Changes the Writing Classroom: Students Authorizing the Self, Authoring Together." *Composition Studies/Freshman English News* 23.1 (Spring 1995): 54–62.

————, ed. *Elements of Alternate Style: Essays on Writing and Revision.* Portsmouth, NH: Boynton/Cook-Heinemann, 1997.

————. "I-Witnessing in Composition: Turning Ethnographic Data into Narratives." *Rhetoric Review* 11.1 (1992): 147–58.

————. *Released into Language: Options for Teaching Creative Writing.* Urbana, IL: NCTE, 1990.

————. "Risk-Taking and Radical Revision—Exploring Writing Identities Through Advanced Composition and Poetry Portfolios." *Portfolios in Practice: Voices from the Classroom.* Ed. Kathleen Yancey. Urbana, IL: NCTE, forthcoming.

————. *The Subject Is Writing: Essays by Teachers and Students.* Portsmouth, NH: Boynton/Cook-Heinemann, 1993.

————. "Teaching Grammar for Writers in a Process Workshop Classroom." *The Place of Grammar in Writing Instruction: Past, Present, Future.* Eds. Susan Hunter and Ray Wallace. Portsmouth, NH: Boynton/Cook-Heinemann, 1995. 176–87.

Bishop, Wendy, and Hans Ostrom, eds. *Colors of a Different Horse: Rethinking Creative Writing, Theory and Pedagogy.* Urbana, IL: National Council of Teachers of English, 1994.

Bishop, Wendy, and Sandra Teichman. "Tales of Two Teachers: Writing Together in Writing Classrooms" "The First Tale: Writing with a Writing Workshop" by Wendy Bishop; copublished with "The Second Tale: Writing with a First-Year Writing Classroom" by Sandra Teichman. *English Leadership Quarterly* 15.3 (Oct. 1993): 2–5

Bissex, Glenda. *GNYS AT WRK: A Child Learns to Write and Read.* Cambridge: Harvard University Press, 1980.

Bitzer, Lloyd. "The Rhetorical Situation." *Philosophy and Rhetoric* 1 (1968): 1–14.

Bizzell, Patricia. *Academic Discourse and Critical Consciousness.* Pittsburgh: University of Pittsburgh Press, 1992.

Blakeslee, Ann. "Inventing Scientific Discourse." Dissertation, Carnegie Mellon University, 1992.

Bleecker, Ann Eliza. *The Posthumous Works of Ann Eliza Bleecker in Prose and Verse to Which is Added, A Collection of Essays, Prose and Poetical, by Margaretta V. Faugeres*. New York: T. and J. Swords, 1793 (microfilm).

Bleich, David. "Ethnography and the Study of Literacy: Prospects for Socially Generous Research." *Into the Field: Sites of Composition Studies*. Ed. Ann Ruggles Gere. New York: MLA, 1993. 176–92.

Bloom, Lynn Z. "I Want a Writing Director." *College Composition and Communication* 43.2 (1992): 176–78.

———. "Teaching College English as a Woman." *College English* 54.7 (Nov. 1992): 818–25.

———. "Textual Terror, Textual Power: Teaching Literature Through Writing Literature." *When Writing Teachers Teach Literature*. Ed. Art Young and Toby Fulwiler. Portsmouth, NH: Heinemann, 1995, 77–86.

———. "Why Don't We Write What We Teach? And Publish It?" [1990]. Rpt. *Composition Theory for the Postmodern Classroom*. Ed. Gary A. Olson and Sidney I. Dobrin. Albany: SUNY Press, 1994, 143–55.

Bloom, Lynn Z, and Ning Yu. "American Autobiography: The Changing Critical Canon." *a/b: Auto/Biography* 9.2 (Fall 1994): 157–70.

Boden, Diedre, and Don Zimmerman. *Talk & Social Structure*. Berkeley: University of California Press, 1991.

Bolter, Jay David. *Writing Space*. Hillsdale, NJ: Lawrence Erlbaum, 1991.

Bourdieu, Pierre. *Distinction: A Social Critique of the Judgment of Taste*. Trans. Richard Nice. Cambridge: Harvard University Press, 1984.

———. *Language and Symbolic Power*. Cambridge: Harvard University Press, 1991.

Boyd, Richard. "Imitate Me; Don't Imitate Me: Mimeticism in David Bartholomae's 'Inventing the University.'" *Journal of Advanced Composition* 11.2 (1991): 335–45.

Brandt, Deborah. "The Cognitive as the Social: An Ethnomethodological Approach to Writing Process Research." *Written Communication* 9 (1992): 315–55.

———. *Literacy as Involvement: The Acts of Writers, Readers, and Texts*. Carbondale: Southern Illinois University Press, 1990.

Bridwell-Bowles, Lillian. "Discourse and Diversity: Experimental Writing Within the Academy." *College Composition and Communication* 43.3 (Oct. 1992): 349–68.

———. "Freedom, Form, Function: Varieties of Academic Discourse." *College Composition and Communication* 46.1 (Feb. 1995): 46–62.

Bristol, Michael D. *Carnival and Theater: Plebeian Culture and the Structure of Authority in Renaissance England*. New York: Routledge, 1985.

Britton, James. *Language and Learning: The Importance of Speech in Children's Development*. Portsmouth, NH: Boynton/Cook, 1993.

Britton, James, Tony Burgess, Nancy Martin, Alex McLeod, and Harold Rosen. *The Development of Writing Abilities (11-18)*. Urbana, IL: NCTE, 1978.

Brodkey, Linda. *Academic Writing as a Social Practice*. Philadelphia, Temple University Press, 1987.

————. "Writing Critical Ethnographic Narratives." *Anthropology Education Quarterly* 18.2 (1987): 67–76.

————. "Writing Ethnographic Narratives." *Written Communication* 4 (1987): 27–50.

————. "Writing on the Bias." *College English* 56.5 (Sept. 1994): 527–47.

Brooke, Robert. *Writing and Sense of Self: Identity Negotiation in Writing Workshops*. Urbana, IL: NCTE, 1991.

Brooke, Robert, Ruth Mirtz, and Rick Evans. *Small Groups in Writing Workshops: Invitations to a Writer's Life*. Urbana, IL: NCTE, 1994.

Bruffee, Kenneth A. "Collaborative Learning and the 'Conversation of Mankind.'" *College English* 46.7 (Nov. 1988): 635–52.

Bruner, Jerome. *Acts of Meaning*. Cambridge: Harvard University Press, 1990.

————. *Actual Minds, Possible Worlds*. Cambridge: Harvard University Press, 1986.

————. "The Role of Dialogue in Language Acquisition." *The Child's Conception of Language*. Eds. A. Sinclair, R. J. Jarvella, and W. J. M. Levelt. New York: Springer-Verlag, 1978. 241–55.

Bruss, Elizabeth. *Autobiographical Acts: The Changing Situation of a Literary Genre*. Baltimore: Johns Hopkins University Press, 1976.

Brutus, Dennis. *Stubborn Hope*. Washington: Three Continents, 1983.

Bullock, Richard, and John Trimbur, eds. *The Politics of Writing Instruction: Postsecondary*. Portsmouth, NH: Boynton/Cook-Heinemann, 1991.

Burke, Kenneth. *Language as Symbolic Action*. Berkeley: University of California Press, 1966.

————. *A Rhetoric of Motives*. Berkeley: University of California Press, 1969.

————. *The Rhetoric of Religion: Studies in Logology*. Berkeley: University of California Press, 1961.

Cadow, Hunter. "New Historicism." *The Johns Hopkins Guide to Literary Theory and Criticism*. Eds. Michael Groden and Martin Kreiswirth. Baltimore: The Johns Hopkins University Press, 1994. 534–40.

Caesar, Terry. *Conspiring with Forms: Life in Academic Texts*. Athens: University of Georgia Press, 1992.

Calkins, Lucy. *The Art of Teaching Writing*. Portsmouth, NH: Heinemann, 1986.

————. *Lessons from a Child*. Portsmouth, NH: Heinemann, 1983.

Campbell, Karlyn, and Kathleen Jamieson. *Deeds Done in Words*. Chicago: University of Chicago Press, 1990.

————. "Form and Genre in Rhetorical Criticism: An Introduction." *Form and Genre: Shaping Rhetorical Action*. Eds. Karlyn Campbell and Kathleen Jamieson. Falls Church, VA: Speech Communication Association, 1978.

Carby, Hazel V. "The Multicultural Wars." *Black Popular Culture*. Ed. Gina Dent. Seattle: Bay Press, 1992.

Carter, Michael. "The Idea of Expertise: An Exploration of Cognitive and Social Dimensions of Writing." *College Composition and Communication* 41 (1990): 265–86.

Casanave, Christin. "Local Interactions: Constructing Contexts for Composing in a Graduate Sociology Program." *Academic Writing in a Second Language*. Eds. G. Braine and D. Belcher. Ablex, forthcoming.

Caywood, Cynthia, and Gillian Overing, eds. *Teaching Writing: Pedagogy, Gender, and Equity*. New York: SUNY Press, 1987.

Cazden, Courtney. "Peekaboo as an Instructional Model: Discourse Development at Home and at School." *Papers and Reports of Child Language Development* 17 (1979): 1–29.

<ccrmitta>. "Email." Writing Center Discussion List [online]. Available email: WCENTER <LISTPROC@UNICORN.ACS.TTU.EDU>. 1 Nov. 1993.

Chabram-Dernersesian, Angie. "I Throw Punches for My Race, but I Don't Want to Be a Man: Writing Us—Chica-nos (Girl, Us)/ Chicanas—Into the Movement Script." *Cultural Studies*. Eds. Lawrence Grossberg, Cary Nelson, and Paula Treichler. London: Routledge, 1992, 81–95.

Chien, Irene. "Autobiography and Feminist Discourse in Grrrl Zines." Unpublished paper.

Chisiri-Strater, Elizabeth. *Academic Literacies: The Public and Private Discourse of University Students*. Portsmouth, NH: Boynton/Cook-Heinemann, 1991.

Chodorow, Nancy. *Feminism and Psychoanalytic Theory*. New Haven: Yale University Press, 1991.

Chordas, Nina. "Classrooms, Pedagogies, and the Rhetoric of Equality." *College Composition and Communication* 43 (1992): 214–24.

Christensen, Francis. "A Generative Rhetoric of the Sentence." *College Composition and Communication* 14 (1963): 155–61.

Christie, Frances. "Genres as Choice." *The Place of Genre in Learning: Current Debates*. Ed. Ian Reid. Deakin, Australia: Deakin University, 1987, 22–34.

Cintron, Ralph. "Wearing a Pith Helmet at a Sly Angle: Or, Can Writing Researchers Do Ethnography in a Postmodern Era?" *Written Communication* 10.3 (1993): 371–412.

Cixous, Helene. *Three Steps on the Ladder of Writing*. New York: Columbia University Press, 1993.

Clark, Beverly Lyon, and Sonja Wiedenhaupt. "On Blocking and Unblocking Sonja: A Case Study in Two Voices." *College Composition and Communication* 43 (Feb. 1992): 55–74.

Clark, Gregory. *Dialogue, Dialectic, and Conversation: A Social Perspective on the Function of Writing*. Carbondale: Southern Illinois University Press, 1990.

Clark, Gregory, and Stephen Doheny-Farina. "Public Discourse and Personal Expression." *Written Communication* 7.4 (1990): 456–81.

Clark, Gregory, and S. Michael Halloran. "Transformations of Public Discourse in Nineteenth-Century America." *Oratorical Culture in Nineteenth-Century America: Transformations in the Theory and Practice of Rhetoric.* Eds. Gregory Clark and Michael Halloran. Carbondale: Southern Illinois University Press, 1993. 1–26.

Clifford, James. "On Ethnographic Authority." *Representations* 1 (1983): 118–46.

Clifford, James, and George Marcus. *Writing Culture: The Poetics and Politics of Ethnography,* Berkeley: University of California Press, 1986.

Cohen, Ralph. "Genre Theory, Literary History, and Historical Change." *Theoretical Issues in Literary History*. Ed. David Perkins. Cambridge: Harvard University Press, 1991, 85–113.

———. "History and Genre." *New Literary History* 17 (1986): 203–18.

Colins, Gail. "The Freddy Krueger in Your Computer." *Working Woman* (Apr. 1994): 62.

Connor, Ulla. "Learning Discipline Specific Writing." Paper delivered at the American Association of Applied Linguistics, Baltimore, March 1994.

Connors, Robert J. "The Modes of Discourse: An Historical Overview." Paper at CCCC, March 1981. ERIC ED 202005.

———. "Personal Writing Assignments." *College Composition and Communication* 38:2 (May 1987): 166–83.

Connors, Robert J., and Andrea Lunsford. "Teachers' Rhetorical Comments on Student Papers." *College Composition and Communication* 44.2 (May 1993): 200–23.

Cooke, Michael G. *Afro-American Literature in the Twentieth Century: The Achievement of Intimacy*. New Haven: Yale University Press, 1984.

Cooper, Marilyn, and Cynthia Selfe. "Computer Conferences and Learning: Authority, Resistance, and Internally Persuasive Discourse." College English 52 (Oct. 1991): 847–69.

Cope, Bill, and Mary Kalantzis. "Introduction." *The Powers of Literacy: A Genre Approach to Teaching Writing*. Eds. Bill Cope and Mary Kalantzis. Pittsburgh: University of Pittsburgh Press, 1993, 1–21.

———. "Histories of Pedagogy, Cultures of Schooling." *The Powers of Literacy: A Genre Approach to Teaching Writing*. Eds. Bill Cope and Mary Kalantzis. Pittsburgh: University of Pittsburgh Press, 1993, 38–62.

———. "The Power of Literacy and the Literacy of Power." *The Powers of Literacy: A Genre Approach to Teaching Writing*. Eds. Bill Cope and Mary Kalantzis. Pittsburgh: University of Pittsburgh Press, 1993, 63–89.

Cott, Nancy. *The Bonds of Womanhood: "Women's Sphere" in New England, 1780–1835*. New Haven: Yale University Press, 1977.

Crow Dog, Mary, and Richard Erdoes. *Lakota Woman*. New York: Harper Perennial, 1990.

Crowley, Tony. *Standard English and the Politics of Language*. Urbana: University of Illinois Press, 1989.

Crusius, Timothy. *Discourse: A Critique and Synthesis of Major Theories*. New York: MLA, 1989.

⟨csjhs⟩. "Email." Writing Center Discussion List [online]. Available email: WCENTER <LISTPROC@UNICORN.ACS.TTU.EDU>. 8 Nov. 1993.

⟨csjhs⟩. "P\R." Writing Center Discussion List [online]. Available email: WCENTER <LISTPROC@UNICORN.ACS.TTU.EDU>. 8 Jul. 1994.

Davidson, Cathy. *36 Views of Mount Fuji: On Finding Myself in Japan*. New York: Dutton, 1993.

Davis, Robert Con, and Ronald Schleifer. "Series Editors' Foreword." *Postmodern Genres*. Norman, OK: University of Oklahoma Press, 1988.

de Lauretis, Teresa. "Technology of Gender." *Technologies of Gender: Essays on Theory, Film, and Fiction*. Bloomington: Indiana University Press, 1987.

Derrida, Jacques. "The Law of Genre." *Critical Inquiry* 7 (1980): 55–81.

Detweiler, Jane. "Narratives of the Novice." This volume.

Devitt, Amy J. "Generalizing About Genre: New Conceptions of an Old Concept." *College Composition and Communication* 44.4 (Dec. 1993): 573–86.

————. "Intertextuality in Tax Accounting: Generic, Referential, and Functional." *Textual Dynamics of the Professions: Historical and Contemporary Studies of Writing in Professional Communities*. Eds. Charles Bazerman and James Paradis. Madison: University of Wisconsin Press, 1991, 336–57.

————. *Standardizing Written English: Diffusion in the Case of Scotland 1520–1659*. Cambridge: Cambridge University Press, 1989.

Didion, Joan. "Why I Write." *The Living Language*. Linda Morris, Hans Ostrom, Linda Young, eds. New York: Harcourt, Brace, Jovanovich, 1984.

DiPardo, Anna. "Narrative Knowers, Expository Knowledge: Discourse as a Dialectic." *Written Communication* 7 (1990): 59–95.

Doheney-Farina, Stephen. "Writing in an Emerging Organization: An Ethnographic Study." *Written Communication* 3 (1986): 158–85.

Douglass, Frederick. *The Narrative and Selected Writings*. [1845.] Rpt. Ed. Michael Meyer. New York: Random House, 1984.

DuBois, W. E. B. *The Autobiography of W. E. B. DuBois: A Solioquy on Viewing My Life from the Last Decade of Its First Century*. New York: International Publishers, 1968.

————. *The Souls of Black Folk: Essays and Sketches*. 17th ed. Chicago: A. C. McClurg, 1931.

Dubrow, Heather. *Genre*. London: Methuen, 1982.

Dudley-Evans, Tony. "Genre Analysis: An Investigation of the Introduction and Discussion Sections of M.Sc. Dissertations." *Talking About Text*. Ed. M. Coulthard. Birmingham: English Language Research, 1986.

Duras, Marguerite. "Home Making." *Ourselves Among Others,* 3rd ed. Ed. Carol J. Verberg. Boston: Bedford–St. Martin, 1994, 152–61.

Ede, Lisa, and Andrea Lunsford. *Singular Texts/Plural Authors*: Perspectives on Collaborative Writing. Carbondale: Southern Illinois University Press, 1990.

Ehrlich, Gretel. *The Solace of Open Spaces.* New York: Penguin, 1985.

Eichhorn, Sara Farris, Karen Hayes, Adriana Hernandez, Susan C. Jarratt, Karen Powers-Stubbs, and Marian M. Sciachitano. "A Symposium on Feminist Experiences in the Composition Classroom." *College Composition and Communication* 43.3 (Oct. 1992): 297–322.

Elbow, Peter. "Being a Writer vs. Being an Academic: A Conflict in Goals." *College Composition and Communication* 46.1 (Feb. 1995): 72–83.

———. ed. *Landmark Essays on Voice and Writing.* Davis, CA: Hermagagoras Press, 1994.

———. "Reflections on Academic Discourse: How It Relates to Freshmen and Colleagues." *College English* 53.2 (Feb. 1991): 135–55.

———. *What Is English.* New York and Urbana: MLA and NCTE, 1990.

———. *Writing Without Teachers.* New York: Oxford University Press, 1971.

Eldred, Janet Carey, and Ron Fortune. "Exploring the Implications of Metaphors for Computer Networks and Hypermedia." *Re-imagining Computers and Composition.* Eds. Gail Hawisher and Paul LeBlac. Portsmouth, NH: Boynton/Cook-Heinemann, 1992.

Ellison, Ralph. *Invisible Man.* New York: Random House, 1952.

———. *Shadow and Act.* New York: Random House, 1953.

Elmer-DeWitt, Philip. "Bards of the Internet." *Time,* July 1994: 66–67.

Equiano, Olaudah. *The Interesting Narrative of the Life of Olaudah Equiano.* Boston: Bedford Books of St. Martin's Press, 1995.

Fahnestock, Jeanne. "Genre and Rhetorical Craft." *Research in the Teaching of English* 27:3 (1993): 50–56.

Faigley, Lester. *Fragments of Rationality: Postmodernity and the Subject of Composition.* Pittsburgh: Pittsburgh University Press, 1992.

———. "Judging Writing, Judging Selves." *College Composition and Communication* 40 (1989): 395–413.

Felski, Rita. *The Gender of Modernity.* Cambridge: Harvard University Press, 1995.

Field, Norma. *The Splendor and Longing in the Tale of Genji.* Princeton: Princeton University Press, 1987.

Fields, Mamie and Karen E. Fields. *Lemon Swamp and Other Places: A Carolina Memoir.* New York: Free Press, 1985.

Fish, Stanley. "Anti-Foundationalism, Theory Hope, and the Teaching of Composition." *Doing What Comes Naturally: Change, Rhetoric, and the Practice of Theory in Literary and Legal Studies.* Durham, NC: Duke University Press, 1989, 342–55.

Fisher, John H. "Chancery and the Emergence of Standard Written English in the Fifteenth Century." *Speculum* 52 (1977): 870–99.

Fishman, Stephen, and Lucille P. McCarthy. "Is Expressivism Dead? Reconsidering Its Romantic Roots and Its Relation to Social Constructionism." *College English* 54.6 (1992): 647–61.

Flower, Linda. *The Construction of Negotiated Meaning: A Social Cognitive Theory of Writing*. Carbondale, IL: Southern Illinois University Press, 1993.

———. "Context, Cognition, and Theory Building." *College Composition and Communication*. 40 (1989): 282-311.

Flower, Linda, David L. Wallace, Linda Norris, and Rebecca E. Burnett, eds. *Making Thinking Visible: Writing, Collaborative Planning, and Classroom Inquiry*. Urbana, IL: NCTE, 1994.

Flynn, Elizabeth. "Composing as a Woman." *College Composition and Communication* 39 (1988): 423–35.

———. "Composing 'Composing as a Woman': A Perspective on Research." *College Composition and Communication* 41 (1990): 83–89.

———. "Review: Feminist Theories/Feminist Composition." *College English* 57.2 (Feb. 1995): 201–12.

Flynn, Elizabeth, and Patrocinio P. Schweickart, eds. *Gender and Reading: Essays on Readers, Texts, and Contexts*. Baltimore: Johns Hopkins University Press, 1986.

Fontaine, Sheryl, and Susan Hunter. "Rendering the 'Text' of Composition." *Journal of Advanced Composition* 12.2 (1992): 395–406.

Foucault, Michel. *The Archeology of Knowledge*. Trans. A. M. Sheridan Smith. New York: Pantheon, 1972.

———. *The Order of Things*. New York: Random House, 1970.

Fowler, Alastair. *Kinds of Literature: An Introduction to the Theory of Genres and Modes*. Oxford: Oxford University Press, 1982.

Fox-Genovese, Elizabeth. *Within the Plantation Household: Black and White Women of the Old South*. Chapel Hill: University of North Carolina Press, 1988.

Frankenberg, Ruth. *White Women, Race Matters: The Social Construction of Whiteness*. Minneapolis: University of Minnesota Press, 1993.

Freadman, Anne. "Anyone for Tennis?" *The Place of Genre in Learning: Current Debates*. Ed. Ian Reid. Deakin University (Australia): Centre for Studies in Literary Education, 1987, 91–124.

Freed, Richard C., and Glenn H. Broadhead. "Discourse Communities, Sacred Texts, and Institutional Norms." *College Composition and Communication* 38.2 (1987): 154–65.

Freedman, Aviva. "Argument as Genre and Genres of Argument." *Perspectives on Written Argumentation*. Ed. D. Berrill. Norfolk, NJ: Hampton Press, 1995.

———. "Learning to Write Again: Discipline-Specific Writing at University." *Carleton Papers in Applied Language Studies* 4 (1987): 95–116.

———. "Reconceiving Genre." *Text* 8/9 (1990): 279–92.

————. "Show and Tell? The Role of Explicit Teaching in Learning New Genres." *Research in the Teaching of English* 27 (1993): 222–51.

————. "The What, Where, When, Why and How of Classroom Genres." *Reconceiving Writing, Rethinking Writing Instruction.* Ed. Joseph Petragla. Mahwah, NJ: Erlbaum, 1995, 121–44.

Freedman, Aviva, C. Adam, and G. Smart. "Wearing Suits to Class: Simulating Genres and Simulations as Genre." *Written Communication* 11 (1994): 193–226.

Freedman, Aviva, and Peter Medway. "Introduction: New Views of Genre and Their Implications for Education." *Learning and Teaching Genre.* Eds. Aviva Freedman and Peter Medway. Portsmouth, NH: Boynton/Cook-Heinemann, 1994, 1–22

————, eds. *Learning and Teaching Genre.* Portsmouth, NH: Boynton/Cook-Heinemann, 1994.

————. *Rethinking Genre.* London: Taylor & Francis, 1994.

Freedman, Aviva, and Ian Pringle. "Contexts for Developing Argument." *Narrative and Argument.* Ed. R. Andrews. Milton Keynes: Open University Press, 1989.

Freedman, Diane P., Olivia Frey, and Frances Murphau Zauhar, eds. *The Intimate Critique: Autobiographical Literary Criticism.* Durham, NC: Duke University Press, 1993.

Freire, Paulo. *Pedagogy of the Oppressed.* [1969.] Rpt. New York: Continuum, 1990.

Freud, Sigmund. "Mourning and Melancholia." [1917.] *The Standard Edition of the Complete Psychological Works,* 19. London: Hogarth, 1953.

Frey, Olivia. "Equity and Peace in the New Writing Class." *Teaching Writing: Pedagogy, Gender, and Equity.* Eds. Cynthia Caywood and Gillian Overing. New York: SUNY Press, 1987, 93–106.

Fujii, James. *Complicit Fictions: The Subject in the Modern Japanese Prose Narrative.* Berkeley: University of California Press, 1993.

Fuller, Steve. *Philosophy, Rhetoric, and the End of Knowledge: The Coming of Science and Technology Studies.* Madison: University of Wisconsin Press, 1993.

Fulwiler, Toby. "Propositions of a Personal Nature." *Writers on Writing.* Vol. 2. Ed. Tom Waldrep. New York: Random House, 1988, 85–88.

————. "Provocative Revision." *The Writing Center Journal* 12.2 (Spring 1992): 190–204.

Fulwiler, Toby, et al. *Writing Personal Voice.* Boston: Blair Press, forthcoming.

Fuss, Diana. *Essentially Speaking: Feminism, Nature, and Difference.* New York: Routledge, 1989.

Gallop, Jane. *Thinking Through the Body.* New York: Columbia University Press, 1988.

Gannett, Cinthia. *Gender and the Journal: Diaries and Academic Discourse.* Albany: SUNY Press, 1992.

Garber, Eugene. "Every Classroom a Nexus of Discourses." *Second Thoughts,* 1990: n. pag.

Gates, Henry Louis. *Colored People: A Memoir*. New York: Knopf, 1994.

————. "The Master's Pieces: On Canon Formation and the African-American Tradition." *The Politics of Liberal Education*. Eds. Darryl Gless and Barbara Herrnstein Smith. Durham, NC: Duke University Press, 1992, 95–117.

————. *The Signifying Monkey: A Theory of Afro-American Literary Criticism*. New York: Oxford University Press, 1988.

Gates, Henry Louis, Jr., and George Houston Bass. *Mule Bone*. New York: Pantheon, 1992. [This reissue of the play on which Langston Hughes and Zora Neale Hurston collaborated contains a detailed discussion of their artistic and personal differences.]

Gebhardt, Richard. "Editor's Column: Diversity in a Mainline Journal." *College Composition and Communication* 43.1 (Feb. 1992): 7–10.

————. "Thoughts on Confidentiality and Submissions." *College Composition and Communication* 44 (1993): 7–8.

Gebhardt, Richard C., Carol Berkenkotter, Philip Arrington, Douglas Hesse, Sheryl L. Fontaine, and Susan Hunter. "Symposium on Peer Reviewing in Scholarly Journals." *Rhetoric Review* 13.2 (1995): 237–75.

Geertz, Clifford. *The Interpretation of Cultures: Selected Essays*. New York: Basic Books, 1973.

————. "Thick Description: Toward an Interpretive Theory of Culture." *The Interpretation of Cultures*. Ed. Clifford Geertz. New York: Basic Books, 1973, 3–30.

————. *Works and Lives: The Anthropologist as Author*. Stanford, CA: Stanford University Press, 1988.

Geisler, Cheryl. "Exploring Academic Literacy: An Experiment in Composing." *College Composition and Communication* 43.1 (Feb. 1992): 39–54.

Gere, Anne Ruggles. "Kitchen Tables and Rented Rooms: The Extracurriculum of Composition." *College Composition and Communication* 45.1 (Feb. 94): 75–92.

Giddens, Anthony. *The Constitution of Society*. Berkeley: University of California Press, 1984.

Giffen, Allison. "'Til Grief melodious grow': The Poems and Letters of Ann Eliza Bleecker." *Early American Literature* 28 (1993): 222–41.

Gilbert, Sandra, and Susan Gubar. *The Madwoman in the Attic: The Woman Writer and the 19th-Century Literary Imagination*. New Haven: Yale University Press, 1979.

Gilligan, Carol. *In a Different Voice: Psychological Theory and Women's Development*. Cambridge: Harvard University Press, 1982.

Giltrow, Janet and Michele Valiquette. "Genres and Knowledge: Students' Writing in the Disciplines." *Learning and Teaching Genre*. Eds. Aviva Freedman and Peter Medway. Portsmouth, NH: Boynton/Cook-Heinemann, 1994, 47–62.

Goffman, Erving. *Asylums: Essays on the Social Situation of Mental Patients and Other Inmates*. New York: Doubleday, 1961.

Goldberg, Natalie. *Writing Down the Bones*. Boston: Shambala, 1986.

Gordon, Lewis R., ed. *Existence in Black: An Anthology of Black Existential Philosophy.* New York: Routledge, 1997.

Gould, Stephen Jay. *Wonderful Life: The Burgess Shale and the Nature of History.* New York: Norton, 1989.

Graff, Gerald. *Beyond the Culture Wars: How Teaching the Conflicts Can Revitalize American Education.* New York: Norton, 1992.

————. *Professing Literature.* Chicago: University of Chicago Press, 1987.

Graff, Gerald, and Bruce Robbins. "Cultural Criticism." *Redrawing the Boundaries: The Transformation of English and American Studies.* Eds. Stephen Greenblatt and Giles Gunn. New York: MLA, 1992, 419–36.

Graham, Robert. *Reading and Writing the Self: Autobiography in Education and the Curriculum.* New York: Teachers College Press, 1991.

Graves, Donald. *Writing: Teachers and Children at Work.* Portsmouth, NH: Heinemann, 1983.

Green, Bill. "Gender, Genre, and Writing Pedagogy." *The Place of Genre in Learning: Current Debates.* Ed. Ian Reid. Deakin, Australia: Deakin University, 1987, 83–92.

Green, Bill, and Allison Lee. "Writing Geography: Literacy, Identity, and Schooling." *Learning and Teaching Genre.* Eds. Aviva Freedman and Peter Medway. Portsmouth, NH: Boynton/Cook-Heinemann, 1994, 207–24.

Gumperz, John. "Contextualization and Understanding." *Rethinking Context.* Eds. A. Duranti and C. Goodwin. Cambridge: Cambridge University Press, 1992.

Gyanranjan. "Our Side of the Fence and Theirs." *Ourselves Among Others.* 3rd. ed. Ed. Carol J. Verberg. Boston: Bedford–St. Martin's, 1994, 134–41.

Haas, W. "Introduction: On the Normative Character of Language." *Standard Languages: Spoken and Written.* Ed. W. Haas. Totowa, NJ: Barnes and Noble, 1982, 1–36.

Haefner, Joel. "Democracy, Pedagogy, and the Personal Essay." *College English* 54.2 (Feb. 1992): 127–37.

Hairston, Maxine. "Diversity, Ideology, and Teaching Writing." *College Composition and Communication* 43.2 (May 1992): 179–93.

Halliday, Michael. *Language as Social Semiotic: The Social Interpretation of Language and Meaning.* London: Edward Arnold, 1978.

————. *Spoken and Written English.* Oxford: Oxford University Press, 1989.

Halliday, Michael, and Ruqaiya Hasan. *Language, Context, and Text: Aspects of Language in a Social-Semiotic Perspective.* 2nd ed. Oxford: Oxford University Press, 1989.

Halliday, Michael, and James Martin. *Writing Science.* Pittsburgh, University of Pittsburgh Press, 1993.

Hanks, Thomas. "Foreword." *Situated Learning: Legitimate Peripheral Participation.* Eds. J. Lave and E. Wegner. Cambridge: Cambridge University Press, 1991, 11–21.

Hanks, William F. "Discourse Genres in a Theory of Praxis." *American Ethnologist* 14 (1987): 668–92.

Haraway, Donna. *Primate Visions: Gender, Race, and Nature in the World of Modern Science.* New York: Routledge, 1989.

Haswell, Janis, and Richard Haswell. "Gendership and the Miswriting of Students." *College Composition and Communication* 42.2 (May 1995): 223–54.

Hrdy, Sarah Blaffer. *The Woman That Never Evolved.* Cambridge: Harvard University Press, 1981.

Harrell, Jackson, and Wil A. Linkugel. "On Rhetorical Genre: An Organizing Perspective." *Philosophy and Rhetoric* 11 (1978): 262–81.

Harris, Joseph. "From the Editor: Writing from the Moon." *College Composition and Communication* 45 (1994): 161–63.

Harris, Sharon M. "Mary White Rowlandson." *The Heath Anthology of American Literature.* Ed. Paul Lauter. 2nd ed. Lexington, MA: Heath, 1994, 340–42.

<harrism>. "Email." Writing Center Discussion List [online]. Available email: WCENTER <LISTPROC@UNICORN.ACS.TTU.EDU>. 9 Nov. 1993.

Hartwell, Patrick. "Grammar, Grammars, and the Teaching of Grammar." *College English* 47 (1985): 105–27.

Hasan, Ruqaiya. "The Structure of Text." *Language, Context, and Text.* Eds. M. Halliday and R. Hasan. Geelong, Australia: Deakin University Press, 1985.

Hawisher, Gail. "Electronic Meetings of the Minds: Research, Electronic Conferences, and Composition Studies." *Re-Imagining Computers and Composition: Teaching and Research in the Virtual Age.* Eds. Gail Hawisher and Paul LeBlanc. Portsmouth, NH: Boynton/Cook-Heinemann, 1992.

Hawisher, Gail, and Paul LeBlanc, eds. *Re-Imagining Computers and Composition: Teaching and Research in the Virtual Age.* Portsmouth, NH: Boynton/Cook-Heinemann, 1992.

Hawisher, Gail, and Charles Moran. "Electronic Mail and the Writing Instructor." *College English* 55 (Oct. 1993): 627–43.

Hawisher, Gail, and Cynthia Selfe. "The Rhetoric of Technology and the Electronic Writing Class." *College Composition and Communication* 42 (Feb. 1991): 55–65.

Hayes, John R. "A Psychological Perspective Applied to Literacy Studies." *Multidisciplinary Perspectives on Literacy Research.* Eds. Richard Beach, Judith L. Green, Michael L. Kamil, and Timothy Shanahan. Urbana, IL: NCRE and NCTE, 1992, 125–40.

Heap, James L. "Ethnomethodology and the Possibility of a Metaperspective on Literacy Research." *Multidisciplinary Perspectives on Literacy Research.* Eds. Richard Beach, Judith L. Green, Michael L. Kamil, and Timothy Shanahan. Urbana, IL: NCRE and NCTE, 1992, 35–56.

Heath, Shirley Brice. "Standard English: Biography of a Symbol." *Standards and Dialects in English.* Eds. Timothy Shopen and Joseph M. Williams. Cambridge: Winthrop, 1980, 3–32.

————. *Ways with Words: Language, Life, and Work in Communities and Class-rooms*. Cambridge, Cambridge University Press, 1983.

Heilbrun, Carolyn. *Writing a Woman's Life*. New York: Norton, 1988.

Hernadi, Paul. *Beyond Genre*. Ithaca, NY: Cornell University Press, 1972.

Herndl, Carl G. "Writing Ethnography: Representation, Rhetoric, and Institutional Practices." *College English* 55.3 (1991): 320–32.

Herren, Jerry. "Writing for My Father." *College English* 54.8 (Dec. 1992): 928–37.

Herrington, Ann. "Writing in Academic Settings: A Study of the Context for Writing in Two College Chemical Engineering Courses." *Research in the Teaching of English* 19 (1985): 331–59.

Hesford, Wendy. "Writing Identities: The 'Essence' of Difference in Multicultural Classrooms." *Writing in Multicultural Settings*. Eds. Johnnella Butler, Juen Guerra, and Carol Severino. New York: MLA, forthcoming.

Hillocks, George. "Reconciling the Qualitative and Quantitative." *Multidisciplinary Perspectives on Literacy Research*. Eds. Richard Beach, Judith L. Green, Michael L. Kamil, and Timothy Shanahan. Urbana, IL: NCRE and NCTE, 1992, 57–65.

Himley, Margaret. "Genre as Generative: One Perspective on One Child's Early Writing Growth." *The Structure of Written Communication: Studies in Reciprocity Between Writers and Readers*. Ed. Martin Nystrand. Orlando: Harcourt, 1986, 137–58.

Holquist, Michael. *Dialogism: Bakhtin and His World*. London: Routledge, 1990.

hooks, bell. "Essentialism and Experience." *American Literary History* 3 (1991): 172–83.

————. *Talking Back: Thinking Feminist Thinking Black*. Boston: South End Press, 1989.

————. *Yearning: Race, Gender, and Cultural Politics*. Boston: South End Press, 1990.

Hopkins, Evans D. "Time and Punishment: From the Other Side of the Iron Bars, the Case for Parole." *The Washington Post*, 19 Dec. 1993: C1.

Hult, Christine A. "Over the Edge: When Reviewers Collide." *Writing on the Edge* 5.2 (Spring 1994): 24–28.

Hunston, Susan. "Evaluation and Ideology in Scientific Writing." *Register Analysis; Theory and Practice*. Ed. M. Ghadessy. London: Pinter, 1988.

Hunt, Russell. "Speech Genres, Writing Genres, School Genres, and Computer Genres." *Learning and Teaching Genre*. Eds. Aviva Freedman and Peter Medway. Portsmouth, NH: Boynton/Cook-Heinemann, 1994.

Hunter, Susan, and Ray Wallace. "From the Editors." *Dialogue* 1.1 (1993): 5.

Hurtado, Aida. "Relating to Privilege: Seduction and Rejection in the Subordination of White Women and Women of Color." *Signs* 14.41 (1989): 833–55.

Jacobs, Harriet A. *Incidents in the Life of a Slave Girl*. [1861.] Rpt. ed. Jean Fagan Yellin. Cambridge: Harvard University Press, 1987.

Jamieson, Kathleen Hall. *Deeds Done in Words: Presidential Rhetoric and the Genres of Governance.* Chicago and London: University of Chicago Press, 1990.

JanMohamed, Abdul R. "Some Implications of Paulo Freire's Border Pedagogy." *Between Borders: Pedagogy and the Politics of Cultural Studies.* Eds. Henry Giroux and Peter McLaren. New York: Routledge, 1994, 242–52.

Jarratt, Susan. "Feminism and Composition: The Case for Conflict." *Contending with Words: Composition and Rhetoric in a Postmodern Age.* Eds. Patricia Harkin and John Schilb. New York: MLA, 1991, 105–23.

——— . "On the Other Hand: Comments on Clark and Doheny-Farina." *Written Communication* 8.1 (1991): 114–24.

Jay, Paul, ed. *The Selected Correspondence of Kenneth Burke and Malcolm Cowley, 1915-1981.* Berkeley: University of California Press, 1988.

Jelliffe, S. E. *Psychopathology of Forced Movements and the Oculogyric Crises of Lethargic Encephalitis.* New York: Nervous and Mental Disease Publishing, 1932.

⟨johnmc⟩. "Elements of email distribution." Megabyte University Discussion List [online]. Available email: MBU-L <LISTPROC@UNICORN.ACS.TTU.EDU. 5 Jul. 1994.

Jones, Ann Rosalind. "Surprising Fame: Renaissance Gender Ideologies and Women's Lyric." *The Poetics of Gender.* Ed. Nancy Miller. New York: Columbia University Press, 1986.

Joseph, John Earl. *Eloquence and Power: The Rise of Language Standards and Standard Languages.* London: Pinter, 1987.

Journet, Debra. "Boundary Rhetoric and Disciplinary Genres: Re-Drawing the Map in Interdisciplinary Writing." This volume.

——— . "Ecological Theories as Cultural Narratives: F. E. Clements' and H. A. Gleason's 'Stories' of Community Succession." *Written Communication* 8 (1991) : 446–72.

——— . "Forms of Discourse and the Sciences of the Mind: Sacks, Luria, and the Role of Narrative in Neurological Case Histories." *Written Communication* 7 (1990): 171–99.

——— . "Interdisciplinary Discourse and 'Boundary Rhetoric': The Case of S. E. Jelliffe." *Written Communication* 10 (1993): 510–41.

Kaplan, Caren. "Deterritorializations: The Rewriting of Home and Exile in Western Feminist Discourse." *Cultural Critique* 6 (1987). 187–98.

——— . "Resisting Autobiography: Outlaw Genres and Transnational Subjects." *De/Colonizing the Subject: The Politics of Gender in Women's Autobiography.* Ed. Sidonie Smith and Julia Watson. Minneapolis: University of Minnesota Press, 1992, 115–38.

Kaufer, David, and Cheryl Geisler. "Novelty in Academic Writing. *Written Communication* 6.3 (1989): 286–311.

Kay, Dennis. *Melodious Tears: The English Funeral Elegy from Spenser to Milton.* New York: Clarendon, 1990.

Kerby, Anthony Paul. *Narrative and the Self*. Bloomington: Indiana University Press, 1991.

Kermode, Frank. *The Sense of an Ending: Studies in the Theory of Fiction*. New York: Oxford University Press, 1967.

Kikuta, Shigeo. "Waka to monogatari." *Waka no Sekai*. Eds. Ogiwata Tadao, et al. Tokyo: Ofusha, 1968, 7–25.

Kimball, Bruce A. *The "True Professional Ideal" in America: A History*. Cambridge: Blackwell, 1992.

Kingston, Maxine Hong. *The Woman Warrior: Memoirs of a Girlhood Among Ghosts*. [1975.] Fpt. New York: Vintage, 1977.

Kinneavy, James L. *A Theory of Discourse*. New York: W. W. Norton, 1971.

Kirsch, Gesa. *Women Writing the Academy: Audience, Authority, and Transformation*. Studies in Writing and Rhetoric. Carbondale: Southern Illinois University Press, 1993.

Kirsch, Gesa, and Patricia A. Sullivan. *Methods and Methodology in Composition Research*. Carbondale: Southern Illinois University Press, 1992.

Klein, Julie Thompson. *Interdisciplinarity: History, Theory and Practice*. Detroit: Wayne State University Press, 1990.

Kleine, Michael. "Beyond Triangulation: Ethnography, Writing, and Rhetoric." *Journal of Advanced Composition* 10 (1990): 117–25.

Kolodny, Annette. *The Lay of the Land: Metaphor as Experience and History in American Life and Letters*. Chapel Hill: University of North Carolina Press, 1975.

Kondo, Dorrine. *About Face*. New York: Routledge, 1997.

———. *Crafting Selves: Power, Gender, and Discourse of Identity in a Japanese Workplace*. Chicago: Chicago University Press, 1990.

———. "The Stakes: Feminism, Asian Americans, and the Study of Asia." *Committee on Women in Asia Studies Newsletter* 9.3 (1991): 2–9.

Konishi, Jun'ichiro. *A History of Japanese Literature: Volume Two: The Early Middle Ages*. Trans. Aileen Gatten. Princeton: Princeton University Press, 1986.

Krapp, George Philip. "Standards of Speech and Their Values." *Modern Philology* 11 (1913–14): 57–70.

Kress, Gunther. "Genre as Social Process." *The Powers of Literacy: A Genre Approach to Teaching Writing*. Eds. B. Cope and M. Kalantzis. Pittsburgh: University of Pittsburgh Press, 1993, 22–37.

———. "Genre in a Social Theory of Language: A Reply to John Dixon." *The Place of Genre in Learning: Current Debates*. Ed. Ian Reid. Deakin, Australia: Deakin University, 1987, 35–45.

Kress, Gunther, and Terry Threadgold. "Towards a Social Theory of Genre." *Southern Review* 21 (1988): 215–43.

Kuhn, Thomas. *The Structure of Scientific Revolutions*. Chicago: University of Chicago Press, 1970.

Lakoff, George, and Mark Turner. *More Than Cool Reason: A Field Guide to Poetic Metaphor.* Chicago: University of Chicago Press, 1989, 63 ff.

Landau, Misia. "Human Evolution as Narrative." *American Scientist* 72 (1984): 262–68.

Lanham, Richard. *The Electronic Word: Democracy, Technology, and the Arts.* Chicago: University of Chicago Press, 1993.

Larson, Richard. "Classifying Discourse: Limitations and Alternatives." *Essays on Classical Rhetoric and Modern Discourse.* Ed. Robert Conners. Carbondale: University of Illinois Press, 1984, 203–14.

Lauter, Paul. "Reconstructing American Literature: Curricular Issues." *Canons and Contexts.* New York: Oxford University Press, 1991, 97–113.

————. "To the Reader." *The Heath Anthology of American Literature.* Lexington, MA: Heath, 1990, I, xxxiii–xliii.

Leggo, Carl. "Questions I Need to Ask Before I Advise My Students to Write in Their Own Voices." *Rhetoric Review* 10.1 (Fall 1991): 143–52.

Leitch, Vincent. "(De)Coding (Generic) Discourse." *Genre* 24 (Spring 1991): 83–98.

Lejeune, Philippe. "The Autobiographical Pact." *On Autobiography.* Minneapolis: University of Minnesota Press, 1989, 3–30.

Lewis, David Levering. *When Harlem Was in Vogue.* New York: Knopf, 1981. Rpt. Oxford: Oxford University Press, 1989.

<lffunkhouser>. "Truck-flattened smiley." Copyediting Discussion List [online]. Available email: COPYEDITING-L <LISTSERV@CORNELL.EDU>. 12 Feb. 1994.

Linde, Charlotte. *Life Stories: The Creation of Coherence.* New York: Oxford University Press, 1993.

Lindemann, Erika. "Freshman Composition: No Place for Literature." *College English* 55.3 (March 1993): 311–16.

————. "Three Views of English 101." *College English* 57.3 (March 1995): 287–302.

<listproc>. "Subscribe CCCCC-L Michael S." Email to M. Spooner [online]. Available email: <mspooner@cc.usu.edu>. 22 Jun. 1994.

Loban, Stephany, and Kevin Jackson. "What Goes On in the Mind of a Writer." *The Subject Is Writing.* Ed. Wendy Bishop. Portsmouth, NH: Boynton/Cook-Heinemann, 1993, 124–31.

Lomax, Michael. "Countee Cullen: A Key to the Puzzle." *The Harlem Renaissance Reconsidered.* Ed. Victor A. Kramer. New York: AMS, 1987.

Looser, Devoney. "Composing as an 'Essentialist'? New Directions for Feminist Composition Theories." *Rhetoric Review* 12.1 (Fall 1993): 54–69.

Lorde, Audre. *Sister Outsider: Essays and Speeches by Audre Lorde.* Freedom, CA: Crossing Press, 1984.

Love, Monifa A. "Freedom in the Dismal." Thesis. Tallahassee: Florida State, 1993.

Lu, Min-Zhan. "Conflict and Struggle: The Enemies or Preconditions of Basic Writing?" *College English* 54(8) (1992): 887–913.

———. "From Silence to Words: Writing as Struggle." *College English* 49(4) (1987): 437–48.

———. "Representing and Negotiating Differences in the Contact Zone." Paper presented at Oberlin College, February 1994.

Luckmann, Thomas. "On the Communicative Adjustment of Perspectives, Dialogue and Communicative Genres." *The Dialogical Alternative*. Ed. Astri Heen Wold. Oslo: Scandinavian University Press, 1992.

Luhmann, Niklas. *Ecological Communication*. Chicago: University of Chicago Press, 1989.

Lunsford, Andrea. "Composing Ourselves: Politics, Commitment, and the Teaching of Writing." *College Composition and Communication* 4 (1990): 71–82.

Lunsford, Andrea, and Lisa Ede. "On the Other Hand: Comments on Clark and Doheny-Farina." *Written Communication* 8.1 (1991): 114–24.

Luria, A. R. *The Man with a Shattered World*. Trans. L. Solotaroff. New York: Basic Books, 1972.

———. *The Mind of a Mnemonist*. Trans. L. Solotaroff. New York: Basic Books, 1968.

Lyon, Arabella. "Interdisciplinarity: Giving Up Territory." *College English* 54 (1992): 681–93.

⟨lysana⟩. "Virtual communities." Cybermind Discussion List [online]. Available email: CYBERMIND <LISTSERV@WORLD.STD.COM>. 6 Jul. 1994.

Macrorie, Ken. *The I-Search Paper*. Revised edition of *Searching Writing*. Portsmouth, NH: Boynton/Cook, 1988.

———. "Process, Product, and Quality." *Taking Stock: The Writing Process Movement in the '90s*. Eds. Lad Tobin and Thomas Newkirk. Portsmouth, NH: Boynton/Cook-Heinemann, 1994, 69–82.

MacKinnon, Catherine A. *Toward a Feminist Theory of the State*. Cambridge: Harvard University Press, 1989.

Mairs, Nancy. "On Being a Cripple." *Plaintext: Deciphering a Woman's Life*. [1986.] Rpt. New York: Perennial, 1987, 9–20.

———. *Remembering the Bonehouse: An Erotics of Space and Place*. New York: Harper, 1989.

<malgosia>. "Virtual communities." Cybermind Discussion List [online]. Available email: CYBERMIND <LISTSERV@WORLD.STD.COM>. 4 Jul. 1994.

Mani, Lata. "Multiple Mediations: Feminist Scholarship in the Age of Multinational Reception." *Feminist Review* 35 (Summer 1990): 38–56.

⟨marius⟩. "Virtual communities." Cybermind Discussion List [online]. Available email: CYBERMIND <LISTSERV@WORLD.STD.COM>. 5 Jul. 1994.

Martin, James R. *English Text: System and Structure*. Philadelphia: John Benjamins, 1992.

Martin, James R., and Joan Rothery. "Grammar: Making Meaning in Writing." *The Powers of Literacy: A Genre Approach to Teaching Writing*. Eds. Bill Cope and Mary Kalantzis. Pittsburgh: University of Pittsburgh Press, 1993, 137–53.

Maxwell, Nicholas. *From Knowledge to Wisdom*. London: Basil Blackwell, 1987.

May, Rollo. *The Courage to Create*. New York: Norton, 1975.

Mayberry, Bob. "Opening Doors." *Composition Studies/Freshman English News* 23.1 (Spring 1995): 678–93.

Mayr, Ernst. *The Growth of Biological Thought: Diversity, Evolution, and Inheritance*. Cambridge: Harvard University Press, 1982.

McCall, Nathan. *Makes Me Wanna Holler: A Young Black Man in America*. New York: Random House, 1994.

McCarthy, Lucille P. "A Stranger in Strange Lands: A College Student Writing Across the Curriculum." *Research in the Teaching of English* 21.3 (1987): 233–65.

McCarthy, Lucille P., and Stephen M. Fishman. "Boundary Conversations: Conflicting Ways of Knowing in Philosophy and Interdisciplinary Research." *Research in the Teaching of English* 25.4 (1991): 419–68.

McKay, Claude. *A Long Way from Home*. New York: Harcourt, 1970.

McQuade. "Composition and Literary Studies." *Redrawing the Boundaries: The Transformation of English and American Literary Studies*. New York: MLA, 1992.

————. "Living in–and on–the Margins." *College Composition and Communication* 43 (Feb. 1992): 11–22.

Mehta, Ved. "Pom's Engagement." Ed. Carol J. Verberg. *Ourselves Among Others*. 3rd. ed. Boston: Bedford–St. Martin's, 1994, 142–51.

Menchú, Rigoberta. *I, Rigoberta Menchú: An Indian Woman in Guatemala*. Ed. Elisabeth Burgos-Debray. Trans. Ann Wright. New York: Verso, 1984.

Merrill, Robert, Thomas J. Farrell, Eileen E. Schell, Valerie Balester, Chris M. Anson, and Greta Gaard. "Symposium on the 1991 Progress Report from the CCCC Committee on Professional Standards." *College Composition and Communication* 43.2 (May 1992): 154–75.

Messer-Davidow, Ellen, David R. Shumway, and David J. Sylvan, eds. *Knowledges: Historical and Critical Studies in Disciplinarity*. Charlottesville: University Press of Virginia, 1993.

Meyer, Sheree L. "Refusing to Play the Confidence Game: The Illusion of Mastery in the Reading/Writing of Texts." *College English* 55 (1993): 46–63.

Miller, Carolyn R. "Genre as Social Action." *Quarterly Journal of Speech* 70 (May 1984): 151–67.

Miller, Nancy. *Getting Personal: Autobiographical Acts and Other Feminist Occasions*. New York: Routledge, 1991.

Miller, Susan. *Rescuing the Subject: A Critical Introduction to Rhetoric and the Writer*. Carbondale, IL: Southern Illinois University Press, 1989.

————. *Textual Carnivals: The Politics of Composition*. Carbondale: Southern Illinois University Press, 1991.

Miner, Earl. *The Princeton Companion to Classical Japanese Literature*. Princeton: Princeton University Press, 1985.

Minh-ha, Trinh T. *Woman, Native, Other, Writing Postcoloniality and Feminism*. Bloomington: Indiana University Press, 1989.

Mink, Louis. "History and Fiction as Modes of Comprehension." *New Literary History* 1 (1970): 541–58.

Miyake, Lynne. "If I Were 'She' and 'She' Were 'I'": The Narration of *Kagero nikki*." Combined Western and Southwestern conferences of the Association for Asian Studies, Mexico City, Mexico, October 21–22, 1993.

————. The Narrative Triad in *The Tale of Genji:* Narrator, Reader, and Text." *Approaches to Teaching Murasaki Shikibu's The Tale of Genji*. New York: MLA, 1994, 77–87.

————. "*The Tosa Diary*: In the Interstices of Gender and Criticism." *The Woman's Hand: Gender and Theory in Japanese Women's Writing*. Stanford: Stanford University Press, forthcoming.

Miyoshi, Masao. *Off Center: Power and Culture Relations Between Japan and the United States*. Cambridge: Harvard University Press, 1991.

Moffett, James. *Teaching the Universe of Discourse*. Boston: Houghton Mifflin, 1968.

Montrose, Louis. "New Historicisms." *Redrawing the Boundaries: The Transformation of English and American Literary Studies*. Eds. Stephen Greenblatt and Giles Gunn. New York: MLA, 1992, 392–418.

Moran, Charles. "Computers and English: What Do We Make of Each Other?" *College English* 54 (Mar. 1992): 193.

<mspooner>. "Early final thoughts." Email to K. Yancey [online]. Available email: <mspooner@press.usu.edu>. 13 Dec. 1994.

<mullanne>. "Email." Writing Center Discussion List [online]. Available email: WCENTER <LISTPROC@UNICORN.ACS.TTU.EDU>. 5 Nov. 1993.

Murphy, James J. "Rhetorical History as a Guide to the Salvation of American Reading and Writing: A Plea for Curricular Courage." *The Rhetorical Tradition and Modern Writing*. Ed. James J. Murphy. New York: MLA, 1982, 3–12.

Murray, Donald M. "Internal Revision: A Process of Discovery." *Research on Composing: Points of Departure*. Eds. Charles Cooper and Lee Odell. Urbana, IL: NCTE, 1978, 85–103.

————. *The Literature of Tomorrow: An Anthology of Student Fiction, Poetry, and Drama*. New York: Holt, 1990.

————. "A Preface on Rejection." *Writing on the Edge* 5.2 (Spring 1994): 29–30.

————. "Pushing the Edge." *Writing on the Edge* 5.2 (Spring 1994): 31–41.

————. *Shoptalk: Learning to Write with Writers*. Portsmouth, NH: Boynton/Cook-Heinemann, 1990.

————. *A Writer Teaches Writing: A Practical Method of Teaching Composition.* 2nd ed. Boston: Houghton, 1968, 1985.

Murray, Pauli. *Proud Shoes: the Story of an American Family.* New York: Harper and Row, 1978.

Myers, Greg. *Writing Biology: Texts on the Social Construction of Scientific Knowledge.* Madison: University of Wisconsin Press, 1990.

Nelson, Cary and Michael Berube. *Higher Education Under Fire: Politics, Economics, and the Crisis of the Humanities.* New York: Routledge, 1994.

Nelson, Jeannie. "This Was an Easy Assignment: Examining How Students Interpret Academic Writing Tasks." *Research in the Teaching of English* 24 (1990): 362–96.

Newkirk, Thomas. "The Narrative Roots of the Case Study." *Methods and Methodology in Composition Research.* Eds. Gesa Kirsch and Patricia A. Sullivan. Carbondale: Southern Illinois University Press, 1992, 130–52.

<newmann> "Email." Writing Center Discussion List [online]. Available email: WCENTER <LISTPROC@UNICORN.ACS.TTU.EDU>. 29 Oct. 1993.

North, Stephen. *The Making of Knowledge in Composition: Portrait of an Emerging Field.* Upper Montclair, NJ: Boynton/Cook, 1985.

————. "On Book Reviews in Rhetoric and Composition." *Rhetoric Review* 10.2 (Spring 1992): 348–63.

Ochs, Elinor. *Culture and Language Development.* Cambridge: Cambridge University Press, 1988.

Olney, James. *Metaphors of Self: The Meaning of Autobiography.* Princeton: Princeton University Press, 1972.

Olson, Gary A. "Jane Tompkins and the Politics of Writing, Scholarship, and Pedagogy." *Journal of Advanced Composition* 15.1 (1995): 1–17.

O'Reilley, Mary Rose. *The Peaceable Classroom.* Portsmouth, NH: Boynton/Cook-Heinemann, 1993.

Ostriker, Alicia Suskin. *Stealing the Language: The Emergence of Women's Poetry in America.* Boston: Beacon Press, 1986.

Ostrom, Hans. "Grammar J, as in Jazzing Around: The Roles Play Plays in Style." *Elements of Alternate Style.* Ed. Wendy Bishop. Portsmouth, NH: Boynton/Cook-Heinemann, 1997.

Pascal, Roy. *Design and Truth in Autobiography.* Cambridge: Harvard University Press, 1960.

Perloff, Marjorie. "Introduction." *Postmodern Genres.* Norman, OK: University of Oklahoma Press, 1988.

Pigman, G. W. *Grief and English Renaissance Elegy.* Cambridge: Cambridge University Press, 1985.

Plutarch. "Consolation to His Wife." *The Art of the Personal Essay from the Classical Era to the Present.* Ed. Phillip Lopate. New York: Anchor, 1994.

Polanyi, Michael. *Personal Knowledge.* New York: Harper, 1964.

Polier, Nicole, and William Roseberry. "Tristes Tropes: Post-Modern Anthropologists Encounter the Other and Discover Themselves." *Economy and Society* 18.2 (1989): 245–64.

Pratt, Mary Louise. "Arts of the Contact Zone." *Profession 91.* New York: MLA, 1991, 33–40.

———. "Fieldwork in Common Places." *Writing Culture: The Poetics and Politics of Ethnography.* Eds. James Clifford and George E. Marcus. Berkeley: University California Press, 1986, 27–50.

Prince, Gerald. "Narratology." *The Johns Hopkins Guide to Literary Theory and Criticism.* Eds. Michael Groden and Martin Kreiswirth. Baltimore: Johns Hopkins University Press, 1994, 524–28.

Prior, Paul. "Contextualizing Writing and Response in a Graduate Seminar. *Written Communication* 8.3 (1991): 267–310.

Proposal for a Ph.D. in English. The University at Albany, State University of New York, 1991.

Ramazani, Jahan. "'Daddy I have had to kill you': Plath, Rage and the Modern Elegy." *PMLA* 108 (1993): 1142–56.

Rampersad, Arnold. *The Life of Langston Hughes.* 2 vols. New York: Oxford University Press, 1988 and 1990.

Rankin, Elizabeth. "The Second Motion of the Mind: Reviewing, Mentoring, Judgment, and Generosity." *Writing on the Edge* 5.2 (Spring 1994): 42–52.

———. *Seeing Yourself as a Teacher: Conversations with Five New Teachers in a University Writing Program.* Urbana, IL: NCTE, 1994.

Reid, Ian, ed. *The Place of Genre in Learning: Current Debates.* Deakin University (Australia): Centre for Studies in Literary Education, 1987.

Reischauer, Edwin O. *The Japanese Today: Change and Continuity.* Cambridge: Harvard University Press, 1988.

Reynolds, Nedra. "*Ethos* as Location: New Sites for Understanding Discursive Authority." *Rhetoric Review* 11:2 (Spring 93): 325–38.

Rich, Adrienne. "Notes Toward a Politics of Location." *Blood, Bread, and Poetry: Selected Prose 1979–1985.* New York: Norton, 1986.

———. "When We Dead Awaken: Writing as Re-vision." *On Lies, Secrets, and Silence: Selected Prose 1966–1978.* New York: Norton, 1979.

Ricoeur, Paul. *Time and Narrative.* Trans. Kathleen Blamey and David Pellauer. Vol. 3. Chicago: University Chicago Press, 1988.

Rief, Linda. *Seeking Diversity: Language Arts with Adolescents.* Portsmouth, NH: Heinemann, 1992.

Ritchie, Joy. "Confronting the Essential Problem: Reconnecting Feminist Theory and Pedagogy" *Journal of Advanced Composition* 10 (1990): 249–73.

Roberts, R. H. and J. M. N. Good, eds. *The Recovery of Rhetoric: Persuasive Discourse and Disciplinarity in the Human Sciences.* Charlottesville: University Press of Virginia, 1993.

Robinson, Lillian. "Treason Our Text: Feminist Challenges to the Literary Canon." *The Feminist Criticism: Essays on Women, Literature, and Theory.* Ed. Elaine Showalter. New York: Pantheon, 1985.

Rodrigues, Raymond, and Dawn Rodrigues. *Teaching Writing with a Word Processor.* Urbana, IL: NCTE, 1986.

Rodrigues, Richard. *Hunger of Memory: The Education of Richard Rodrigues: An Autobiography.* Boston: Godine, 1982.

Rogoff, Barbara. *Apprenticeship in Thinking.* New York: Oxford University Press, 1990.

Rorty, Richard. *Philosophy and the Mirror of Nature.* Princeton, NJ: Princeton University Press, 1979.

Rosch, Eleanor. "Principles of Categorization." *Cognition and Categorization.* Eds. E. Rosch and B. B. Lloyd. Hillsdale: Erlbaum, 1978, 27–48.

Rose, Gillian. *Feminism and Geography.* Minneapolis: University of Minnesota Press, 1993.

Rose, Mike. *Lives on the Boundary: The Struggles and Achievements of America's Underprepared.* New York: Macmillan, 1989.

Rowlandson, Mary. *A Narrative of the Captivity and Restauration of Mrs. Mary Rowlandson.* [1682.] Rpt. *The Heath Anthology of American Literature.* Ed. Paul Lauter. 2nd ed. Lexington, MA: Heath, 1994, 343–66.

Sacks, Oliver. *Awakenings.* 2nd ed. New York: Dutton, 1983.

———. *A Leg to Stand On.* New York: Summit, 1984.

Sacks, Peter M. *The English Elegy: Studies in the Genre from Spenser to Yeats.* Baltimore: Johns Hopkins University Press, 1985.

Said, Edward W. *The World, the Text, and the Critic.* Cambridge: Harvard University Press, 1983.

Schenk, Celeste. "Feminism and Deconstruction: Reconstructing the Elegy." *Tulsa Studies in Women's Literature* 5 (1986): 13–27.

Schiesari, Juliana. *The Gendering of Melancholia: Feminism, Psychoanalysis, and the Symbolics of Loss in Renaissance Literature.* Ithaca, NY: Cornell University Press, 1992.

Schilb, John. "Ideology and Composition Scholarship." *Journal of Advanced Composition* 8 (1988): 22–29.

Scholes, Robert. *Textual Power: Literary Theory and the Teaching of English.* New Haven: Yale University Press, 1985.

Scholes, Robert, Nancy R. Comley, and Gregory L. Ulmer. *Text Book: An Introduction to Literary Language.* 2nd ed. New York: St. Martin's, 1993.

Schryer, Catherine. "Records as Genre." *Written Communication* 10 (1993): 200–34.

Schuster, Charles. "The Politics of Promotion." *The Politics of Writing Instruction: Postsecondary.* Eds. Richard Bullock and John Trimbur. Portsmouth, NH: Boynton/Cook-Heinemann, 1991, 85–96.

Seabrook, John. "Email from Bill." *The New Yorker.* Jan. 10, 1994: 48–62.

————. "My First Flame." *The New Yorker.* Jun. 6, 1994: 70–79.

Searle, John. *Speech Acts.* Cambridge: Cambridge University Press, 1969.

Sedgwick, Eve Kosofsky. *Epistemology of the Closet.* Berkeley: University of California Press, 1990.

————. *Tendencies.* Durham, NC: Duke University Press, 1993.

Selfe, Cynthia, and Richard J. Selfe, Jr. "The Politics of the Interface: Power and Its Exercise in the Electronic Contact Zone." *College Composition and Communication.* 45 (Dec. 1994): 480–504.

Selzer, Jack, ed. *Understanding Scientific Prose.* Madison: University of Wisconsin Press, 1993.

Shafer, Roy. "Narration in the Psychoanalytic Dialogue." *On Narrative.* Ed. W. J. T. Mitchell. Chicago: University of Chicago Press, 25–49.

Shellnut, Eve. *The Writing Room: Keys to the Craft of Fiction and Poetry.* Marietta, GA: Longstreet Press, 1989.

Shopen, Timothy, and Joseph M. Williams, eds. *Standards and Dialects in English.* Cambridge: Winthrop, 1980.

Shucard, Alan R. *Countee Cullen.* Boston: Twayne, 1984.

<skeevers>. "Signature." Business Communication Discussion List [online]. Available email: BIZCOM <LISTSERV@EBBS.ENGLISH.VT.EDU>. 6 Jun. 1994.

Slevin, James. "Genre Theory, Academic Discourse, and Writing Within Disciplines." *Audits of Meaning.* Ed. Louise Z. Smith. Portsmouth, NH: Boynton/Cook-Heinemann, 1988, 3–16.

Smart, Graham. "Genre as Community Invention." *Writing in the Workplace.* Ed. R. Spilka. Carbondale: Southern Illinois University Press, 1993.

Smith, Barbara Herrnstein. *Contingencies of Value: Alternative Perspectives for Critical Theory.* Cambridge, MA: Harvard University Press, 1988.

Smith, Henry Nash. *Virgin Land.* [1950.] Cambridge: Harvard University Press, 1970.

Smith, Sidonie. "Maxine Hong Kingston's Woman Warrior: Filiality and Woman's Autobiographical Storytelling." *Feminisms: An Anthology of Literary Theory and Criticism.* Eds. Robyn R. Warhol and Diane Price Herndl. New Brunswick, NJ: Rutgers University Press, 1993, 1058–79.

————. *Subjectivity, Identity, and the Body: Women's Autobiographical Practices in the Twentieth Century.* Bloomington: Indiana University Press, 1993.

Smith-Rosenberg, Carroll. "The Female World of Love and Ritual: Relations Between Women in Nineteenth-Century America." [1975.] Rpt. in *Disorderly Conduct: Visions of Gender in Victorian America.* New York: Knopf, 1985, 53–76.

Sobel, Kathryn Wooten. Interview, April 22, 1994, Bloomington, IN.

Sommers, Nancy. "Between the Drafts." *College Composition and Communication* 43.1 (Feb. 1992): 23–31.

————. "I Stand Here Writing." *College English* 55.4 (Apr. 1993): 420–28.

Sontag, Susan. "The Anthropologist as Hero." *Against Interpretation.* Ed. Susan Sontag. New York: Farrar, 1966, 69–81.

Spain, Daphne. *Gendered Spaces.* Chapel Hill: University of North Carolina Press, 1992.

Spellmeyer, Kurt. *Common Ground: Dialogue, Understanding, and the Teaching of Composition.* Englewood Cliffs, NJ: Prentice Hall, 1993.

Spivak, Gayatri Chakravorty. *In Other Worlds: Essays in Cultural Politics.* New York: Routledge, 1987.

————. *The Post-Colonial Critic: Interviews, Strategies, Dialogues.* Ed. Sarah Harasym. New York: Routledge, 1990.

Sprengnether, Madelon. *The Spectral Mother: Freud, Feminism, and Analysis.* Ithaca, NY: Cornell University Press, 1990.

Stein, Gertrude. *Everybody's Autobiography.* [1937.] Rpt. New York: Vintage, 1937.

Stranger, Carol. "The Sexual Politics of the One-to-One Tutorial Approach and Collaborative Learning." *Teaching Writing: Pedagogy, Gender, and Equity.* Eds. Cynthia Caywood and Gillian Overing. New York: SUNY Press, 1987, 3–4.

Strelka, Joseph P. *Theories of Literary Genre.* University Park: Pennsylvania State University Press, 1978.

Strenski, Ellen. "Disciplines and Communities, 'Armies' and 'Monasteries,' and the Teaching of Composition." *Rhetoric Review* 8 (1989): 137–45.

Sullivan, Patricia A. "Feminism and Methodology in Composition Studies." *Methods and Methodology in Composition Research.* Eds. Gesa Kirsch and Patricia A. Sullivan. Carbondale: Southern Illinois University Press, 1992, 37–61.

————. "From Student to Scholar: A Contextual Study of Graduate-Student Writing in English." Dissertation, Ohio State University, 1988.

————. "Writing in the Graduate Curriculum: Literary Criticism as Composition." *Journal of Advanced Composition* 11.2 (Fall 1991): 283–99.

Swales, John M. *Genre Analysis: English in Academic and Research Settings.* Cambridge: Cambridge University Press, 1990.

<swilbur>. "Beauty in cyberspace?" Cybermind Discussion List [online]. Available email: CYBERMIND <LISTSERV@WORLD.STD.COM>. 5 Jul. 1994.

Tate, Gary. "Notes on the Dying of a Conversation." *College English* 57.3 (March 1995): 303–09.

————. "A Place for Literature in Freshman English." *College English* 55.3 (March 1993): 317–21.

Taylor, John R. *Linguistic Categorization.* Oxford: Clarendon, 1989.

Taylor, Paul. "Social Epistemic Rhetoric and Chaotic Discourse." *Re-imagining Computers and Composition.* Eds. Gail Hawisher and Paul LeBlanc. Portsmouth, NH: Boynton/Cook-Heinemann, 1992.

Tedesco, Janis. "Women's Ways of Knowing/Women's Ways of Composing." *Rhetoric Review.* 9.2 (1991): 245–56.

Tedlock, Barbara. "From Participant Observation to Observation of Participation: The Emergence of Narrative Ethnography." *Journal of Anthropological Research* 47.1 (1991): 69–94.

The Independent Commission of Inquiry on the U.S. Invasion of Panama. *The U.S. Invasion of Panama: The Truth Behind Operation "Just Cause."* Boston: South End, 1991.

Thompson, Robert Ferris. *Flash of the Spirit: African and Afro-American Art and Philosophy.* New York: Random House, 1983.

Tobin, Lad. *Writing Relationships: What Really Happens in the Composition Class.* Portsmouth, NH: Boynton/Cook-Heinemann, 1993.

Todorov, Tzvetan. *Genres in Discourse.* Trans. Catherine Porter. New York: Cambridge University Press, 1990.

——— . "The Origin of Genres." Trans. Lynn Moss and Bruno Braunrot. *New Literary History* 8 (1976): 159–70.

Tokarczyk, Michelle, and Elizabeth Fay. *Working-Class Women in the Academy: Laborers in the Knowledge Factory.* Amherst: University of Massachusetts Press, 1993.

Tompkins, Jane. "Me and My Shadow." *New Literary History* 19 (Autumn 1987): 169–78.

——— . "Pedagogy of the Distressed." *College English* 52 (Oct. 1990): 653–60.

——— . "Postcards from the Edge." *Journal of Advanced Composition* 13.2 (1993): 449–57.

Toomer, Jean. *Cane.* [1923.] New York: Harper, 1969.

Torogovnick, Marianna. "Experimental Critical Writing." *Profession* 90 (1990): 27–29.

Toulmin, Stephen, Richard Rieke, and Alan Janik. *An Introduction to Reasoning.* New York: Macmillan, 1979.

Turnbull, Colin. *The Human Cycle.* New York: Simon & Schuster, 1983.

Verburg, Carol J., ed. *Ourselves Among Others: Cross-Cultural Readings for Writers.* 2nd ed. Boston: Bedford–St. Martin's, 1991.

Vernon, Victoria. "Introduction." *Daughters of the Moon: Wish, Will, and Social Constraint in Fiction by Modern Japanese Women.* Berkeley: University of California Press, 1988.

Villanueva, Victor, Jr. *Bootstraps, from an American Academic of Color.* Urbana, IL: NCTE, 1993.

Vygotsky, Lev. *Thought and Language.* Trans. Alex Kozulin. Cambridge: MIT Press, 1986.

Wagar, W. Warren. *Terminal Visions: The Literature of Last Things.* Bloomington: Indiana University Press, 1982.

Walker, Alice. *In Search of Our Mother's Gardens.* San Diego: Harcourt, 1983.

Walker, Cheryl, ed. "Introduction." *American Women Poets of the Nineteenth Century: An Anthology.* New Brunswick, NJ: Rutgers University Press, 1992.

————. *The Nightingale's Burden: Women Poets and American Culture Before 1900*. Bloomington: Indiana University Press, 1982.

Warhol, Robyn R., and Diane Price Herndl, eds. *Feminisms: An Anthology of Literary Theory and Criticism*. New Brunswick, NJ: Rutgers University Press, 1993.

Warner, Michael. *The Letters of the Republic: Publication and the Public Sphere in Eighteenth-Century America*. Cambridge: Harvard University Press, 1990.

Watts, Emily Stipes. *The Poetry of American Women from 1632 to 1945*. Austin, TX: University of Texas Press, 1977.

Weathers, Winston. *An Alternate Style: Options in Composition*. Rochelle Park, NJ: Hayden, 1980.

————. "Grammars of Style: New Options in Composition." *Rhetoric and Composition: A Sourcebook for Teachers and Writers*. 3rd ed. Ed. Richard L. Graves. Portsmouth, NH: Boynton/Cook-Heinemann, 1990, 200–14.

Wellek, Rene and Austin Warren. *Theory of Literature*. [1942.] Rpt. New York: Harcourt, 1949.

Welsh-Huggins, Pamela J. Interview, April 22, 1994, Bloomington, IN.

Wertsch, James V. *Voices of the Mind: A Sociocultural Approach to Mediated Action*. Cambridge: Harvard University Press, 1991.

White, Hayden. *The Content of Form: Narrative Discourse and Historical Representation*. Baltimore: Johns Hopkins University Press, 1987.

Wideman, John Edgar. *Brothers and Keepers*. New York: Holt, 1984.

————. *Hurry Home*. New York: Harcourt, 1970.

Wiesel, Eli. "Why I Write: Making No Become Yes." [1985.] Rpt. in *The Essay Connection: Readings for Writers*. Ed. Lynn Z. Bloom. 4th ed. Lexington, MA: Heath, 1995, 41–46.

Willard, Charles A. "Argument Fields." *Advances in Argumentation Theory and Research*. Eds. James R. Cox and Charles A. Willard. Carbondale: Southern Illinois University Press, 1982, 24–77.

Williams, Joseph M. "The Phenomenology of Error." *College Composition and Communication* 32 (1981): 152–68.

Williams, Oscar. *A Little Treasury of Modern Poetry*. New York: Scribners, 1970, 616.

Williams, Patricia J. *The Alchemy of Race and Rights*. Cambridge: Harvard University Press, 1992.

Wills, Gary. *Lincoln at Gettysburg: The Words That Remade America*. New York: Simon & Schuster, 1992.

Wittgenstein, Ludwig. *Philosophical Investigations*. 3rd. ed. Trans. G.E.M. Anscombe. New York: Macmillan, 1958.

Wittig, Rob. *Invisible Rendezvous: Connection and Collaboration in the New Landscape of Electronic Writing*. Hanover, NH: Wesleyan University Press, 1994.

Worsham, Lynn. "Writing Against Writing: The Predicament of Ecriture Feminine in Composition Studies." *Contending with Words: Composition and Rhetoric in a*

Postmodern Age. Eds. Patricia Harkin and John Schilb. New York: MLA, 1991, 82–104.

Wright, Richard. *Black Boy: A Record of Childhood and Youth.* New York: Harper & Brothers, 1945.

Wyche-Smith, Susan, and Shirley K. Rose. "One Hundred Ways to Make the Wyoming Resolution a Reality: A Guide to Personal and Political Action." *College Composition and Communication* 41.3 (Oct. 1990): 318–24.

X., Malcolm. *The Autobiography of Malcolm X.* with the assistance of Alex Haley. New York: Grove Press, 1965.326.

Yates, JoAnne. *Control Through Communication: The Rise of System in American Management.* Baltimore: Johns Hopkins University Press, 1989.

Yates, JoAnne, and Wanda Orlikowski. "Genres of Organizational Communication: A Structurational Approach." *Academy of Management Review* 17 (1992): 299–

Yeats, William Butler. *Interviews and Recollections.* Ed. E. H. Mikhail. New York: Barnes, 1977.

————. *Words for Music Perhaps and Other Poems.* Dublin: Cuala, 1932.

Young, Arthur, and Toby Fulwiler. *When Writing Teachers Teach Literature.* Portsmouth, NH: Boynton/Cook-Heinemann, 1995.

Zamierowski, Mark. "The Virtual Voice in Network Culture." *Voices on Voice: Perspectives, Definition, Inquiry.* Ed. Kathleen Yancey. Urbana, IL: NCTE, 1994.

Zawacki, Terry Myers. "Recomposing as a Woman—An Essay in Different Voices." College Composition and Communication 43.1 (Feb. 1992): 32–38.

Zitkala-Sa (Gertrude Bonnin). "The School Days of an Indian Girl." Rpt. in *American Indian Stories.* Lincoln: University of Nebraska Press, 1921, 47–80.

Contributors

Charles Bazerman is Professor of English at the University of California, Santa Barbara. His books include *Constructing Experience, Shaping Written Knowledge: The Genre and Activity of the Experimental Article in Science*, and *The Informed Writer*. He also coedited *Textual Dynamics of the Professions* and *Landmark Essays in Writing Across the Curriculum*. His research interests include the psychosocial dynamics of writing, the rhetoric of science and technology, and rhetorical theory. Currently he is completing a new freshman writing textbook, entitled *Involved: Writing for College, Writing for Your Self*, and a study of the rhetorical and representational work that made Edison's incandescent light a social reality, entitled *The Languages of Edison's Light*.

Wendy Bishop is Professor of English at Florida State University, where she teaches composition and rhetoric and creative writing. She is the author of ethnographic writing research and writes on the theory and pedagogy of creative writing. With Hans Ostrom, she coedited and contributed to *Colors of a Different Horse: Rethinking Creative Writing, Theory and Pedagogy* (NCTE, 1994). Currently, she's completing *Thirteen Ways of Looking for a Poem: A Guide to Writing Poetry* (HarperCollins), *Ethnographic Writing Research: Writing It Down, Writing It Up, and Reading It* (Boynton/Cook). She edited *Elements of Alternate Style: Essays on Writing and Revision* (Boynton/Cook, 1997).

Lynn Bloom is Professor of English and Aetna Chair of Writing at the University of Connecticut, Storrs. She is the author of *Doctor Spock: Biography of a Conservative Radical* (1972), coauthor of *American Autobiography 1945–1980: A Bibliography* (1982, with Tobias Briscoe), and numerous articles, including the autobiographical "Teaching College English as a Woman" (1992) and "Growing Up with Dr. Spock" (1994). She is currently writing *Coming to Life: Reading, Researching, Writing Autobiography.* Her recent research on autobiography has been supported by grants and fellowships from the National Endowment for the Humanities.

Robert Brooke is Professor of English at the University of Nebraska–Lincoln, where he teaches writing and critical theory and serves as director of the Nebraska Writing Project. His publications include *Small Groups in Writing Workshops* (1994, with Ruth Mirtz and Rick Evans), *Writing and Sense of Self* (1991), and the Braddock Award article "Underlife and Writing Instruction" (*CCC* 1987).

JoAnn Campbell works primarily in nineteenth-century composition and literacy history. She has edited a collection of writing by Gertrude Buck, *Towards a Feminist Rhetoric*, published by the University of Pittsburgh Press, and is an Assistant Professor of English at Indiana University.

Gregory Clark is Professor of English at Brigham Young University. He is a theorist and historian of rhetoric with particular interest in its ethics and its practice in the United States. He wrote *Dialogue, Dialectic, and Conversation* (1990), coedited *Oratorical Culture in Nineteenth-Century America* (1993), and has published articles in various journals in rhetoric and composition.

Jane Detweiler is an Assistant Professor of English, specializing in composition and rhetoric, at the University of Nevada–Reno. She is coauthor, with Brenda Jo Bruggemann and Margaret Strain, of a collaborative annotated bibliography for graduate students new to the field ("The Profession"). Her dissertation study, *Storied Rhetorics: Narrative Genres in Qualitative Composition Research*, focuses on the role of conventional naturalistic rhetorics in the work of writing researchers—and in the development of the discipline. As with her other studies, this project inquires into the ways professional and personal narrations of experience are related.

Amy Devitt is an Associate Professor of English and Director of Freshman-Sophomore English at the University of Kansas. She teaches courses at the undergraduate and graduate level in writing, composition theory, and English language studies. She has published a book on *Standardizing Written English* with Cambridge University Press (1989) and several articles in various collections and journals. Most recently her work on genre theory has appeared in *College Composition and Communication*, in *Generalizing About Genre: New Conceptions of an Old Concept* (1993) and in *Genre, Genres, and the Teaching of Genre* (1996).

Aviva Freedman is Professor of Linguistics and Applied Language Studies at Carleton University, Ottawa, Canada. She has written, coedited, and coauthored several books and many articles on rhetorical theory and writing research, including *Reinventing the Rhetorical Tradition* (1980), and *Learning to Write: First Language/Second Language* (1982). She has recently written a number of articles and chapters in books on "genre," as well as coedited two books with Peter Medway, *Genre in the New Rhetoric* (1994); and *Learning and Teaching Genre* (1994). Currently, she is involved in a six-year, large-scale research study comparing academic and workplace discourse.

Allison Giffen is an Assistant Professor at New Mexico State University. She has published in *Early American Literature* and has essays forthcoming in *The Emily Dickinson Journal* and *The Garland Encyclopedia of Nineteenth-Century American Poets*. She is currently at work on a book entitled *The Poetics of Loss: American Women Poets and the Elegiac Voice*.

Thomas P. Helscher has taught writing in both the undergraduate and graduate programs at the University of Virginia and UCLA. He is currently a research analyst candidate at the Los Angeles Institute and Society for Psychoanalytic Studies and is at work on a book on genre and psychoanalysis.

Wendy S. Hesford is an Assistant Professor in the English Department at Indiana University, where she teaches courses in composition and literacy studies. She has articles forthcoming in two MLA anthologies: *Feminism and Composition* (ed. Jarratt and Worsham) and *Writing in Multicultural Settings* (ed. Butler, Guerra, and Severino). She is currently working on a book-length project entitled *Reframing Autobiography: Pedagogy and the Politics of Identity.*

Evans Derrell Hopkins was born on June 23, 1954 in segregated Danville, Virginia. At age 17, he joined the Black Panther Party, traveling to Oakland, California in 1972 to write for the party newspaper. In 1981, he was given a life sentence for robbery by an all-white Danville jury. Since 1982, he has contributed commentary, reportage, and poetry to national and regional publications including *The New Yorker, Slate Magazine, The Washington Post, The Atlanta Journal/Constitution,* and *Southern Exposure.* He has recently been released after 16 years of confinement and is looking toward publication of his autobiography and prison memoir and production of his work for film and theatre.

Dale Jacobs received his B.A. (1988) and M.A. (1993) from the University of Alberta. He earned a Ph.D. in composition and rhetoric at the University of Nebraska–Lincoln. His current research focuses on re-visioning the relationships between critical pedagogy, student cultures, and teacher identities. He has presented papers at conferences such as the Kentucky Narrative Conference, the National Writing Centers Association Conference, and the Pedagogy of the Oppressed Conference. "Coming to Composition, or a Collaborative Metanarrative of Professional Life," an essay coauthored with Kate Ronald, will be published in *Professional Writes of Passage: Enculturation Processes in Composition and Rhetoric,* edited by Jane Detweiler and Lauren Sewell. Jacobs is Assistant Professor of English at East Carolina University.

Debra Journet is Professor and Chair of English at the University of Louisville, where she teaches in the doctoral program in rhetoric and composition. Her primary research interests are in the rhetoric of the physical and human sciences, and she has published essays on genre, interdisciplinarity, and narrative. Her work has appeared in such journals as *Written Communication, Social Epistemology, Mosaic,* and *Technical Communication Quarterly.* She is currently completing a book on the role of narrative in evolutionary biology and neurology.

Michael Kuhne is a full-time English instructor at Minneapolis Community and Technical College. He will soon complete his dissertation—an exploration of the intersections between liberation pedagogy, liberation theology, and composition studies—at the University of Minnesota. His research interests include the rhetoric of theology, first-year composition, and literacy narratives.

Carrie Shively Leverenz is Assistant Professor of English at Florida State University, where she also directs the Reading/Writing Center and Computer-Supported Writing Classrooms. Her research and teaching interests include multicultural literacy, collaboration, feminist theory and pedagogy, and teacher training. She has published articles in *The Journal of Advanced Composition, Rhetoric Society Quarterly*, and *Pre/Text*.

Monifa A. Love recently completed her doctorate in English at the Florida State University. *Provisions,* a volume of her poetry, was published by Lotus Press in 1989. She is a recipient of a 1995 Zora Neale Hurston/Richard Wright Outstanding Fiction Award and the winner of the third round of the Plover Nivola Series. Her novel, *Freedom in the Dismal,* will be published by Plover Press in 1998. She is the founder of Crossroads, a performance poetry ensemble and she frequently collaborates with her husband, visual artist Ed Love.

William Lyne teaches African-American literature at Western Washington State University in Bellingham, Washington. His essay "The Signifying Modernist: Ralph Ellison and the Limits of the Double-Consciousness" appeared in *PMLA*, and he is at work on a book about African-American literature and theories of cultural criticism.

Ruth Mirtz is an Assistant Professor of Rhetoric and Composition and directs the First Year Writing Program at Florida State University. She teaches undergraduate and graduate composition and theory courses. She recently coauthored *Small Groups in Writing Workshops: Invitations to a Writer's Life* with Robert Brooke and Rick Evans.

Lynne Miyake teaches Japanese language classes and courses on Japanese women writers and Japanese and Japanese-American autobiography at Pomona College. Her research interests include Heian narratives, narratology, literary theory, gender, and feminist criticism. Miyake has published articles on narratology, women's voice, and gender-bending narration, and is presently working on a book manuscript involving Heian narratives. Miyake has been a Japanese Ministry of Education Scholar, an Affiliated Scholar at the UCLA Center for the Study of Women, and a recipient of a Japan Foundation Grant, the Harriet Barnard Summer Fellowship at Pomona College, and the National Endowment for the Humanities Sabbatical Grant.

Myka is the creation of Michael Spooner, Director of the Utah State University Press, and Kathleen Yancey, Assistant Professor of English at UNC-Charlotte. In a more conventional style, they wrote "Concluding the Text," in Yancey's collection *Voices on Voice* (1994). But the process of writing "Postings" they found created a collaborated authorial persona: a single persona that isn't Spooner, Yancey, or some combination thereof. The persona, collaborative singular, is singularly named: Myka. And this observation took them, naturally, to their next project: ways that collaboration produces a/the collective persona.

Stephen North (author of *The Making of Knowledge in Composition* [1987]), Lori Anderson, Barbara Chepaitis, David Coogan, Lale Davidson, Ron Maclean, Cindy Parrish, Jonathan Post, Beth Weatherby, and Amy Schoch have all done their doctoral work in English at SUNY Albany. North, Anderson, and Chepaitis continue to teach and write in Albany; Coogan at Illinois Institute of Technology (Chicago); Davidson at Adirondack Community College (upstate New York); Weatherby at Southwest State University (Minnesota); and Maclean in Boston. Parrish and Post are based in Stephentown, New York, and are involved in a range of community projects, with a special interest in Native American issues. Schoch is a project manager for the New York State Department of Economic Development.

Hans Ostrom is the author of *Langston Hughes: A Study of the Short Fiction* (1993), *Lives and Moments: An Introduction to Short Fiction* (1991), and a variety of other anthologies and articles. His novel, *Three to Get Ready,* was published in 1990, and with Wendy Bishop he published *Water's Night,* a chapbook of poetry. Ostrom is Professor of English at the University of Puget Sound. He has taught at Gutenberg University in Germany and in 1994 was a Fulbright Senior Lecturer at Uppsala University in Sweden. His novel, *Honoring Juanita,* is forthcoming.

Irvin Peckham is an Assistant Professor of English at the University of Nebraska at Omaha. He has published essays in *English Journal, Composition Studies, Wings,* and *This Fine Place So Far from Home*—a collection of essays by working-class academics. His research interests involve the ways in which unfamiliar genres are learned in business writing.

Brad Peters is an Associate Professor and Director of Composition at California State University Northridge, where he teaches composition theory and rhetoric. His contributions to other Boynton/Cook-Heinemann anthologies focus on cultural studies, race, gender, and connections between teaching composition and literature. He also publishes on medieval rhetorics of resistance and reclaiming women in *rhetorica.*

Eileen Schell is Assistant Professor of English at Syracuse University. She has published pieces in *College Composition and Communication, Composition*

Studies, and *Discourse: Theoretical Studies in Media and Culture*. She is currently completing a book-length feminist analysis of women's work as part-time writing instructors entitled *Gypsy Academics and Motherteachers: Women, Teaching, and Contingent Labor in Composition Studies*, forthcoming from Boynton/Cook-Heinemann in 1997.

Carol Severino is an Associate Professor of Rhetoric at the University of Iowa, where she directs the Writing Lab and teaches courses on contrastive rhetorics and on the politics of literacy. She has published in the *Journal of Basic Writing*, the *Writing Center Journal*, and *The Journal of Second Language Writing*. With Juan Guerra and Johnnella Butler, she has coedited *Writing in Multicultural Settings* (forthcoming). She has recently completed a history of academic opportunity programs in urban settings to be published by Lawrence Erlbaum Associates.

Michael Spooner, see **Myka**.

Kathleen Yancey, see **Myka**.